Preference, production, and capital

Preference, production, and capital

Selected papers of Hirofumi Uzawa

HIROFUMI UZAWA
University of Tokyo

The right of the University of Cambridge to print and sell all manner of books was granted by Henry VIII in 1534. The University has printed and published continuously since 1584.

CAMBRIDGE UNIVERSITY PRESS
Cambridge
New York New Rochelle Melbourne Sydney

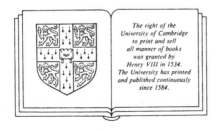

CAMBRIDGE
UNIVERSITY PRESS

32 Avenue of the Americas, New York NY 10013-2473, USA

Cambridge University Press is part of the University of Cambridge.

It furthers the University's mission by disseminating knowledge in the pursuit of education, learning and research at the highest international levels of excellence.

www.cambridge.org
Information on this title: www.cambridge.org/9780521361743

First published 1988

A catalogue record for this publication is available from the British Library

Library of Congress Cataloguing in Publication data

Uzawa, Hirofumi, 1928–

Preference, production, and capital : selected papers of
Hirofumi Uzawa/Hirofumi Uzawa.

p. cm.

ISBN 0-521-36174-5

1. Economics -Mathematical models. I. Title.
HB 135.U9 1988
330'.028 –dc19 88–9725
CIP

ISBN 978-0-521-36174-3 Hardback
ISBN 978-0-521-02224-8 Paperback

Contents

Foreword

In 1954 or thereabouts, I received in the mail a letter and a manuscript from Japan. The letter came from a young man, Hirofumi Uzawa, who identified himself as a graduate student in mathematics at the University of Tokyo. The manuscript referred to an unpublished paper by Leonid Hurwicz and myself, distributed as a RAND Corporation paper, which proposed what amounted to an iterative method of solving concave programs based on a partial analogy to the competitive market. We had only been able to show that the method was locally stable; if the starting point was sufficiently close to the optimum, the method would indeed converge to it. Uzawa's manuscript showed elegantly and simply that the Euclidean distance to the optimum was bound to be decreasing and therefore our process must converge globally. The letter stated with characteristic modesty that undoubtedly the author's paper contained errors, and he would be grateful to have them pointed out. Of course, there were no errors. I immediately looked over what small research budget I then had from the Office of Naval Research and found enough to invite him to spend the next year at Stanford. How fortunate to have had the opportunity of making such a good decision even once in a lifetime.

Uzawa promptly took a leading role in the development of economic theory. His earliest work took off from current topics, such as concave programming and the existence and stability of competitive equilibrium. In each case, he brought new insights and new points of view. Thus his concept of the Edgeworth barter process brought to stability analysis a deeper rooting in the underlying economics, the gradual realization of gains from trade.

In his subsequent work, he became the creator of new topics. The interest in growth theory, starting with Robert Solow's papers, was given a new turn by Uzawa's introduction of the two-sector model. It put on the agenda a whole new field of the interaction between economic growth and economic structure, and the possible complications of the dynamics have remained a live topic, one undergoing revival today with the aid of new tools of nonlinear dynamic analysis. Part of his inspiration, and characteristic of Uzawa's breadth of viewpoint, was his interest in the post-Keynesian analysis of growth that Joan Robinson and Nicholas Kaldor had developed.

He next played a powerful role in the development of optimal growth theory, partly extending his two-sector work, partly emphasizing the role of the public sector. Simultaneously with his work on growth models, he maintained a steady interest in the foundations of the theories of consumption and production. His papers on rational choice and the integrability of demand functions clarified greatly, and put on a new and rigorous footing, the earlier work of Samuelson and Houthakker. In a more applied vein, he gave the definitive analysis of constant-elasticity-of-substitution production functions with more than two factors of production.

After several years as a Research Associate, he was appointed to the Economics Department at Stanford. He immediately became a great influence on a distinguished generation of students (especially David Cass, Harl Ryder, and Karl Shell, who have themselves had such influence on economic theory) – a tribute to his devotion to his students and to his ability to lead without dominating. My wife and I were glad of our friendship with Hirofumi and his wife, Hiroko. His commitment to research was combined with deep social concerns, making him an almost ideal colleague. He subsequently left Stanford to be equally influential at Chicago, before his eventual return to the University of Tokyo. His analytic concerns have gone in different, more policy-oriented directions, especially with regard to pollution. But our friendship has remained unbroken, though renewed in person only on the infrequent occasions of our visits to each other's countries.

The papers in this volume are a permanent part of the heritage of economic theory. Each has been and will be cited time and again, for its insights have retained their relevance.

Kenneth J. Arrow

Preface

The papers collected here deal with various topics in economic theory, ranging from preference and consumption, duality and production, equilibrium, capital, and growth, to the theory of social overhead capital. They all have a common theme: to try to formulate the working of economic forces in a capitalist economy in terms of mathematical models and to explore their static, dynamic, and welfare implications.

Most of the papers were published during the 1960s and a few in the early 1970s. Economic theory since then has made significant progress, both in the refinement and elaboration of analytical methods and in the enlargement of the scope of economic inquiries. In particular, institutional and social aspects of the contemporary economic systems have been explicitly incorporated into the formal framework of the economic theory, and their implications for the mechanism of economic processes have been fully explored. However, the analytical methods developed in the papers and the theoretical implications derived thereby still seem to retain value, particularly in tracing the origin of some of the contemporary works in economic theory.

This volume represents work done while I was affiliated with Stanford University, the University of California at Berkeley, and the University of Chicago. During this period, I was extremely fortunate in being able to work with Professor Kenneth J. Arrow, whose intellect influenced almost all the work I was then doing. I should like to take this opportunity to acknowledge my intellectual and personal indebtedness to him. I was equally fortunate in being associated with Professor Leonid Hurwicz, who inspired me to continue to work in the field of pure economic theory. I should like to express my gratitude to him and to the many economists from whose association I have benefited.

I should also like to thank various institutions such as the National Science Foundation, the Ford Foundation, and the Office of Naval Research for their generous financial support while I was engaged in the research in economic theory of which the papers here collected are a sample.

Preferences and demand

Chapter 1 deals with the logical foundations of the theory of consumer behavior and their implications for the structure of the demand functions. It postulates the rationality of consumer behavior in terms of a set of axioms concerning preference relations and completely characterizes the structure of demand functions derived from them.

Whereas Chapter 1 gives a logical, axiomatic approach to the theory of consumer behavior, Chapter 2 is concerned with a more classical approach where the correspondence between preferences and demand functions is discussed in terms of the integrability of demand functions. The precise mathematical conditions under which demand functions can be integrated to preference relations are explicitly derived.

Chapter 3 extends the preference analysis to the situation where intertemporal allocations of scarce resources are compared. It is an attempt to formulate the Fisherian theory of time preference in such a manner that problems of portfolio analysis are rigorously handled and applied to macroeconomic analysis.

Duality and production

The duality principles discussed in Chapters 1 and 2 have a counterpart in the theory of cost and production. In Chapter 4, the duality relationships between production functions and cost functions are explicitly formulated and the one-to-one correspondence between them is established. Chapter 5 applies the duality principle to characterize the class of production functions for which elasticities of substitution are all constant regardless of factor prices.

Chapter 6 deals with the problems of technological inventions and their implications for the stability of growth processes in a capitalist economy. The relationships between Hicks-neutrality and Harrod-neutrality are clarified and it is shown that Harrod-neutrality is a more natural concept when we address ourselves to the stability of growth equilibrium. In Chapter 7 a model is formulated where an advancement of technological knowledge is attained only by engaging scarce resources in research activities. Under the assumption of the Harrod-neutrality of technological progress, the pattern of the allocations of scarce resources optimum from a social point of view are examined.

Concave programming

Chapter 8 gives an elementary proof for an extended version of the Kuhn-Tucker Theorem in concave programming. Chapter 9 proves the global stability of the Arrow-Hurwicz gradient method in concave programming when certain qualifying constraints are imposed, and the method used for the stability property is applied to show the convergence of an iterative method for concave programming.

Chapter 10 discusses the Heckscher-Ohlin-Lerner-Samuelson theory of factor-price equalization and shows that complete factor-prize equalization occurs only in the case in which the factor endowments in countries are precisely the ones that arise in an equilibrium position of world trade when the factors of production as well as the commodities can move internationally.

Equilibrium and stability

Chapter 11 shows that Walras's Existence theorem – the fundamental theorem in general equilibrium analysis – is equivalent to Brouwer's Fixed-Point Theorem, one of the basic theorems in mathematics. In Chapter 12, the classical adjustment processes of Edgeworth are explicitly formulated and the stability properties are examined.

Theory of economic growth

In Chapters 13 and 14, processes of capital accumulation in a capitalist economy are formulated in terms of the two-sector model of economic growth, where the economy is composed of two different sectors, one producing consumption goods and the other producing investment goods. The stability problem of growth equilibria is discussed under certain assumptions concerning the institutional behavioral characteristics.

Chapter 15 emphasizes the crucial roles played by the institutional and behavioral structure in the processes of economic growth. A two-class model of a private-enterprise market economy is formulated where business firms and households compose two distinct classes. The Fisherian theory of time preference and the Veblen-Penrose theory of the growth of the firm are formulated in precise mathematical forms and their implications for the stability of growth equilibrium are discussed. In Chapter 16, the analytical framework developed in Chapter 15 is used to clarify the relationships between the neoclassical and Keynesian theories of economic growth.

Optimum growth

Chapters 13 and 14 develop the problem of dynamic optimality in terms of the two-sector growth model, and clarify the structure of optimum resource allocations. Chapter 17 applies the technique of the optimum growth theory to examine whether or not the resource allocation process in a decentralized market economy is dynamically optimum.

Chapter 18 applies the technique of optimum economic growth to the problem of fiscal policy in the aggregative model of economic growth.

The standard economic theory is concerned with a decentralized private-enterprise economy where market mechanism and private ownership of means of production are the two major instruments for the allocation of scarce resources. Chapter 19 introduces the concept of social overhead capital and formulates a model of an economy where social overhead capital plays a central role in the processes of both static and dynamic resource allocation.

PART I

Preference and demand

CHAPTER 1

Preference and rational choice in the theory of consumption

The purpose of this paper is to study the logical foundations of the theory of consumer behavior. Preference relations, in terms of which the rationality of consumer behavior is postulated, are precisely defined as irreflexive, transitive, monotone, convex, and continuous relations over the set of all conceivable commodity bundles. A demand function associates with prices and incomes those commodity bundles that the consumer chooses subject to budgetary restraints. It will be shown that if a demand function with certain qualitative regularity conditions satisfies Samuelson's Weak Axiom of Consumer Behavior, there exists a preference relation from which the demand function is derived. On the other hand, the demand functions derived from preference relations satisfy Samuelson's Weak Axiom and those regularity conditions other than the Lipschitz condition with respect to income.

1 Introduction

The pure theory of consumer behavior is concerned with the structure of choices of commodity bundles made by a *rational* consumer when he is confronted with various prices and incomes. A large part of the theory is devoted to explaining the contents in which the *rationality* of a consumer's behavior is understood (e.g., Hicks ([7], Chap. 1), Samuelson ([18], Chap. 5), Wold and Juréen ([24], Part 2), and Robertson ([14], Part 1,

From *Proceedings of the First Stanford Symposium on Mathematical Methods in the Social Sciences*, Stanford University Press, 1960, and *Preferences, Utility, and Demand*, edited by J. Chipman, L. Hurwicz, M. Richter, and H. Sonnenschein, Harcourt, Brace, Jovanovich, 1971, pp. 1–17, reprinted with permission.

The author is grateful to Kenneth J. Arrow, David Gale, Paul A. Samuelson, and particularly to Hendrik S. Houthakker and Leonid Hurwicz for their valuable comments and suggestions. The original version contained a number of logical errors which have been pointed out to the author by Professor Hurwicz, and the present version incorporates the lines of proof suggested by him.

especially pp. 13–20). According to the contributions of Pareto [13], Slutsky [21], Hicks and Allen [9], Wold [23], and others, it is now fairly generally agreed that the rationality of a consumer's behavior may be described by postulating that the consumer has a definite preference over all conceivable commodity bundles and that he chooses those commodity bundles that are optimum with respect to his preference subject to budgetary constraints. The structure of those demand functions that are derived from a consumer's preference relations has been investigated by Slutsky [21], Hicks and Allen [9], Hotelling [10], Hicks ([7], Chap. 2), Samuelson ([18], Chap. 5), and others.

Samuelson's "revealed preference" approach, on the other hand, directly postulates the rationality of a consumer's behavior in terms of demand function. In [16], [17], and ([18], pp. 107–117), he shows that almost all properties of the demand functions derived from preferences are consequences of the so-called Weak Axiom of Consumer Behavior (the term introduced in [20]):

If at the price and income of situation 0 *commodity bundle* x^1 *could be chosen but commodity bundle* x^0 *actually has been chosen* (x^0 *is revealed preferred to* x^1), *then at the price and income of situation* 1 *at which commodity bundle* x^1 *is chosen it is impossible to choose commodity bundle* x^0 (x^1 *is not revealed preferred to* x^0).

The integrability condition[1] or the symmetry of the substitution matrix, however, has not been shown to be implied by the Weak Axiom except in the case of two commodities.[2]

It has been the contribution of Ville [22] and Houthakker [11] to show that a necessary and sufficient condition for a demand function to be derived from a consumer's preference is the so-called Strong Axiom of Consumer Behavior:

If for a finite sequence of commodity bundles $x^0, x^1, \ldots, x^s$ *each commodity bundle* x^t *is revealed preferred to commodity bundle* x^{t+1} ($t = 0, 1, \ldots, s-1$), *then commodity bundle* x^s *is not revealed preferred to commodity bundle* x^0.

Houthakker's Strong Axiom obviously implies Samuelson's Weak Axiom. The existing literature, however, is not sufficient[3] to determine whether or not Samuelson's Weak Axiom is strong enough to imply Houthakker's Strong Axiom. In a recent paper [2], Arrow investigates the problem in a general theory of demand and shows that for those demand

[1] For the integrability problem the reader may consult Georgescu–Roegen [6], Samuelson [20], or Wold and Juréen [24].

[2] For the two-commodity case it has been shown by Samuelson [19] that the Weak Axiom implies the Strong Axiom. See also Rose [15].

[3] See Arrow ([2], p. 121, especially footnote 4). It may be noted that an example given in Hicks ([8], pp. 110–111) is not sufficient to deny the statement.

functions whose domain of definition contains every set consisting of a finite number of commodity bundles, the Weak Axiom implies the Strong Axiom. The demand functions that appear in consumption theory, however, are not defined for sets of a finite number of commodity bundles. The main purpose of this chapter is to prove that for demand functions with certain qualitative regularity conditions, Samuelson's Weak Axiom implies Houthakker's Strong Axiom. The whole theory of rational consumer behavior may, therefore, be built on the basis of Samuelson's Weak Axiom of Consumer Behavior.

In Section 2 we are concerned with giving a rigorous definition for a consumer's demand functions. A consumer's demand function $h(p, M)$ is a function that is defined for any positive price vector $p = (p_1, p_2, \ldots, p_n)$ and positive income M and has a value in the set of conceivable commodity bundles. It will be supposed furthermore that any positive commodity bundle may be chosen under suitable prices and incomes, and that the total expenditure is equal to income M.

In Section 3 a system of axioms for a consumer's preference relation will be postulated. A preference relation is defined as a relation over the set of all conceivable commodity bundles that is irreflexive, transitive, monotone, convex, and continuous. A demand function will be derived by associating with prices and incomes those commodity bundles that are optimum under a given preference relation in the budget sets.

In Section 4 we show that if a demand function satisfies the Strong Axiom of Consumer Behavior, it is possible to find a preference relation P^* from which the original demand function is derived. It is also noted that the preference relation P^* is uniquely determined by the demand function $h(p, M)$. The relation P^* is generated by successive applications of revealed preference relations.

In order to find a condition under which the Strong Axiom is implied by the Weak Axiom, we introduce the function $M^b = \rho_{b,a}(M^a)$, which maps an income M^a at price p^a into an income M^b at price p^b. It will be shown in Section 5 that a demand function satisfies the Strong Axiom if and only if the Weak Axiom holds and the function $\rho_{b,a}(M^a)$ is strictly increasing.

In Section 6 we shall be concerned with the Pareto-Slutsky-Hicks-Allen approach to the theory of consumer choice. It will be shown that if there is a consumer's preference relation P, then a demand function is uniquely determined and satisfies the Strong Axiom of Consumer Behavior and the regularity conditions other than the Lipschitz condition with respect to income. The preference relation P^*, generated by the derived demand function, coincides with the original preference relation P.

Finally, in Section 7 it will be noted that the symmetry of the substitution matrix may be proved directly in terms of demand functions.

2 Demand functions

We are concerned with an individual consumer or a group of consumers faced with the problem of choosing a commodity bundle subject to market prices and incomes. Suppose there are n commodities, labeled $i = 1, 2, \ldots, n$, and the individual consumer under consideration may conceivably choose every commodity i in any amount not less than a given quantity x_i^0. A *commodity bundle* $x = (x_1, x_2, \ldots, x_n)$ is an n-vector whose ith component x_i specifies the amount of commodity i to be consumed. The set of all conceivable commodity bundles will be denoted by Ω. By changing the origin of the scale, if necessary, we may without loss of generality assume that minimum available quantities are all zero: $x_i^0 = 0\,(i = 1, 2, \ldots, n)$. Now Ω is the set of all nonnegative n-vectors:

$$\Omega = \{x = (x_1, x_2, \ldots, x_n) : x \geqq 0\}.^4$$

Market prices of commodities are described by a *price vector* $p = (p_1, p_2, \ldots, p_n)$, where p_i denotes the price of commodity i $(i = 1, 2, \ldots, n)$. We assume throughout the paper that *price vectors have all positive components*. For a given price vector $p = (p_1, p_2, \ldots, p_n)$ and a given income M, the *budget set* $X(p, M)$ is the set of all commodity bundles whose market values evaluated at p do not exceed income M:

$$X(p, M) = \{x = (x_1, x_2, \ldots, x_n) : x \in \Omega, px \leqq M\}.$$

The demand function of the consumer describes the relation of price vectors and incomes to those commodity bundles that the consumer chooses. Precisely, a function $x = h(p, M) = (h_1(p, M), h_2(p, M), \ldots, h_n(p, M))$ is defined as a *demand function* if the following conditions are met:

D.I *The vector $x = h(p, M)$ is a commodity bundle in Ω defined for any price vector $p = (p_1, p_2, \ldots, p_n)$ and positive income M;*

D.II *Any positive commodity bundle $x = (x_1, x_2, \ldots, x_n)$ is chosen for a*

[4] We use the conventional vector notations: for any two vectors $x = (x_1, x_2, \ldots, x_n)$ and $y = (y_1, y_2, \ldots, y_n)$,

$$x \geqq y \text{ means } x_i \geqq y_i \quad (i = 1, 2, \ldots, n),$$
$$x \geq y \text{ means } x \geqq y \text{ but } x \neq y,$$
$$x > y \text{ means } x_i > y_i \quad (i = 1, 2, \ldots, n),$$
$$xy = \sum_{i=1}^{n} x_i y_i,$$

and $\|x\|$ stands for the length of vector $x = (x_1, x_2, \ldots, x_n)$:

$$\|x\| = \left(\sum_{i=1}^{n} x_i^2\right)^{1/2}.$$

suitable price vector $p=(p_1,p_2,\ldots,p_n)$ *and suitable income* $M{:}x=h(p,M)$;

D.III *The commodity bundle* $x=h(p,M)$ *satisfies the budget equation* $ph(p,M)=M$ *for all* $p>0$ *and* $M>0$.

In what follows, the condition D.II will sometimes be replaced by the following more stringent condition:

D.II′ *For any positive commodity bundle* $x=(x_1,x_2,\ldots,x_n)$ *the price vector* $p=(p_1,p_2,\ldots,p_n)$, *at which commodity bundle* x *is chosen, exists and is determined uniquely except for a scalar multiple.*

We need furthermore to assume that demand functions satisfy certain regularity conditions. In particular, we assume

D.IV *The demand function* $h(p,M)$ *satisfies the Lipschitz condition*[5] *with respect to positive income* M.

The condition D.IV implies that $h(p,M)$ is continuous with respect to M.

The Lipschitz condition is satisfied, for example, if the function $h(p,M)$ has a bounded derivative $\partial h_i/\partial M$ with respect to income M. For demand functions, the Lipschitz condition is also satisfied at those price vectors p and incomes M at which no commodity is inferior. In fact, the budget relation D.III implies that for any variation ΔM in income,

$$\sum_{i=1}^{n} p_i \Delta x_i = \Delta M,$$

where $\Delta x_i = h_i(p, M+\Delta M) - h_i(p,M)$ $(i=1,2,\ldots,n)$. If there is no inferior commodity at (p,M) we have $\Delta x_i/\Delta M \geqq 0$ $(i=1,\ldots,n)$ for sufficiently small income variation ΔM. Hence we have $\Delta x_i/\Delta M \leqq 1/p_i$ $(i=1,2,\ldots,n)$.

A commodity bundle x^0 is defined as *revealed preferred* to a commodity bundle x^1 if

$$p^0x^0 \geqq p^0x^1, \quad x^0 \neq x^1, \tag{1}$$

where $x^0=h(p^0,M^0)$ and $x^1=h(p^1,M^1)$ for suitable p^0,p^1 and M^0,M^1. The relation (1) will be denoted by x^0Rx^1.

It is noted that, by D.II,

$$\text{For any positive commodity bundles } x, y \in \Omega, x \geq y \text{ implies } xRy. \tag{2}$$

[5] A function $h(p,M)$ is said to satisfy the Lipschitz condition with respect to M at (p^0,M^0) if there exist real numbers $\varepsilon>0$ and K such that, for all positive p with $\|p-p^0\|<\varepsilon$ and all nonnegative M', M'' with $|M'-M^0|<\varepsilon$ and $|M''-M^0|<\varepsilon$, we have

$$\|h(p,M')-h(p,M'')\| \leqq K|M'-M''|.$$

The Lipschitz condition with respect to M is said to be satisfied if it is satisfied at all (p^0,M^0).

A commodity bundle x is defined as *indirectly revealed preferred* to a commodity bundle y if there is a finite set of commodity bundles $x^1, x^2, \ldots, x^s$ such that

$$xRx^1, x^1Rx^2, \ldots, x^sRy. \tag{3}$$

The relation (3) will be denoted by xR^*y. The relation R^* may be called the *indirect revealed preference relation* generated by the demand function $h(p, M)$.

It is easily seen that the relation R^* is transitive:

$$xR^*y \text{ and } yR^*z \text{ imply } xR^*z. \tag{4}$$

To postulate the regularity condition required to investigate the structure of the demand functions derived from preference relations, we introduce a function $M^b = \rho_{b,a}(M^a)$ associated with two arbitrary price vectors p^a and p^b. For any positive income M^a at price p^a, the income $M^b = \rho_{b,a}(M^a)$ is defined as the supremum of those incomes M at price p^b such that the commodity bundle $x^a = h(p^a, M^a)$ is indirectly revealed preferred to the corresponding commodity bundles $x = h(p^b, M)$. In symbols,

$$\rho_{b,a}(M^a) = \sup\{M : h(p^a, M^a)R^*h(p^b, M)\}. \tag{5}$$

The function $\rho_{b,a}(M^a)$ is always a nondecreasing function of M^a. The regularity condition will be formulated as follows:

(R) *For any price vectors p^a and p^b the function $\rho_{b,a}(M^a)$ is strictly increasing.*

Let the function $\rho'_{b,a}(M^a)$ be defined by

$$\rho'_{b,a}(M^a) = \inf\{M : h(p^b, M)R^*h(p^a, M^a)\}. \tag{6}$$

Then, as can be shown, for a demand function satisfying D.I–D.IV and the Weak Axiom (W), the regularity condition (R) is equivalent to the following:

(R)′ *For any price vectors p^a and p^b the function $\rho_{b,a}(M^a)$ is finite and the function $\rho'_{b,a}(M^a)$ is continuous.*

By using the revealed preference relation R, we can state Samuelson's Weak Axiom of Consumer Behavior as

(W) x^0Rx^1 *implies* $\overline{x^1Rx^0}$.

Houthakker's Strong Axiom of Consumer Behavior, on the other hand, may be formulated in terms of the derived relation R^* by

(S) xR^*y *implies* $\overline{yR^*x}$.

3 Preference relations

It is customary in modern theory of consumer choice to assume that a rational consumer has a preference relation on the set of all conceivable commodity bundles and that he chooses those commodity bundles that are optimum with respect to his preference. In this section, preference relations on the set of commodity bundles are rigorously defined in terms of a system of axioms.[6]

A relation[7] P defined on the set Ω of all conceivable commodity bundles will be called a *preference relation* if the following axioms are satisfied:

P.I *Irreflexivity: For any* $x \in \Omega$, *we have* $\overline{xPx}$.

P.II *Transitivity: For any* $x, y, z \in \Omega$, *the relations* xPy *and* yPz *imply* xPz.

P.III *Monotonicity: For any* $x, y \in \Omega$ *such that* $x \geq y$, *we have* $\overline{yPx}$.

P.IV *Convexity:*[8] *For any* x, $y \in \Omega$ *such that* $x \neq y$ *and* $\overline{xPy}$, *we have* $(1-\lambda)x + \lambda y P x$ *for all* $0 < \lambda < 1$.

P.V *Continuity: For any* $x^0 \in \Omega$ *the set* $\{x : x \in \Omega, x^0 P x\}$ *is an open set in* Ω.

A preference relation on the set Ω_0 of all positive commodity bundles is similarly defined.[9]

Axiom P.I, in view of P.II, may be replaced by

P.I′ *Asymmetry: For any* $x, y \in \Omega$, *the relation* xPy *implies* $\overline{yPx}$.

Note that Continuity Axiom P.V introduced above is weaker than the usual continuity condition, which requires in addition to P.V the following:

P.VI *For any* $x^0 \in \Omega$, *the set* $\{x : x \in \Omega, xPx^0\}$ *is on open set in* Ω.

Axioms P.V and P.VI are, respectively, equivalent to

P.V′ *For any* $x^0 \in \Omega$, *the set* $\{x : x \in \Omega, \overline{x^0 P x}\}$ *is a closed set.*

P.VI′ *For any* $x^0 \in \Omega$, *the set* $\{x : x \in \Omega, \overline{xPx^0}\}$ *is a closed set.*

If a preference relation P satisfies Axioms P.I–P.VI, then there exists a continuous function $u(x)$ defined on Ω such that

$$\text{For any } x, y \in \Omega,\ xPy \text{ if and only if } u(x) > u(y). \qquad (7)$$

[6] The techniques of symbolic logic in terms of which preference relations are defined were first, in economic analysis, employed extensively by Arrow [1].

[7] By a relation P is meant here a binary relation; i.e., for any two elements x and y in Ω, either xPy or $\overline{xPy}$, where $\overline{xPy}$ means the negation of xPy.

[8] Convexity Axiom P.IV in the present form was suggested by Houthakker.

[9] Any preference relation P on Ω induces a preference relation on Ω_0. However, there exists a preference relation on Ω_0 of which it is impossible to find an extension on Ω. For example, let the relation P on Ω_0 be defined by xPy if and only if $x_1 x_2 \cdots x_n > y_1 y_2 \cdots y_n$. Then P is a preference relation on Ω_0 but it is impossible to extend it to Ω. This example is due to Arrow.

In fact, let the relation P' be defined by $xP'y$, if and only if $\overline{yPx}$. Then it is shown that

For any $x, y \in \Omega$, $xP'y$ and/or $yP'x$. (8)

For any $x, y, z \in \Omega$, the relations $xP'y$ and $yP'z$ imply $xP'z$. (9)

For any $x \in \Omega$, $\{y{:}yP'x\}$ and $\{y{:}xP'y\}$ are closed in Ω. (10)

The relations (8) and (10) are restatements of P.I′ and P.V–P.VI, respectively. In order to prove (9) suppose, to the contrary, that there are commodity bundles x, y, and z so that $xP'y$ and $yP'z$, but $\overline{xP'z}$ $(x \neq y)$. By Axiom P.IV, $(1-\lambda)x + \lambda yPy$ for all $0 < \lambda < 1$. But by Axiom P.V, there is a positive number λ_0 such that $zP(1-\lambda_0)x + \lambda_0 y$. Hence zPy, which is a contradiction.

By applying Debreu's theorem [4, Theorem I, p. 162], therefore, we can find a continuous function $u(x)$ satisfying (7). Axioms P.III and P.IV imply that $u(x)$ is monotone and strictly quasi-concave. On the other hand, let $u(x)$ be any continuous, monotone, strictly quasi-concave function defined on Ω. Then the relation P defined by (7) is a preference relation satisfying Axioms P.I–P.VI.

Let p be a price vector and M an income. A commodity bundle x^0 is called *optimum* with respect to a preference relation P in the budget set $X(p, M)$ if $x^0 \in X(p, M)$ and $x^0 Px$ for all commodity bundles $x \in X(p, M)$, $x \neq x^0$.

A demand function $h(p, M)$ is defined as *derived* from a preference relation P if for every price vector p and positive income M the commodity bundle $h(p, M)$ is optimum with respect to P in the budget set $X(p, M)$.

4 Preference relations generated by demand functions

Theorem 1. Let $h(p, M)$ be a demand function satisfying D.I–D.IV and the Strong Axiom (S). Then the indirect revealed preference relation R^*, generated by $h(p, M)$, is a preference relation on the set Ω_0 of all positive commodity bundles (i.e., R^* satisfies Axioms P.I–P.V) and the demand function $h(p, M)$ is derived from R^*.

Any preference relation from which the demand function $h(p, M)$ is derived coincides with R^* on Ω_0.

Proof. As is noted in (2) and (4), the relation R^* satisfies P.II and P.III. P.I′ is identical with the Strong Axiom (S). We shall prove here that P.IV and P.V hold for the relation P^*.

In order to prove P.IV, we need the following:

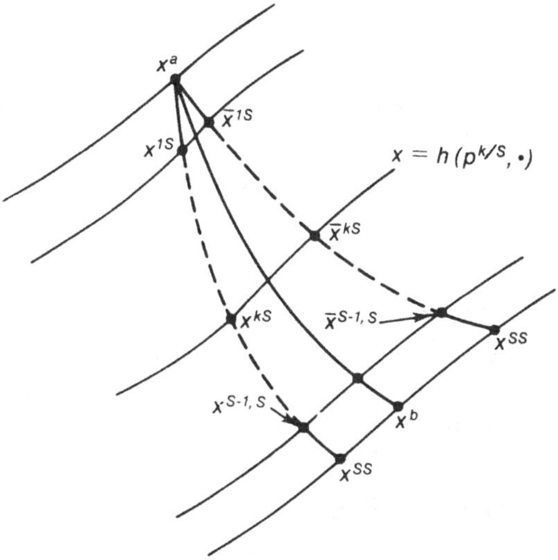

Figure 1.1

Lemma 1. Let the demand function $h(p, M)$ satisfy D.I–D.IV and the Strong Axiom (S). Then, for any price vectors p^a and p^b, we have

$$h(p^a, M^a)R^*h(p^b, M) \quad \text{for all } M < \rho_{b,a}(M^a), \tag{11}$$

and

$$h(p^b, M)R^*h(p^a, M^a) \quad \text{for all } M > \rho_{b,a}(M^a), \tag{12}$$

where $\rho_{b,a}(M^a)$ is defined by (5).

Proof.[10] It may be first noted that the conclusions, (11) and (12), of Lemma 1 are established if the ρ- and ρ'-functions defined by (5) and (6) are identical:

$$\rho_{b,a}(M^a) = \rho'_{b,a}(M^a) \quad \text{for all positive } M^a. \tag{13}$$

The relation (13) will be shown by using the upper and lower income sequences originally introduced by Houthakker [11]. For any positive integer S, let us define the sequence of incomes $\bar{M}^{0S}, \bar{M}^{1S}, \ldots, \bar{M}^{SS}$ recursively by (Figure 1.1).

$$\bar{M}^{k+1,S} = p^{(k+1)/S}\bar{x}^{kS}, \bar{x}^{kS} = h(p^{k/S}, \bar{M}^{kS}), \quad k = 0, 1, \ldots, S-1,$$
$$\bar{M}^{0S} = M^a, \bar{x}^{0S} = x^a = h(p^a, M^a), \tag{14}$$

[10] The present proof of Lemma 1 is based on a slight modification of the technique used by Houthakker [11].

where

$$p^t = p^a + t(p^b - p^a), \qquad (0 \leqq t \leqq 1). \tag{15}$$

On the other hand, let the sequence $M^{0S}, M^{1S}, \ldots, M^{SS}$ be defined by recursively solving (Figure 1.1)

$$M^{kS} = p^{k/S}x^{k+1,S}, x^{k+1,S} = h(p^{(k+1)/S}, M^{k+1,S}), \quad k = 0, 1, \ldots, S-1,$$
$$M^{0S} = \bar{M}^{0S}. \tag{16}$$

For given positive M^{kS}, the right-hand side of equation (16), when regarded as a function of $M^{k+1,S}$, approaches zero as $M^{k+1,S}$ approaches zero and attains a value as large as possible by increasing $M^{k+1,S}$. Hence, by the continuity of $h(p, M)$ with respect to M, it is always possible to solve equation (16) with respect to $M^{k+1,S}$.

The Strong Axiom (S) implies that

$$\rho_{b,a}(M^a) \leqq \rho'_{b,a}(M^a) \quad \text{for all } M^a > 0. \tag{17}$$

Hence, we have from (14), (16), and (17) that

$$M^{SS} \leqq \rho_{b,a}(M^a) \leqq \rho'_{b,a}(M^a) \leqq \bar{M}^{SS}. \tag{18}$$

The equality (13) will be therefore shown if we can establish

$$\lim_{S \to \infty} (\bar{M}^{SS} - M^{SS}) = 0. \tag{19}$$

To see (19), let us first consider the upper income sequence $\bar{M}^{kS}$. We get from (14) and the budget equation D.III that

$$\bar{M}^{k+1,S} - \bar{M}^{kS} = p^{(k+1)/S}\bar{x}^{kS} - p^{k/S}\bar{x}^{kS}$$
$$= \frac{1}{S}(p^b - p^a)\bar{x}^{kS}. \tag{20}$$

On the other hand, from the definition (16) of the lower income sequence M^{kS}, we get

$$M^{k+1,S} - M^{kS} = p^{(k+1)/S}x^{k+1,S} - p^{k/S}x^{k+1,S}$$
$$= \frac{1}{S}(p^b - p^a)x^{k+1,S}. \tag{21}$$

Substracting (21) from (20) and using the notation

$$\nu^{kS} = \bar{M}^{kS} - M^{kS}, \nu^{0S} = 0$$

(where $\nu^{kS} \geqq 0$ from the Strong Axiom (S)), we get

$$\nu^{k+1,S} - \nu^{kS} = \frac{1}{S}(p^b - p^a)(\bar{x}^{kS} - x^{k+1,S}), \qquad k = 0, 1, \ldots, S-1. \tag{22}$$

Summing (22) over $k=0,1,\ldots,j-1$, yields

$$v^{jS}=\frac{1}{S}(p^b-p^a)\{(\bar{x}^{0S}-x^{1S})+(\bar{x}^{1S}-x^{2S})+\cdots+(\bar{x}^{j-1,S}-x^{jS})\}$$

$$=\frac{1}{S}(p^b-p^a)\left\{(x^a-x^{jS})+\sum_{k=1}^{j-1}(\bar{x}^{kS}-x^{kS})\right\}. \tag{23}$$

Since $x^a R^* x^{jS}$, we have by the Strong Axiom that

$$p^{j/S}x^a \geqq p^{j/S}x^{jS}. \tag{24}$$

Let

$$\bar{p}=\max\{p^a,p^b\}, \qquad \underline{p}=\min\{p^a,p^b\},$$

where $\bar{p}=(\bar{p}_1,\bar{p}_2,\ldots,\bar{p}_n)$ is defined in the obvious way by $\bar{p}_j=\max\{p_j^a,p_j^b\}$, and similarly for $\underline{p}$. Then, for any $j=0,1,\ldots,S$, we get from (24)

$$\bar{p}x^a \geqq \underline{p}x^{jS};$$

hence, x^{jS} is contained in the compact set

$$\Gamma=\{x: x\geqq 0, \underline{p}x\leqq \bar{p}x^a\}$$

(which is defined independently of S). Let

$$A=\max_{x\in\Gamma}|(p^b-p^a)(x^a-x)|. \tag{25}$$

On the other hand, since $h(p,M)$ is Lipschitzian with respect to M,

$$|\bar{x}^{kS}-x^{kS}|=|h(p^{k/S},\bar{M}^{kS})-h(p^{k/S},M^{kS})|$$
$$\leqq K|\bar{M}^{kS}-M^{kS}|, \tag{26}$$

where K is a Lipschitzian constant.

The relation (23), together with (25) and (26), yields

$$v^{jS}\leqq\frac{1}{S}\{A+B(v^{1S}+\cdots+v^{j-1,S})\}, \qquad j=1,2,\ldots,S; \tag{27}$$

where

$$B=K|p^b-p^a|.$$

From (27), we can get the following recursive formula

$$v^{jS}\leqq\frac{A}{S}\left(1+\frac{B}{S}\right)^{j-1}, \qquad j=1,2,\ldots,S, \tag{28}$$

in particular,

$$v^{SS}\leqq\frac{A}{S}\left(1+\frac{B}{S}\right)^{S-1}. \tag{29}$$

Since

$$\lim_{S\to\infty}\left(1+\frac{B}{S}\right)^{S-1}=e^{B},$$

the inequality (29), by taking the limit as S goes to infinity, implies the desired property (19). ■

Proof of P.IV. Let $x^a = h(p^a, M^a), x^b = h(p^b, M^b)$, and $x^c = h(p^c, M^c)$ be positive commodity bundles such that

$$\overline{x^a R^* x^b}, \qquad x^a \neq x^b,$$

$$x^c = (1-c)x^a + cx^b, \qquad (0 < c < 1). \tag{30}$$

Then, either $p^c x^c \geqq p^c x^a$ or $p^c x^c > p^c x^b$. If $p^c x^c \geqq p^c x^a$, we have $x^c R x^a$. If $p^c x^c > p^c x^b$, then by the continuity of $h(p, M)$ with respect to M we have

$$x^c R h(p^b, M^b + \varepsilon) \quad \text{for sufficiently small } \varepsilon > 0. \tag{31}$$

On the other hand, by applying Lemma 1, the relation (30) implies

$$h(p^b, M^b + \varepsilon) R^* x^a \quad \text{for all positive } \varepsilon > 0. \tag{32}$$

The relation (31), together with (32), implies that $x^c R^* x^a$. ■

Proof of P.V. Let x^b be any positive commodity bundle such that $x^0 R^* x^b$. By the definition (3) of R^* there is a commodity bundle x^1 such that (Figure 1.2)

$$x^0 = x^1 \quad \text{or} \quad x^0 R^* x^1 \tag{33}$$

and

$$p^1 x^1 \geqq p^1 x^b, \qquad x^1 \neq x^b, \tag{34}$$

where p^1 is the price vector at which the commodity bundle x^1 is chosen.

Consider the commodity bundle x^2 defined by $x^2 = x^1/2 + x^b/2$. By the relation (34), we have

$$p^1 x^1 \geqq p^1 x^2, \qquad x^1 \neq x^2. \tag{35}$$

The Weak Axiom (W), together with (35), implies that $p^2 x^1 > p^2 x^2$, where p^2 is a price vector at which x^2 is chosen. Hence, $p^2 x^2 > p^2 x^b$. Therefore, there is a neighborhood V^b of commodity bundle x^b such that

$$p^2 x^2 > p^2 x \quad \text{for all commodity bundles } x \text{ in } V^b. \tag{36}$$

The relations (33), (35), and (36) imply that $x^0 R^* x$ for all commodity bundles x in V^b. Hence, the set $\{x^a : x^a > 0, x^0 R^* x^a\}$ is an open set. ■

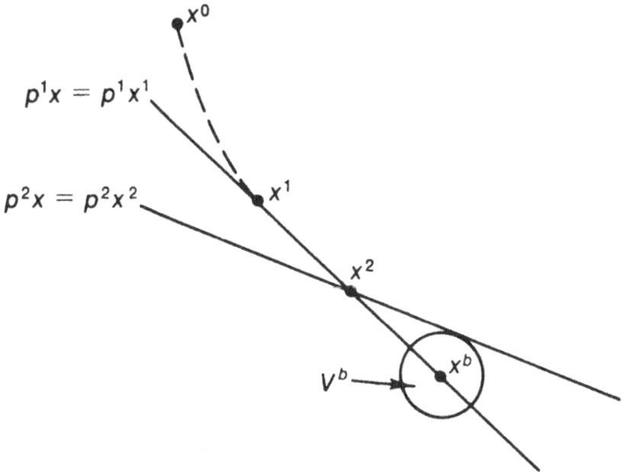

Figure 1.2

As is noted from the above proof, Axiom P.V holds for R^* whenever $h(p, M)$ satisfies the Weak Axiom.

We have now established that the indirect revealed preference ordering R^* is a preference ordering satisfying all the axioms P.I–P.V. We shall now show that the demand function $h(p, M)$ originally given is derived from the indirect revealed preference ordering R^*. In fact, if $x^0 = h(p^0, M^0)$, then, for all commodity bundles $x \neq x^0$ from the budget set $X(p^0, M^0)$, $x^0 R x$ and a fortiori $x^0 R^* x$. On the other hand, let x^0 be a commodity bundle in the budget set $X(p^0, M^0)$ for which $x^0 R^* x$ for all $x \neq x^0$ from the budget set $X(p^0, M^0)$. Then $x^0 = h(p^0, M^0)$; otherwise, $x^0 R^* h(p^0, M^0)$ contradicting the Strong Axiom.

In order to prove the uniqueness, let P be any preference relation on Ω_0 from which the demand function $h(p, M)$ is derived. By definition,

$$xRy \text{ implies } xPy. \tag{37}$$

Since P is transitive, (37) implies that

$$xR^*y \text{ implies } xPy. \tag{38}$$

On the other hand, we shall show that

$$\overline{xR^*y} \text{ implies } \overline{xPy}. \tag{39}$$

In fact, let x and y be commodity bundles such that $\overline{xR^*y}$. Then, by Lemma 1, there exists a sequence $\{y^\nu\}$ of commodity bundles such that

$$\lim_\nu y^\nu = y, y^\nu R^* x, \qquad (\nu = 1, 2, \ldots).$$

Hence, by (38) and P.V′ we have $\overline{xPy}$.

The relations (38) and (39) show that $R^* = P$. Thus the proof of Theorem 1 is completed. ■

It is not known whether or not the relation R^*, generated by a demand function $h(p, M)$ with D.I–D.IV and the Strong Axiom, satisfies Axiom P.VI. However, the relation R^* satisfies the following:

P.VI″ *Let $x^a = h(p^a, M^a)$ and $x^b = h(p^b, M^b)$ be positive commodity bundles such that*

$$x^a R^* x^b. \tag{40}$$

Then there exists a positive number δ such that

$$h(p^a, M^a - \delta) R^* x^b. \tag{41}$$

Axiom P.VI″ is a direct consequence of Lemma 1 proved in relation with Theorem 1 above. Indeed, the relation (40) implies that

$$\rho_{ba}(M^a) > M^b.$$

Then, because of the continuity of $\rho_{ba}(M^a)$ with respect to M^a, there should exist a positive number δ such that

$$\rho_{ba}(M^a - \delta) > M^b,$$

which implies (41).

By using the relation P.VI″ we can prove the following:

Theorem 2. Let a demand function $h(p, M)$ satisfy D.I–D.IV. Then the Strong Axiom (S) implies the continuity of the demand function $h(p, M)$ with respect to price vector p and income M.

Proof. We shall first show that for any price vector p and positive income M, we have $x^0 = h(p, M)$ if and only if

$$px^0 = M \tag{42}$$

and

$$x^0 R^* x \quad \text{for all } x \text{ such that } px < px^0. \tag{43}$$

Suppose to the contrary that there is commodity bundle x^0 satisfying (42) and (43), but $x^0 \neq h(p, M)$. Then, by the definition of R^*, we have $h(p, M) R^* x^0$. Hence, by P.VI″, there is a positive number δ such that $h(p, M - \delta) R^* x^0$, where $ph(p, M - \delta) = M - \delta < M = px^0$, contradicting (43) and the Strong Axiom (S).

In order to prove the continuity of $h(p, M)$ with respect to p and M, let $\{(p^\nu, M^\nu)\}$ be a sequence converging to (p, M). It suffices to show that any limiting commodity bundle x^0 of the sequence $\{h(p^\nu, M^\nu)\}$ satisfies (42) and (43). Since $p^\nu h(p^\nu, M^\nu) = M^\nu$, the relation (42) obviously holds for x^0. Let x be an arbitrary commodity bundle such that $px < M$. Then there exists an integer ν_0 such that $p^\nu x < M^\nu$ for all $\nu \geqq \nu_0$. Since $h(p^\nu, M^\nu)$ is optimum with respect to R^* in the budget set $X(p^\nu, M^\nu)$, we have $\overline{xR^*h(p^\nu, M^\nu)}$. Hence, by Axiom P.V,

$$\overline{xR^*x^0} \quad \text{for all } x \text{ such that } px < M. \tag{44}$$

The relation (44) implies the relation (43). Otherwise, there would be a commodity bundle x^1 such that

$$\overline{x^0 R^* x^1}, \qquad px^1 < M. \tag{45}$$

Let $x^2 = x^0/2 + x^1/2$. Then, by (45) and P.IV, we have $x^2 R^* x^0$, where $px^2 < M$, contradicting (44). ■

The indirect revealed preference relation R^* does not necessarily satisfy Axiom P.VI, even if the demand function $h(p, M)$ satisfies the Strong Axiom. We can easily construct an example of a two-dimensional demand function $h(p, M)$ that satisfies the Strong Axiom and D.I–D.III but that is not derived by any preference relation satisfying P.VI. We may, however, prove the following:

Theorem 3. Let $h(p, M)$ be a demand function satisfying D.I, D.II′, D.III, D.IV, and the Strong Axiom (S). Then the indirect revealed preference relation R^* satisfies Axioms P.I–P.VI on Ω_0.

Proof. In view of Theorem 1, it suffices to show that P.VI holds for the relation R^*. Let $x^a = h(p^a, M^a)$ and $x^0 = h(p^0, M^0)$ be commodity bundles such that $x^a R^* x^0$. Then by P.VI″ there is a commodity bundle x^1 such that (Figure 1.3)

$$x^1 = x^0 \quad \text{or} \quad x^1 R^* x^0 \tag{46}$$

and

$$p^a x^a > p^a x^1. \tag{47}$$

Let x^2 be defined by $x^2 = x^a/2 + x^1/2$.

The Weak Axiom (W), together with (47), implies that

$$p^2 x^2 > p^2 x^1, \tag{48}$$

$$p^a x^a > p^a x^2. \tag{49}$$

We now show that there is a neighborhood V^a of commodity bundle x^a

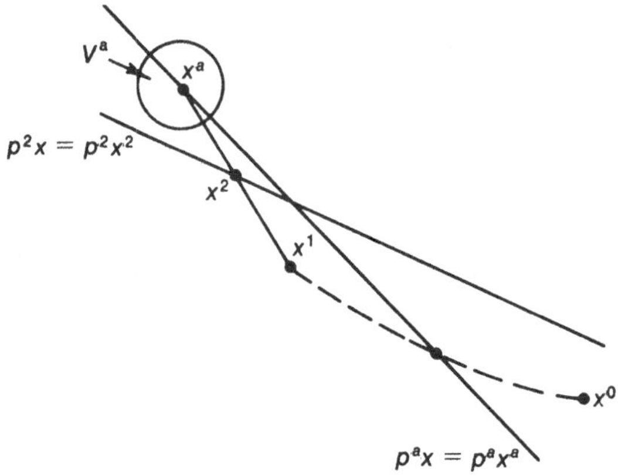

Figure 1.3

such that

$$p^c x^c > p^c x^2 \quad \text{for all commodity bundles } x^c \text{ in } V^a \text{ and corresponding price vectors } p^c. \tag{50}$$

Otherwise, there would be a bounded sequence $\{(p^v, M^v)\}$ of positive price vectors p^v and positive incomes M^v for which

$$\lim_{v \to \infty} h(p^v, M^v) = x^a \quad \text{and} \quad p^v h(p^v, M^v) \leqq p^v x^2. \tag{51}$$

Let (p^*, M^*) be an arbitrary limiting point[11] of the sequence $\{(p^v, M^v)\}$. Then the continuity of the function $h(p, M)$ and (51) imply that $x^a = h(p^*, M^*)$ and $p^* h(p^*, M^*) \leqq p^* x^2$, contradicting D.II′ and (49).

The relations (46), (48), and (50) imply that $x^a R^* x^0$ for all commodity bundles $x^a \in V^a$. Hence, the set $\{x^a : x^a > 0,\ x^a R^* x^0\}$ is an open set in Ω_0. ■

5 Equivalence of the Weak Axiom and the Strong Axiom

Theorem 4. Let a demand function $h(p, M)$ satisfy D.I–D.IV. Then the Strong Axiom (S) holds if and only if the Weak Axiom (W) and the regularity condition (R) both hold.

Proof. Let $h(p, M)$ satisfy the Strong Axiom. The Weak Axiom is obviously

[11] The components of the limiting price vector p^* may always be assumed to be positive. For a proof, see Chapter 4 by H. Sonnenschein in *Preferences, Utility, and Demand*, edited by Chipman, Hurwicz, Richter, and Sonnenschein: Harcourt, Brace, Jovanovich, 1971.

implied by the Strong Axiom. In order to prove (R), let us suppose to the contrary that there are two price vectors p^a and p^b such that

$$M^b = \rho_{b,a}(M_1^a) = \rho_{b,a}(M_2^a) \quad \text{for some } M_1^a < M_2^a. \tag{52}$$

Then we have

$$\rho_{a,b}(M^b) \geqq M_2^a > M_1^a. \tag{53}$$

Otherwise, by Lemma 1, we would have $h(p^a, M_2^a)R^*h(p^b, M^b)$. Hence, by P.V and the continuity of $h(p^b, M)$ with respect to M, there exists a positive number δ such that $h(p^a, M_2^a)R^*h(p^b, M^b + \delta)$, contradicting (52).

The relation (53) now implies, by P.VI″, that there exists a positive number δ' such that $\rho_{a,b}(M^b - \delta') > M_1^a$; that is,

$$h(p^b, M^b - \delta')R^*h(p^a, M_1^a). \tag{54}$$

On the other hand, (52) implies, by Lemma 1, that $h(p^a, M_1^a)R^*h(p^b, M^b - \delta')$, contradicting (54) and the Strong Axiom (S).

We shall next prove that the Weak Axiom, together with (R), implies the Strong Axiom. Let $h(p, M)$ satisfy the Weak Axiom and (R). In order to prove the Strong Axiom, it suffices to show that for any positive commodity bundle x^0, the set

$$C = \{x : x > 0, x^0R^*x, xR^*x^0\} \tag{55}$$

is empty. Suppose to the contrary that there exists a positive commodity bundle $x^0 = h(p^0, M^0)$ for which the set C defined by (55) is not empty.

Let us first show that there is a positive number ε such that

$$h(p^0, M^0 + \varepsilon) \in C. \tag{56}$$

In fact, as is noted in the proof of Theorem 1, the Weak Axiom implies that the set $\{x : x > 0, x^0R^*x\}$ is open, so that $x^0R^*x^0$ implies the existence of a neighborhood V of x^0 such that x^0R^*x for all $x \in V$.

Let $x^b = h(p^b, M^b)$ be an arbitrary commodity bundle in C and $\bar{M}^b$ be defined by

$$\bar{M}^b = \sup\{M : h(p^b, M) \in C\}. \tag{57}$$

Then the relation (57) may be written as

$$\bar{M}^b = \rho_{b,0}(M^0), \tag{58}$$

where $\rho_{b,0}$ is the function associated with price vectors p^0 and p^b.

By (R), the relation (58) implies $\bar{M}^b < \rho_{b,0}(M^0 + \varepsilon)$.

Let δ be a positive number such that $\bar{M}^b + \delta < \rho_{b,0}(M^0 + \varepsilon)$. Then, by the definition of $\rho_{b,0}(M^0 + \varepsilon)$,

$$x^0R^*h(p^b, \bar{M}^b + \delta). \tag{59}$$

On the other hand, we have $h(p^b, \bar{M}^b + \delta)R^*x^0$, which together with (59) contradicts the definition (57) of $\bar{M}^b$. ■

6 Demand functions derived from preference relations

In this section we show that given any preference relation on the set of all nonnegative commodity bundles, it is possible to derive the corresponding demand function. First, we shall prove

> **Theorem 5.** Let P be a preference relation on the set Ω of all nonnegative commodity bundles satisfying Axioms P.I–P.V. Then there exists a demand function $h(p, M)$ which satisfies D.I, D.III, and the Strong Axiom (S).

Proof. Let $X = X(p, M)$ be the budget set with positive price vector p and positive income M. Since p is a positive price vector, the set X is compact (i.e., bounded and closed) and convex.

It will first be shown that there exists a commodity bundle $x^0 \in X$ such that

$$\overline{xPx^0} \quad \text{for all } x \in X. \tag{60}$$

For any $x \in X$, let the set C_x be defined by $C_x = \{z : z \in X, \overline{xPz}\}$. Then, for any finite number of commodity bundles $x^1, x^2, \ldots, x^r$,

$$C_{x^1} \cap \cdots \cap C_{x^r} \quad \text{is nonempty.} \tag{61}$$

In fact, for $r = 1$, the set C_{x^1} is nonempty since, by P.I, $x^1 \in C_{x^1}$. Assume that the relation (61) is valid for $r - 1$ commodity bundles $x^1, x^2, \ldots, x^{r-1}$. Then there is a commodity bundle z such that $z \in C_{x^s}$ $(s = 1, 2, \ldots, r-1)$. If $\overline{x^r P z}$, then z belongs to the intersection $C_{x^1} \cap \cdots \cap C_{x^r}$. If $x^r P z$, then $\overline{x^s P x^r}$ $(s = 1, 2, \ldots, r-1)$. Hence,

$$x^r \in C_{x^1} \cap \cdots \cap C_{x^r}$$

and the relation (61) is valid for r commodity bundles.

By P.V, the set C_x is closed in the compact set X. Therefore, we have [12]

$$\bigcap_{x \in X} C_x \neq \varnothing.$$

[12] If $\{C_\alpha\}$ is a class of closed subsets of a compact set X, and if any finite number of C_α's has a nonempty intersection, then the intersection of all C_α's is nonempty. This proposition is fundamental for compact sets.

Let x^0 be any commodity bundle in

$$\bigcap_{x \in X} C_x.$$

Then, by the definition of C_x, we have (60).

Now we shall show that commodity bundle x^0 satisfying (60) is optimum in $X(p, M)$. Let us suppose to the contrary that there is a commodity bundle x^1 such that $x^1 \in X, x^1 \neq x^0, \overline{x^0 P x^1}$. Let $z = x^0/2 + x^1/2$. Then $z \in X$. But, by P.IV, we have zPx^0, which contradicts (60).

The optimum commodity bundle x^0 is uniquely determined in the budget set $X(p, M)$. In fact, if x^1 were another commodity bundle optimum with respect to P in the budget set $X(p, M)$, then $x^0 P x^1$ and $x^1 P x^0$, contradicting P.I′.

Let $h(p, M)$ be the function that associates the optimum commodity bundle x^0 with positive price vector p and positive income M. It is evident that the function $h(p, M)$ satisfies D.I and D.III.

We next show that the Strong Axiom (S) holds. Let us suppose to the contrary that there is a commodity bundle x^0 such that

$$x^0 R^* x^0. \tag{62}$$

But for any two commodity bundles x and y,

$$xR^*y \text{ implies } xPy.$$

Hence, (55) implies $x^0 P x^0$, contradicting Axiom P.I. ∎

Theorem 6. Let P be a preference relation on the set Ω of all nonnegative commodity bundles satisfying Axioms P.I–P.VI. Then there exists a demand function $h(p, M)$ that is derived from the preference relation P. The demand function $h(p, M)$ satisfies D.I–D.III and the Strong Axiom (S), and is continuous with respect to price vectors p.

Proof. It suffices to prove that the derived demand function $h(p, M)$ satisfies D.II and is continuous with respect to p.

In order to see that D.II is satisfied, let x^0 be any positive commodity bundle. Let $B = \{x : x \in \Omega, xPx^0\}$. By P.II–P.IV, the set B is convex. Since x^0 is not contained in the interior of B, there exists, by a separation theorem on convex sets (e.g., see Fenchel [5, p. 47]), a nonzero vector p such that

$$px \geqq px^0 \quad \text{for all } x \in B. \tag{63}$$

Since $x \in B$ for all x such that $x \geqq x^0$, the vector p must have all nonnegative components.

The continuity axiom P.VI, however, shows that

$$px > px^0 \quad \text{for all } x \in B. \tag{64}$$

Indeed, suppose to the contrary that for some x we have $x \in B$ and $px = px^0$. Since xPx^0, by P.VI, there exists a neighborhood V of x such that zPx^0 for all $z \in V$. Since p is a nonzero vector, there exists a commodity bundle $z \in V$ such that $px^0 > pz$ and zPx^0, which contradicts (63). The relation (64) may be rewritten as follows: $\overline{xPx^0}$ for every commodity bundle x such that $px \leqq px^0$. Hence, x^0 is the optimum commodity bundle associated with p and M. The relation (64) and P.III show that all the components of the vector p are positive.

Finally, we prove that the demand function $h(p, M)$ is continuous with respect to p. As is noted in Section 4, it will suffice to show that for any price vector p and positive income M, a commodity bundle x^0 is optimum in the budget set $X(p, M)$ if and only if

$$px^0 = M \tag{65}$$

and

$$x^0 Px \quad \text{for all positive commodity bundles } x \text{ such that } px^0 > px. \tag{66}$$

In fact, let x^0 satisfy the conditions (65) and (66). For any commodity bundle x in $X(p, M)$ there exists a sequence $\{x^\nu\}$ of positive commodity bundles such that

$$px^0 > px^\nu, \quad \lim_\nu x^\nu = x.$$

Hence, by (66) and P.I we have $\overline{x^\nu P x^0}$ for all $\nu = 1, 2, \ldots$. Then, by P.VI′ we have $\overline{xPx^0}$ for all $px \leqq px^0$, which implies that $x^0 = h(p, M)$. ■

7 The Slutsky equations and demand functions

The structure of demand functions derived by preferences, as investigated by Slutsky [21], Hicks and Allen [9], Hotelling [10], and others, is concerned with the properties of the so-called Slutsky terms or the substitution terms K_{ij}:

$$K_{ij} = \frac{\partial x_i}{\partial p_j} + x_j \frac{\partial x_i}{\partial M}, \quad i, j = 1, 2, \ldots, n.$$

The two main properties derived by Slutsky [21] are: the negative semidefiniteness of the substitution matrix $[K_{ij}]$,

$$\sum_{i,j} K_{ij} c_i c_j \leqq 0, \quad \text{for all } c = (c_1, c_2, \ldots, c_n), \tag{67}$$

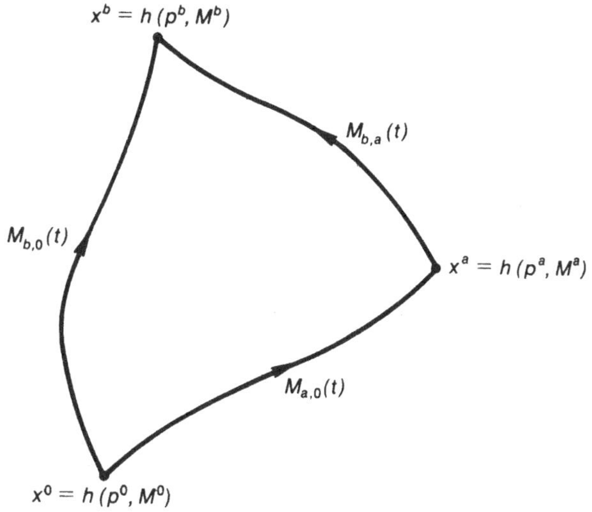

Figure 1.4

with strict inequality unless $c = \lambda p$, with λ real; and the symmetry of the substitution matrix $[K_{ij}]$,

$$K_{ij} = K_{ji}, \qquad i,j = 1, 2, \ldots, n. \tag{68}$$

It is shown by Samuelson [18, pp. 113–115] that the negative semidefiniteness (67) is a direct consequence of the Weak Axiom (W). It may be of some interest to give a proof of the symmetry of the substitution matrix (68) directly in terms of demand functions.

Let p^0 and M^0 be a price vector and an income that are arbitrarily fixed, and let x^0 be the corresponding commodity bundle. We consider the following differential equation:[13]

$$\frac{dM_{a,0}}{dt} = (p^a - p^0)h(p^t, M), \qquad M_{a,0}(0) = M^0, \tag{69}$$

where $p^t = p^0 + t(p - p^0)$, with $0 \leqq t \leqq 1$ (Figure 1.4).

Since the demand function $h(p, M)$ is continuous with respect to p and M (Theorem 2) and satisfies a Lipschitz condition with respect to M, it can be shown that the Houthakker lower-income sequence introduced in the proof of Lemma 1 converges to the solution of the differential equation (69). In addition, the solution to the differential equation (69) is continuous and uniquely determined with respect to the initial condition M^0.

[13] The function $M(p) = M_{x^0}(p)$ was introduced by McKenzie [12]. In [12], however, $M_{x^0}(p)$ is defined in terms of preference relations.

The proof of Lemma 1 also shows that $M(p^b) = \rho_{p^b,p^0}(M^0)$ is equal to the value $M_{b,a}(1)$ at $t = 1$ of the solution $M_{b,a}(t)$ to the following differential equation:

$$\frac{dM_{b,a}}{dt} = (p^b - p^a)h[p^a + t(p^b - p^a), M_{b,a}], \tag{70}$$

with initial value $M_{b,a}(0) = M_{a,0}(1)$.

Let p^a be an arbitrary price vector, and consider a price vector p^b such that $p^b - p^a = e^i$, where $e^i = (e_1^i, e_2^i, \ldots, e_n^i)$, with $e_j^i = 0$, $j \neq i$, $e_i^i = 1$.

Then the differential equation (70) may be written

$$\frac{dM_{b,a}}{dt} = h_i(p^a + te^i, M_{b,a}), \qquad M_{b,a}(0) = M_{a,0}(1). \tag{71}$$

Evaluating (71) at $t = 0$, we get

$$\left[\frac{dM_{b,a}}{dt}\right]_{t=0} = h_i(p^a, M^a).$$

On the other hand,

$$\begin{aligned}\left[\frac{dM_{b,a}}{dt}\right]_{t=0} &= \lim_{t\to 0} \frac{M_{b,a}(t) - M_{b,a}(0)}{t} \\ &= \lim_{t\to 0} \frac{M(p^a + te^i) - M(p^a)}{t} \\ &= \left[\frac{\partial M}{\partial p_i}\right]_{p=p^a}.\end{aligned}$$

We have, therefore,

$$\frac{\partial M(p)}{\partial p_i} = h_i[p, M(p)], \qquad i = 1, 2, \ldots, n, \tag{72}$$

for all positive price vectors p.

Differentiating both sides of equation (72) with respect to p_j, we have

$$\frac{\partial}{\partial p_j}\frac{\partial M(p)}{\partial p_i} = \frac{\partial h_i}{\partial p_j} + \frac{\partial h_i}{\partial M}\frac{dM}{\partial p_j} = \frac{\partial h_i}{\partial p_j} + \frac{\partial h_i}{\partial M}h_j(p, M) = K_{ij}(p).$$

Since

$$\frac{\partial^2 M(p)}{\partial p_j \partial p_i} = \frac{\partial^2 M(p)}{\partial p_i \partial p_j}$$

whenever such partial derivatives both exist and one of them is continuous, we have the symmetry condition (68) for the substitution matrix $[K_{ij}(p)]$.

References

[1] Arrow, K. J., *Social Choice and Individual Values*, New York: John Wiley and Sons, 1951.
[2] ———, "Rational Choice Functions and Ordering," *Economica*, N.S., **26**, 1959, 121–127.
[3] Coddington, E. A., and N. Levinson, *Theory of Ordinary Differential Equations*, New York: McGraw-Hill, 1955.
[4] Debreu, G., "Representation of a Preference Ordering by a Numerical Function," in *Decision Processes*, R. M. Thrall, C. H. Coombs, and R. L. Davis, Eds., New York: John Wiley and Sons, 1954, pp. 159–165.
[5] Fenchel, W., *Convex Cones, Sets, and Functions*, Princeton, N.J.: Princeton University, Department of Mathematics, 1953.
[6] Georgescu-Roegen, N., "The Pure Theory of Consumers' Behavior," *Quarterly Journal of Economics*, **50**, 1936, 545–593.
[7] Hicks, J. R., *Value and Capital*, 2d ed., Oxford: Oxford University Press, 1946.
[8] ———, *A Revision of Demand Theory*, Oxford: Oxford University Press, 1956.
[9] ———, and R. G. D. Allen, "A Reconsideration of the Theory of Value," *Economica*, N.S., **1**, 1934, 52–76, 196–219.
[10] Hotelling, H., "Demand Functions with Limited Budgets," *Econometrica*, **3**, 1935, 66–78.
[11] Houthakker, H. S., "Revealed Preference and the Utility Function," *Economica*, N.S., **7**, 1950, 159–174.
[12] McKenzie, L. W., "Demand Theory without a Utility Index," *Review of Economic Studies*, **24**, 1956–57, 185–189.
[13] Pareto, V., *Manuel d'économie politique*, 2d ed., Paris: Giard, 1927.
[14] Robertson, D. H., *Utility and All That, and Other Essays*, London: Allen and Unwin, 1952.
[15] Rose, H., "Consistency of Preference: The Two-Commodity Case." *Review of Economic Studies*, **35**, 1958, 124–125.
[16] Samuelson, P. A., "A Note on the Pure Theory of Consumer's Behaviour," *Economica*, N.S., **5**, 1938, 61–71, 353–354.
[17] ———, "The Empirical Implications of Utility Analysis," *Econometrica*, **6**, 1938, 344–356.
[18] ———, *Foundations of Economic Analysis*, Cambridge, Mass.: Harvard University Press, 1947.
[19] ———, "Consumption Theory in Terms of Revealed Preference," *Economica*, N.S., **15**, 1948, 243–253.
[20] ———, "The Problem of Integrability in Utility Theory," *Economica*, N.S., **17**, 1950, 355–385.
[21] Slutsky, E. E., "Sulla teoria del bilancio del consumatore," *Giornale degli Economisti*, **51**, 1915, 1–26; trans. by O. Ragusa, "On the Theory of the Budget of the Consumer," in *Readings in Price Theory*, G. J. Stigler and K. E. Boulding, Eds., Homewood, Ill.: Irwin, 1952.

[22] Ville, J., "Sur les conditions d'existence d'une ophélimité totale et d'un indice du niveau des prix," *Annales de l'Université de Lyon*, **9**, 1946, Sec. A(3), 32–39; trans. by P. K. Newman, "The Existence-Conditions of a Total Utility Function," *Review of Economic Studies*, **19**, 1951–52, 123–128.
[23] Wold, H., "A Synthesis of Pure Demand Analysis," *Skandinavisk Aktuarietid-skrift*, **26**, 1943, 85–118, 220–263; **27**, 1944, 69–120.
[24] ———, and L. Juréen, *Demand Analysis*, New York: John Wiley and Sons, 1953.

CHAPTER 2

On the integrability of demand functions

1 Introduction

This paper deals with the properties of demand functions derived from utility maximization. Such properties may be either "finite" (involving finite sets of points) or "infinitesimal" (involving the derivatives of the demand functions). The "revealed preference" approach, pioneered by P. A. Samuelson and developed by H. S. Houthakker, is of the "finite" type. In what follows, we shall confine ourselves to the "infinitesimal" type of analysis, dealing with "substitution terms." This analysis has been carried out in terms of the "direct" demand functions (quantities taken as functions of prices and incomes) by Slutsky, Hicks, Allen, Samuelson, and the "indirect" demand function (relative prices as functions of the quantities taken) by the "rediscovered" Antonelli, and also by Samuelson. The present paper deals only with the "direct" demand functions.

Perhaps the most familiar result, found in Hicks's Appendix in *Value and Capital* as well as in Samuelson's *Foundations*, is the fact that utility maximization (subject, of course, to the budget constraint) implies the symmetry and negative semidefiniteness of the Slutsky–Hicks substitution term matrix (derived from the "direct" demand functions). But much more remarkable is the converse proposition that, under certain regularity assumptions, if the demand function has a symmetric, negative semidefinite substitution term matrix, then it is generated by the maximization of a utility function.

In his *Foundations of Economic Analysis* [8], p. 116, Samuelson formulates the converse proposition and provides suggestions for a proof. He says

The assumption that the form in (96) be symmetrical and negative semi-definite completely exhausts the empirical implications of the utility analysis. All other

Written jointly with L. Hurwicz; *Preferences, Utility, and Demand*, edited by J. Chipman, L. Hurwicz, M. Richter, and H. Sonnenschein, Harcourt, Brace, Jovanovich, 1971, pp. 114–48; reprinted with permission.

demand restrictions can be derived as theorems from this single assumption. These are bold statements, but they are substantiated by the fact that it is possible to work backwards from the assumption of (96) to an integrable preference field displaying the properties necessary for a maximum. [The matrix in Samuelson's (96) was that of the Slutsky–Hicks substitution terms.]

A detailed justification of this assertion was subsequently given in Samuelson's 1950 *Economica* article on the problem of integrability in utility theory, specifically in its mathematical notes. But the method of proof chosen required the utilization of single-valued[1] indirect demand functions and hence called for an important additional assumption on the rank of the Slutsky matrix so as to guarantee the *invertibility* of the (direct) demand function. (See [9].)

The present paper vindicates Samuelson's original statement by performing the integration operations on the direct (rather than indirect) demand functions, thus avoiding the invertibility assumption. The basic result is contained in Theorem 2 which states, roughly, that a single-valued differentiable demand function arises from the maximization of a utility function subject to the budget constraint if the Slutsky substitution matrix is symmetric and negative semidefinite. It is furthermore shown that this utility function is monotone and its indifference surfaces are strictly convex to the origin (Theorem 4) and that it is upper semicontinuous (Theorem 5). These results utilize the following additional assumptions: The whole budget is spent and the derivatives of the demand function with respect to income satisfy a boundedness property. If a further (e.g., "modified Lipschitzian") assumption is made, the utility function is continuous, not merely upper semicontinuous (Theorem 6). The extent to which this assumption may be redundant has not yet been completely investigated.

A simple example is provided to show that invertibility is not implied by our assumptions. In the example, the indifference curves have kinks, so that there does not exist a single-valued indirect demand function. Although the example given involves only two commodities, higher dimensional examples of this type can also be constructed.

Theorem 1 shows to what extent the assumptions made are necessary for utility maximization subject to the budget constraint; if the demand function is single-valued and differentiable and if the whole budget is spent, the Slutsky matrix must be symmetric and negative semidefinite. This result differs from those due to Slutsky, Hicks, and Samuelson in that no assumptions are made about the differentiability properties of the utility function that is being maximized. Both the conclusions and the assump-

[1] In this paper, the term *function* is used in a broad sense compatible with multivaluedness, i.e., as a synonym for what Debreu calls a *correspondence*. A point-valued correspondence (a function in the narrow sense) is here referred to as a *single-valued function*.

tions of Theorem 1 are stronger than those found in McKenzie's "Demand Theory Without a Utility Index" [6]. (See, however, footnote 10 below.)

In essence, we exploit the fact that the existence of the utility function, under the assumptions made, is *equivalent*[2] to the existence of a concave function (the "income compensation" function) whose derivatives equal the corresponding components of the (direct) demand function. (The necessity, long known, is shown in connection with Theorem 1; the sufficiency, in connection with Lemma 8.)

In order to show that the assumptions made are sufficient to integrate the demand functions, the (integrability) Existence Theorem III is proved in the Appendix. This theorem, which does not seem to be available in the required form in the mathematical literature, guarantees the existence of the integrals *in the large* for the so-called Pfaffian systems when the dependent variable (income) is nonnegative. The results obtained here can be generalized by relaxing the regularity conditions on the demand functions. In particular, it is possible to guarantee the integrability of the demand functions with conditions weaker than differentiability.

2 Notation and assumptions

We shall be concerned with a finite number of commodities, to be labeled $1, 2, \ldots, n$. The quantities of the n commodities will be in general represented by an n-vector ("bundle") $x = (x_1, x_2, \ldots, x_n)$, where x_i stands for the quantity of the ith commodity. We shall be dealing only with nonnegative bundles $x \geqq 0$ (without always mentioning this explicitly).[3] Prices of all the n commodities are always assumed to be positive, and they are represented by an n-vector $p = (p_1, p_2, \ldots, p_n)$, where p_i stands for the price of the ith commodity in terms of a certain accounting unit. The set of all positive price vectors will be denoted by Π; that is,

$$\Pi = \{p = (p_1, p_2, \ldots, p_n) : p_i > 0, i = 1, 2, \ldots, n\}.$$

A demand function $x = \xi(p, m)$ specifies the relationships between

[2] The related statement found (without proof or reference) in Fourgeaud and Nataf [3], p. 345, came to our attention only after this paper was completed.

[3] Conventional vector notation will be used: For any two vectors $u = (u_1, u_2, \ldots, u_n)$ and $v = (v_1, v_2, \ldots, v_n)$,

$u \geqq v$ means $u_i \geqq v_i$, for all $i = 1, 2, \ldots, n$;
$u \geq v$ means $u \geqq v$, but $u \neq v$;
$u > v$ means $u_i > v_i$, for all $i = 1, 2, \ldots, n$.

Furthermore,

$$u \cdot v = uv = \sum_{i=1}^{n} u_i v_i.$$

quantities x of the n commodities to be consumed on the one hand and the prices p and income m on the other.

It will be assumed that the demand function $\xi(p,m)$ is defined for all positive vectors p and nonnegative m; we write

$$\Omega = \{(p,m): p > 0, m \geqq 0\}.$$

In what follows, we shall be referring to the following conditions.

(A) *$\xi(p,m)$ is a single-valued n-vector function defined on Ω, and $\xi(p,m) \geqq 0$, for all $(p,m)\in\Omega$.*

(B) *The budget equation is satisfied:*
$p\xi(p,m) = m$, for all $(p,m)\in\Omega$.

(D) *For each $i = 1, 2, \ldots, n$, the function $\xi^i(p,m)$ possesses a differential on Ω.*[4]

(E) *For any a', a'' with $0 < a' < a''$, there exists a positive $K_{a',a''}$ such that, for each $i = 1, 2, \ldots, n$, the inequality*

$$|\xi^i_m(p,m| \leqq K_{a',a''}, \qquad \textit{for all } (p,m)\in\Omega, a' \leqq p_j \leqq a'', \quad j = 1, 2, \ldots, n,$$

[4] Let the function f be defined on a subset S of the n-dimensional Euclidean space R^n and let $x^0 = (x^0_1, x^0_2, \ldots, x^0_n)$ be a point in S which is an accumulation point of S.

f is said to possess a differential at x^0 if there exist n numbers $\phi^i(x^0)$, $i = 1, 2, \ldots, n$, such that, for every $\varepsilon > 0$, there exists a $\delta > 0$ such that, for all $x = (x_1, x_2, \ldots, x_n)$, $x \in S$, $0 < \|x - x^0\| < \delta$, the inequality

$$\frac{|f(x) - f(x^0) - \sum \phi^i(x^0)\cdot(x_i - x^0_i)|}{\|x - x^0\|} < \varepsilon$$

holds; here $\|x - x^0\|$ stands for the norm of the vector $x - x^0$; for example,

$$\|x - x^0\| = \left|\sum_{i=1}^{n} (x_i - x^0_i)^2\right|^{1/2}$$

or

$$\|x - x^0\| = \max_i |x_i - x^0_i|.$$

When x^0 is an interior point of S,

$$\phi^i(x^0) = \left.\frac{\partial f}{\partial x_i}\right|_{x = x_0}$$

and is finite.

In the present application, the differentiability of $\xi^i(p,m)$ over Ω implies that the differential $d\xi^i$ satisfies

$$d\xi^i(p^0, m^0; p - p^0, m - m^0) = \sum_{j=1}^{n} \xi^i_{pj}(p^0, m^0)\cdot(p_j - p^p_j) + \xi^i_m(p^0, m^0)\cdot(m - m^0),$$

where $\xi^i_{pj}(p^0, m^0)$ and $\xi^i_m(p^0, m^0)$ are partial derivatives of ξ^i with respect to p_j or m, respectively, evaluated at (p^0, m^0). The derivatives $\xi^i_m(p^0, 0)$ are one-sided. (See Graves, pp. 76–77, [4].)

holds, where $\xi^i_m(p, m)$ is the partial derivative of $\xi^i(p, m)$ with respect to m.

The set of all commodity bundles $\xi(p, m)$, $(p, m) \in \Omega$, will be referred to as the *range*, to be denoted by X; that is,

$$X = \{\xi(p, m) : (p, m) \in \Omega\}.$$

Given a demand function $\xi(p, m) = (\xi^1(p, m), \xi^2(p, m), \ldots, \xi^n(p, m))$, the Slutsky terms $S_{ij}(p, m)$ at $(p, m) \in \Omega$ are defined by

$$S_{ij}(p, m) = \xi^i_j(p, m) + \xi^i_m(p, m)\xi^j(p, m), \qquad i, j = 1, 2, \ldots, n, \tag{1}$$

where $\xi^i_j = \partial \xi^i / \partial p_j$, $\xi^i_m = \partial \xi^i / \partial m$.

The Slutsky term $S_{ij}(p, m)$ is defined as a function of the price vector p and income m.

We may refer to the $n \times n$ matrix

$$S(p, m) = \begin{pmatrix} S_{11}(p, m) & S_{12}(p, m) & \cdots & S_{1n}(p, m) \\ \vdots & \vdots & & \vdots \\ S_{n1}(p, m) & S_{n2}(p, m) & \cdots & S_{nn}(p, m) \end{pmatrix}$$

as the *Slutsky-Hicks matrix*. The *Slutsky-Hicks matrix functions* S then associates with points (p, m) of Ω the matrix $S(p, m)$. The following two conditions on S will be considered.

(S) *Symmetry*[5]

$$S(p, m) = S'(p, m), \quad \text{for all } (p, m) \in \Omega;$$

that is,

$$S_{ij}(p, m) = S_{ji}(p, m), \quad \text{for all } i, j = 1, 2, \ldots, n, \text{ and all } (p, m) \in \Omega.$$

(N) *Negative semidefiniteness*

$$v'S(p, m)v \leqq 0, \quad \text{for all } (p, m) \in \Omega \text{ and all } n\text{-vectors } v = (v_1, v_2, \ldots, v_n);$$

that is,

$$\sum_{i,j=1}^{n} v_i S_{ij}(p, m) v_j \leqq 0, \quad \text{for all } (p, m) \in \Omega \text{ and all } v_1, v_2, \ldots, v_n.$$

3 Necessary conditions for utility maximization

The following Theorem 1 states conditions under which utility maximization implies the symmetry and negative semidefiniteness of the Slutsky-Hicks substitution term matrix. These conditions are: The quantity

[5] The prime denotes a transpose.

demanded uniquely maximizes the consumer's satisfaction (whether represented by an ordering or a numerical utility indicator); the demand function is single-valued; the whole budget is spent; and the demand function is differentiable.

Unlike, for example, in Hicks's Appendix in *Value and Capital* or in Samuelson's *Foundations*, nothing is assumed about the differentiability properties of the utility function.

The method of proof, involving the use of the "income compensation" function, is very close to that used by McKenzie in his "Demand Theory Without a Utility Index" [6].[6] A remark bearing on the relationship of Theorem 1 to McKenzie's results is found in footnote 10.

Theorem 1. Let $\succcurlyeq$ be a transitive reflexive connected[7] relation ("preference relation") defined on a set D ("consumption set") of nonnegative n-vectors x ("commodity bundles").

Let ξ be a (single-valued) function ("demand function") on Ω into D such that $\xi(p,m)$ is the unique maximizer of "satisfaction" (represented by $\succcurlyeq$) over D subject to the budget inequality $p\cdot x \leqq m$.[8]

In addition to (A), let the demand function ξ satisfy the budget equality (B) and the differentiability condition (D).

Then the Slutsky matrix $S(p,m)$ is defined and satisfies the conditions of symmetry (S) and negative semidefiniteness (N) for every element (p,m) of Ω.

Proof. Let (p^0,m^0) be a point of Ω and $x^0 = \xi(p^0,m^0)$. Define a subset K of the nonnegative commodity space by

$$K = \{x : x \in D \text{ and } x \succcurlyeq x^0\}. \tag{2}$$

We define the function μ on Π by

$$\mu(p) = \inf_{x \in K} px. \tag{3}$$

[It is sometimes convenient to write more explicitly $\mu(p;p^0,m^0)$ for $\mu(p)$.] Since K is composed of nonnegative vectors, for any $p \in \Pi$ and $x \in K$, px is a nonnegative number; therefore a nonnegative $\mu(p)$ exists for all $p \in \Pi$.

[6] See also footnote 9.

[7] "$\succcurlyeq$ is connected on D" means that, for any two distinct bundles $(x' \neq x'')$ in D, either $x' \succcurlyeq x''$ or $x'' \succcurlyeq x'$ or both. Since $\succcurlyeq$ is also assumed reflexive, we have $x' \succcurlyeq x''$ or $x'' \succcurlyeq x'$, or both, for any two x', x'' in D, whether distinct or not. We shall write $x' \succ x''$ to mean $x' \succcurlyeq x''$ and $x'' \not\succcurlyeq x'$; $x' \sim x''$ to mean $x' \succcurlyeq x''$ and $x'' \succcurlyeq x'$.

[8] That is, $\xi(p,m)$ is in D, $p\cdot\xi(p,m) \leqq m$, and $\xi(p,m) \succ x$ for any x in D satisfying the conditions $p\cdot x \leqq m$ and $x \neq \xi(p,m)$.

The function μ thus defined is a concave function on Π (see, e.g., Fenchel [2], p. 60, Proposition 7). Hence it is continuous on Π (see, e.g., Fenchel [2], p. 75, Proposition 23).

In turn, define

$$X(p) = \xi(p, \mu(p)), \quad \text{for all } p \in \Pi. \tag{4}$$

The function $X(p)$ is continuous on Π, since ξ and μ are both continuous. Note that, in view of (B),

$$pX(p) = \mu(p), \quad \text{for all } p \in \Pi. \tag{5}$$

We shall now show that, for any $p' \in \Pi$,

$$pX(p) \leqq pX(p'). \tag{6}$$

By definition of $\mu(\cdot)$, there exists a sequence $\{x^1, x^2, \dots\}$ such that

$$x^i \succcurlyeq x^0, \quad \text{for every } i \in \{1, 2, \dots\}$$

and

$$\lim_{i \to \infty} p' \cdot x^i = \mu(p') = \inf_{x \in K} p' \cdot x.$$

Hence, for every $\varepsilon > 0$, there exists i_ε such that

$$p' \cdot x^i < \mu(p') + \varepsilon \quad \text{for all } i \geqq i_\varepsilon.$$

Consider now $x_\varepsilon \equiv \xi[p', \mu(p') + \varepsilon]$. By hypothesis of the theorem, x_ε is the unique satisfaction maximizer subject to $p' \cdot x \leqq \mu(p') + \varepsilon$. Therefore, $p' \cdot x^i < \mu(p') + \varepsilon$ yields

$$x_\varepsilon \succ x^i;$$

hence, $x_\varepsilon \in K$.

On the other hand, since $\xi(p, m)$ is continuous with respect to m,

$$x_\varepsilon \to X(p') \quad \text{as} \quad \varepsilon \to 0.$$

Consider the first the case $X(p) \in K$. By (5), $X(p)$ minimizes (with respect to x) over K the function px. Since $x_\varepsilon \in K$, this implies

$$pX(p) \leqq px_\varepsilon \quad \text{for all } \varepsilon;$$

hence, by continuity,

$$pX(p) \leqq pX(p'),$$

since $x_\varepsilon \to X(p')$.

Consider now the case $X(p) \notin K$. Here $X(p) \prec x^0$. Since $x^i \succcurlyeq x^0$, and $x_\varepsilon \succ x^i$, we have

$$x_\varepsilon \succ X(p).$$

Now suppose $pX(p) > pX(p')$. Then, by continuity, for sufficiently small ε,

$$pX(p) > px_\varepsilon.$$

Thus, x_ε is more desirable than $X(p)$, and, at the price p, cheaper. It follows that $X(p)$ does not maximize satisfaction subject to $px \leqq \mu(p)$, hence $X(p) \neq \xi(p, \mu(p))$ which contradicts the definition of $X(p)$. Thus we have proved (6).

We next prove that, for every $j = 1, 2, \ldots, n$, the partial derivative $\partial\mu/\partial p_j$ exists and is continuous, and we have[9]

$$\frac{\partial \mu}{\partial p_j} = X^j(p), \qquad j = 1, 2, \ldots, n. \tag{7}$$

Consider two price vectors p and $p + \Delta p$, and the corresponding bundles $X(p)$ and $X(p + \Delta p)$. By (6),

$$p \cdot X(p) \leqq p \cdot X(p + \Delta p).$$

Writing

$$\Delta X(p) = X(p + \Delta p) - X(p),$$

(6) becomes

$$p \cdot X(p) \leqq p \cdot (X(p) + \Delta X(p)),$$

and hence

$$p \cdot \Delta X(p) \geqq 0. \tag{8}$$

We then have

$$\begin{aligned} \Delta\mu(p) &= \mu(p + \Delta p) - \mu(p) \\ &= (p + \Delta p)(X(p) + \Delta X(p)) - pX(p) \\ &= p \cdot \Delta X(p) + \Delta p \cdot X(p) + \Delta p \cdot \Delta X(p) \\ &\geqq \Delta p \cdot X(p) + \Delta p \cdot \Delta X(p) \qquad [\text{by}(8)]. \end{aligned} \tag{9}$$

Now take a special Δp, viz.

$$\Delta p = (0, \ldots, 0, \Delta p_j, 0, \ldots, 0), \qquad \Delta p_j > 0.$$

Then

$$\frac{\Delta \mu}{\Delta p_j} \geqq X^j(p) + \Delta X^j(p). \tag{10}$$

[9] An early statement of a relation underlying the basic equality (7) is already found in Slutsky [10], p. 41, in the form $ds = x_i dp_i$, where s is used for our m. See, however, Mosak [7] concerning Slutsky's concept of compensation for "apparent loss" versus our "actual loss."

Since $\mu(p)$ is a concave function of p, it possesses both left- and right-hand derivatives (see, e.g., Fenchel [2], pp. 71, 79 ff.).

On the other hand, by the continuity of $X^j(p)$,

$$\lim_{\Delta p_j \to 0} \Delta X^j(p) = 0;$$

hence, by letting $\Delta p_j \to 0$ in (10), we get

$$\lim_{\substack{\Delta p_j \to 0 \\ \Delta p_j > 0}} \frac{\Delta \mu}{\Delta p_j} \geqq X^j(p). \tag{11}$$

Analogously, taking

$$\Delta p = (0, \ldots, 0, \Delta p_j, 0, \ldots, 0), \qquad \Delta p_j < 0,$$

we obtain from (9),

$$\lim_{\substack{\Delta p_j \to 0 \\ \Delta p_j < 0}} \frac{\Delta \mu}{\Delta p_j} \leqq X^j(p). \tag{12}$$

Combining (11) and (12), we get

$$\lim_{\substack{\Delta p_j \to 0 \\ \Delta p_j < 0}} \frac{\Delta \mu}{\Delta p_j} \leqq X^j(p) \leqq \lim_{\substack{\Delta p_j \to 0 \\ \Delta p_j > 0}} \frac{\Delta \mu}{\Delta p_j}. \tag{13}$$

On the other hand, since $\mu(p)$ is a concave function of p, we have

$$\lim_{\substack{\Delta p_j \to 0 \\ \Delta p_j < 0}} \frac{\Delta \mu}{\Delta p_j} \geqq \lim_{\substack{\Delta p_j \to 0 \\ \Delta p_j > 0}} \frac{\Delta \mu}{\Delta p_j}. \tag{14}$$

The inequalities (13) and (14) together show that the partial derivative $\partial\mu/\partial p_j$ exists and is equal to $X^j(p)$, so that (7) holds.

Since $X^j(p)$ is continuous, $\mu_j = \partial\mu/\partial p_j$ is also continuous. (See Bonnesen and Fenchel [1], p. 26.)

Now, because of the differentiability assumption (D) for ξ and the just established continuous differentiability of μ, we may apply the chain rule to the partial differentiation of X^j with respect to p_i to get

$$\begin{aligned} X_i^j(p) \equiv \frac{\partial X^j}{\partial p_i} &= \xi_i^j(p, \mu(p)) + \xi_m^j(p, \mu(p))\mu_i(p) \\ &= \xi_i^j(p, \mu(p)) + \xi_m^j(p, \mu(p))\xi^i((p), \mu(p)) \\ &= S_{ji}(p, \mu(p)). \end{aligned} \tag{15}$$

The relations (7) and (15) imply that (writing $\mu_{ji} = \partial^2\mu/\partial p_i \partial p_j$)

$$\mu_{ji} = S_{ji}(p, \mu(p)), \qquad i,j = 1, 2, \ldots, n, \quad \text{for all } p \in \Pi. \tag{16}$$

We shall now show that the value of μ at $p = p^0$ is m^0; that is, that

$$m^0 = \mu(p^0). \tag{17}$$

In fact, we have [by definition of x^0 and of $\mu(\cdot)$, with $\mu(p^0) \equiv \mu(p^0; p^0, m^0)$]

$$m^0 \geqq \mu(p^0).$$

Suppose $m^0 > \mu(p^0)$; then there would exist a vector x^1 such that

$$x^1 \in D, \qquad m^0 = p^0 x^0 > p^0 x^1, \qquad x^1 \succcurlyeq x^0.$$

Such x^1 then would belong to $\xi(p^0, m^0)$, contradicting the assumption (A).

It follows, from (16) and (17), that [with $\mu_{ji}(p^0) \equiv \mu_{ji}(p^0; p^0, m^0)$], for every $(p^0, m^0) \in \Omega$,

$$\mu_{ji}(p^0) = S_{ji}(p^0, m^0). \tag{18}$$

Since $\mu_j(p)$ is differentiable, we may apply Young's theorem ([13], Section 19, pp. 22–23) to get

$$\mu_{ji}(p^0) = \mu_{ij}(p^0), \qquad i, j = 1, 2, \ldots, n, \quad p^0 \in \Pi. \tag{19}$$

Using (18) and (19), we get the symmetry condition (S).

The matrix

$$\begin{pmatrix} \mu_{11}(p) & \mu_{12}(p) & \cdots & \mu_{1n}(p) \\ \vdots & \vdots & & \vdots \\ \mu_{n1}(p) & \mu_{n2}(p) & \cdots & \mu_{nn}(p) \end{pmatrix}$$

is defined [by (16)] and negative semidefinite for all $p \in \Pi$, because μ is a concave twice differentiable function (see, e.g., Fenchel [2], pp. 87–88). Hence, using (18), we find that the Slutsky matrix $(S_{ij}(p^0, m^0))$ is negative semidefinite for all $(p^0, m^0) \in \Omega$.[10] ■

4 Sufficient conditions for utility maximization

The following Theorem 2 shows that the symmetry and negative semidefiniteness of the Slutsky–Hicks substitution terms, in conjunction with certain regularity properties, suffice to guarantee the existence of a utility function generating the given demand function. The required regularity

[10] In trying to relate Theorem 1 to the results of [6], it is interesting to inquire about the consequences of weakening the assumption that the demand function $\xi(p, m)$ is differentiable to mere continuity of $\xi(p, m)$. The results obtained in the first part of our proof do not use differentiability of $\xi(p, m)$ and remain valid. Thus there still exists a family of ("income compensation") functions $\mu(p; p^0, m^0)$ indexed by (p^0, m^0). Writing again $\mu(p) = \mu(p; p^0, m^0)$, the function $\mu(p)$ is still concave and we have [with $\mu'(p)$ denoting the vector of partial derivatives of $\mu(p)$] $\mu'(p) = X(p)$ where, by definition, $X(p) = \xi[p, \mu(p)]$.

properties are: The whole budget is spent; the demand function is single-valued and differentiable; and its derivatives with respect to income satisfy a boundedness condition. Theorem 2 follows from Lemmas 1–8 established below.

The basic idea of the proof is to show that, under the above assumptions, there exists a family of functions ("income compensation" functions) whose derivatives with regard to prices equal the corresponding demand functions. The income compensation functions are then used to construct a utility indicator which turns out to have been maximized, subject to the budget constraint, by the initially given demand function.

It is then shown that, under the same assumptions, this utility function is upper semicontinuous (Theorem 5) and monotone, and that its indifference surfaces are convex to the origin (Theorem 4). In Theorem 6, lower semicontinuity (hence, continuity) is obtained with the help of additional assumptions.

The procedures used permit the construction of alternative utility indicators through the use of different "base prices" in the income compensation function. Theorem 3 shows that these alternative indicators define the same ordering of commodity bundles.

Theorem 2. Let the demand function $\xi(p, m)$ satisfy conditions (A), (B), (D), and (E). If the Slutsky-Hicks terms $S_{ij}(p, m)$ satisfy

As pointed out by McKenzie, it follows from the concavity of $\mu(p)$ (by the theorem due to A.D. Alexandrov) that $X(p)$ is almost everywhere differentiable. Furthermore, where $X(p)$ is differentiable (i.e., almost everywhere) the compensated demand function $X(p)$ has a matrix of derivatives

$$\| X_j^i(p) \|$$

which is symmetric and negative semidefinite.

It is not clear, however, how [without assumptions stronger than the continuity of $\xi(p, m)$] one could infer, as in [6], that the matrix

$$\| S_{ij}(p, m) \|$$

is symmetric and negative semidefinite almost everywhere.

In particular, it is not obvious what differentiability properties $\xi(p, m)$ would have even if $X(p)$ were everywhere differentiable. The nature of the difficulty is seen from the following ($n = 2$) example. Let $\xi^1(p, m)$ be given by

$$\xi^1(p, m) = \frac{m \cdot f(m^2)}{2p \cdot f(p)} \qquad (p = p_2/p_1)$$

where $f(z)$ is a nowhere differentiable function varying between $\frac{1}{2}$ and 1. Here the differential equation $\mu'(p) = \xi(p, m)$ has a solution $\mu(p) = p^{1/2}$ which is everywhere twice differentiable. (However, since it has not been shown that solutions through *all* initial points (p^0, m^0) are concave, this is not a counter-example.)

[Appearing after the completion of this paper, Hartman's bracketed remark in Theorem 9.1(iii), [5], pp. 329–330, implies that $\| S_{ij}(p, m) \|$ is symmetric and negative semidefinite almost everywhere when $\xi(p, m)$ is locally uniformly Lipschitzian in (p, m).]

conditions (S) and (N), then there exists a utility function u defined on the range X of the demand function $\xi(p, m)$ such that the value of $\xi(p, m)$ of the demand function at (p, m) uniquely maximizes $u(x)$ over the budget set

$$\{x : x \in X, p \cdot x \leqq m\}.$$

4.1. To prove Theorem 2, let us first consider the following system of partial differential equations:

$$\frac{\partial m}{\partial p_i} = \xi^i(p, m), \qquad i = 1, 2, \ldots, n; \tag{20'}$$

or, in vector notation,

$$\frac{\partial m}{\partial p} = \xi(p, m). \tag{20''}$$

By applying Existence Theorem III in the Appendix we obtain Lemma 1.

Lemma 1. Let the demand function $\xi(p, m)$ satisfy the conditions (A), (D), (E), and (S). Then the system (20) is uniquely integrable; that is, for any $(p^*, m^*) \in \Omega$, there uniquely exists a function $\mu(p; p^*, m^*)$ defined for all $p \in \Pi$ such that

$$\mu(p^*; p^*, m^*) = m^*, \tag{21}$$

$$\mu_i(p; p^*, m^*) = \xi^i(p, \mu(p; p^*, m^*)), \qquad i = 1, 2, \ldots, n, \tag{22}$$

for all $p \in \Pi$. [Here $\mu_i(p; p^*, m^*)$ denotes the partial derivative of $\mu(p; p^*, m^*)$ with respect to the ith component of p.]

For every fixed $p \in \Pi$, $\mu(p; p^*, m^*)$ is continuous with respect to (p^*, m^*).

The "income compensation" function μ may be used to compare various price-income combinations; namely, a price-income combination (p', m') may be defined to be "preferred to" (p'', m'') if, for some fixed p^*, the income $\mu(p^*; p', m')$ is greater than $\mu(p^*; p'', m'')$. The following two lemmas will show that the relation thus defined is in fact an ordering and is independent of the choice of the base price vector p^*. The use of the term "income compensation" function in the sense of (3) above is justified by Lemma 8.

Lemma 2. Let (p', m'), $(p'', m'') \in \Omega$. If

$$\mu(p^0; p', m') = \mu(p^0; p'', m''), \quad \text{for some } p^0 \in \Pi, \tag{23}$$

then

$$\mu(p; p', m') = \mu(p; p'', m''), \quad \text{for all } p \in \Pi. \tag{24}$$

Proof. The assertion of the Lemma is implied by the uniqueness of the solution $\mu(p; p^*, m^*)$ of the system (20). ■

Lemma 3. Let (p', m'), $(p'', m'') \in \Omega$. If

$$\mu(p^0; p', m') < \mu(p^0; p'', m''), \quad \text{for some } p^0 \in \Pi, \tag{25}$$

then

$$\mu(p; p', m') < \mu(p; p'', m''), \quad \text{for all } p \in \Pi. \tag{26}$$

Proof. Suppose there exist $p^0, p^1 \in \Pi$ such that the relation (25) is satisfied for p^0, but $\mu(p^1; p', m') \geqq \mu(p^1; p'', m'')$.

Let $p^t = p^0 + t(p^1 - p^0)$, $0 \leqq t \leqq 1$, and the function $\varphi(t)$ be defined by

$$\varphi(t) = \mu(p^t; p', m') - \mu(p^t; p'', m'').$$

Then $\varphi(t)$ is a continuous[11] function of t and we have the inequalities:

$$\varphi(0) < 0, \qquad \varphi(1) \geqq 0.$$

Hence there exists a number τ such that $0 < \tau \leqq 1$ and $\varphi(\tau) = 0$; that is,

$$\mu(p^\tau; p', m') = \mu(p^\tau; p'', m'').$$

This, by Lemma 2, implies that

$$\mu(p; p', m') = \mu(p; p'', m''), \quad \text{for all } p \in \Pi,$$

thus contradicting (25). ■

4.2. The income compensation function $\mu(p^*; p, m)$ may now be used to construct, on the range X of the demand function $\xi(p, m)$, the utility function $u(x)$ promised in Theorem 2. Namely, for some fixed p^*, and any x in X, we shall define $u(x)$ as equal to $U_{p^*}(x)$ where

$$U_{p^*}(x) = \mu(p^*; p, m), \tag{27}$$

and (p, m) is any pair with a price vector p and income m for which $x = \xi(p, m)$.

That $U_{p^*}(x)$ qualifies as a utility function follows from Lemma 8. But we must first show that, for given p^*, the value of $U_{p^*}(x)$ defined by (27) is

[11] The continuity of $\varphi(t)$ follows from the continuity of $\mu(p; p^*, m^*)$ as a function of p. This property of μ is implied by Lemma 1.

uniquely determined, independently of the choice of (p, m) satisfying $x = \xi(p, m)$. This follows from Lemma 7 whose proof is preceded by lemmas concerning the properties of the income compensation function μ.

Lemma 4. Let (p^0, m^0) and (p^1, m^1) be two arbitrary pairs of price vectors and incomes such that

$$x^0 = \xi(p^0, m^0) \neq x^1 = \xi(p^1, m^1) \tag{28}$$

and

$$m^1 \geqq \mu(p^1; p^0, m^0). \tag{29}$$

Then

$$p^0 x^1 > p^0 x^0. \tag{30}$$

Proof. *Case 1.* Let us first establish (30) for the case where (29) holds with equality sign, that is, where

$$m^1 = \mu(p^1; p^0, m^0). \tag{31}$$

We define

$$p^t = p^0 + t(p^1 - p^0), \qquad 0 \leqq t \leqq 1, \tag{32}$$

$$m^t = \mu(p^t; p^0, m^0), \qquad x^t = \xi(p^t, m^t), \tag{33}$$

$$\psi(t) = p^0 x^t. \tag{34}$$

Differentiating (34) with respect to t, we get (in vector notation)

$$\begin{aligned}\psi'(t) &= p^0\left(\frac{\partial \xi}{\partial p} + \frac{\partial \xi}{\partial m}\cdot\frac{\partial \mu}{\partial p}\right)\frac{dp^t}{dt} \\ &= p^0 S(p^t, m^t)(p^1 - p^0),\end{aligned} \tag{35}$$

where all partial derivatives are evaluated at (p^t, m^t) and $S(p, m)$ is the (n, n) matrix of Slutsky terms.

Differentiating the budget equation $p^t x^t = m^t$ with respect to t, we get

$$p^t S(p^t, m^t)(p^1 - p^0) = 0. \tag{36}$$

Subtract (36) from (35) to get

$$\begin{aligned}\psi'(t) &= -(p^t - p^0)S(p^t, m^t)(p^1 - p^0) \\ &= -t(p^1 - p^0)S(p^t, m^t)(p^1 - p^0).\end{aligned} \tag{37}$$

The equality (37), together with assumption (N), implies that

$$\psi'(t) \geqq 0, \quad \text{for all } 0 \leqq t \leqq 1. \tag{38}$$

Therefore

$$\psi(0) \leqq \psi(1). \tag{39}$$

We shall now show that (39) holds with a strict inequality sign, which is equivalent to (30). Suppose (39) holds with equality. Then from (38) and (39), we have

$$\psi'(t) = 0, \quad \text{for all } 0 < t \leqq 1,$$

which, in view of (37), implies that

$$(p^1 - p^0)S(p^t, m^t)(p^1 - p^0) = 0, \quad \text{for all } 0 < t \leqq 1. \tag{40}$$

Since $S(p^t, m^t)$ is negative semidefinite, (40) yields[12]

$$S(p^t, m^t)(p^1 - p^0) = 0, \quad \text{for all } 0 < t \leqq 1. \tag{41}$$

But since $x^t = \xi(p^t, m^t)$, we get by differentiation

$$\frac{dx^t}{dt} = \left(\frac{\partial \xi}{\partial p} + \frac{\partial \xi}{\partial m}\frac{\partial \mu}{\partial p}\right)\frac{dp^t}{dt} = S(p^t, m^t)(p^1 - p^0), \quad \text{for all } 0 < t \leqq 1. \tag{42}$$

The equations (41) and (42) together imply that

$$\frac{dx^t}{dt} = 0, \quad \text{for all } 0 < t \leqq 1;$$

hence,

$$x^1 = x^t, \quad 0 < t \leqq 1. \tag{43}$$

Since x^t is continuous at $t = 0$, we have

$$x^1 = x^0, \tag{44}$$

thus contradicting (28).

Case 2. It remains to consider the case where (29) holds as a strict inequality, that is, where

$$m^1 > \mu(p^1; p^0, m^0). \tag{45}$$

Here, substituting $m^1 = \mu(p^1; p^1, m^1)$ in (45) and using Lemma 3, we have

$$\mu(p^0; p^1, m^1) > \mu(p^0; p^0, m^0) = m^0. \tag{46}$$

Write $m^* = \mu(p^0; p^1, m^1)$; then, by an argument similar to that used above

[12] In general, let A be a nonnegative semidefinite symmetric (n, n) matrix. Then there exists a symmetric matrix B such that $A = B^2$. Hence, $xAx = 0$ implies $(xB)(Bx) = 0$. Therefore $Bx = 0$, which by pre-multiplying with B yields $Ax = BBx = 0$.

to establish (39), we obtain the inequality

$$m^* \leqq p^0 x^1. \tag{47}$$

Combining (46) and (47), we get

$$p^0 x^0 = m^0 < m^* \leqq p^0 x^1. \quad \blacksquare$$

Lemma 5. Weak Axiom of Revealed Preference.[13] Let

$$x^0 = \xi(p^0, m^0), \qquad x^1 = \xi(p^1, m^1).$$

If

$$p^0 x^0 \geqq p^0 x^1, \qquad x^0 \neq x^1, \tag{48}$$

then

$$p^1 x^0 > p^1 x^1. \tag{49}$$

Proof. From (48) we obtain, by Lemma 4, $\mu(p^1; p^1, m^1) = m^1 < \mu(p^1; p^0, m^0)$; then, in view of Lemma 3, we have

$$\mu(p^0; p^1, m^1) < \mu(p^0; p^0, m^0) = m^0. \tag{50}$$

Applying Lemma 4 to (50), we get (49). ■

Lemma 6. For any $x \in X$, the set $\{(p, m) \in \Omega : \xi(p, m) = x\}$ is convex.[14]

Proof. Let

$$\xi(p^0, m^0) = \xi(p^1, m^1) = \bar{x},$$

so that

$$m^0 = p^0 \bar{x}, \qquad m^1 = p^1 \bar{x}.$$

Define

$$p(t) = p^0 + t(p^1 - p^0), \tag{51}$$

$$m(t) = m^0 + t(m^1 - m^0), \tag{52}$$

[13] The Strong Axiom of Revealed Preference can be established directly by a method analogous to that used in the proof of Lemma 5.

[14] In fact, it can be seen from the proof of Theorem 6 below that the following more general property holds:

If

$$\xi(p^1, m^1) = \lim_{\nu \to \infty} \xi(p^\nu, m^\nu) = \bar{x}, \qquad \lim_{\nu \to \infty} (p^\nu, m^\nu) = (p^0, m^0),$$

then

$$\xi(p(t), m(t)) = \bar{x}, \quad \text{for all } 0 < t \leqq 1,$$

where $p(t)$, and $m(t)$ are defined respectively by (51) and (52).

and

$$x(t) = \xi[p(t), m(t)]. \tag{53}$$

Then

$$p(t)\bar{x} = m(t) = p(t)x(t). \tag{54}$$

We want to prove

$$x(t) = \bar{x}, \quad \text{for all } 0 \leqq t \leqq 1. \tag{55}$$

Suppose, for some $0 < t < 1$, $x(t) \neq \bar{x}$. Noting (54) and applying Lemma 5, we get

$$p^0\bar{x} < p^0 x(t) \tag{56}$$

and

$$p^1\bar{x} < p^1 x(t). \tag{57}$$

Multiplying (56) by $(1 - t)$ and (57) by t, we get

$$p(t)\bar{x} < p(t)x(t),$$

which contradicts (54). Therefore, relation (55) must hold; that is, the set

$$\{(p, m) : \xi(p, m) = \bar{x}\}$$

is convex. ■

Lemma 7. If $\xi(p^0, m^0) = \xi(p^1, m^1)$, then $\mu(p; p^0, m^0) = \mu(p; p^1, m^1)$ for all p.

Proof. Let $p(t)$ and $m(t)$ be defined by equations (51) and (52). Then, by Lemma 6,

$$\xi(p(t), m(t)) = \xi(p^0, m^0), \quad \text{for all } 0 \leqq t \leqq 1.$$

Hence,

$$\frac{dm(t)}{dt} = \xi(p(t), m(t))\frac{dp(t)}{dt}, \quad \text{for all } 0 \leqq t \leqq 1. \tag{58}$$

The relation (58) shows that the path $\{(p(t), m(t)) : 0 \leqq t \leqq 1\}$ lies on a solution to (20). Applying Lemma 2 we then get

$$\mu(p(t); p^0, m^0) = m(t), \quad \text{for all } 0 \leqq t \leqq 1.$$

Therefore,

$$\mu(p^1; p^0, m^0) = m(1) = m^1;$$

hence, by Lemma 2,

$$\mu(p; p^0, m^0) = \mu(p; p^1, m^1), \quad \text{for all } p. \qquad ■$$

4.3. Theorem 2 then follows directly from Lemma 8.

Lemma 8. Let the demand function $\xi(p,m)$ satisfy conditions (A), (B), (D), (E), (S), and (N). For any price vector p^*, $U_{p^*}(x)$ defined by (27) is a single-valued function defined on the range X, and for any price vector p and income m,

$$U_{p^*}[\xi(p,m)] > U_{p^*}(x) \qquad \text{for all } x \in X \text{ such that } px \leqq m, x \neq \xi(p,m). \tag{59}$$

Proof. The single-valuedness of the function $U_{p^*}(x)$ follows from Lemmas 1, 2, and 7. To establish (59), let

$$x^0 = \xi(p^0, m^0), \qquad p^0 x^0 = m^0,$$
$$x^1 = \xi(p^1, m^1), \qquad p^1 x^1 = m^1,$$

and

$$p^0 x^1 \leqq m^0, \qquad x^1 \neq x^0.$$

Then, by Lemma 4 (contrapositive)

$$m^1 < \mu(p^1; p^0, m^0),$$

hence, since $m^1 = \mu(p^1; p^1, m^1)$ by Lemma 1,

$$\mu(p^1; p^1, m^1) < \mu(p^1; p^0, m^0).$$

Therefore, by Lemma 3,

$$\mu(p; p^1, m^1) < \mu(p; p^0, m^0), \quad \text{for all } p;$$

in particular,

$$\mu(p^*; p^1, m^1) < \mu(p^*; p^0, m^0)$$

which, by definition (27) of $U_{p^*}(\cdot)$, is equivalent to

$$U_{p^*}(x^0) > U_{p^*}(x^1). \qquad \blacksquare$$

5 An invariance property of the utility functions

Two real-valued functions, $f(a)$ and $g(a)$, defined on a set A are said to *induce the same ordering on A* if: for all $a', a'' \in A$, $f(a') > f(a'')$ if and only if $g(a') > g(a'')$.

Theorem 3. For any two positive price vectors, p^* and p^{**}, the functions U_{p^*} and $U_{p^{**}}$ induce the same ordering on the range X of the demand function $\xi(p,m)$.

Proof. By definition, for any $x, x' \in X$,

$$\begin{cases} U_{p^*}(x) > U_{p^*}(x') & \text{if, and only if,} \quad \mu(p^*; p, m) > \mu(p^*; p', m'), \\ U_{p^{**}}(x) > U_{p^{**}}(x') & \text{if, and only if,} \quad \mu(p^{**}; p, m) > \mu(p^{**}; p', m'), \end{cases} \tag{60}$$

where

$$x = \xi(p, m), \qquad x' = \xi(p', m').$$

On the other hand, we have from Lemma 3,

$$\mu(p^*; p, m) > \mu(p^*; p', m') \tag{61}$$

if, and only if,

$$\mu(p^{**}; p, m) > \mu(p^{**}; p', m').$$

The relations (60) and (61) together imply that, for any $x, x' \in X$,

$$U_{p^*}(x) > U_{p^*}(x') \quad \text{if, and only if,} \quad U_{p^{**}}(x) > U_{p^{**}}(x')$$

that is, U_{p^*} and $U_{p^{**}}$ induce the same ordering on X. ∎

6 Monotonicity and convexity

The indifference sets of a real-valued function $f(a)$ defined on a set A of vectors are said to be *strictly convex toward the origin* if, for any $a^0 \in A$, there exists a positive vector q such that

$$qa^0 < qa, \quad \text{for all } a \in A \text{ satisfying } f(a) = f(a^0),\ a \neq a^0.$$

Theorem 4. For any price vector p^*, $U_{p^*}(x)$ is monotone with respect to the vectorial ordering of X, and the indifference sets of the function U_{p^*} are strictly convex toward the origin. ("Monotone" means "monotone increasing.")

Proof. Monotonicity follows from Lemma 8 above. To prove that the indifference sets of the function U_{p^*} are strictly convex toward the origin, it suffices to show that for any $(p^0, m^0) \in \Omega$,

$$p^0 x > p^0 x^0, \quad \text{for all } x \in X \text{ satisfying } U_{p^*}(x) = U_{p^*}(x^0). \tag{62}$$

To establish (62), let x^1 be any bundle in X satisfying

$$U_{p^*}(x^1) = U_{p^*}(x^0).$$

Let

$$x^0 = \xi(p^0, m^0), \qquad x^1 = \xi(p^1, m^1).$$

Define $\psi(t)$ by equation (34) above. Then, adapting the procedure used to derive (30) from (34), we get

$$\psi(0) < \psi(1), \quad \text{whenever} \quad x^0 \neq x^1;$$

that is, (62) holds. ■

7 Upper semicontinuity of the utility function $U_{p*}(\cdot)$

In this section, we shall establish the following.

Theorem 5. Under the assumptions of Theorem 2, the function $U_{p*}(x)$ is upper semicontinuous[15] in x, for every choice of p^*.

Proof.[16] To demonstrate the upper semicontinuity of U_{p*}, one has to show that, for every real α, the set

$$\{x : x \in X, U_{p*}(x) < \alpha\}$$

is open; that is, given any $x^1 \in X$ and satisfying

$$U_{p*}(x^1) < \alpha, \tag{63}$$

there exists a positive number S such that

$$U_{p*}(x) < \alpha, \quad \text{for all } x \text{ satisfying } \|x - x^1\| < S. \tag{64}$$

Let $x^1 = \xi(p^1, m^1)$, for some positive price vector p^1 and income m^1. Then (63) means

$$\mu(p^*; p^1, m^1) < \alpha.$$

Because of the continuity of $\mu(p^*; p^1, m)$ with respect to m, it follows that there exists a positive number ε such that

$$\mu(p^*; p^1, m^1 + \varepsilon) < \alpha. \tag{65}$$

On the other hand, $p^1 x^1 = m^1$ and $p^1 x$ is continuous with respect to x. Hence, there exists a positive number S such that

$$p^1 x < m^1 + \varepsilon, \quad \text{for all } x \text{ satisfying } \|x - x^1\| < S. \tag{66}$$

Let $x^\varepsilon = \xi(p^1, m^1 + \varepsilon)$; then, Lemma 8 and (66) imply that

$$U_{p*}(x) < U_{p*}(x^\varepsilon), \quad \text{for all } x \text{ satisfying } \|x - x^1\| < S. \tag{67}$$

[15] A function f defined on a set D is said to be *upper semicontinuous* if, for every real number α, the upper contour set $\{x : x \in D, f(x) \geqq \alpha\}$ is closed in D.

[16] This closely parallels the proof in [12] of the fact that R^* satisfies P.V. of [12]. However, in the present proof we do not assume the range X of the function $\xi(p, m)$ to be a convex set.

By construction of x^{ε} and (27), the inequality (65) may be written as

$$U_{p^*}(x^{\varepsilon}) < \alpha,$$

which, together with (67), yields (64). ■

8 Lower semicontinuity of the utility function $U_{p^*}(\cdot)$

In this section, we shall show that the utility function $U_{p^*}(x)$ is also lower semicontinuous[17] in x for every choice of p^*, but this result will involve a strengthening of the previously made assumptions.

Theorem 6. The utility function $U_{p^*}(x)$ is lower semicontinuous in x for every choice of p^* if, in addition to the assumptions (A), (B), (D), and (E) of Theorem 2, we also have any one of the following three conditions:

a. If the sequence $p^{\nu} > 0$, $\nu = 1, 2, \ldots$, converges to some p^0 such that $p^0 \neq 0$, $p^0 \not> 0$, then the sequence x^{ν}, $\nu = 1, 2, \ldots$, where $x^{\nu} = \xi[p^{\nu}, \mu(p^{\nu}; p, m)]$, is unbounded for every choice of (p, m), $p > 0$, $m \geqq 0$;

b. There exists a single-valued inverse demand function; that is,

$$\xi(p', m') = \xi(p'', m'')$$

implies $m' = m'' = 0$ or $(p'/m') = (p''/m'')$;

c. $\xi(p, m)$ is Lipschitzian with respect to the boundary; that is, for every p^0 such that $p^0 \geqq 0$, $p^0 \neq 0$, and $p^0 \not> 0$, there exist positive numbers ε and $K = K_{\varepsilon, p^0}$ such that

$$\| \xi(p, m') - \xi(p, m'') \| < K |m' - m''|$$

for all $m', m'' \geqq 0$ and all $p > 0$, $\| p - p^0 \| < \varepsilon$.

Remark 1. Hypothesis (a) involves the use of the function μ whose existence is assured because Theorem 6 incorporates the assumptions of Theorem 2. All elements x^{ν}, $\nu = 1, 2, \ldots$, have the same utility. Thus, hypothesis (a) requires that when one or more (but not all) of the prices tend to zero while income is so compensated as to leave the consumer at a constant utility level, some of the quantities demanded tend to infinity. Hypothesis (a) applies to Example in Section 9 below which would not be covered by hypotheses (b) or (c).

[17] A function f defined on a set D is said to be *lower semicontinuous* if, for every real number α, the lower contour set $\{x : x \in D, f(x) \leqq \alpha\}$ is closed in D.

Remark 2. Hypothesis (b) is that of *invertibility*, used by Samuelson in [9]. For a proof of lower semicontinuity in this case, see Uzawa [12], Theorem 2, and Sonnenschein [11].

Proof. Suppose that the utility function $U_{p*}(x)$ is not lower semicontinuous. Then there exists a number α such that the set

$$\{x \in X : U_{p*}(x) \leqq \alpha\}$$

is not closed in the relative topology of X; namely, there exists a sequence of vectors $\bar{x}, x^1, x^2, \ldots,$ such that

$$\bar{x} \in X \quad \text{and} \quad x^\nu \in X, \qquad \nu = 1, 2, \ldots,$$

satisfying

$$\bar{x} = \lim_{\nu \to \infty} x^\nu, \tag{68}$$

$$U_{p*}(x^\nu) \leqq \alpha, \quad \text{for all } \nu, \text{ and } U_{p*}(\bar{x}) = \bar{\alpha} > \alpha. \tag{69}$$

Since $\bar{x}$ and the x^ν are all in X, there exist $(\bar{p}, \bar{m})$ and (p^ν, m^ν), $\nu = 1, 2, \ldots,$ such that

$$\bar{x} = \xi(\bar{p}, \bar{m}), \qquad \bar{p} \cdot \bar{x} = \bar{m}, \tag{70}$$

$$x^\nu = \xi(p^\nu, m^\nu), \qquad p^\nu \cdot x^\nu = m^\nu, \tag{71}$$

where $\bar{p} > 0$, $p^\nu > 0$, and $\bar{m} \geqq 0$, $m^\nu \geqq 0$. (Note that, by the monotonicity of U_{p*}, $U_{p*}(x^\nu) < U_{p*}(\bar{x})$ implies $\bar{x} \geq 0$, hence $\bar{m} > 0$.) Since the function $\xi(p, m)$ is homogeneous of degree zero in (p, m),[18] we may assume, without loss of generality, that $\|(p^\nu, m^\nu)\| = 1$, for all ν. Since the sequence (p^ν, m^ν) is bounded, we may assume, by taking a subsequence if necessary, that it converges to a certain point (p^0, m^0); that is,

$$\lim_{\nu \to \infty} (p^\nu, m^\nu) = (p^0, m^0). \tag{72}$$

We have then from (69), (70), and (71) that

$$p^0 \cdot \bar{x} = \lim_{\nu \to \infty} p^\nu \cdot x^\nu = \lim_{\nu \to \infty} m^\nu = m^0. \tag{73}$$

Because of the nonnegativity of (p^ν, m^ν), the limit (p^0, m^0) is nonnegative and in addition $\|(p^0, m^0)\| = 1$. Hence, because $p^0 \cdot \bar{x} = m^0$, p^0 is nonzero; that is, $p^0 \geq 0$.

However, we must have $p^0 \ngtr 0$. Otherwise, the function $\xi(p, m)$ would be

[18] The homogeneity of the demand function $\xi(p, m)$ follows from the Weak Axiom of Revealed Preference, established in Lemma 5 above. See Samuelson [8], pp. 111–112.

defined and continuous at (p^0, m^0); hence,

$$\bar{x} = \lim_{\nu \to \infty} \xi(p^\nu, m^\nu) = \xi(p^0, m^0).$$

On the other hand, conditions (69) imply that

$$U_{p^*}(x^\nu) = \mu(p^*; p^\nu, m^\nu) \leqq \alpha, \quad \text{for all } \nu.$$

Because of the continuity of $\mu(p^*; p, m)$ in (p, m),

$$U_{p^*}(\bar{x}) = \mu(p^*; p^0, m^0) = \lim \mu(p^*; p^\nu, m^\nu) \leqq \alpha,$$

contradicting conditions (69) assumed above.

Therefore, we have

$$p^0 \geqq 0, \qquad p^0 \not> 0, \quad \text{and} \quad \bar{p} > 0. \tag{74}$$

Define $m^{*\nu} = \mu(p^\nu; p^*, \alpha)$ and $x^{*\nu} = \xi(p^\nu, m^{*\nu})$, $\nu = 1, 2, \ldots$. Then $x^{*\nu} \to \bar{x}$ and hence $x^{*\nu} = \xi[p^\nu, \mu(p^\nu; p^*, \alpha)]$ are bounded, thus contradicting hypothesis (a) of Theorem 6. [Without loss of generality, set $\alpha = \sup_\nu U_{p^*}(x^\nu)$.]

Let us now define

$$p(t) = (1-t)p^0 + t\bar{p}, \tag{75}$$

$$\bar{M}(t) = (1-t)m^0 + t\bar{m}, \quad \text{for } 0 \leqq t \leqq 1. \tag{76}$$

Then $p(t)$ is positive for all $0 < t \leqq 1$, and

$$p(0) = p^0, \qquad p(1) = \bar{p}$$
$$\bar{M}(0) = m^0, \qquad \bar{M}(1) = \bar{m}.$$

We shall now show that

$$\bar{x} = \xi(p(t), \bar{M}(t)), \quad \text{for all } 0 < t \leqq 1. \tag{77}$$

To establish (77), let us first note, in view of (70) and (73), that

$$p(t)\bar{x} = (1-t)p^0\bar{x} + t\bar{p}\bar{x} = \bar{M}(t).$$

Now for some $0 < t \leqq 1$, consider any vector x satisfying the budget inequality

$$p(t)x \leqq \bar{M}(t), \tag{78}$$

which is equivalent to

$$(1-t)p^0x + t\bar{p}x \leqq (1-t)m^0 + t\bar{m}, \qquad 0 < t \leqq 1.$$

Hence, we have either $p^0x < m^0$ or $\bar{p}x \leqq \bar{m}$.

If $p^0x < m^0$, we have from (72) that

$$p^\nu x < m^\nu, \quad \text{for sufficiently large } \nu,$$

and so

$$U_{p^*}(x) < U_{p^*}(x^\nu) < U_{p^*}(\bar{x}).$$

On the other hand, if $\bar{p}x \leqq \bar{m}$, then from (70) one gets

$$U_{p^*}(x) < U_{p^*}(\bar{x}).$$

In either case, the utility level associated with x is lower than that for $\bar{x}$; therefore, the vector $\bar{x}$ is the most desired one in the budget set defined by (78), thus implying (77).

Since $p^0 \not> 0$, (77) implies $\bar{x} = \xi(\bar{p}, \bar{m}) = \xi(p(\frac{1}{2}), \bar{M}(\frac{1}{2}))$, with $\bar{m} > 0$, $\bar{M}(\frac{1}{2}) > 0$ and $p(\frac{1}{2})/\bar{M}(\frac{1}{2}) \neq \bar{p}/\bar{m}$, thus contradicting hypothesis (b) of Theorem 6.

It now remains to show that the existence of a sequence x^ν, satisfying (68) and (69), contradicts hypothesis (c) of Theorem 6. We construct the functions $M(t)$ and $X(t)$ to be defined as follows:

$$M(t) = \mu[p(t); p^*, \alpha], \; X(t) = \xi[p(t), M(t)], \quad \text{for } 0 < t \leqq 1, \tag{79}$$

where $p(t)$ is defined by (75).

Then we have

$$U_{p^*}[X(t)] = \alpha, \; p(t)X(t) = M(t).$$

It follows from (69) and (79), that

$$U_{p^*}(x^\nu) \leqq U_{p^*}[X(t)].$$

On the other hand, x^ν is the unique maximizer of $U_{p^*}(x)$ subject to the budget inequality $p^\nu x \leqq m^\nu$. Hence, we must have

$$m^\nu \leqq p^\nu X(t), \quad \text{for all } \nu = 1, 2, \ldots, \text{ and } 0 < t \leqq 1. \tag{80}$$

For any fixed value of t, taking the limit of both sides of (80) as ν tends to infinity, we get

$$m^0 \leqslant p^0 X(t).$$

Therefore,

$$M(t) = p(t)X(t) = (1-t)p^0X(t) + t\bar{p}X(t) \geqq (1-t)m^0, \quad \text{for all } 0 < t \leqq 1. \tag{81}$$

On the other hand, we have from (77) and (69) that

$$\bar{M}(t) = \mu(p(t); p^*, \bar{\alpha}), \quad \text{for all } 0 < t \leqq 1, \tag{82}$$

with $\alpha < \bar{\alpha}$. Hence, by the definition (79) of $M(t)$ and Lemma 3, we have

$$M(t) < \bar{M}(t), \quad \text{for all } 0 < t \leqq 1. \tag{83}$$

Combining (81) and (83), one gets

$$(1-t)m^0 \leqq M(t) < \bar{M}(t), \quad \text{for all } 0 < t \leqq 1. \tag{84}$$

Both $(1-t)m^0$ and $\bar{M}(t)$ converge to m^0, as t tends to 0. Hence, the inequalities (84) imply that $M(t)$ also converges to m^0, that is,

$$\lim_{t\to 0} M(t) = m^0 = \lim_{t\to 0} \bar{M}(t). \tag{85}$$

Differentiating equations (79) and (82), we get

$$M'(t) = p'(t)\xi[p(t), M(t)],$$
$$\bar{M}'(t) = p'(t)\xi[p(t), \bar{M}(t)], \quad \text{for all } 0 < t \leqq 1,$$

where $p'(t) = (\bar{p} - p^0)$. Hence, both functions $M(t)$ and $\bar{M}(t)$ constitute solutions to the same ordinary differential equation, say

$$\frac{dm}{dt} = (\bar{p} - p^0)\xi[(1-t)p^0 + t\bar{p}, m].$$

We may, therefore, apply a fundamental result in the theory of ordinary differential equations[19] to get the following inequality:

$$|\bar{M}(1) - M(1)| \leqq K'|\bar{M}(t) - M(t)|, \quad \text{for all } 0 < t \leqq 1, \tag{86}$$

where

$$K' = \exp[K|1-t|],$$

and K is the Lipschitzian constant in hypothesis (c) of Theorem 6.

Considering the limit of (86) as t tends to 0, and taking into account (85), we get

$$\bar{M}(1) = M(1),$$

where

$$\bar{M}(1) = \bar{m} = \mu[\bar{p}; p^*, \bar{\alpha}], \qquad M(1) = \mu[\bar{p}; p^*, \alpha].$$

But then Lemma 2 yields $\bar{\alpha} = \alpha$, thus contradicting (69). ■

[19] Graves, [4], p. 155, Theorem 2: "Suppose that $y(x)$ and $z(x)$ are continuous functions with piecewise continuous derivatives on the interval $a \leqq x \leqq b$. Suppose also that $f(x, y)$ is continuous in x and satisfies a Lipschitz condition in y, with constant K, on a domain D containing the graphs of $y(x)$ and $z(x)$. Suppose finally that

$$\| y'(x) - z'(x) - f(x, y(x)) + f(x, z(x)) \| \leqq \varepsilon$$

at the points of $[a, b]$ where $y'(x)$ and $z'(x)$ exist and are continuous. Then, for each ξ and x on the interval $[a, b]$, we have

$$\| y(x) - z(x) \| \leqq \| y(\xi) - z(\xi) \| e^{K|x-\xi|} + \frac{\varepsilon}{K}(e^{K|x-\xi|} - 1).\text{"}$$

9 An example

It is interesting to note that, because the invertibility of the direct demand function $\xi(p, m)$ has not been assumed, "kinked" indifference surfaces are not ruled out by the conditions of the preceding theorems. To establish this fact, we give a two-commodity example, satisfying the assumptions, with "kinked" indifference curves. Examples involving more commodities can also be constructed. Let $u(x, y)$ be defined on the positive quadrant by

$$\text{i. } u(x, y) = \begin{cases} y[3 - 2(1 - t) - (1 - t)^{3/2}], & \text{for } x \leqq y \\ x\left[3 - 2\left(1 - \dfrac{1}{t}\right) - \left(1 - \dfrac{1}{t}\right)^{3/2}\right], & \text{for } x > y, \end{cases}$$

where $t = x/y$. Then,

ii. $u(x, y)$ is homogeneous of degree one.

iii. u_x, u_y are positive for all $(x, y) > (0, 0)$.

It suffices to show (iii) for $x \leqq y$. Let

$$\phi(t) = 3 - 2(1 - t) - (1 - t)^{3/2}, \qquad 0 \leqq t \leqq 1.$$

Then

$$\phi'(t) = 2 + \tfrac{3}{2}(1 - t)^{1/2} > 0,$$

$$\phi''(t) = -\tfrac{3}{4}(1 - t)^{-1/2} < 0, \quad \text{for } 0 \leqq t < 1$$

$$u(x, y) = y\phi(t)$$

$$u_x = \phi'(t) > 0$$

$$\begin{aligned} u_y &= \phi(t) - t\phi'(t) \\ &= 1 - (1 - t)^{3/2} - \frac{3t}{2}(1 - t)^{1/2} \\ &= 1 - \tfrac{3}{2}(1 - t)^{1/2} + \tfrac{1}{2}(1 - t)^{3/2} > 0, \quad \text{for all } 0 < t \leqq 1. \end{aligned}$$

iv. $u(x, y)$ is concave.

This is established by using the following facts. For $0 < x < y$, we have

$$u_{xx} = \frac{1}{y}\phi''(t) < 0$$

$$u_{xy} = -\frac{1}{y}t\phi''(t)$$

$$u_{yy} = \frac{1}{y}t^2\phi''(t) < 0,$$

$$\begin{vmatrix} u_{xx} & u_{xy} \\ u_{yx} & u_{yy} \end{vmatrix} = 0.$$

On the other hand, at $x = y$, we have

$$\left(\frac{u_x}{u_y}\right)_- = 2, \qquad \left(\frac{u_x}{u_y}\right)_+ = \frac{1}{2}.$$

Hence the indifference curves are "kinked" along the 45°-line in the (x, y)-plane, and so the direct demand function is not invertible.

v. The demand functions (for normalized p and m) are given by:

For $p > 2$,

$$\begin{cases} x = \dfrac{t}{pt+1} m \\ y = \dfrac{1}{pt+1} m, \end{cases}$$

where t is the solution of

$$(1-t)^{3/2} - 3\left(1 + \frac{1}{p}\right)(1-t)^{1/2} + 2\left(1 - \frac{2}{p}\right) = 0, \qquad 0 < t < 1. \tag{*}$$

For $\frac{1}{2} \leqq p \leqq 2$,

$$\begin{cases} x = \dfrac{1}{p+1} m \\ y = \dfrac{1}{p+1} m. \end{cases}$$

This is seen as follows:

$$p = \frac{u_x}{u_y} \text{ may be written as}$$

$$p = \frac{2 + \frac{3}{2}(1-t)^{1/2}}{1 - \frac{3}{2}(1-t)^{1/2} + \frac{1}{2}(1-t)^{3/2}}$$

which implies (*) above.

The solution to (*) is uniquely determined. Let

$$\psi(v) = v^3 - 3\left(1 + \frac{1}{p}\right)v + 2\left(1 - \frac{2}{p}\right).$$

Then,

$$\psi(0) = 2\left(1 - \frac{2}{p}\right) > 0, \quad \text{for } p > 2,$$

$$\psi(1) = -\frac{7}{p} < 0, \quad \text{for } p > 0,$$

$$\psi'(v) = 3\left[v^2 - \left(1 + \frac{1}{p}\right)\right] < 0, \quad \text{for all } 0 \leqq v \leqq 1.$$

Therefore, $\psi(v) = 0$ has a unique solution in $[0, 1]$.

vi. $\dfrac{\partial x}{\partial p}, \dfrac{\partial y}{\partial p}$ are continuous at $p = 2$.

From (v), for $p > 2$,

$$\frac{\partial x}{\partial p} = -\frac{t^2 m}{(pt+1)^2} + \frac{m}{(pt+1)^2}\frac{dt}{dp}$$

$$\frac{\partial y}{\partial p} = -\frac{tm}{(pt+1)^2} - \frac{pm}{(pt+1)^2}\frac{dt}{dp}.$$

But differentiating (*) with respect to p, one gets

$$\frac{dt}{dp}\left[-\frac{3}{2}(1-t)^{1/2} + \frac{3}{2}\left(1 + \frac{1}{p}\right)(1-t)^{-1/2}\right] + \frac{3(1-t)^{1/2}}{p^2} + \frac{4}{p^2} = 0;$$

hence,

$$\frac{dt}{dp}\left[-\frac{3}{2}(1-t) + \frac{3}{2}\left(1 + \frac{1}{p}\right)\right] = -\frac{3(1-t)}{p^2} - \frac{4(1-t)^{1/2}}{p^2}.$$

Therefore,

$$\lim_{p \to 2}\left(\frac{dt}{dp}\right) = 0,$$

because

$$\lim_{p \to 2} t = 1.$$

Hence,

$$\lim_{\substack{p \to 2 \\ p > 2}} \frac{\partial x}{\partial p} = -\frac{m}{9},$$

$$\lim_{\substack{p \to 2 \\ p > 2}} \frac{\partial y}{\partial p} = -\frac{m}{9}.$$

On the other hand, for $x = y = m/(p+1)$ for $\frac{1}{2} \leqq p \leqq 2$, we get

$$\frac{\partial x}{\partial p} = \frac{\partial y}{\partial p} = -\frac{m}{(p+1)^2};$$

hence,

$$\left(\frac{\partial x}{\partial p}\right)_{p=2}=\left(\frac{\partial y}{\partial p}\right)_{p=2}=-\frac{m}{9};$$

that is, the demand functions have continuous partial derivatives with respect to p at $p=2$.

vii. Similarly, we can show that

$$\frac{\partial x}{\partial m}=\frac{\partial y}{\partial m}=\frac{1}{3}$$

both for $p>2$ and $p\leqq 2$ sides.

Thus the substitution terms satisfy the assumptions of Theorem 2, even though there is a "kink" and no invertibility of the direct demand function.

References

[1] Bonnesen, T., and W. Fenchel, *Theorie der konvexen Körper*, Ergebnisse der Mathematik 3, 1, Berlin: Julius Springer, 1934, New York: Chelsea Publishing Company, 1948.

[2] Fenchel, W., "Convex Cones, Sets, and Functions," Lecture Notes, Princeton University, 1953.

[3] Fourgeaud, C., and A. Nataf, "Consommation en prix et revenu réels et théorié des choix," *Econometrica*, **27**, 1959, 329–354.

[4] Graves, L. M., *The Theory of Functions of Real Variables*, 2nd ed., New York: McGraw-Hill, 1956.

[5] Hartman, P., "Frobenius Theorem under Carathéodory Type Conditions," *Journal of Differential Equations*, **7**, 1970, 307–333.

[6] McKenzie, L. W., "Demand Theory Without a Utility Index," *Review of Economic Studies*, **24**, 1956–57, 185–189.

[7] Mosak, J. L., "On the Interpretation of the Fundamental Equation of Value Theory," in *Studies in Mathematical Economics and Econometrics*, O. Lange, F. McIntyre, and O. Yntema, Eds., Chicago: University of Chicago Press, 1942, pp. 69–74.

[8] Samuelson, P. A., *Foundations of Economic Analysis*, Cambridge, Mass.: Harvard University Press, 1947.

[9] ———, "The Problem of Integrability in Utility Theory," *Economica*, N.S., **17**, 1950, 355–385.

[10] Slutsky, E. E., "On the Theory of the Budget of the Consumer," in *Readings in Price Theory*, G. J. Stigler and K. E. Boulding, Eds., Chicago: Irwin, 1952, pp. 27–56.

[11] Sonnenschein, H., "On the Lower Semicontinuity of Utility Functions Derived from Demand Data," in *References, Utility, and Demand*, J. Chipman, L. Hurwicz, M. Richter, and H. Sonnenschein, Eds., New York: Harcourt, Brace, & Jovanovich, 1971, Chapter 4.

[12] Uzawa, H., "Preference and Rational Choice in the Theory of Consumption," in *Mathematical Methods in the Social Sciences*, K. J. Arrow, S. Karlin, and P.

Suppes, Eds., Stanford: Stanford University Press, 1960, pp. 129–148, Chapter 1, this volume.
[13] Young, W. H., *The Fundamental Theorems of the Differential Calculus*, New York: Hafner, 1960.

Appendix

Our analysis in the main text is based on a theorem concerning the existence of solutions to a certain system of partial differential equations. The existing literature, however, does not precisely cover the present case. We, therefore, derive an existence theorem needed in the text of our paper and indicate the relationship of our results to those due to other authors.

We are concerned with the conditions under which the system of partial differential equations[1]

$$\frac{\partial z}{\partial x_i} = f^i(x_1, x_2, \ldots, x_n, z), \qquad i = 1, 2, \ldots, n, \tag{A1}$$

has a unique solution with a preassigned value z^0 at a given point

$x^0 = (x_1^0, x_2^0, \ldots, x_n^0)$.[2]

To state the problem more precisely, let Π be a nonempty set of n-dimensional vectors $x = (x_1, x_2, \ldots, x_n)$ and Θ a nonempty set of real numbers z. The functions $f^1(x, z)$, $f^2(x, z)$ are defined on the nonempty Cartesian product

$$\Omega = \{(x, z) : x \in \Pi, z \in \Theta\} = \Pi \times \Theta.$$

Definition 1. A real-valued function $z = \omega(x)$ defined on a set $\Pi^* \subseteq \Pi$ is called *a solution* (*on* Π^*) of the system of partial differential equations (A1) *with the initial condition* $(x^0, z^0) \in \Omega$ if the domain of definition Π^* of the function $\omega(x)$ contains x^0, and

$$\omega_i(x) = f^i(x, \omega(x)), \qquad i = 1, 2, \ldots, n, \qquad \text{for all } x \in \Pi^*, \tag{A2}$$

$$\omega(x^0) = z^0, \tag{A3}$$

where $\omega_i(x)$ stands for the partial derivative of $\omega(x)$ with respect to x_i, evaluated at x.

If there is only one solution $\omega(x)$ (on the given Π^*) of the system (A1) with the initial condition (x^0, z^0), it may be more explicitly written as

[1] In this appendix, z is assumed one-dimensional. The results obtained here are, however, easily extended to the case of multi-dimensional z.

[2] For brevity, vector notation such as $x = (x_1, x_2, \ldots, x_n)$ and $x^0 = (x_1^0, x_2^0, \ldots, x_n^0)$ is used whenever advisable.

$\omega(x; x^0, z^0)$, so that the equation (A3) becomes $\omega(x^0; x^0, z^0) = z^0$. It may be noted that the relation (A2) in particular implies that $f^i(x, \omega(x))$, $i = 1, 2, \ldots, n$, are defined for all $x \in \Pi^*$, that is, that $\omega(x) \in \Theta$ for all $x \in \Pi^*$.

One of the main results on this subject has been obtained by Nikliborc [3].

Nikliborc's Theorem. Let the functions $f^i(x, z)$ be defined on the set $\Omega = \Pi \times \Theta$ where (for some $a > 0$, $b > 0$)

$$\Pi = \{x = (x_1, x_2, \ldots, x_n) : |x_i - x_i^0| \leqq a,\ i = 1, 2, \ldots, n\}, \tag{A4}$$

and

$$\Theta = \{z : |z - z^0| \leqq b\}. \tag{A5}$$

Let the following conditions be satisfied:

(CD) For each $i = 1, 2, \ldots, n$, the partial derivatives of the first order $f^i_j(x, z)$ and $f^i_z(x, z)$ of $f^i(x, z)$ with respect to $x_j (j = 1, 2, \ldots, n)$ and z exist and are continuous on Ω.

(S) The symmetry condition holds:

$$f^i_j(x, z) + f^i_z(x, z) f^j(x, z) = f^j_i(x, z) + f^j_z(x, z) f^i(x, z), \quad i, z = 1, 2, \ldots, n,$$

for all $(x, z) \in \Omega$.

Then there uniquely exists a continuous solution $\omega(x) = \omega(x; x^0, z^0)$ of the system (A1) with the initial condition (x^0, z^0), for which the domain of definition Π^* is given by

$$\Pi^* = \{x = (x_1, x_2, \ldots, x_n) : |x_i - x_i^0| \leqq \min(a, b/nM), \quad i = 1, 2, \ldots, n\}, \tag{A6}$$

where

$$M = \sup\{|f^i(x, z)| : i = 1, 2, \ldots, n, (x, z) \in \Omega\}. \tag{A7}$$

The following theorem due to Tsuji [5] has broader applicability since it only requires that $f^i(x, z)$ possess a differential without demanding that derivatives be continuous. (Note, however, that Tsuji's domains are defined by *strict* inequalities.)

Tsuji's Theorem. Let the functions $f^i(x, z)$ be all defined on the set $\Omega = \Pi \times \Theta$, where (for some $a > 0, b > 0$)

$$\Pi = \{x = (x_1, x_2, \ldots, x_n) : |x_i - x_i^0| < a, i = 1, 2, \ldots, n\}, \tag{A8}$$

and

$$\Theta = \{z : |z - z^0| < b\}. \tag{A9}$$

Let the following conditions be satisfied together with (S):

(UB) For each $i = 1, 2, \ldots, n$, the function $f^i(x, z)$ is uniformly bounded in Ω, that is, the number M defined by (A7) is finite;

(D) For each $i = 1, 2, \ldots, n$, the function $f^i(x, z)$ possesses a differential at very point of Ω;[3]

(UD) For each $i = 1, 2, \ldots, n$, the partial derivative $f^i_z(x, z)$ is uniformly bounded in Ω; that is, there exists a finite number K such that

$$|f^i_z(x, z)| \leqq K, \quad \text{for all } (x, z) \in \Omega.$$

Then there uniquely exists a continuous solution $\omega(x) = \omega(x; x^0, z^0)$ of the system (A1) with the initial condition (x^0, z^0) for which the domain of definition is Π^* is given by

$$\Pi^* = \{x = (x_1, x_2, \ldots, x_n) : |x_i - x_i^0| < \min(a, b/nM), \quad i = 1, 2, \ldots, n\}. \tag{A10}$$

In both Nikliborc's and Tsuji's Theorems, the domain of definition Π^* for the solution $\omega(x)$ may differ from the x component Π of Ω in which the functions $f^i(x, z)$ are originally defined. Furthermore, the z component Θ of the domain Ω is restricted to a bounded interval; this condition is not satisfied for the demand functions generated by nonsatiated preference orderings. In connection with both of these limitations, the following existence theorem due to Thomas [4] is helpful for our purpose.

Thomas's Theorem.[4] Let the functions $f^i(x, z)$ be defined on the set $\Omega = \Pi \times \Theta$ where

$$\Omega = \{x = (x_1, x_2, \ldots, x_n) : a' < x_i < a'', \ i = 1, 2, \ldots, n\}, \quad a' < a'', \tag{A11}$$

and

$$\Theta = \{z : -\infty < z < +\infty\}. \tag{A12}$$

Let the conditions (CD), (UD), and (S) be satisfied. Then, for any point $(x^0, z^0) \in \Omega$, there uniquely exists a continuous solution $\omega(x) = \omega(x; x^0, z^0)$ of the system (A1), with the initial condition (x^0, z^0), for which the domain of definitions is Π.

[3] See footnote 4, for a definition of differentials.

[4] We are stating a special case of Thomas's result; in the latter the set II can be taken as any open simply connected set.

The question naturally arises if the condition (CD) in Thomas's Theorem can be weakened to the total differentiability condition (D) used by Tsuji. In fact, we shall prove the following:

Existence Theorem I. Let the functions $f^i(x, z)$ be all defined on the set $\Omega = \Pi \times \Theta$ where

$$\Pi = \{x = (x_1, x_2, \ldots, x_n): a' \leqq x_i \leqq a'', i = 1, 2, \ldots, n\}, \qquad a' < a'', \tag{A13}$$

and

$$\Theta = \{z: -\infty < z < +\infty\}. \tag{A14}$$

If the conditions (D), (UD), and (S) are satisfied, then, for any point $(x^0, z^0) \in \Omega$, there uniquely exists a solution $\omega(x) = \omega(x; x^0, z^0)$ of the system (A1), with initial condition (x^0, z^0), defined on Π.

The solution $\omega(x; x^0, z^0)$ is continuous with respect to x and with respect to the initial condition (x^0, z^0).[5]

Proof. We shall show that it is possible to modify Nikliborc's proof in [3] so that the solution $\omega(x)$ is defined on Π and only the conditions (D) and (UD) are required.

We may without loss of generality assume that

$$\Pi = \{x = (x_1, x_2, \ldots, x_n): |x_i| \leqq a, i = 1, 2, \ldots, n\}, \qquad a > 0, \tag{A15}$$

and $(x^0, z^0) = (0, 0)$.

For any point $x \in \Pi$, let us define a sequence of approximating functions $\{z^{(r)}(x): r = 0, 1, 2, \ldots\}$ by the following recursive formula

$$z^{(0)}(x) = 0, \tag{A16}$$

$$z^{(r+1)}(x) = \int_0^1 \sum_{k=1}^n f^k(tx, z^{(r)}(tx))x_k \, dt, \qquad r = 0, 1, 2, \ldots \tag{A17}$$

As in Nikliborc's proof ([3], pp. 44–45), we obtain from (A16) and (A17) the inequalities

$$|z^{(r)}(x) - z^{(r-1)}(x)| \leqq \frac{M(x)}{K} \frac{\left\{K \sum_{i=1}^n \|x_i\|\right\}^r}{r!} \leqq \frac{M}{K} \cdot \frac{\left\{K \sum_{i=1}^n \|x_i\|\right\}^r}{r!}, \quad \text{for } r = 1, 2, \ldots, \tag{A18}$$

[5] In fact, ω is continuous in $(x; x^0, z^0)$ jointly. See Hartman, [2] (p. 94, Theorem 2.1). Even without additional assumptions, properties stronger than continuity [e.g., Lipschitz continuity with respect to $(x; x^0, z^0)$] can be established ([2], p. 109, Theorem 8.1). If $f(x, z)$ is assumed continuously differentiable with respect to z, $\omega(x; x^0, z^0)$ is also continuously differentiable in all its arguments ([2], p. 104, Theorem 6.1 and p. 128, Theorem 6.1).

where

$$M(x) = \max\{|f^i(tx,0)|: i=1,2,\ldots,n, 0 \leqq t \leqq 1\},$$
$$M = \max\{M(x): x\in\Pi\}, \tag{A19}$$

and K is the number introduced in (UD).

Therefore the sequence $\{z^{(r)}(x): r=1,2,\ldots\}$ is uniformly convergent. Let us now define the function $\omega(x)$ by

$$\omega(x) = \lim_{r\to\infty} z^{(r)}(x), \qquad x\in\Pi. \tag{A20}$$

The function $\omega(x)$ is defined for all $x\in\Pi$ and, since the convergence in (A20) is uniform for $x\in\Pi$, it is continuous on Π. Taking the limit in (A17) as r tends to infinity, we get

$$\omega(x) = \int_0^1 \sum_{k=1}^n f^k(tx, \omega(tx))x_k dt, \quad \text{for all } x\in\Pi. \tag{A21}$$

Since the chain rule for partial differentiation is guaranteed by the condition (D), we get, differentiating (A17) with respect to x_i,

$$\frac{\partial z^{(r+1)}}{\partial x_i} = \int_0^1 \left\{ f^{i(r)} + \sum_{k=1}^n \left[f_i^{k(r)} + f_z^{k(r)} \frac{\partial z^{(r)}}{\partial x_i} \right] tx_k \right\} dt, \tag{A22}$$

where $f^{i(r)} = f^i(tx, z^{(r)}(tx))$, and so on.

Integrating (A22) by parts and using the condition (S), we get (as in Nikliborc's proof [3], pp. 45–46)

$$\frac{\partial z^{(r+1)}}{\partial x_i} = f^i(x, z^{(r)}(x)) - \int_0^1 \sum_{s\neq i} tx_s \left[f_z^{i(r)}\left(\frac{\partial z^{(r)}}{\partial x_s} - f^{s(r)}\right) \right.$$
$$\left. - f_z^{s(r)}\left(\frac{\partial z^{(r)}}{\partial x_i} - f^{i(r)}\right)\right] dt. \tag{A23}$$

We have from (A23) by mathematical induction

$$\sum_{i=1}^n \left| \frac{\partial z^{(r)}}{\partial x_i} - f^i(x, z^{(r)}(x)) \right| \leq nM(x) \frac{\left\{3Kn \sum_{i=1}^n \|x_i\|\right\}^r}{r!}$$
$$\leq nM \frac{\left\{3Kn \sum_{i=1}^n \|x_i\|\right\}^r}{r!}, \tag{A24}$$

for $r = 1, 2, \ldots,$ where $M(x)$ and M are defined by (A19).

Hence, for each i,

$$f^i(x, \omega(x)) = \lim_{r \to \infty} f^i(x, z^{(r)}(x)) = \lim_{r \to \infty} \frac{\partial z^{(r)}(x)}{\partial x_i}, \tag{A25}$$

uniformly on Π.

Therefore, for each i, the partial derivative $\omega_i(x) = \partial\omega(x)/\partial x_i$ of the function $\omega(x)$ exists at every point x of Π and

$$\omega_i(x) = f^i(x, \omega(x)), \qquad i = 1, 2, \ldots, n, \qquad x \in \Pi. \tag{A26}$$

On the other hand, from (A16) and (A17), we have

$$\omega(0) = 0. \tag{A27}$$

The relations (A26) and (A27) together mean that the continuous function $\omega(x)$ is a solution on Π of the system (A1) with the initial condition (0, 0).

The proof of uniqueness of the solution is similar to Nikliborc's ([3], pp. 48–49). Continuity with respect to initial values then follows from uniqueness, since $\omega(x; x^0, z^0)$ is the solution of an ordinary differential equation through (x^0, z^0). (See Hartman ([2], p. 94, Theorem 2.1.) ■

To handle the demand functions defined for *nonnegative* incomes (corresponding to $z \geqq 0$), we shall prove the following:

Existence Theorem II. Let the functions $f^i(x, z)$ be all defined on the set $\Omega = \Pi \times \Theta$ where

$$\Pi = \{x = (x_1, x_2, \ldots, x_n) : a' \leqq x_i \leqq a'', i = 1, 2, \ldots, n\}, \qquad a' < a'', \tag{A28}$$

and

$$\Theta = \{z : 0 \leqq z < +\infty\}. \tag{A29}$$

If the conditions (D), (UD), and (S) are satisfied together with[6]

$$f^i(x, 0) = 0, \qquad i = 1, 2, \ldots, n, \quad \text{for all } x \in \Pi, \tag{O}$$

then, for any initial condition $(x^0, z^0) \in \Omega$, there uniquely exists a continuous solution $\omega(x) = \omega(x; x^0, z^0)$ of the system (A1) defined on Π.

The solution $\omega(x; x^0, z^0)$ is continuous with respect to x and also with respect to the initial condition (x^0, z^0).

[6] In applying the results of this appendix we interpret $f^i(x, z)$ of this theorem as the quantity demanded of commodity i given the price vector x and income z. Hence condition (O) states that demand equals zero for all goods whenever income equals zero. This will be so if the budget equation holds with positive prices and nonnegative commodity bundles.

Proof. For each i, define a function $f^i_*(x,z)$ by

$$f^i_*(x,z) = \begin{cases} f^i(x,z), & \text{for } x \in \Pi, z \geqq 0, \\ -f^i(x,-z), & \text{for } x \in \Pi, z < 0. \end{cases} \tag{A30}$$

For each i, the function $f^i_*(x,z)$, is defined on the set $\Omega^* = \Pi \times \Theta^*$, where $\Theta^* = \{z: -\infty < z < \infty\}$.

The functions $f^i_*(x,z)$ satisfy the conditions (D), (UD), and (S). The conditions (UD) and (S) follow from the definition (A30). To verify (D), it suffices to consider the existence of a differential for $f^i_*(x,z)$ at $(x,0)$.

The function $f^i(x,z)$ possesses a differential at $(x,0)$, $x \in \Pi$; hence for any positive number ε, there exists a positive number δ such that, for $x \in \Pi$, $z \geqq 0$,

$$\left| f^i(x',z') - f^i(x,0) - \sum_{k=1}^{n} f^i_k(x,0)(x'_k - x_k) - f^i_z(x,0)z' \right|$$
$$< \varepsilon(\|x'-x\| + |z'|) \quad \text{for all } 0 < \|x'-x\| + |z'| < \delta. \tag{A31}$$

[Here

$$f^i_z(x,0) = \lim_{z \downarrow 0} \frac{|f^i(x,z) - f^i(x,0)|}{z}$$

is a partial right-hand derivative of $f^i(x,z)$ with respect to z, evaluated at $z=0$. If x is on the boundary of Π, $f^i_k(x,0)$ may also be a one-sided derivative.]

But the condition (O) holds for $f^i(x,z)$, so that

$$f^i(x,0) = 0, \quad f^i_k(x,0) = 0, \quad \text{for all } i,k = 1,2,\ldots,n, \quad \text{and all } x \in \Pi. \tag{A32}$$

In view of (A32), the inequality (A31) reduces to

$$|f^i(x',z') - f^i_z(x,0)z'| < \varepsilon(\|x'-x\| + z'),$$
$$\text{for all } 0 < \|x'-x\| + z' < \delta, x' \in \Pi, z' \geqq 0. \tag{A33}$$

The inequality (A33) implies

$$|-f^i(x',-z') - f^i_z(x,0)|z'|| < \varepsilon(\|x'-x\| + (-z')),$$
$$\text{for all } \|x'-x\| + (-z') < \delta, z' \leqq 0. \tag{A34}$$

The relations (A33) and (A34), together with (A30) and (A32), yield

$$\left| f^i_*(x',z') - f^i_*(x,0) - \sum_{k=1}^{n} f^i_{*k}(x,0)(x'_k - x_k) - f^i_{*z}(x,0)z' \right|$$
$$< \varepsilon\{\|x'-x\| + |z'|\}, \quad \text{for all } 0 < \|x'-x\| + |z'| < \delta, x' \in \Pi; \tag{A35}$$

thus the function $f^i_*(x,z)$ possesses a differential at $(x,0)$.

Now consider the system of partial differential equations

$$\frac{\partial z^*}{\partial x_i} = f^i_*(x, z^*), \qquad i = 1, 2, \dots, n. \tag{A36}$$

The functions $f^i_*(x, z)$ satisfy the conditions (D), (UD), and (S). Hence, by applying Existence Theorem I, there uniquely exists a continuous solution $\omega(x; x^0, z^0)$ defined on Π. In particular, because of (O) and the uniqueness of the solution, we have

$$\omega(x; x^0, 0) = 0, \quad \text{for all } x^0, x \in \Pi. \tag{A37}$$

Let (x^0, z^0) be an arbitrary point in Ω; that is, $x^0 \in \Pi$ and $z^0 \geqq 0$. We shall show that $z^0 > 0$ implies

$$\omega(x; x^0, z^0) > 0, \quad \text{for all } x \in \Pi. \tag{A38}$$

In fact, suppose there exists a point $x^1 \in \Pi$ such that

$$\omega(x^1; x^0, z^0) \leqq 0. \tag{A39}$$

Then define

$$\varphi(t) = \omega(x^t; x^0, z^0), \qquad \text{where } x^t = (1-t)x^0 + tx^1, 0 \leqq t \leqq 1.$$

From (A38) and (A39), we get

$$\varphi(0) > 0, \qquad \varphi(1) \leqq 0,$$

which, by the continuity of $\varphi(t)$, yield the existence of a number $\bar{t}$ such that

$$\varphi(\bar{t}) = 0;$$

that is,

$$\omega(x^{\bar{t}}; x^0, z^0) = 0. \tag{A40}$$

By the uniqueness of the solution of the system (A1), we have from (A40)

$$z^0 = \omega(x^0; x^{\bar{t}}, 0) = 0;$$

thus contradicting $z^0 > 0$.

Therefore, for any initial condition $(x^0, z^0) \in \Omega$, the solution $\omega(x; x^0, z^0)$ of the system (A36) becomes the solution of the original system (A1). ■

Remark. It is possible directly to prove Existence Theorem II, by modifying the existence theorem of the type discussed in Graves ([1], p. 152, Theorem 1).

By applying Existence Theorem II to a sequence of bounded subsets of II we can prove the following:

Existence Theorem III. Let the functions $f^i(x, z)$ be all defined on the set $\Omega = \Pi \times \Theta$, where

$$\Pi = \{x = (x_1, x_2, \ldots, x_n) : x_i > 0,\ i = 1, 2, \ldots, n\}. \qquad \text{(A41)}$$

and

$$\Theta = \{z : 0 \leqq z < \infty\}. \qquad \text{(A42)}$$

Let the following condition be satisfied together with (D), (S), and (O): (UD′). For any numbers a' and a'' satisfying $0 < a' < a''$, there exists a (finite) number $K_{a'a''}$ such that

$$|f^i_z(x, z)| \leqq K_{a'a''}, \qquad i = 1, 2, \ldots, n, \qquad \text{for all } (x, z) \in \Omega$$

satisfying $a' \leqq x_j \leqq a''$ $(j = 1, 2, \ldots, n)$ and $0 \leqq z < +\infty$.

Then, for any initial condition $(x^0, z^0) \in \Omega$, there uniquely exists a unique continuous solution $\omega(x) = \omega(x; x^0, z^0)$ of the system (A1) defined on Π.

The solution $\omega(x; x^0, z^0)$ is continuous with respect to x and also with respect to the initial conditions (x^0, z^0).

References

[1] Graves, L. M., *The Theory of Functions of Real Variables*, New York: McGraw-Hill, 1956.

[2] Hartman, P., *Ordinary Differential Equations*, New York: Wiley, 1964.

[3] Nikliborc, W., "Sur les équations linéaires aux différentielles totales," *Studia Mathematica*, **1**, 1929, 41–49.

[4] Thomas, T. Y., "Systems of Total Differential Equations Defined over Simply Connected Domains," *Annals of Mathematics*, **35**, 1936, 730–734.

[5] Tsuji, M., "On a System of Total Differential Equations," *Japanese Journal of Mathematics*, **19**, 1948, 383–393.

CHAPTER 3

Time preference, the consumption function, and optimum asset holdings

1 Introduction

The problem of demand for money and other assets has been recently studied by Douglas (1966) and Sidrauski (1965) within the framework of a rational individual faced with the choice of a consumption schedule which is optimal with respect to the individual's time preference structure. In both papers, the intertemporal utility function upon which the consumer's choice is based is represented by a discounted integral of the stream of instantaneous utility levels, where future utilities are discounted by a rate which is kept constant independently of time profile of the utility stream associated with each consumption schedule. Thus, if a consumer is permitted to hold his assets either in the form of real cash balances or in the form of perpetuities yielding a constant rate of interest and if his instantaneous utility function is linear and homogeneous, he will either postpone his consumption until the very last moment or will consume as much as possible, according to whether the subject rate of discount is lower than the rate of interest. The only case in which the individual would desire to possess two types of assets simultaneously is one where his subject rate of discount is precisely equal to the rate of interest. Douglas has avoided this difficulty by having the level of bond holdings as one of the components for instantaneous utility level, while Sidrauski has introduced real capital as an alternative asset for which the rate of return varies with the amount held. In this paper, we shall instead start with an analysis of an individual's time preference structure, to derive a certain specific formulation regarding the rate by which he discounts future levels. We shall then proceed to examine the behavior of an individual consumer

From *Value, Capital, and Growth: Papers in Honour of Sir John Hicks*, edited by J. N. Wolfe, The University of Edingburgh Press, 1968, pp. 485–504; reprinted with permission.

I am indebted to Harry Johnson, Michael Lav, John Scadding, and Miguel Sidrauski for their comments and criticisms.

who decides the allocation of his income between consumption and savings and the choice of portfolio balances in such manner that the resulting consumption stream is most preferred in terms of his time preference structure. The analysis will be first carried out for the simple case in which the individual is permitted to hold his assets only in the form of bonds for which the expected rate of interest is constant, and then for a more general case in which he may hold his assets in the form of money and bonds and other types for which the rates of return may vary.

2 Time preference

The analysis presented here is based upon a re-examination of the concept of time preference, which originates with Boehm-Bawerk (1884–89) and Fisher (1907), and for which an elaborated analysis has been recently done by Koopmans (1960). It is the rate by which future income (or utility) is discounted to the present, summarizing the preference structure of an individual economic unit regarding present and future consumption. To define the concept of time preference more precisely, let us first consider a special case where future consumption is concentrated at a certain time, say t. The preference structure of an individual unit then is described in terms of indifference curves, as typically depicted in Figure 3.1, where the horizontal axis represents the utility level u_0 resulting from present consumption, while the utility level of future consumption u_t is measured along the vertical axis. Each indifference curve is assumed to be convex toward the origin and to intersect with the horizontal axis (by a linear transition, if necessary).

Let u_0 and u_t be the levels of present and future utility, to be represented by a point A in Figure 3.1, and let U be the level of present utility at the point B at which the indifference curve through A intersects with the horizontal axis. Thus an increase in present utility from u_0 to U exactly compensates a decrease in future utility from u_t to 0. The ratio $u_t/(U - u_0)$, if we subtract one, represents the rate by which future utility is discounted to make it comparable with the present utility.

We may then define the rate of *time preference* $\Delta_{0,t}$:

$$\Delta_{0,t} = \frac{u_t}{U - u_0} - 1; \tag{1}$$

namely,

$$U = u_0 + \frac{u_t}{1 + \Delta_{0,t}}, \tag{2}$$

and the level U may be used to describe the preference structure of the

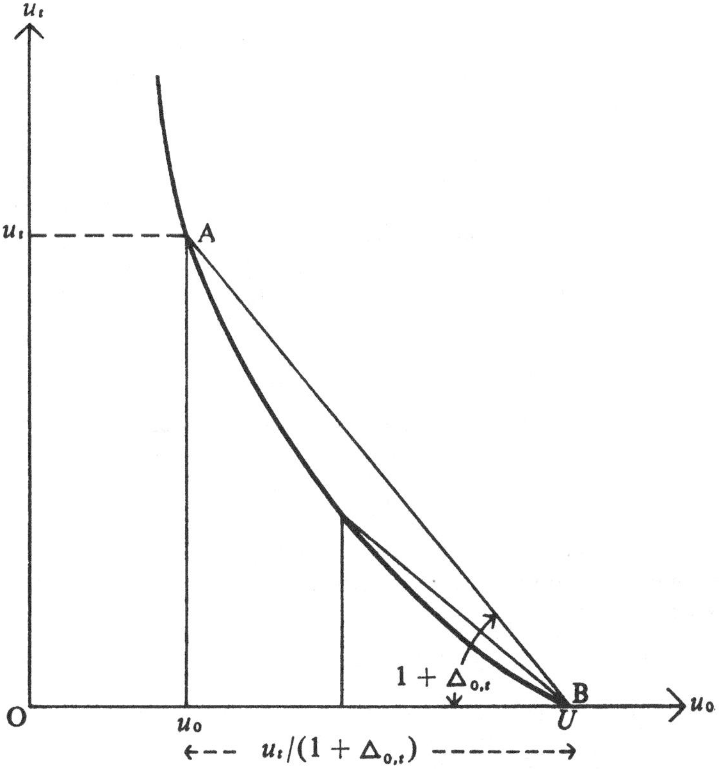

Figure 3.1

individual in consideration. The rate of time preference $\Delta_{0,t}$ depends upon the utility levels of present and future consumption, and it is easily seen that an increase in the present utility along the indifference curve will result in a decrease in the rate of time preference; namely, the higher the level of real income today, the lower is the rate by which the individual discounts tomorrow's real income.

The concept of time preference is extended to the general case where future consumption is made at various time points, say $t = 1, \ldots, n$. Any utility stream is represented by a vector with $n + 1$ components, $(u_0, u_1, \ldots, u_n)$, where u_0 is the utility level for present consumption and $u_1, \ldots, u_n$ refer to those for future consumption. Assuming that each indifference surface always intersects with the u_0-axis, it is possible to find n rates of time preference, $\Delta_{0,1}, \ldots, \Delta_{0,n}$, such that

$$U = u_0 + \frac{u_1}{1 + \Delta_{0,1}} + \cdots + \frac{u_n}{1 + \Delta_{0,n}} \tag{3}$$

represents the level of present utility which is indifferent with the given utility stream $(u_0, u_1, \ldots, u_n)$. The rate of time preference $\Delta_{0,t}$ now depends upon the entire time profile of the utility stream, to be indicated by the functional notation

$$\Delta_{0,t} = \Delta_{0,t}(u_0, \ldots, u_n) \qquad t = 1, \ldots, n. \tag{4}$$

In what follows, we shall confine ourselves to time preference which satisfies certain consistency and independency postulates. First, we shall postulate that the rate of time preference $\Delta_{0,t}$ for utility at time t is independent of the utility levels beyond time t; namely, the function $\Delta_{0,t}$ may be specified as

$$\Delta_{0,t} = \Delta_{0,t}(u_0, u_1, \ldots, u_t) \qquad t = 1, \ldots, n. \tag{5}$$

The concept of time preference then may be extended to discount utility at time t to one at time s, whenever $s < t$:

$$\Delta_{s,t} = \Delta_{s,t}(u_s, \ldots, u_t) \qquad s < t. \tag{6}$$

Second, it is assumed that the discounting procedure based on the time preference function (6) is independent of the manner in which it is done; in particular, it is required that

$$1 + \Delta_{0,t} = (1 + \Delta_{0,s})(1 + \Delta_{s,t}), \qquad 0 < s < t < n. \tag{7}$$

The relation (7) yields

$$\frac{1 + \Delta_{0,t}(u_0, \ldots, u_t)}{1 + \Delta_{0,t-1}(u_0, \ldots, u_{t-1})} = 1 + \Delta_{t-1,t}(u_{t-1}, u_t), \qquad 0 < t < n, \tag{8}$$

indicating that the logarithmic increase in the rate of time preference (plus one) depends upon the utility levels for consumption at time $t-1$ and t.

Finally, the structure of time preference remains invariant through the entire period, and the relations (8) may be written as:

$$\frac{1 + \Delta_{0,t}(u_0, \ldots, u_t)}{1 + \Delta_{0,t-1}(u_0, \ldots, u_{t-1})} = 1 + \delta(u_{t-1}, u_t), \tag{9}$$

with a certain function δ.

If consumption is made continuously over an infinite time period, the structure of time preference is in general described in terms of the intertemporal utility functional:

$$U = \int_0^\infty u_t e^{-\Delta_t}\, dt, \tag{10}$$

where the rate of time preference Δ_t depends upon the time profile of a continuous utility stream $u_t(0 < t < \infty)$, and the relation (8) then may be transformed to the following:

$$\dot{\Delta}_t = \delta(u_t), \qquad (\Delta_0 = 0). \tag{11}$$

It will be assumed that $u(c)$ is a concave utility function satisfying

$$u(c) > 0, \qquad u'(c) > 0, \qquad u''(c) < 0, \quad \text{for } c > 0. \tag{12}$$

It is assumed that the function δ, to be referred to simply as the time preference function, satisfies the following conditions:

$$\delta(u) > 0, \qquad \delta'(u) > 0, \qquad \delta''(u) > 0, \quad \text{for all } u > 0, \tag{13}$$

and

$$\delta(u) - \delta'(u)u > 0. \tag{14}$$

The condition (14) above indicates that between two stationary consumption streams the one with higher level of instantaneous utility is preferred. The second assumption in (13) requires that an increase in the consumption level at a certain future date will increase the rate of discount for all consumption made afterward, while the third assumption is required to derive a continuous consumption function, as discussed in detail below.

3 Optimum savings and consumption schedule

The specific structure of time preference, as derived in the previous section, will now be used to examine the pattern of behavior for an individual consumer with regard to transitory, as well as permanent, adjustments of his holdings of cash and other assets. We shall begin with a simple case in which the individual consumer is allowed to hold his assets only in the form of interest-yielding bonds. It is simply assumed that bonds are quoted in terms of real output and yield interests, payable in output, at whatever rate will prevail in the market at the time of payments. At a certain moment of time 0, the consumer possesses a fixed sum of bonds, say b_0, and expects to receive wages w_t. The income stream he expects to receive then depends upon the amounts of accumulated savings, in the form of bond holdings, and he is primarily concerned with attaining the time path of consumption which is most preferred, in terms of his time preference structure, among all the feasible consumption paths consistent with his initial asset holdings and the state of expectations regarding future rates of interest and wage payments.

Let b_t be the amount of bonds the consumer plans to hold at each moment of time t. Then the level y_t of his income (in real terms) at time

t is given by

$$y_t = r_t b_t + w_t, \tag{15}$$

which will be divided between consumption c_t and savings $\dot{b}_t$; namely,

$$y_t = c_t + \dot{b}_t, \tag{16}$$

with the initial bond holdings b_0.

The optimum paths of consumption and bond holdings thus are determined, among other, relative to the state of expectations regarding to real wages, real transfer payments, and real rate of interest, all of which in general vary through time. However, it will be assumed in the rest of the paper that the consumer expects real wages, real transfer payments, and real rate of interest to remain at certain constant, permanent levels such that the resulting patterns of consumption and savings coincide with those which would have been derived under more general circumstances. Such a procedure in fact would be justified only after we have made a thorough examination of the general case, but it will be adopted here as a first approximation to enable us to get some insight into the complex structure of optimum resource allocation over time.

The analytical framework may now be summarized before we proceed to examine its structure in detail. We consider an individual consumer who possesses a fixed amount of assets to be held in the form of bonds. He expects the real rate of interest to be constant, r, and to receive wage payments fixed in real terms, w. His utility level u_t at each moment of time t is related to consumption c_t:

$$u_t = u(c_t), \tag{17}$$

and he is concerned with maximizing the total utility:

$$\int_0^\infty u_t e^{-\Delta_t} \, dt \tag{18}$$

subject to the constraints:

$$\dot{\Delta}_t = \delta(u_t), \qquad \text{with } \Delta_0 = 0, \tag{19}$$

$$\dot{b}_t = y_t - c_t, \qquad \text{with given } b_0, \tag{20}$$

where the real income y_t is given by

$$y_t = rb_t + w. \tag{21}$$

4 Solution of the optimum problem

The first step in simplifying the optimum problem consists of a transformation of the time variable t into one in terms of which the rate of time preference becomes constant; namely,[1] if we take Δ as the independent variable instead of t in the maximand and (18), we get, in view of (19), that

$$\int_0^\infty ue^{-\Delta}dt = \int_0^\infty \frac{u}{\delta(u)}e^{-\Delta}d\Delta, \tag{22}$$

while the differential equation (19) is transformed to

$$\overset{\circ}{b}\left(=\frac{db}{d\Delta}\right)=\frac{y-c}{\delta(u)}, \quad \text{with a given } b(0)=b_0, \tag{23}$$

where $\overset{\circ}{b}$ in general indicates $db/d\Delta$.

Since the real rate of interest r is constant through time, the differential equation (23) is reduced to one involving y instead of b; that is,

$$\overset{\circ}{y}\left(=\frac{dy}{d\Delta}\right)=\frac{r}{\delta(u)}(y-c), \tag{24}$$

with the given initial condition $y(0)=rb_0+w$.

The optimum problem now is converted to that of maximizing (22) subject to the differential equation (23) or (24). In the present form, it is possible to apply the mathematical techniques of the calculus of variations, as developed by, e.g. Ramsey (1928) and Koopmans (1963).

By introducing the imputed price of investment $\lambda=\lambda(\Delta)$ for each level of accumulated rate of time preference, the imputed value of income H is defined by:

$$H=u(c)+\lambda(y-c). \tag{25}$$

The present value of the imputed income H, to be discounted at the prevailing rate of preference $\delta=\delta(u(c))$, is given by

$$\frac{H}{\delta(u)}e^{-\Delta}. \tag{26}$$

The optimum consumption c is determined at the level at which the present value (26) of the imputed income is maximized; namely, by taking the first order condition, we get

$$u'(c)-\lambda-\frac{\delta'(u)u'(c)}{\delta(u)}H=0. \tag{27}$$

The solution c to the first order condition (27) in fact is a maximum of (26), as is easily seen from the assumptions (12–14).

[1] The transformation introduced here is similar to what Allais (1966) has termed the psychological time.

To explain the condition (27), let us rewrite it as

$$u' = \lambda + \frac{\delta' u'}{\delta} H, \tag{28}$$

the left-hand side of which is nothing but the marginal utility of consumption, while the right-hand side is the sum of the imputed value of investment λ and the marginal increase in the present value of the imputed income due to a marginal decrease in the rate of time preference.

The differential equation describing the dynamic path of the imputed price $\lambda = \lambda(\Delta)$ is obtained from the Euler-Lagrange condition; namely, we have

$$\frac{\mathring{\lambda}}{\lambda} = \frac{\delta(u) - r}{\delta(u)}, \tag{29}$$

which indicates that capital gains are always equal to the interest charges minus the competitive rent.

The optimum path of the asset accumulation is then characterized as one which, by a proper choice of imputed prices λ, constitutes a bounded solution to the system of differential equations (24) and (29), together with (27). The structure of the differential equations (24) and (29), however, is more easily analyzed by transforming them into those involving y and c. Let us denote

$$\phi(y, c, \lambda) = u'(c) - \frac{\delta(u(c))u'(c)}{\delta(u(c))} H, \tag{30}$$

which by a differentiation yields

$$\phi_y \mathring{y} + \phi_c \mathring{c} + \phi_\lambda \mathring{\lambda} = 0, \tag{31}$$

along the path satisfying (27).

Substituting (24) and (29) into (31) and re-arranging, we get

$$\mathring{c} = \frac{r - \delta - \delta' u'(y - c)}{\delta\left(\dfrac{u'\delta''(u + u'(y - c))}{\delta - u\delta'} - \dfrac{u''}{u'}\right)}, \tag{32}$$

where $\delta' = \delta'(u)$, $u' = u'(c)$, etc.

The rate of change in income level y is zero if and only if $c = y$; namely, the $\mathring{y} = 0$ curve is described by the 45° line starting at the origin on the (c, y)-plane, as indicated in Figure 3.2. Real income y tends to increase below the $\mathring{y} = 0$ curve, while it tends to decrease above the $\mathring{y} = 0$ curve. On the other hand, the $\mathring{c} = 0$ curve is characterized by:

$$r - \delta(u) - \delta'(u)u'(c)(y - c) = 0, \tag{33}$$

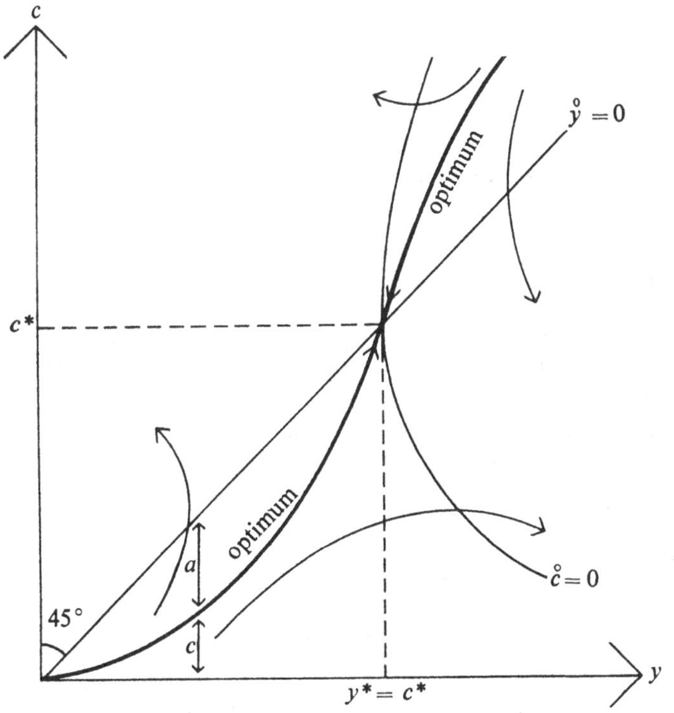

Figure 3.2

or

$$y = c + \frac{1}{\delta' u'}(r - \delta). \tag{34}$$

To see the shape of the $\mathring{c} = 0$ curve, differentiate (34) with respect to c to get

$$\left(\frac{dy}{dc}\right)_{\mathring{c}=0} = -\frac{r-\delta}{\delta' u'}\left(\frac{\delta'' u'}{\delta'} + \frac{u''}{u'}\right), \tag{35}$$

which vanishes whenever $\delta((u(c)) = r$. We can see from (35), $y \gtreqless c$ according to $r \gtreqless \delta$. Therefore the $\mathring{c} = 0$ curve is in general shaped as illustrated in Figure 3.2. Since $\mathring{x} > 0$ if and only if (c, y) lies on the right-hand side of the $\mathring{c} = 0$ curve, the solution paths to the system (24) and (29) have the structure typically illustrated in Figure 3.2 by arrowed curves. It is then easily seen that there are two solution paths which converge to the stationary point at which the $\mathring{y} = 0$ and $\mathring{c} = 0$ curves intersect, as indicated by heavy arrowed curves in Figure 3.2. Let the solution paths converging to the stationary point be denoted by

$$c = c(y, r), \tag{36}$$

since a change in r will in general shift such curves.

The optimum time paths of consumption and assets then are determined in terms of the $c(y, r)$ curves thus obtained:

$$\left.\begin{aligned} c_t &= c(y, r) \\ \dot{y}_t &= r(y_t - c_t) \end{aligned}\right\}. \tag{37}$$

The function (36) specifies the optimum level c of consumption for given level of income y and real rate of interest r, and it will be referred to as the *short-run consumption function.* On the other hand, the stationary level of consumption c^* (which in turn is equal to the stationary level y^* of income) is determined by the real rate of interest r:

$$c^* = c^*(r), \tag{38}$$

which will be referred to as the *long-run consumption function.*

5 The long-run consumption function $c^*(r)$

The long-run level of consumption c^* has been defined as that level of consumption which would have been eventually reached if the real rate of interest were to remain at a certain constant level r, throughout the whole period of adjustment. It is independent of the initial level of the asset holding or of initial income level, since it is determined at the level at which the rate of time preference is equal to the real rate of interest, that is

$$\delta(u(c^*)) = r. \tag{39}$$

The long-run level c^* of real consumption thus is one for which the rate of time preference $\delta(u(c^*))$ is precisely equal to the market (real) rate of interest r. The determination of c^* is now typically described in Figure 3.3, where the first quadrant is simply copied from Figure 3.2. In the second quadrant, the horizontal axis represents the utility level u, while the vertical axis in the third quadrant measures the rate of time preference δ. The utility level for each consumption is specified by the $u(c)$-curve, while the $\delta(u)$-curve relates the rate of time preference δ with the utility level u. For a given real rate of interest r, the long-run level $c^*(r)$ of consumption is thus uniquely determined, and the higher the real rate of interest r, the higher is the corresponding long-run level of consumption, hence the higher will be the long-run level of real income $c^* = y^*$. More precisely,

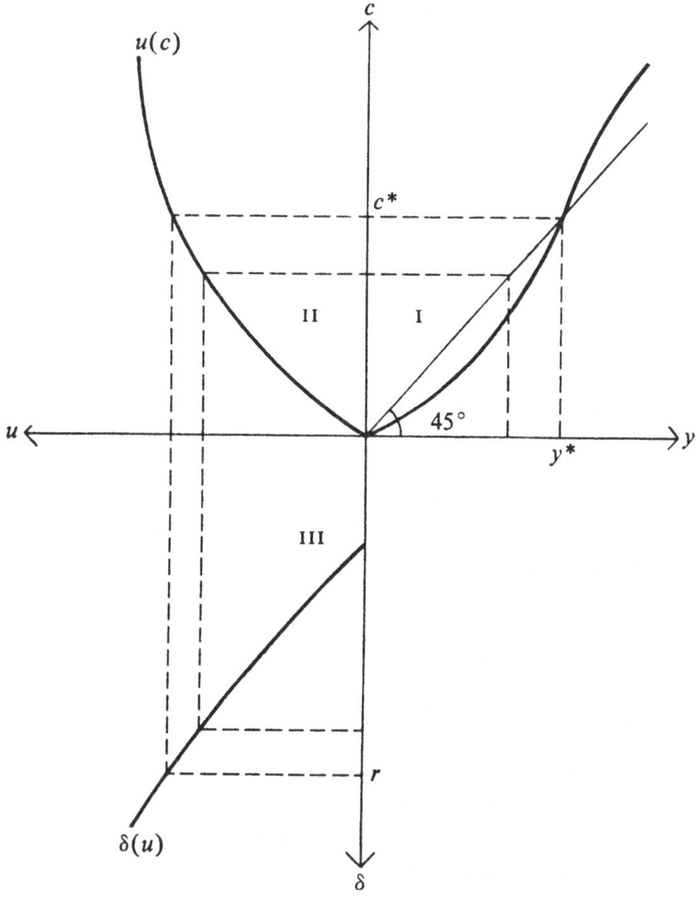

Figure 3.3

differentiate (39) to get

$$\frac{dc^*}{c^*} = \frac{1}{\varepsilon^*}\frac{dr}{r}, \tag{40}$$

where ε^* is the elasticity of the rate of time preference with respect to the level of consumption:

$$\varepsilon^* = \left[\frac{\delta'(u)u'(c)c}{\delta(u)}\right]_{c=c^*} = \left[\frac{\delta'(u)u}{\delta(u)}\frac{u'(c)c}{u(c)}\right]_{c=c^*}, \tag{41}$$

which, in view of (12–14), lies between 0 and 1. Namely, a percentage increase in the real rate of interest r increases the long-run level c^* more than proportionally. The long-run level of bond holdings b^*, on the other hand, is determined by the relation:

$$c^* = y^* = rb^* + w, \tag{42}$$

which, by a differentiation, yields

$$dc^* = r\,db^* + b^*\,dr + dw. \tag{43}$$

We have from (40) and (43) that

$$\frac{db^*}{b^*} = \frac{(1/\varepsilon^*)c^* - rb^*}{rb^*}\frac{dr}{r} - \frac{w}{rb^*}\frac{dw}{w}, \tag{44}$$

which implies

$$\frac{\partial b^*}{\partial r} > 0, \quad \frac{\partial b^*}{\partial w} < 0; \tag{45}$$

namely, the long-run level of bond holdings b^* will be increased whenever there is an increase in the rate of interest r or a decrease either in real wages or transfer payments.

6 The short-run consumption function $c(y, r)$

In Section 4, we have shown that the optimum level of consumption c is uniquely determined for given income y and real rate of interest r. The structure of the short-run consumption $c(y, r)$ is illustrated in Figure 3.4, where part of Figure 3.2 has been reproduced. It is first seen that an increase in income y is always associated with an increase in the optimum level of computation, that is,

$$\partial c/\partial y > 0. \tag{46}$$

Second, it can be shown that a decrease in the real rate of interest r shifts the optimum path uniformly to the left, thus resulting an increase in optimum consumption for a given level of income y, that is,

$$\partial c/\partial r < 0. \tag{47}$$

Since an increase in r results in an upward movement (along the 45° line) of the long-run level of consumption, the proposition (47) will be proved if we can show that the slope of the optimum path is always increased whenever there is an increase in r; in other words, it suffices to show that

$$\frac{\partial}{\partial r}\left(\frac{dc}{dy}\right)_{\text{opt.}} > 0, \qquad y < y^*. \tag{48}$$

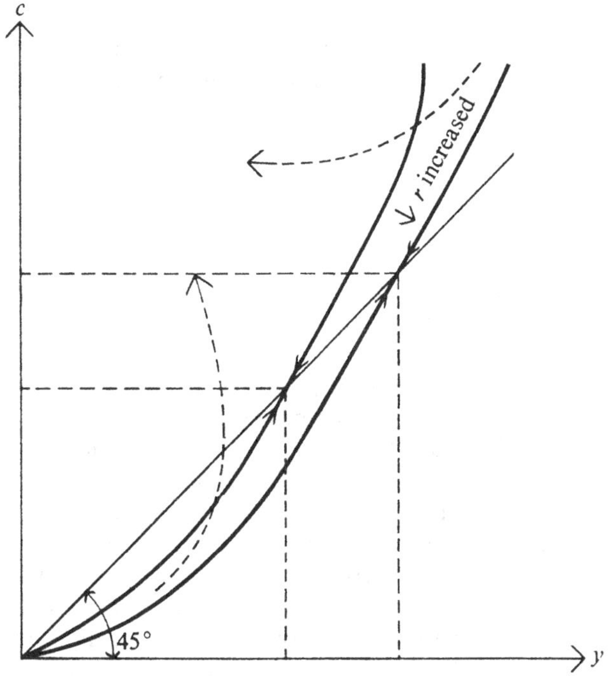

Figure 3.4

To see (48), let us first derive an explicit formula for the slope of the optimum path from (24) and (29):

$$\left(\frac{dc}{dy}\right)_{\text{opt.}} = \frac{1}{y-c} \frac{1 - \dfrac{\delta + \delta' u'(y-c)}{r}}{\dfrac{u'\delta''(u + u'(y-c))}{\delta - u\delta'} - \dfrac{u''}{u'}}, \tag{49}$$

which is increased whenever r is increased. Similarly, we can show that, when $y > y^*$, an increase in r always decreases the slope of the short-run consumption schedule.

The structure of the short-run consumption $c(y, r)$ typically illustrated in Figure 3.4 enables us to infer about the relative magnitude of consumption compared with real income. Optimum consumption $c(y, r)$ is less than real income y if and only if the real income is less than the long-run level of real income y^*, while the latter is the case if and only if the rate of time preference $\delta(u(y))$ when all real income y is spent on consumption is still less than the market real rate of interest; namely, savings are positive if and only if the rate of time preference $\delta(u(y))$ when real income y is all spent on consumption is less than the real rate of interest. Hence, we can particularly show that the marginal propensity to consume is greater than or equal to unity at the long-run level of real income, that is,

$$\left(\frac{\partial c}{\partial y}\right)_{y=y^*} \geqslant 1. \tag{50}$$

7 Demand for money and other assets

The analysis presented above may be extended without much difficulty to a more general case in which each individual consumer is permitted to hold his assets either in the form of cash, from which he derives certain utility, or in the form of bonds, interest payments for which will be annually added to his income. At a certain moment of time, say 0, the consumer has a fixed amount, A_0, of assets, to be given in dollar terms, and expects to receive wages W_t for indefinite future all in money terms. The expected income stream will now depend upon the expected rates of interest as well as upon the way in which his asset holdings are divided between cash and bond. The consumer is again concerned with the time-path of consumption which is most preferred among all feasible time-paths of consumption.

Let M_t and B_t be respectively the amounts of cash balances and bond holdings the consumer plans to possess at each moment of time t. The total monetary value A_t of his asset holdings will then be

$$A_t = M_t + \pi_t B_t, \tag{51}$$

where π_t is the market price of bonds which the consumer expects to prevail at time t. On the other hand, the level of his nominal income Y_t at time t will be composed of interests and wages payments:

$$Y_t = i_t B_t + W_t, \tag{52}$$

where i_t is the coupon rate of interest; that is, the unit of bond is expected to yield interests in the amount i_t at time t.

The money income Y_t will be divided between consumption expenditure C_t, increases in cash balances $\dot{M}_t$, and in bond holdings $\dot{B}_t$:

$$Y_t = C_t + \dot{M}_t + i_t \dot{B}_t. \tag{53}$$

It is assumed that the level of utility depends upon the amount of real cash balances as well as upon real consumption (Patinkin, 1956; Archibald and Lipsey, 1958–9, pp. 1–23; Douglas, 1966; Sidrauski, 1965). If p_t is the general price level expected at time t, real consumption c_t and real cash balances m_t will be

$$c_t = C_t/p_t, \quad m_t = M_t/p_t,$$

and the utility level u_t will be given by

$$u_t = u(c_t, m_t).$$

The optimum plan then is the one which maximizes the total utility defined by (10) among all possible paths of consumption and real cash balances consistent with his initial value A_0 of assets and the state of his expectations regarding increases in the general price level and in the price of bond, as well as regarding the bond rate of interest. Let the expected money rate of interest and rate of increase in the general price level be denoted by

$$\rho_t = \frac{i_t}{\pi_t} + \frac{\dot{\pi}_t}{\pi_t}, \quad \psi_t = \frac{\dot{p}_t}{p_t}.$$

To simplify the formulation, we introduce the following real variables (which are in general denoted by small letters):

$a_t = A_t/p_t$: real value of the asset holdings,
$b_t = \pi_t B_t/p_t$: the market value of the bond holdings in real terms,
$m_t = M_t/p_t$: real cash balances,
$c_t = C_t/p_t$: real consumption,
$w_t = W_t/p_t$: the expected real wages,
$y_t = Y_t/p_t$: real income.

Then the relations (51–53) may be rewritten as:

$$a_t = m_t + b_t, \tag{54}$$

$$\begin{aligned} c_t + \dot{m}_t + \dot{b}_t &= (\rho_t - \psi_t)b_t + w_t - m_t\psi_t \\ &= r_t b_t + w_t - \psi_t m_t, \end{aligned} \tag{55}$$

where $r_t = \rho_t - \psi_t$ is the expected real rate of interest.

In view of (54), the equation (55) is reduced to

$$\dot{a}_t = (r_t a_t + w_t) - (\rho_t m_t + c_t), \tag{56}$$

of which the first term on the right-hand side, $r_t a_t + w_t$, corresponds to the concept of real income, while the second term, $\rho_t m_t + c_t$, represents the virtual level of consumption, being the sum of the alternative cost of holding real cash balances at m_t and of real consumption c_t.

The optimum paths of consumption, real cash balances, and bond holdings thus are determined relative to the state of expectations regarding real wages, real rate of interest, and money rate of interest which will be again assumed to be fixed at certain levels.

We consider an individual consumer who possesses a fixed amount ($a_0 = A_0/p_0$) in real terms to be held either in the form of real cash balances or in the form of bonds. He expects the real and money rates of interest to be constant, r and ρ, respectively, and to receive wage and transfer payments fixed in real terms, w and τ. His utility level at each moment of time t, u_t is related to consumption c_t and real cash balances m_t:

$$u_t = u(c_t, m_t), \tag{57}$$

and he is concerned with maximizing the total utility:

$$\int_0^{\infty} u_t e^{-\Delta_t} dt \tag{58}$$

subject to the constraints:

$$\dot{\Delta}_t = \delta(u_t), \qquad \text{with } \Delta_0 = 0, \tag{59}$$

$$\dot{a}_t = y_t - x_t, \qquad \text{with given } a_0, \tag{60}$$

$$a_t = m_t + b_t, \tag{61}$$

where real income y_t and the virtual level of consumption x_t are respectively defined by

$$y_t = ra_t + w, \tag{62}$$

$$x_t = c_t + \rho m_t. \tag{63}$$

It may be first noted that, along any optimum path, consumption c and real cash balances m are determined so as to maximize the level of utility $v(c, m)$ subject to the constraint that

$$c + \rho m = x. \tag{64}$$

Such a combination (c, m) of consumption and real cash balances is obtained at the point at which the marginal rate of substitution between them is equal to the money rate of interest ρ:

$$\frac{u_m}{u_c} = \rho, \tag{65}$$

so that c and m are uniquely determined by the level of virtual consumption x. In Figure 3.5, the horizontal axis represents real cash balances m, while the level of real consumption is measured along the vertical axis, and the optimum combination (c, m) of consumption and real cash balances moves along the income-consumption path, as the virtual level of consumption x is increased from zero to infinity; we may write:

$$c = c(x, \rho), \qquad m = m(x, \rho), \tag{66}$$

to indicate their dependency upon the money rate of interest ρ. The

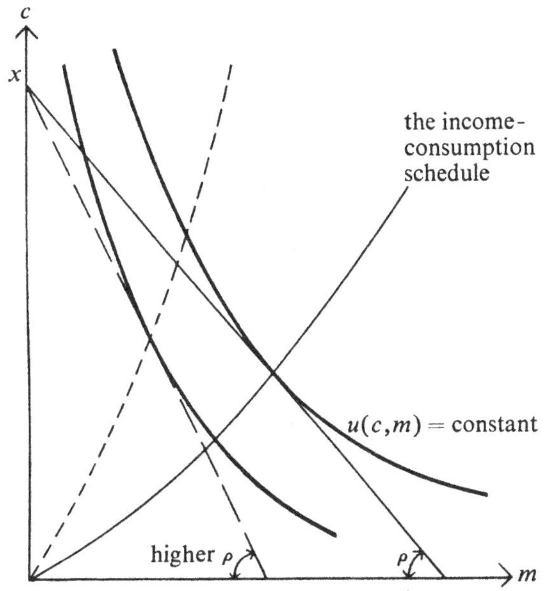

Figure 3.5

maximum level of utility will then be denoted by

$$u(c, m) = U(x, \rho). \tag{67}$$

It will be assumed that both consumption and real cash balances are superior goods in the sense that an increase in the virtual level of consumption x will increase both optimum consumption and real cash balances:

$$\frac{\partial c}{\partial x} > 0, \quad \frac{\partial m}{\partial x} > 0. \tag{68}$$

The effect of an increase in the money rate of interest ρ is, on the other hand, to shift the income-consumption path uniformly upward; it will be assumed that

$$\frac{\partial c}{\partial \rho} > 0, \quad \frac{\partial m}{\partial \rho} < 0. \tag{69}$$

It is easily seen that the utility function $u(x) = U(x; \rho)$ satisfies the following conditions

$$u(x) > 0, \qquad u'(x) > 0, \qquad u''(x) < 0, \quad \text{for all } x > 0. \tag{70}$$

In terms of the new utility function $u(x) = U(x, \rho)$, the optimum problem is reduced to one in which the total utility (58) is maximized subject to the constraints (59) and (60), where

$$u_t = U(x_t; \rho). \tag{71}$$

The optimum path of the virtual level of consumption x_t and the real income y_t will then be obtained with the aid of the following differential equations:

$$\dot{y} = r(y - x), \tag{72}$$

$$\dot{x} = \frac{r - \delta - \delta' u'(y - x)}{\dfrac{u'\delta''[u + u'(y - x)]}{\delta - \delta' u} - \dfrac{u''}{u'}}, \tag{73}$$

where $u' = u'(x) = \partial U/\partial x$ denotes the marginal utility of virtual consumption x, etc. The stable solution paths of the differential equations (72–3) determine the short-run consumption schedule; namely, let

$$x = x(y, r, \rho) \tag{74}$$

represent the stable branches of the solution paths, as illustrated by the heavy arrowed curves in Figure 3.2, where real consumption c is now replaced by the virtual level of consumption x for the vertical axis.[2] Then the optimum path of asset accumulation is attained by adjusting the virtual level of consumption according to the schedule (74) and by determining the allocation of the virtual level of consumption x between real consumption c and real cash balances m in such a manner that the marginal rate of substitution between real consumption and real cash balances is equal to the money rate of interest ρ; namely,

$$c(y, r, \rho) = c(x, \rho),$$
$$m(y, r, \rho) = m(x, \rho),$$

where $x = x(y, r, \rho)$.

The effects of a change in the real rate of interest r upon the short-run consumption and demand for real cash balances are easily examined, since it does not involve a change in the shape of the utility function $u(x) = U(x; \rho)$. By applying the analysis presented for the simpler case, an increase in the real rate of interest r is shown to decrease the virtual level of short-run consumption x, thus resulting with decreases both in real consumption and real cash balances, that is,

$$\frac{\partial c}{\partial r} < 0, \quad \frac{\partial m}{\partial r} < 0. \tag{75}$$

[2] Such a curve will shift whenever there is a change either in the real rate of interest r or in the money rate of interest ρ, to be indicated by the functional notation (74).

On the other hand, an increase in real income y is easily shown to result in increases in both real consumption and real cash balances; that is,

$$\frac{\partial c}{\partial y} > 0, \quad \frac{\partial m}{\partial y} > 0. \tag{76}$$

The long-run virtual level of consumption x^* is determined at the level at which the rate of time preference is equated to the real rate of interest r:

$$\delta(u(x^*)) = r;$$

the long-run levels of real consumption c^* and real cash balances m^* are then determined by the real rate of interest r, together with the money rate of interest ρ upon which the shape of the utility function $u(x)$ depends; that is,

$$c^* = c^*(r, \rho), \qquad m^* = m^*(r, \rho).$$

The long-run levels c^* and m^* are more precisely characterized by the requirements

$$u_m - \rho u_c = 0,$$
$$\delta(u(c, m)) = r,$$

which, by a differentiation, yield

$$\begin{pmatrix} u_{mc} - \rho u_{cc}, & -(\rho u_{cm} - u_{mm}) \\ 1 & \rho \end{pmatrix} \begin{pmatrix} dc^* \\ dm^* \end{pmatrix} = \begin{pmatrix} u_c & d\rho \\ (1/\delta' u_c) & dr \end{pmatrix};$$

hence,

$$\frac{\partial c^*}{\partial \rho} = \frac{\rho u_c}{\Delta^*} > 0, \quad \frac{\partial c^*}{\partial r} = \frac{\rho u_{cm} - u_{mm}}{\Delta^*} \frac{1}{\delta' u_c} > 0,$$

$$\frac{\partial m^*}{\partial \rho} = -\frac{u_c}{\Delta^*} < 0, \quad \frac{\partial m^*}{\partial r} = \frac{u_{cm} - \rho u_{cc}}{\Delta^*} \frac{1}{\delta' u_c} > 0,$$

where $\Delta^* = -\rho^2 u_{cc} + \rho u_{cm} - u_{mm} > 0.$

Thus an increase in the real rate of interest increases both the long-run levels of real comsumption and real cash balances, while an increase in the money rate of interest results with an increase in the long-run level of real consumption and a decrease in the long-run real cash balances.

References

Allais, M. (1966), "A Restatement of the Quantity Theory of Money: the Hereditary, Relativistic and Logistic Formulation of the Demand for Money," *American Economic Review* 56.

Archibald, G. C. and Lipsey, R. G. (1958), "Monetary and Value Theory: a Critique of Lange and Patinkin," *Review of Economic Studies* 26, 1–22.
Boehm-Bawerk, E. von (1884–89), *Positive Theory of Capital*. Tr. by G. D. Huncke. South Holland, Ill. (1959).
Douglas, A. J. (1966), "Studies in Monetary Dynamics. (Doctoral dissertation, Stanford University).
Fisher, I. (1907), *The Rate of Interest*, New York.
Koopmans, T. C. (1960), "Stationary Ordinary Utility and Impatience," *Econometrica* 28, 287–309.
——— (1965), "On a Concept of Optimum Economic Growth," *Semaine d'Etude sur le Role de l'Analyse Econometrique dans la Formulation de Plans de Development*, 225–87.
Patinkin, D. (1956), *Money, Interest and Price*. Evanston, Ill.
Ramsey, F. P. (1928), "A Mathematical Theory of Savings," *Economic Journal* 38, 543–59.
Sidrauski, M. (1965), "Inflation, Optimum Consumption, and Real Cash Balances" (Paper presented at the New York meetings of the Econometric Society, 1965).

PART II

Duality and production

CHAPTER 4

Duality principles in the theory of cost and production

1 Introduction

The theory of production, as typically described by Samuelson [2, (IV, 57--89)], is primarily concerned with the optimum allocation of factors of production that minimizes the total cost for each output, and with the nature of the cost curves derived from production processes under neoclassical hypotheses. However, it is customary in econometric studies of production structure to specify the form of production functions, up to a certain parametric class (such as Cobb-Douglas or Constant Elasticities of Substitution), and then estimate the parameters, through the cost curves which are usually derived by minimization of total cost.[1] It is of some interest to see if production functions are uniquely determined by curves of minimum total cost and to characterize the class of total cost curves which are derived from production functions with neoclassical properties. This dual determination of production functions from cost curves has been established by Shephard [3], and in the present note we are interested in extending some of his results as well as formulating explicitly the conditions for cost curves that are derived from neoclassical production processes by a minimization of total cost.[2]

2 The structure of cost functions

The model of production dealt with in this note consists of one output and a finite number of inputs, say $1, \ldots, n$. The structure of production is characterized by specifying the set of all combinations of inputs which

From *International Economic Review*, Vol. 5 (1964), pp. 216–20; reprinted with permission.

[1] See, e.g., K. J. Arrow, H. B. Chenery, B. S. Minhas and R. M. Solow [1].

[2] In terms of the formulation presented in this note, it is easily seen that our duality theorems are equally applicable to the theory of consumer's behavior; one has only to regard level of utility as output, and consumption of goods as input.

result in a given quantity of outputs. Let $A(y)$ be the set of all input vectors $x=(x_1,\dots,x_n)$ which could possibly produce output y. The boundary of $A(y)$ is the familiar isoquant corresponding to the given level of output y.

Assumptions

(A) For each $y \geqq 0$, the set $A(y)$ is a nonempty, closed set consisting of nonnegative n-vectors $x=(x_1,\dots,x_n)$.
(B) Marginal rates of substitution are nonincreasing, i.e., for each $y \geqq 0$, the set $A(y)$ is a convex set.
(C) Disposal activities are costless, i.e.,

$$\text{for each } y \geqq 0,\ x \in A(y) \text{ and } x' \geqq x \text{ imply } x' \in A(y); \tag{1}$$

$$y_1 \geq y_2 \text{ implies } A(y_1) \subset A(y_2). \tag{2}$$

The producer is assumed to choose those combinations of inputs that minimize the value of inputs computed at prevailing market prices. Let $p=(p_1,\dots,p_n)$ be the vector of market prices whose i-th component, p_i, stands for the price of the ith input.

The cost minimization problem is:

Find the input vector $x=(x_1,\dots,x_n)$ that minimizes the total cost px, subject to $x \in A(y)$.

Because of the assumption (A), minimum total cost always exists and is uniquely determined by the given level of output, y, and by the market price vector, $p=(p_1 \dots, p_n)$. We may, therefore, denote minimum cost by $c(p,y)$, and refer to it as the *(total) cost function*. $c(p,y)$ is formally defined as

$$c(p,y) = \min\{px : x \in A(y)\}. \tag{3}$$

Theorem 1. Let the production possibility sets $A(y)$ satisfy the conditions (A) and (C). Then the cost function $c(p,y)$ specified by (3) satisfies the following conditions:

(A′) $c(p,y)$ is defined for all $p \geq 0$ and $y > 0$, and is continuous, nonnegative, and homogeneous of first degree with respect to p;
(B′) $c(p,y)$ is a concave function with respect to the price vector p;
(C′) $c(p,y)$ is a nondecreasing function with respect to level of output y.

Proof. (A′) and (C′) are trivially implied by (A) and (C). In order to see that $c(p,y)$ satisfies (B′), let p^0 and p^1 be two price vectors, and

$$p^t = (1-t)p^0 + tp^1, \qquad 0 \leqq t \leqq 1.$$

By definition (3), we have

$$c(p^0, y) \leqq p^0 x, \quad \text{for all } x \in A(y), \tag{4}$$

and

$$c(p^1, y) \leqq p^1 x, \quad \text{for all } x \in A(y). \tag{5}$$

Multiplying (4) and (5) by $(1-t)$ and t, respectively, and adding, we have

$$(1-t)c(p^0, y) + tc(p^1, y) \leqq p^t x, \quad \text{for all } x \in A(y),$$

which implies that

$$(1-t)c(p^0, y) + tc(p^1, y) \leqq c(p^t, y), \quad \text{for all } 0 \leqq t \leqq 1.$$

Hence, the function $c(p, y)$ is concave with respect to p. ■

To investigate the determination of the production possibility set $A(y)$ from the cost function $c(p, y)$, let us introduce the set $B(y)$ associated with the function $c(p, y)$ by

$$B(y) = \{x : px \geqq c(p, y), \quad \text{for all } p \geq 0\}. \tag{6}$$

Theorem 2. Let the production possibility set $A(y)$ satisfy the conditions (A), (B), and (C). Then, for any level of output y, the production possibility set $A(y)$ coincides with the set $B(y)$ defined by (6).

Proof. Let $x^0 \in A(y)$. Then, by definition (3),

$$c(p, y) \leqq px^0, \quad \text{for all } p \geq 0.$$

Hence, by (6), $x^0 \in B(y)$.

On the other hand, let $x^0 \notin A(y)$. Since the set $A(y)$ is a closed, convex set, there is nonzero vector p^0 such that

$$p^0 x^0 < \min\{p^0 x : x \in A(y)\}.$$

But by (C), p^0 becomes nonnegative; hence,

$$p^0 x^0 < c(p^0, y).$$

By definition (6), then, we have

$$x^0 \notin B(y).$$ ■

3 The structure of production

In section 2 we discussed the structure of cost functions derived from given production possibility sets. In this section, we start with a given cost function and see if the structure of production is uniquely determined.

Let $c(p, y)$ be a function defined for price vector p and level of output y. The production possibility set associated with level of output y is defined by (6).

> **Theorem 3.** Let the cost function $c(p, y)$ satisfy the conditions (A′) and (C′). Then the sets $B(y)$ defined by (6) satisfy the conditions (A), (B), and (C).

Proof. Since $c(p, y)$ is homogeneous of first degree with respect to p, the set $B(y)$ defined by (6) is nonempty. The closedness of $B(y)$ is implied by the continuity assumption of $c(p, y)$ and (A) is satisfied. To see that (B) is satisfied by $B(y)$, let x^0 and $x^1 \in B(y)$, and $x^t = (1-t)x^0 + tx^1$, $0 \leqq t \leqq 1$. By definition (6),

$$px^0 \geqq c(p, y), \quad \text{for all } p \geq 0,$$

and

$$px^1 \geqq c(p, y), \quad \text{for all } p \geq 0.$$

Hence,

$$px^t \geqq c(p, y), \quad \text{for all } p \geq 0, \tag{7}$$

namely,

$$x^t \in B(y). \tag{8}$$

(C) is implied by (6) and (C′). ■

> **Theorem 4.** Let the function $c(p, y)$ satisfy the conditions (A′) and (B′). Then the cost function $c^*(p, y)$ derived from the production possibility sets $B(y)$ coincides with $c(p, y)$.

Proof. Let the set R in the $n+1$-dimensional vector space be defined by

$$R = \left\{ \begin{pmatrix} p \\ \alpha \end{pmatrix} : p \geqq 0, \alpha \geqq -c(p, y) \right\}. \tag{9}$$

Because of conditions (A′) and (B′), the set R is a closed convex cone. Therefore, by the duality theorem on closed convex cones, we have

$$R^{++} = R, \tag{10}$$

where

$$R^{+} = \left\{ \begin{pmatrix} x \\ \beta \end{pmatrix} : \begin{pmatrix} p \\ \alpha \end{pmatrix}' \begin{pmatrix} x \\ \beta \end{pmatrix} \geqq 0, \quad \text{for all } \begin{pmatrix} p \\ \alpha \end{pmatrix} \in R \right\}, \tag{11}$$

$$R^{++} = \left\{ \begin{pmatrix} p \\ \alpha \end{pmatrix} : \begin{pmatrix} p \\ \alpha \end{pmatrix}' \begin{pmatrix} x \\ \beta \end{pmatrix} \geqq 0, \quad \text{for all } \begin{pmatrix} x \\ \beta \end{pmatrix} \in R^{+} \right\}. \tag{12}$$

From (6) and (11), we have

$$R^{+} = \left\{ \begin{pmatrix} x \\ \beta \end{pmatrix} : \beta = 0, x \geqq 0, \quad \text{or} \quad \beta > 0, \frac{x}{\beta} \in B(y) \right\}. \tag{13}$$

Hence,

$$R^{++} = \left\{ \begin{pmatrix} p \\ \alpha \end{pmatrix} : p \geqq 0, \alpha \geqq -px, \quad \text{for all } x \in B(y) \right\}. \tag{14}$$

The relation (14), together with (9) and (10), implies that

$$c(p, y) = c^*(p, y).$$ ■

References

[1] Arrow, K. J., H. B. Chenery, B. S. Minhas, and R. M. Solow, "Capital-Labor Substitution and Economic Efficiency," *Review of Economics and Statistics*, XLIII (August, 1961), 225–50.

[2] Samuelson,P. A., *Foundations of Economic Analysis*, Cambridge: Harvard University Press, 1947.

[3] Shephard, R. W., *Cost and Production Functions*, Princeton: Princeton University Press, 1953.

CHAPTER 5

Production functions with constant elasticities of substitution

1 The Arrow-Chenery-Minhas-Solow production function

In the present note, we are concerned with characterizing the class of production functions for which elasticities of substitution are all constant regardless of factor prices. In the case of two factors of production, the characterization of such production functions was discussed by Arrow, Chenery, Minhas, and Solow [2].

Let $f(x_1, x_2)$ be a production function where x_1 and x_2 respectively represent the amounts of factors 1 and 2 employed. Production is assumed to be subject to constant returns to scale and to diminishing marginal rates of substitution. As is discussed in Hicks [3], pp. 241–46, the elasticity of substitution σ may be defined by:

$$\sigma = \frac{\dfrac{\partial f}{\partial x_1}\dfrac{\partial f}{\partial x_2}}{f(x_1, x_2)\dfrac{\partial^2 f}{\partial x_1 \partial x_2}}. \tag{1}$$

It has been shown in [2] that the elasticity of substitution σ is constant regardless of factor inputs x_1 and x_2 if and only if the production function $f(x_1, x_2)$ is of the following form:

$$f(x_1, x_2) = (\alpha_1 x_1^{-\beta} + \alpha_2 x_2^{-\beta})^{-1/\beta}, \tag{2}$$

where α_1 and α_2 are positive constants and

$$\beta = \frac{1}{\sigma} - 1. \tag{3}$$

From *Review of Economic Studies*, Vol. 19 (1963), pp. 291–9; reprinted with permission.

This work was written while the author was a Fellow at the Centre for Advanced Study in the Behavioral Sciences. He is very much indebted to Dan McFadden and Marc Nerlove for valuable comments and suggestions.

The production function of the form (2) was first introduced by Solow [8] as an example to illustrate his model of economic growth.

2 Allen's elasticities of substitution

The elasticity of substitution may be in several ways generalized to the case in which more than two factors of production are involved.[1] In what follows, we shall adapt the definition of partial elasticities of substitution as introduced in Allen [1], pp. 503–9.

Let the number of factors of production be n and $f(x) = f(x_1, \ldots, x_n)$ a production function; $x_1, \ldots, x_n$ represent the amounts of factors of production $1, \ldots, n$ employed. It is again assumed that production is subject to constant returns to scale and to diminishing marginal rates of substitution. Allen's *partial elasticity of substitution* σ_{ij} between two factors of production, say factors i and $j (i \neq j)$, is defined by:

$$\sigma_{ij} = \frac{x_1 f_1 + \cdots + x_n f_n}{x_i x_j} \frac{F_{ij}}{F}, \tag{4}$$

where

$$f_i = \frac{\partial f}{\partial x_i}, f_{ij} = \frac{\partial^2 f}{\partial x_i \partial x_j},$$

$$F = \det \begin{bmatrix} 0, & f_1, \ldots, f_n \\ f_1, & f_{11}, \ldots, f_{1n} \\ & \\ f_n, & f_{n_1}, \ldots, f_{nn} \end{bmatrix}$$

and F_{ij} is the co-factor of the element f_{ij} in the determinant F.

By definition (4), σ_{ij} are symmetric; i.e.,

$$\sigma_{ij} = \sigma_{ji}, \quad \text{for all } i \neq j. \tag{5}$$

Before we investigate the implications of constancy of partial elasticities of substitution σ_{ij}, we shall first transform the definition (4) into one in terms of the unit cost function.

Let $p = (p_1, \ldots, p_n)$ be a vector of prices of factors of production; p_i are assumed all positive. The vector $x = (x_1, \ldots, x_n)$ of factor inputs that minimizes the unit cost

$$\sum_{i=1}^{n} p_i x_i$$

[1] For the definition of the elasticity of substitution, see, e.g., Hicks [3], p. 117; Lerner [4]; Robinson [5], pp. 256–7; Allen [1], pp. 340–3, pp. 503–9.

subject to

$$f(x_1, \ldots, x_n) = 1$$

is uniquely determined. We may write

$$x_1 = x_1(p), \ldots, x_n = x_n(p),$$

$$\lambda = \lambda(p) = \sum_{i=1}^{n} p_i x_i(p).$$

The function $\lambda(p)$ will be referred to as the unit cost function associated with the production function $f(x)$. The factor input functions $x_i(p)$ are all homogeneous of degree zero, while the unit cost function $\lambda(p)$ is homogeneous of degree one.

In what follows it will be assumed that the factor input functions $x_i(p)$ are positive for all $p > 0$ and have continuous partial derivatives of the third order.

The definition (4) may be written as (see Allen [1], p. 508)

$$\sigma_{ij} = \frac{\lambda \dfrac{\partial x_i}{\partial p_j}}{x_i x_j}, \quad \text{for } i \neq j. \tag{6}$$

Since we have the following relations (see, e.g., Samuelson [6], p. 68):

$$x_i = \frac{\partial \lambda}{\partial p_i} \qquad i = 1, \ldots, n, \tag{7}$$

and

$$\frac{\partial x_i}{\partial p_j} = \frac{\partial^2 \lambda}{\partial p_i \partial p_j} \qquad i,j = 1, \ldots, n, \tag{8}$$

the elasticity of substitution σ_{ij} may be written:

$$\sigma_{ij} = \frac{\lambda \dfrac{\partial^2 \lambda}{\partial p_i \partial p_j}}{\dfrac{\partial \lambda \partial \lambda}{\partial p_i \partial p_j}} \quad \text{for } i \neq j, \tag{9}$$

where $\lambda = \lambda(p)$ is the unit cost function.

Let

$$\Lambda = \Lambda(p) = \log \lambda(p); \tag{10}$$

then, the relation (9) is equivalent to the following:

$$\sigma_{ij} - 1 = \frac{\dfrac{\partial^2 \Lambda}{\partial p_i \partial p_j}}{\dfrac{\partial \Lambda \partial \Lambda}{\partial p_i \partial p_j}}, \quad \text{for } i \neq j,$$

or

$$\frac{\partial^2 \Lambda}{\partial p_i \partial p_j} = (\sigma_{ij} - 1) \frac{\partial \Lambda}{\partial p_i} \frac{\partial \Lambda}{\partial p_j}, \quad \text{for } i \neq j. \tag{11}$$

3 A generalization of the Arrow-Chenery-Minhas-Solow production function

The production function which extends the Arrow-Chenery-Minhas-Solow function to the n-factor case may be the following type:

$$f(x_1, \ldots, x_n) = (\alpha_1 x^{-\beta} + \cdots + \alpha_n x^{-\beta})^{-1/\beta}, \tag{12}$$

where $\alpha_1, \ldots, \alpha_n$ are positive constants and β a number greater than -1.

The function $f(x_1, \ldots, x_n)$ is homogeneous of degree one, strictly quasi-concave, and has partial derivatives of any order. The unit cost function associated with the production function $f(x_1, \ldots, x_n)$ is given by:

$$\lambda(p_1, \ldots, p_n) = (\alpha_1^\sigma p_1^{1-\sigma} + \cdots + \alpha_n^\sigma p_n^{1-\sigma})^{1/1-\sigma}, \tag{13}$$

where

$$\sigma = \frac{1}{1 + \beta}. \tag{14}$$

Hence,

$$\sigma_{ij} = \sigma, \quad \text{for all } i \neq j. \tag{15}$$

Therefore, if the production function $f(x_1, \ldots, x_n)$ is of the form (12) *then the partial elasticities of substitution σ_{ij} are independent of factor prices and are identical for all pairs of two factors of production.*

On the other hand, if partial elasticities of substitution σ_{ij} are all constant and identical for different pairs of factors, then the production function $f(x_1, \ldots, x_n)$ is of the form (12).

In order to prove the latter statement, it suffices to show that if elasticities of substitution σ_{ij} are constant and identical, say equal to σ, then the unit cost function $\lambda(p_1, \ldots, p_n)$ must be of the form (13), since by Shephard's duality theorem ([7], pp. 17–22) the unit cost function uniquely determines the production function (in the case of constant returns to scale). In the case where $\sigma = 1$, it is easily shown from (11) that $\Lambda = \log \lambda$ is additive. But the unit cost function $\lambda = \lambda(p_1, \ldots, p_n)$ is homogeneous of degree one; hence it must be the limit of the form (13) as σ tends to one:

$$\lambda(p_1,\ldots,p_n) = p_1^{\alpha'_1}\cdots p_n^{\alpha'_n}, \quad \text{with } \alpha'_1,\ldots,\alpha'_n > 0.$$

In the case where $\sigma \neq 1$, consider the following transformation:

$$z = \lambda^{1-\sigma}, \quad u_i = p_i^{1-\alpha}, \qquad i = 1,\ldots,n.$$

Then from (9) and (15) we have

$$\frac{\partial^2 z}{\partial u_i \partial u_j} = 0, \quad \text{for } i \neq j.$$

But, the function $z = z(u_1,\ldots,u_n)$ is homogeneous of degree one with respect to $u_1,\ldots,u_n$; hence, z is a linear function of $u_1,\ldots,u_n$. Therefore, the unit cost function $\lambda(p_1,\ldots,p_n)$ is of the form (13).

The problem naturally would arise if it were possible to find a production function with more than two factors of production for which elasticities of substitution are all constant but may differ for different pairs of factors of production.

Let $\{N_1,\ldots,N_S\}$ be a partition of the set $\{1,\ldots,n\}$ of n factors of production; namely

$$N_1 \cup \cdots \cup N_S = \{1,\ldots,n\},$$
$$N_s \cap N_t = \text{empty}, \quad \text{for all } s \neq t.$$

The vector $x = (x_1,\ldots,x_n)$ may be correspondingly partitioned into a set of subvectors:

$$x = (x^{(1)},\ldots,x^{(S)}),$$

where $x^{(s)}$ is the subvector of x whose components are x_i, $i \in N_s$. Similarly for price vector $p = (p_1,\ldots,p_n)$:

$$p = (p^{(1)},\ldots,p^{(S)}).$$

Consider now a production function $f(x)$ defined by:

$$f(x) = \prod_{s=1}^{S} f^{(s)}(x^{(s)})^{\rho_s}, \tag{16}$$

where

$$f^{(s)}(x^{(s)}) = \left(\sum_{i \in N_s} \alpha_i x_i^{-\beta_s}\right)^{-1/\beta_s}, \tag{17}$$

$$\alpha_i > 0,$$
$$-1 < \beta_s < \infty, \qquad \beta_s \neq 0,$$
$$\rho_s > 0, \qquad \sum_{s=1}^{S} \rho_s = 1.$$

The production function $f(x)$ defined by (16) is homogeneous of degree one, strictly quasi-concave, and has partial derivatives of any order.

The unit cost function $\lambda(p)$ is easily derived; namely,

$$\lambda(p) = a \prod_{s=1}^{S} [\lambda^{(s)}(p^{(s)})]^{\rho_s}, \tag{18}$$

where a is a positive constant and

$$\lambda^{(s)}(p^{(s)}) = \left(\sum_{i \in N_s} \alpha_i^{\sigma_s} p_i^{1-\sigma_s} \right)^{1/1-\sigma_s} \tag{19}$$

with

$$\sigma_s = \frac{1}{1+\beta_s},$$

is the unit cost function associated with the production function $f^{(s)}(x^{(s)})$, $s = 1, \ldots, S$.

Hence,

$$\Lambda(p) = \log \lambda(p) = A + \prod_{s=1}^{S} \rho_s \Lambda^{(s)}(p^{(s)}), \tag{20}$$

where A is a constant and

$$\Lambda^{(s)}(p^{(s)}) = \frac{1}{1-\sigma_s} \log \left(\sum_{i \in N_s} \alpha_1^{\sigma_s} p_i^{1-\sigma_s} \right), \qquad s = 1, \ldots, S. \tag{21}$$

Partial elasticities of substitution σ_{ij} are calculated from the formula (11); we have

$$\sigma_{ij} = \begin{cases} 1, & \text{if } i \in N_s, j \in N_t, s \neq t, \\ \sigma_s, & \text{if } i, j \in N_s. \end{cases} \tag{22}$$

The foregoing analysis may be summarized by the following:

Theorem 1. Let a production function $f(x)$ be of the form:

$$f(x) = \prod_{s=1}^{S} f^{(s)}(x^{(s)})^{\rho_s} \tag{16}$$

where

$$\rho_s > 0, \quad \sum_{s=1}^{S} \rho_s = 1,$$

and

$$f^{(s)}(x^{(s)}) = \left(\sum_{i \in N_s} \alpha_i x_i^{-\beta_s} \right)^{-1/\beta_s}, \tag{17}$$

$$\alpha_i > 0, \qquad i = 1, \ldots, n,$$
$$-1 < \beta_s < \infty, \quad \beta_s \neq 0, \qquad s = 1, \ldots, S.$$

Then partial elasticities of substitution σ_{ij} are all constant and

$$\sigma_{ij} = \begin{cases} 1, & \text{if } i \in N_s,\ j \in N_t,\ s \neq t, \\ \sigma_s, & \text{if } i, j \in N_s, \end{cases} \tag{22}$$

where

$$\sigma_s = \frac{1}{1 + \beta_s} \neq 1. \tag{23}$$

4 Characterization of production functions with constant elasticities of substitution

In what follows, we shall show that the class of the production functions of the form (16) exhausts all possible linear and homogeneous production functions with constant partial elasticities of substitution; namely, we have:

> **Theorem 2.** Let a production function $f(x)$, $x = (x, \ldots, x_n)$, be homogeneous of degree one, strictly quasi-concave, and possess continuous partial derivatives of third order. If partial elasticities of substitution σ_{ij} are constant for all pairs of factors of production, i and j, then there exists a partition $\{N_1, \ldots, N_S\}$ of the set $\{1, \ldots, n\}$ of n factors of production such that for partial elasticities of substitution σ_{ij} the relations (22) hold and the production function $f(x)$ is of the form (16) with
>
> $$\beta_s = \frac{1}{\sigma_s} - 1, \qquad s = 1, \ldots, S. \tag{24}$$

Proof. Let us first prove that if σ_{ij} are constant for all pairs of factors of production, there exists a partition $\{N_1, \ldots, N_S\}$ of the set $\{1, \ldots, n\}$ such that the relations (22) hold.

Differentiating both sides of the relation (11) with respect to p_k, we get

$$\frac{\partial^3 \Lambda}{\partial p_k \partial p_i \partial p_j} = (\sigma_{ij} - 1) \left\{ \frac{\partial^2 \Lambda}{\partial p_k \partial p_i} \frac{\partial \Lambda}{\partial p_j} + \frac{\partial^2 \Lambda}{\partial p_k \partial p_j} \frac{\partial \Lambda}{\partial p_i} \right\},$$

which, in view of (11), implies that

$$\frac{\partial^3 \Lambda}{\partial p_k \partial p_i \partial p_j} = (\sigma_{ij} - 1)\left\{(\sigma_{ik} - 1) - (\sigma_{jk} - 1)\right\} \frac{\partial \Lambda}{\partial p_i} \frac{\partial \Lambda}{\partial p_j} \frac{\partial \Lambda}{\partial p_k} \tag{25}$$

for all distinct i, j, and k.

Interchanging i and k in (25), we get

$$\frac{\partial^3 \Lambda}{\partial p_i \partial p_k \partial p_j} = (\sigma_{kj} - 1)\{(\sigma_{ki} - 1) - (\sigma_{ji} - 1)\} \frac{\partial \Lambda}{\partial p_k} \frac{\partial \Lambda}{\partial p_j} \frac{\partial \Lambda}{\partial p_i}. \tag{26}$$

Since σ_{ij} are symmetric, $x_i = \partial \lambda / \partial p_i$ positive, and $\partial^3 \Lambda / \partial p_i \partial p_j \partial p_k$ independent of the order of differentiation, we have from (25) and (26) that

$$(\sigma_{ik} - 1)(\sigma_{ij} - \sigma_{kj}) = 0, \tag{27}$$

for all distinct i, j, and k.

Let us now define a binary relation $\sim$ between two factors of production i and k by:

$$i \sim k \text{ if and only if } i = k \text{ or } \sigma_{ik} \neq 1. \tag{28}$$

We shall prove that the relation $\sim$ is an equivalence relation; namely,

$$i \sim i, \tag{29}$$

$$i \sim j \text{ implies } j \sim i, \tag{30}$$

and

$$i \sim j \text{ and } j \sim k \text{ imply } i \sim k. \tag{31}$$

Since (29) and (30) are trivial, we prove only the transitivity relation (31), which may be implied by the following:

$$\text{If, for distinct } i, j, \text{ and } k,\ i \sim j \text{ and } j \sim k, \text{ then } \sigma_{ij} = \sigma_{jk} = \sigma_{ik} \tag{32}$$

Let, for distinct i, j, and k,

$$\sigma_{ij} \neq 1 \quad \text{and} \quad \sigma_{jk} \neq 1. \tag{33}$$

From (27) we have

$$(\sigma_{ij} - 1)(\sigma_{ik} - \sigma_{jk}) = 0, \tag{34}$$

$$(\sigma_{jk} - 1)(\sigma_{ij} - \sigma_{ik}) = 0. \tag{35}$$

The relations (33), (34), and (35) together imply that

$$\sigma_{ik} = \sigma_{ij} = \sigma_{jk} \neq 1.$$

Since the relation $\sim$ is an equivalence relation on the set $\{1,\ldots,n\}$ there exists a partition $\{N_1,\ldots,N_S\}$ of the set $\{1,\ldots,n\}$ such that

$$i \sim j \quad \text{if and only if } i, j \in N_s \text{ for some } s. \tag{36}$$

Hence

$$\sigma_{ij} = 1 \quad \text{if } i \in N_s, j \in N_t, \quad s \neq t. \tag{37}$$

The relation (32) implies the existence of $\sigma_1,\ldots,\sigma_S$ such that

$$\sigma_{ij} = \sigma_s \neq 1, \quad \text{for all } i, j \in N_s, \quad i \neq j. \tag{38}$$

The relations (37) and (38) together imply (22).
From (11) and (22), we have

$$\frac{\partial^2 \Lambda}{\partial p_i \partial p_j} = \begin{cases} 0, & \text{if } i \in N_s, j \in N_s, j \in N_t, s \neq t \\ (\sigma_s - 1) \dfrac{\partial \Lambda}{\partial p_i} \dfrac{\partial \Lambda}{\partial p_j}, & \text{if } i, j \in N_s, i \neq j. \end{cases} \tag{39}$$

Hence, there exist S functions $\psi^{(1)}(p^{(1)}),\ldots,\psi^{(S)}(p^{(S)})$ such that

$$\Lambda(p) = \sum_{s=1}^{S} \psi^{(s)}(p^{(s)}), \tag{40}$$

where

$$\frac{\partial^2 \psi^{(s)}}{\partial p_i \partial p_j} = (\sigma_s - 1) \frac{\partial \psi^{(s)}}{\partial p_i} \frac{\partial \psi^{(s)}}{\partial p_j}, \quad \text{for } i \neq j, \ i, j \in N_s. \tag{41}$$

Let

$$\varphi^{(s)}(p^{(s)}) = e^{\psi^{(s)}(p^{(s)})}, \quad s = 1,\ldots,S.$$

Then

$$\lambda(p) = \prod_{s=1}^{S} \varphi^{(s)}(p^{(s)}), \tag{42}$$

$$\varphi^{(s)} \frac{\partial \varphi^{(s)2}}{\partial p_i \partial p_j} = \sigma_s \frac{\partial \varphi^{(s)}}{\partial p_i} \frac{\partial \varphi^{(s)}}{\partial p_j}, \quad \text{for } i, j \in N_s, \ i \neq j. \tag{43}$$

By considering the transformation

$$\varphi^{(s)} \to \varphi^{(s)1-\sigma_s}, \quad p_i \to p_i^{1-\sigma_s} (i \in N_s),$$

and taking the homogeneity of the unit cost function $\lambda(p)$ into account, we have

$$\varphi^{(s)}(p^{(s)}) = \left(\sum_{i \in N_s} \alpha_i p_i^{1-\sigma_s} \right)^{1/1-\sigma_s}, \quad s = 1,\ldots,S, \quad \text{with } \alpha_i > 0 \quad (i \in N_s). \tag{44}$$

Hence, the unit cost function $\lambda(p)$ is of the form (18). Therefore, by applying Shepherd's duality theorem ([17], pp. 17–22), the production function $f(x)$ must be of the form (16). ■

References

[1] Allen, R. G. D. *Mathematical Analysis for Economists*, London: Macmillan, 1938.

[2] Arrow, K. J., H. B. Chenery, B. S. Minhas, and R. M. Solow, "Capital-Labor Substitution and Economic Efficiency," *Review of Economics and Statistics*, Vol. 63 (1961), pp. 225–50.

[3] Hicks, J. R., *The Theory of Wages*, London: Macmillan, 1932.

[4] Lerner, A. P. "Notes on the Elasticities of Substitution," *Review of Economic Studies*, Vol. 1 (1933–4), pp. 39–44 and pp. 68–71.

[5] Robinson, J., *The Economics of Imperfect Competition*, London: Macmillan, 1933.

[6] Samuelson, P. A., *Foundations of Economic Analysis*, Cambridge: Harvard University Press, 1947.

[7] Shephard, R. W., *Cost and Production Functions*, Princeton: Princeton University Press, 1953.

[8] Solow, R. M., "A Contribution to the Theory of Economic Growth," *Quarterly Journal of Economics*, Vol. 70 (1956), pp. 65–94.

CHAPTER 6

Neutral inventions and the stability of growth equilibrium

1 Introduction

In criticizing Hicks's classification[1] of technical inventions, Harrod has proposed a new definition[2] of neutral inventions primarily intended for applications to the problem of economic growth. According to Harrod, a technical invention is defined as *neutral* if at a constant rate of interest it does not affect the value of the capital coefficient. Harrod's classification has been discussed by J. Robinson [6] who showed graphically that a neutral invention is equivalent to "an all-round increase in the efficiency of labor" ([6], p. 140). The first part of the present article is concerned with precisely formulating Robinson's proposition and characterizing analytically those inventions that are neutral in Harrod's sense.

Harrod's definition of neutral inventions, as indicated above, has been introduced to handle the problem of economic growth. Recent contributions, however, in particular those of Solow [8] and Swan [9], are discussed for the case in which technical inventions are neutral in Hicks's sense.[3] In the second part of this article we consider a neoclassical growth model with neutral inventions in Harrod's sense, and prove the stability of the growth equilibrium in such a model. The aggregate production function underlying the model is assumed only to be subject to constant returns to scale and to diminishing marginal rates of substitution; the Cobb-

From *Review of Economic Studies*, Vol. 28 (1961), pp. 117–24; reprinted with permission.

1 According to Hicks's definition, introduced in [3], pp. 121–2, a technical invention is termed neutral if the ratio of the marginal product of capital to that of labor remains undisturbed at a constant capital-labor ratio.

2 Harrod's criterion was first introduced in his review of Robinson's book [1]; see Kaldor [4], Hicks [3], Robinson [5], pp. 132–6, Harrod [2], pp. 22–7, and Robinson [7], pp. 131–3.

3 Both Solow and Swan are concerned with the Cobb–Douglas production function case. The Cobb–Douglas production function is, as will be seen below, the only case in which Hicks's neutrality coincides with Harrod's neutrality. Hence, in Solow's and Swan's models, technical inventions are neutral in Harrod's sense also.

Douglas condition, as is customarily imposed in recent literature, is not required.

2 Neutral inventions in Harrod's sense

It is assumed that there are two factors of production: capital and labor. Both are assumed to be composed of homogeneous quantities; K and L refer respectively to the capital stock and the labor forces in terms of physical units. The structure of production in each time period t (conveniently referred to as *year* t) is described by the *aggregate production function* $F(K, L, t)$, which specifies the maximum output Y produced by capital K and labor L in year t:

$$Y = F(K, L, t). \tag{1}$$

Production is assumed to be subject to constant returns to scale; namely, the aggregate production function $F(K, L; t)$ is homogeneous of first degree:

$$F(\lambda K, \lambda L, t) = \lambda F(K, L, t), \quad \text{for all } \lambda > 0. \tag{2}$$

Hence, the output per head, to be denoted by y, is uniquely determined by the capital-labor ratio, to be denoted by k:

$$y = f(k, t), \tag{3}$$

where

$$y = Y/L, \tag{4}$$

$$k = K/L, \tag{5}$$

and

$$f(k, t) = F(k, 1, t). \tag{6}$$

We assume that production is subject to the neoclassical conditions; namely, the aggregate production function $F(K, L, t)$ is continuously differentiable with respect to $K.L, t$; capital is always productive, and the marginal rates of substitution are diminishing. The latter two conditions may be represented by

$$f_k(k, t) > 0, \tag{7}$$

and

$$f_{kk}(k, t) < 0, \tag{8}$$

where

$$f_k = \partial f/\partial k, \quad f_{kk} = \partial^2 f/\partial k^2.$$

The Cobb-Douglas function

$$F(K, L, t) = A(t)K^{\alpha(t)}L^{1-\alpha(t)}, \; A(t) > 0, \; 0 < \alpha(t) < 1$$

is the most familiar neoclassical production function.

For a given rate of interest r, the optimum capital-labor ratio in year t, to be denoted by $k(r, t)$, is determined as the one at which the marginal product of capital equals the rate of interest r:

$$f_k[k(r, t), t] = r. \tag{9}$$

The corresponding optimum output per head $y(r, t)$ and capital-output ratio $x(r, t)$ are determined by

$$y(r, t) = f[k(r, t), t], \tag{10}$$

$$x(r, t) = \frac{k(r, t)}{y(r, t)}. \tag{11}$$

The technical invention represented by the aggregate production function $F(K, L, t)$, or equivalently by $f(k, t)$, will be termed *Harrod neutral* if the optimum capital-output ratio $x(r, t)$ is independent of t.

Under the diminishing marginal productivity assumption (8), the definition of the Harrod neutrality may be rephrased as:

$F(K, L; t)$ is Harrod neutral if and only if the marginal product of capital f_k remains undisturbed at a constant capital-output ratio x.

3 Joan Robinson's theorem on neutral inventions

An analytical characterization of the Harrod neutrality is given by the following:

> **Joan Robinson's theorem:** The technical invention represented by $F(K, L; t)$ is Harrod neutral if and only if the production function $F(K, L; t)$ is of the form:
>
> $$F(K, L, t) = G[K, A(t)L], \tag{12}$$
>
> with a positive function $A(t)$.

Proof: By the assumptions (7) and (8), the relation (1) may be transformed into the one concerned with output per head y and capital-output ratio x:

$$y = \varphi(x, t) \tag{13}$$

where

$$k = xy. \tag{14}$$

The marginal product f_k of capital then can be expressed in terms of the function $\varphi(x, t)$ as follows:

Differentiating (13) and (14) with respect to x, y, and k, we have

$$dy = \varphi_x dx, \tag{15}$$

$$dk = x\,dy + y\,dx. \tag{16}$$

Solving (15) and (16) with respect to dy and dk, we get

$$\frac{\partial y}{\partial k} = \frac{\varphi_x}{\varphi + x\varphi_x}. \tag{17}$$

Hence $f(k, t)$ is Harrod neutral if and only if the right-hand side of (17) is independent of t; namely,

$$\frac{\varphi_x}{\varphi + x\varphi_x} = c(x), \tag{18}$$

where $c(x)$ is a function of x only.

From (18), we have

$$\frac{\varphi_x}{\varphi} = \frac{1}{\dfrac{1}{c(x)} - x}. \tag{19}$$

The relation (19) indicates that φ_x/φ is independent of t; hence the function $\varphi(x, t)$ is decomposable:

$$\varphi(x, t) = A(t)\psi(x). \tag{20}$$

From (13) and (20), we have

$$x = \psi^{-1}\left[\frac{y}{A(t)}\right], \tag{21}$$

where ψ^{-1} is the inverse function of ψ.

The relation (21), together with (14), implies

$$\frac{k}{A(t)} = \frac{y}{A(t)}\psi^{-1}\left[\frac{y}{A(t)}\right]; \tag{22}$$

hence,

$$\frac{y}{A(t)} = g\left[\frac{k}{A(t)}\right], \text{ say.} \tag{23}$$

In view of (3) and (4), the relation (23) may be written as

$$Y = G[K, A(t)L],$$

where

$$G(K, L) = g(k)L.$$

On the other hand, let the condition (12) be satisfied. Then, for the function $y = f(k, t)$, we have

$$y = f(k, t) = A(t)g\left[\frac{k}{A(t)}\right], \tag{24}$$

with $g(k) = G(K, L)/L = G(k)$.

Solving (24) with respect to y and x, we get

$$y = A(t)\psi(x)$$

for some $\psi(x)$. Hence

$$\frac{\varphi_x}{\varphi + x\varphi_x} = \frac{\psi'(x)}{\psi(x) + x\psi'(x)},$$

which is independent of t. Then, from (17), $\partial y/\partial k$ is independent of r; hence $F(K, L, t)$ of the form (12) is Harrod neutral. ■

It may be of some interest to compare Harrod's neutrality with Hicks's. According to Hicks [3], a technical invention is defined as *neutral* if the ratio of the marginal product of capital to that of labor remains unchanged at a constant capital-labor ratio. Such a technical invention may be termed *Hicks neutral.* It is possible to characterize the Hicks neutrality in terms of the aggregate production function $F(K, L, t)$; *namely, the technical invention represented by* $F(K, L, t)$ *is Hicks neutral if and only if* $F(K, L, t)$ *is decomposable:*[4]

$$F(K, L, t) = A(t)F(K, L) \tag{25}$$

with some positive $A(t)$.

Corollary to Joan Robinson's theorem: The non-trivial technical invention represented by the aggregate production function $F(K, L.t)$ is both Harrod and Hicks neutral if and only if

$$F(K, L, t) = A(t)K^{\beta}L^{1-\beta}, \tag{26}$$

with some positive $A(t)$ and $0 < \beta < 1$.

Proof: It suffices to show that the production function $y = f(k, t)$ is both

[4] This proposition is well-known; for an analytical proof, see e.g., Uzawa and Watanabe [10].

Harrod and Hicks neutral if and only if

$$y = A(t)k^{\beta}, \ A(t) > 0, \ 0 < \beta < 1. \tag{27}$$

Let $f(k, t)$ be Harrod neutral. Then

$$f(k, t) = B(t)g\left[\frac{k}{B(t)}\right], \tag{28}$$

with positive $B(t)$.

On the other hand, the function $f(k, t)$ is Hicks neutral if and only if

$$\frac{\partial^2 \log f(k, t)}{\partial k \, \partial t} = 0, \quad \text{for all } k \text{ and } t. \tag{29}$$

Let the function $\psi(z)$ be defined by

$$\psi(z) = \log g(e^z); \tag{30}$$

hence,

$$\log f(k, t) = \log B(t) + \psi\left(\log \frac{k}{B(t)}\right). \tag{31}$$

Differentiating (31) with respect to k and t, we get

$$\frac{\partial^2 \log f(k, t)}{\partial k \, \partial t} = \frac{-B'(t)}{kB(t)} \psi''\left[\log \frac{k}{B(t)}\right]. \tag{32}$$

From (32) and (29),

$$\psi''\left[\log \frac{k}{B(t)}\right] = 0, \quad \text{for all } k \text{ and } t.$$

Therefore,

$$\psi(z) = \alpha + \beta z;$$

hence

$$g(k) = e^{\alpha} k^{\beta}.$$

■

4 Stability of the neoclassical growth equilibrium

In this section we shall show the stability of growth equilibrium in a competitive model of economic growth with neutral technical progress in Harrod's sense.

Among the many recent contributions to the neoclassical theory of economic growth, the most important would probably be the one by

Solow [8]; our formulation of a neoclassical growth model here is primarily based on Solow's.

We are concerned with an economy in which a homogeneous output is produced by capital and labor; any part of the output is either consumed by labor or accumulated as capital stock. For the sake of simplicity, it is assumed that capital never depreciates.

Let $K(t)$ and $L(t)$ be the capital stock and the labor force, respectively, and $Y(t)$ the rate of output, all in year t. The annual output $Y(t)$ is uniquely determined by capital stock $K(t)$ and labor force $L(t)$ in terms of the aggregate production function $F(K, L, t)$. It is assumed that the technical invention represented by $F(K, L, t)$ is always Harrod neutral; hence, by Robinson's theorem, the aggregate production function is of the form $F[K, A(t)L]$, where $A(t)$ may be referred to as the *efficiency of labor*. The function $F(K, L)$ satisfies all the neoclassical conditions.

In the neoclassical theory, both capital and labor markets are assumed *perfectly competitive*; hence the distribution of the annual output $Y(t)$ between capital and labor is determined by the marginal products of capital and labor. The return to capital $r(t)$ and the wage $w(t)$, in year t, are given by

$$r(t) = F_K[K(t), A(t)L(t)] \tag{33}$$

and

$$w(t) = F_L[K(t), A(t)L(t)]. \tag{34}$$

We have

$$Y(t) = P(t) + W(t), \tag{35}$$

where $P(t)$ and $W(t)$ are respectively the shares of capital and labor in year t:

$$P(t) = r(t)K(t), \tag{36}$$

$$W(t) = w(t)L(t). \tag{37}$$

It is assumed for the sake of simplicity that labor does not save and capital does not consume. Then the neoclassical growth process may be described by the following system of differential equations:

$$\begin{aligned} Y(t) &= F[K(t), A(t)L(t)], \\ \frac{\dot{K}(t)}{K(t)} &= F_K[(t), A(t)L(t)], \end{aligned} \tag{*}$$

where

$$\dot{K}(t) = \frac{dK(t)}{dt}.$$

It is assumed that both the rate of growth in labor, $\dot{L}/L$, and the rate of increase in the efficiency of labor, $\dot{A}/A$, are exogenously given and constant:

$$\frac{\dot{L}(t)}{L(t)} = \nu > 0, \tag{38}$$

$$\frac{\dot{A}(t)}{A(t)} = \alpha > 0. \tag{39}$$

Let $y(t)$ and $k(t)$ be respectively the output per head and the capital-labor ratio in year t:

$$y(t) = Y(t)/L(t), \tag{40}$$

$$k(t) = K(t)/L(t). \tag{41}$$

The growth process may be transformed into the one with respect to $y(t)$ and $k(t)$:

$$\begin{cases} \dfrac{y(t)}{A(t)} = f\left[\dfrac{k(t)}{A(t)}\right], \\ \dfrac{\dot{k}(t)}{k(t)} = f_k\left[\dfrac{k(t)}{A(t)}\right] - \nu. \end{cases} \tag{**}$$

Let

$$z(t) = \frac{k(t)}{A(t)}.$$

Then

$$\frac{\dot{z}(t)}{z(t)} = f_k[z(t)] - \nu - \alpha. \tag{42}$$

Since

$$f_{kk}(z) < 0, \quad \text{for all } z > 0,$$

the differential equation (42) is globally stable, and the equilibrium z^* is uniquely determined by

$$f_k(z^*) = \nu + \alpha. \tag{43}$$

Therefore, for the solution $[y(t), k(t)]$ of the process (**), both $y(t)/A(t)$ and $k(t)/A(t)$ converge:

$$\lim_{t\to\infty} y(t)/A(t) = y^*, \text{ say},$$

and

$$\lim_{t \to \infty} k(t)/A(t) = z^*.$$

Hence,

$$\lim_{t \to \infty} x(t) = x^*,$$

where

$$x(t) = k(t)/y(t), \quad x^* = z^*/y^*.$$

The above observations lead us to the following:[5]

Equilibrium theorem: Let the initial capital stock K^* and labor forces L^* satisfy

$$f_k[K^*/A(0)L^*] = v + \alpha,$$

where v is the rate of growth in labor, defined by (38), and α is the rate of growth in the efficiency of labor, defined by (39). Then, for the solution $[Y^*(t), K^*(t), L^*(t)]$ to the neoclassical growth process (*), the capital-output ratio $x^* = K^*(t)/Y^*(t)$ remains constant, and the output per head $y^*(t) = Y^*(t)/L^*(t)$ increases at the same constant rate as the capital-labor ratio $k^*(t) = K^*(t)/L^*(t)$. The capital-output ratio x^* is uniquely determind and may be referred to as the equilibrium capital-output ratio of the process (*).

Stability theorem:[6] Let the growth equilibrium exist. Then the neo-classical growth process (*) is globally stable; namely, for the solution $[Y(t), K(t), L(t)]$ to the process (*) with arbitrary initial $K(0)$ and $L(0)$, the capital-output ratio $x(t) = K(t)/Y(t)$ converges to the equilibrium capital-output ratio x^*.

References

[1] Harrod, R. F., "Review of Joan Robinson's *Essays in the Theory of Employment*," *Economic Journal*, Vol. 47 (1937), 326–30.
[2] Harrod, R. F., *Towards a Dynamic Economics*. London, Macmillan, 1948.
[3] Hicks, J. R., *The Theory of Wages*. London: Macmillan, 1932.

[5] If we measure the quantity of labor forces according to efficiency, then our stability theorem below is essentially reduced to the case without technical progress discussed by Solow [8].

[6] It has been pointed out by Professor Robert M. Solow that the stability of the neoclassical growth discussed here crucially hinges on the assumption that the balanced growth exists.

[4] Kaldor, N., "A Case Against Technical Progress?" *Economica*, Vol. 12 (1932), 180–96.
[5] Robinson, J., *Essays in the Theory of Employment*. London: Macmillan, 1937.
[6] Robinson, J., "The Classification of Inventions," *Review of Economic Studies*, Vol. 5 (1937–38), 139–42.
[7] Robinson, J., *The Accumulation of Capital*. Homewood: Richard D. Irwin, 1956.
[8] Solow, R. M., "A Contribution to the Theory of Economic Growth," *Quarterly Journal of Economics*, Vol. 70 (1956), 65–94.
[9] Swan, T. W., "Economic Growth and Capital Accumulation," *Economic Record*, Vol. 32 (1956), 334–61.
[10] Uzawa, H., and Watanabe, T., "A Note on the Classification of Technical Inventions," Technical Report No. 85, Contract No. 225 (50), Applied Mathematics and Statistics Laboratories, Stanford University, 1960.

CHAPTER 7

Optimum technical change in an aggregative model of economic growth

1 A model of endogenous technical change

In this paper we are interested in formulating a model of economic growth in which an advancement in the state of technological knowledge is achieved only by engaging scarce resources in some positive quantities, and in analyzing the pattern of the allocation of scarce resources that results in an optimum growth.

Our discussion is carried out in terms of the aggregative model of economic growth, recently introduced by Solow [**6**, **7**] and Swan [**8**]. The economy is visualized as consisting of two factors of production, labor and capital, which are combined to produce a homogeneous output; any part of the output may be either instantaneously consumed or accumulated as capital stock. The state of technological knowledge existing at each moment of time t is summarized by an aggregate production function, $Y(t) = F(K(t), L_P(t); t)$,which uniquely determines the annual output, $Y(t)$, in terms of the existing capital stock, $K(t)$, and the quantity of labor employed in material production, $L_P(t)$, at time t. Any change in technological knowledge is described by a shift in the aggregate production function. To make the analysis simpler, we shall assume that all changes in technological knowledge are embodied in labor, and that the improvement in labor efficiency does not depend upon the amount of capital to be employed. The aggregate production function at each moment of time, t, then may be written as

$$Y(t) = F[K(t), A(t)L_P(t)], \tag{1}$$

From *International Economic Review*, Vol. 6 (1965), pp. 18–31; reprinted with permission.

The author is greatly indebted to Professor Evsey D. Domar for his valuable comments and suggestions.

where the state of technological knowledge at time t is represented by the efficiency in labor $A(t)$.[1]

It is assumed that various activities in the form of education, health, construction and maintenance of public goods, etc., which result in an improvement in labor efficiency, $A(t)$, are put together as one sector, to be referred to as the educational sector.[2] We postulate that the educational sector employs labor only, and that the impact of activities in the educational sector is uniformly diffused over the whole economy. The rate of improvement in labor efficiency, $\dot{A}(t)/A(t)$, then, may be assumed to be determined by the ratio of labor employed in the educational sector, $L_E(t)$, over the total labor force, $L(t)$,

$$\dot{A}(t)/A(t) = \phi[L_E(t)/L(t)]. \tag{2}$$

It is assumed that the larger the improvement in labor efficiency, the higher the proportion of labor force employed in the educational sector, with nonincreasing marginal returns, namely,

$$\phi'(s) \geqq 0, \quad \phi''(s) \leqq 0, \quad \text{for all } 0 \leqq s \leqq 1. \tag{3}$$

The available labor, $L(t)$, at each moment of time t, is assumed to grow at constant rate v, and to be inelastically supplied, namely,

$$L_P(t) + L_E(t) \leqq L(t), \tag{4}$$

$$\dot{L}(t)/L(t) = v. \tag{5}$$

The rate of capital accumulation, on the other hand, is determined by the quantity of the annual output to be set aside for investment. Let $I(t)$ and $C(t)$ be respectively the annual rates of aggregate investment and consumption. Then we have

$$I(t) + C(t) \leqq Y(t), \qquad I(t), \quad C(t) \geqq 0, \tag{6}$$

and

$$\dot{K}(t)/K(t) = I(t) - \mu K(t), \tag{7}$$

where μ stands for the rate of depreciation of capital.

The stock of capital, $K(0)$, and labor efficiency, $A(0)$, at the beginning are given as data, together with the pattern of population growth, $L(t)$. The time path of the economy is then uniquely determined when we specify

[1] Technological changes described by the shift of form (1) in the aggregate production function are neutral in the Harrod definition introduced in [1]; see [9].

[2] A number of studies, in particular by Professor Theodore W. Schultz [3, 4], have been made recently on the implications of the improvement in the quality of labor upon the pattern of economic growth. The model presented below has been intended primarily to serve as a basis for discussions on the economic effects of education.

the allocation of labor between the educational and productive sectors, $L_E(t)$ and $L_P(t)$, and the division of the annual output, $Y(t)$, between consumption and investment, $C(t)$ and $I(t)$, at each moment of time.

2 Optimum technical change

We are now interested in the problem of finding and characterizing the time path of the optimum economy with respect to the social welfare criterion in terms of the discounted sum of consumption per capita.[3] Let the rate of discount, δ, be given and remain constant, independent of the level of consumption per capita. Then the problem is to find a time path of the economy over which the discounted sum of consumption per capita,

$$\int_0^\infty \frac{C(t)}{L(t)} e^{-\delta t}\, dt, \tag{8}$$

is maximized among all feasible paths resulting from the given initial capital stock, $K(0)$, and labor efficiency, $A(0)$.

It will be assumed in the following that production processes underlying the aggregate production function, $F(K, L)$, are subject to constant returns to scale and to a diminishing marginal rate of substitution between labor and capital. Let output per capita, $y = Y/L$, be related to the capital-labor ratio, $k = K/L$, by the function $y = f(k)$, namely,

$$f(k) = F(K, L)/L = F(k, 1).$$

Then, $f(k)$ is continuously twice-differentiable, and

$$f(k) > 0, \quad f'(k) > 0, \quad f''(k) < 0, \quad \text{for all } k > 0, \tag{9}$$

$$f(0) = 0, \quad f(\infty) = \infty, \tag{10}$$

$$f'(0) = \infty, \quad f'(\infty) = 0. \tag{11}$$

We shall assume that

$$\phi(1) < \delta < \phi(0) + \phi'(0), \tag{12}$$

so that quantity (8) is finite for all feasible paths. If $\delta \leqq \phi(1)$, quantity (8) will be indefinitely increased by allocating all available labor force to the educational sector for a sufficiently long period of time. If $\delta \geqq \phi(0) + \phi'(0)$, then it will be seen that, by using a method similar to the one presented below, optimum growth will be obtained by allocating all available labor to the productive sector.

[3] See T. N. Srinivasan [5] and H. Uzawa [10]. Since labor growth is assumed to be exogeneous, our social welfare criterion, with proper change in the discount rate, may also be regarded as based upon aggregate consumption.

Let us define

$$y(t)=\frac{Y(t)}{L(t)}=\text{output per capita},$$

$$k(t)=\frac{K(t)}{L(t)}=\text{aggregate capital-labor ratio},$$

$$u(t)=\frac{L_P(t)}{L(t)}=\text{labor allocation to the productive sector},$$

$$s(t)=\frac{I(t)}{Y(t)}=\text{investment ratio}.$$

Then our problem is reduced to the following:
Maximize

$$\int_0^\infty (1-s(t))y(t)e^{-\delta t}\,dt, \tag{13}$$

subject to the restraints

$$\dot{k}(t)=s(t)y(t)-\lambda k(t), \tag{14}$$

$$\dot{A}(t)=A(t)\phi(1-u(t)), \tag{15}$$

where

$$y(t)=A(t)u(t)f\left(\frac{k(t)}{A(t)u(t)}\right), \tag{16}$$

$$0\leqq s(t),\ u(t)\leqq 1, \tag{17}$$

and $\delta, \lambda=\nu+\mu$, $k(0)=K(0)/L(0)$, $A(0)$ are given constants, and $u(t)$, $s(t)$ are piecewise continuous.

3 Solving the optimum problem

The problem thus formulated may be solved by Pontryagin's Maximum Principle, as described in L. S. Pontryagin, V. G. Boltyanskii, R. V. Gamkrelidze and E. F. Mishchenko [2]. It is concerned in general with solving problems of the following type:

Given $n+1$ continuously differentiable functions $f^0(x,u), f^1(x,u),\ldots, f^n(x,u)$ defined for n-dimensional vectors $x=(x^1,\ldots,x^n)$ and r-dimensional vectors $u=(u^1,\ldots,u^r)$, find a trajectory $x(t)$ and control $u(t)$, $0\leqq t<\infty$, that maximizes the integral

$$J = \int_0^\infty f^0(x(t), u(t))\, dt,$$

subject to the constraints

$$\dot{x}^i(t) = f^i(x(t), u(t)), \qquad i = 1, \ldots, n,$$
$$u(t) \in U, \quad \text{for all } t,$$

where U is a given set of r-vectors (to be referred to as the control region), $x(t)$ is piecewise continuous, and $x(0)$ takes a pre-assigned value.

Pontryagin's Maximum Principle [**2**, (Theorem 7, p. 69, Theorem 17, pp. 193–94)]: In order that the admissible control $u(t)$ and the corresponding trajectory $x(t)$, $0 \leqq t < \infty$, yield a solution of the optimal problem above, it is necessary that there exist n continuous functions $q^1(t), \ldots, q^n(t)$, such that the following conditions are satisfied:

$$\dot{q}^i(t) = -\frac{\partial H}{\partial x^i}, \qquad i = 1, \ldots, n, \tag{a}$$

$$H(q(t), x(t), u(t)) = \max_{u \in U} H(q(t), x(t), u), \quad \text{for all } t, \tag{b}$$

$$\lim_{t \to \infty} q^i(t) = 0, \tag{c}$$

where the Hamiltonian $H(q, x, u)$ is defined by

$$H(q, x, u) = f^0(x, u) + q^1 f^1(x, u) + \cdots + q^n f^n(x, u).$$

In our present problem, the Hamiltonian is given by

$$H(q, v, k, A, u, s, t)$$
$$= \left[(1 - s) Auf\left(\frac{k}{Au}\right) + q\left(sAuf\left(\frac{k}{Au}\right) - \lambda k \right) + vA\phi(1 - u) \right] e^{-\delta t}. \tag{18}$$

Applying Pontryagin's Maximum Principle, we then derive

Lemma 1. If a time path $(k(t), A(t), u(t), s(t))$, $t \geqq 0$, is optimal, then there exist continuous functions, $q(t)$, $v(t)$, such that

$$\dot{k}(t) = s(t)A(t)u(t)f\left(\frac{k(t)}{A(t)u(t)}\right) - \lambda k(t), \tag{19}$$

with initial condition $k(0) = K(0)/L(0)$,

$$\dot{A}(t) = A(t)\phi(1 - u(t)), \tag{20}$$

with initial condition $A(0)$,

$$\dot{v}(t) = [\delta - \phi(1 - u(t))]v(t)$$
$$- p(t)u(t)\left[f\left(\frac{k(t)}{A(t)u(t)}\right) - \frac{k(t)}{A(t)u(t)} f'\left(\frac{k(t)}{A(t)u(t)}\right)\right], \tag{21}$$

$$u(t) \text{ maximizes } p(t)uf\left(\frac{k(t)}{A(t)u}\right) + v(t)\phi(1-u), \tag{22}$$

subject to $0 \leqq u \leqq 1$,

$$s(t) \text{ maximizes } (1 - s) + sq(t), \tag{23}$$

subject to $0 \leqq s \leqq 1$,

$$\lim_{t\to\infty} q(t)e^{-\delta t} = \lim_{t\to\infty} v(t)e^{-\delta t} = 0, \tag{24}$$

where

$$p(t) = \max(1, q(t)). \tag{25}$$

To simplify the necessary conditions in Lemma 1, let us introduce the ratio of capital to labor measured in terms of the efficiency unit as a new variable $x(t)$

$$x(t) = \frac{k(t)}{A(t)} = \frac{K(t)}{A(t)L(t)}.$$

Then the time paths of the economy are completely specified by $(x(t), u(t), s(t))$ instead of $(k(t), A(t), u(t), s(t))$. Also, in view of (3) and (9), the expression $puf(x/u) + v\phi(1-u)$ is a strictly concave function of u; hence $u(t)$ satisfying (22) is uniquely determined by solving the first-order condition

$$\left[f\left(\frac{x}{u}\right) - \frac{x}{u} f'\left(\frac{x}{u}\right)\right] \leqq \frac{v}{p}\phi'(1-u), \tag{26}$$

with strict equality if $0 \leqq u < 1$.

The function $[f(x/u) - (x/u)f'(x/u)]$ is a decreasing function of u, and approaches infinity as u goes to zero, while the value at $u = 1$ is $[f(x) - xf'(x)] > 0$. On the other hand, it is easily seen that $v \geqq 0$ and the function $(v/p)\phi'(1-u)$ is an increasing function of u, ranging from $v\phi'(1)$ to $(v/p)\phi'(0)$. Hence, the determination of u by condition (26) may be illustrated by Figure 7.1.

Since the solution u to condition (26) is uniquely determined by x and

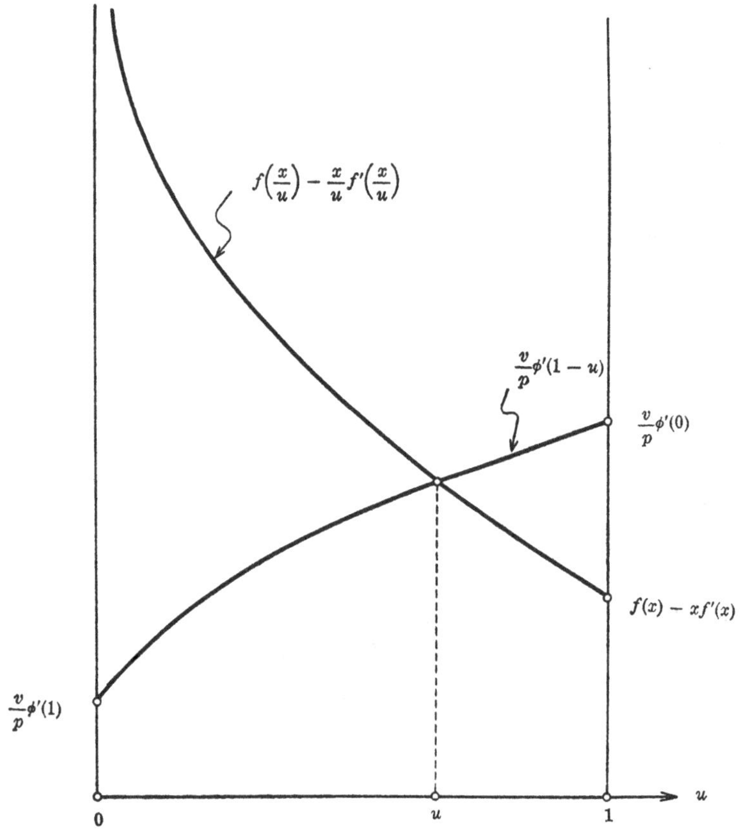

Figure 7.1

v/p, we may write

$$u = \psi\left(x, \frac{v}{p}\right).$$

An increase in x is accompanied by an upward shift in the $f(x/u) - (x/u)f'(x/u)$-curve, while the $(v/p)\phi(1-u)$-curve remains fixed. Hence, as x is increased, u is increased. On the other hand, increasing v/p implies an upward shift in the $(v/p)\phi'(1-u)$-curve, resulting in a decrease in u. We then have

$$\frac{\partial\psi}{\partial x} \geqq 0, \quad \frac{\partial\psi}{\partial(v/p)} \leqq 0, \tag{27}$$

with strict inequality if $u = \psi(x, v/p) < 1$.

Lemma 1 is therefore simplified as follows.

Lemma 2. If a time path $(x(t), u(t), s(t))$ is optimal, then there exist continuous functions $q(t)$, $v(t)$ such that

$$\frac{\dot{x}(t)}{x(t)} = s(t)\frac{f\left(\frac{x(t)}{u(t)}\right)}{\frac{x(t)}{u(t)}} - \lambda - \phi(1-u(t)), \tag{28}$$

with initial condition $x(0) = K(0)/A(0)L(0)$,

$$\dot{q}(t) = (\delta + \lambda)q(t) - f'\left(\frac{x(t)}{u(t)}\right)p(t), \tag{29}$$

$$\dot{v}(t) = [\delta + \phi(1-u(t))]v(t) - p(t)u(t)\left[f\left(\frac{x(t)}{u(t)}\right) - \frac{x(t)}{u(t)}f'\left(\frac{x(t)}{u(t)}\right)\right], \tag{30}$$

$$s(t) = \begin{cases} 0, & \text{if } q(t) < 1, \\ 1, & \text{if } q(t) > 1, \end{cases} \tag{31}$$

$$\lim_{t\to\infty} q(t)e^{-\delta t} = 0, \quad \lim_{t\to\infty} v(t)e^{-\delta t} = 0, \tag{32}$$

$$u(t) = \psi\left(x(t), \frac{v(t)}{p(t)}\right), \tag{33}$$

$$p(t) = \max(1, q(t)). \tag{34}$$

To analyse the conditions in Lemma 1 in detail, let us first consider a particular state of the economy where the differential equations (28)–(30) are singular. It is easily seen that such a case takes place only if $q(t) = 1$. Let (x^*, v^*, u^*, s^*) be obtained by solving the following equations:

$$\phi(1-u^*) + u^*\phi'(1-u^*) = \delta, \quad 0 < u^* < 1, \tag{35}$$

$$f'\left(\frac{x^*}{u^*}\right) = \delta + \lambda, \tag{36}$$

$$f\left(\frac{x^*}{u^*}\right) - \frac{x^*}{u^*}f'\left(\frac{x^*}{u^*}\right) = v^*\phi'(1-u^*), \tag{37}$$

$$s^*\frac{f\left(\frac{x^*}{u^*}\right)}{\frac{x^*}{u^*}} = \lambda + \phi(1-u^*), \quad 0 < s^* < 1. \tag{38}$$

The function $\phi(1-u)+u\phi'(1-u)$ has a positive derivative, $-u\phi''(1-u)$, and takes the values from $\phi(1)$ to $\phi(0)+\phi'(0)$ as u moves from zero to unity. Hence, in view of assumption (12), the value u^* satisfying (35) always exists and is uniquely determined. The value x^* then is uniquely obtained by solving equation (36). v^* is determined by substituting the values of u^*, x^* thus obtained into (37). By assumptions (3) and (9), v^* is always positive, and $u^* = \psi(x^*, u^*)$. Equation (38) finally determines the value of s^*. In view of (35)–(37), equation (38) is reduced to

$$s^* = \frac{\lambda + \phi(1-u^*)}{\lambda + \phi(1-u^*) + \left(1 + \dfrac{v^*}{x^*}\right)u^*\phi'(1-u^*)};$$

hence, $0 < s^* < 1$.

It is easily seen from equations (35)–(38) that the path defined by $x(t) \equiv x^*$, $v(t) \equiv v^*, u(t) \equiv u^*$, $s(t) \equiv s^*, q(t) \equiv 1$ satisfies all the conditions (28)–(34) except for the initial condition on $x(0)$. Such a state (x^*, u^*, s^*) will be referred to as the *balanced state* (with respect to the discount rate δ).

The state of the economy is now classified into two phases according to whether $q(t) < 1$ or $q(t) > 1$.

Phase I: $q(t) < 1$. In this phase, we have

$$p(t) \equiv 1, \quad s(t) \equiv 0. \tag{39}$$

Hence, conditions (28)–(31) in Lemma 1 are reduced to the following:

$$\frac{\dot{x}}{x} = -\lambda - \phi(1-u), \tag{40}$$

$$\frac{\dot{q}}{q} = \delta + \lambda - \frac{f'\left(\dfrac{x}{u}\right)}{q}, \tag{41}$$

$$\frac{\dot{v}}{v} \leqq \delta - \phi(1-u) - u\phi'(1-u), \tag{42}$$

with equality whenever $u < 1$, where, for the sake of simplicity, all variables are denoted without explicit reference to time t and $u = \psi(x, v)$; i.e., u satisfies the equality (26) with $p = 1$.

The paths of (x, v) are determined by differential equations (40) and (42) only, independent of the values of q. To investigate the structure of the solutions to the system of differential equations (40) and (42), let us

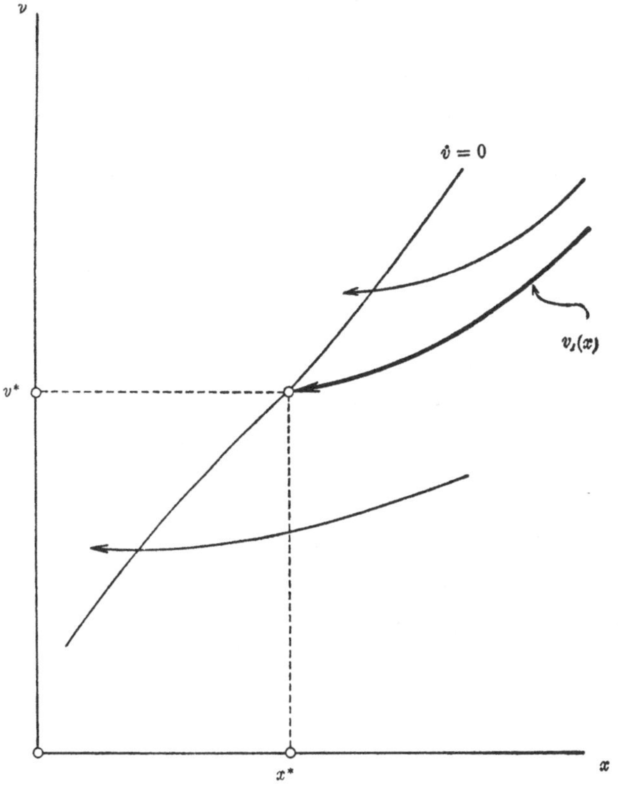

Figure 7.2

consider the function

$$\beta(x, v) = \delta - [\phi(1-u) + u\phi'(1-u)], \tag{43}$$

where $u = u(x, v)$.

Differentiating $\beta(x, v)$ partially with respect to x, and using (27), we get

$$\frac{\partial \beta}{\partial x} = u\phi''(1-u)\frac{\partial u}{\partial x} < 0, \tag{44}$$

and similarly

$$\frac{\partial \beta}{\partial v} = u\phi''(1-u)\frac{\partial u}{\partial v} > 0. \tag{45}$$

As x approaches zero, u also approaches zero; hence, in view of (12), $\beta(x, v) < 0$ if x is sufficiently small. On the other hand, as x becomes larger, the value of u approaches unity; hence again, in view of (12), $\beta(x, v) < 0$ if x is sufficiently large. Similarly, $\beta(x, v) < 0$ if v is sufficiently small, and $\beta(x, v) > 0$ if v is sufficiently large. On the other hand, x is always decreasing in Phase I; hence, the solution paths of (40) and (42) have the pattern illustrated by arrow curves in Figure 7.2.

The balanced state (x^*, v^*) obviously lies on the $\beta(x, v) = 0$ curve. Among the solution paths of the differential equations (40) and (42), there is one which goes through point (x^*, v^*). Such a path is uniquely determined. Let us define the function $v = v_I(x)$ such that $(x, v_I(x))$ lies on the solution path going through (x^*, v^*).

It is also seen that, for any $x > x^*$, there exists a uniquely determined value $q = q_I(x)$, such that the solution $(x(t), v(t), q(t))$ to the differential equations (40)–(42), with initial condition $(x, v_I(x), q_I(x))$, actually reaches the point $(x^*, v^*, 1)$.

Let the initial capital-labor ratio $x(0) = K(0)/A(0)L(0)$ be greater than the balanced ratio x^*. Then define

$$v_I(0) = v_I(x(0)), \quad q_I(0) = q_I(x(0)).$$

Let $(x_I(t), V_I(t), q_I(t))$ be the solution to the differential equations (40)–(42), with initial condition $(x(0), v_I(0), q_I(0))$ and t_I be the time when the solution $(x_I(t), v_I(t), q_I(t))$ reaches the point $(x^*, v^*, 1)$; i.e.

$$x_I(t_I) = x^*, \quad v_I(t_I) = v^*, q_I(t_I) = 1.$$

Now consider the time path $(x(t), v(t), q(t), u(t), s(t))$ defined by

$$\text{For } 0 \leqq t \leqq t_I: x(t) = x_I(t) \quad v(t) = v_I(t), \quad q(t) = q_I(t), \tag{46}$$

$$u(t) = \psi(x_I(t), \quad v_I(t)), \quad s(t) = 0;$$

$$\text{For } t > t_I: x(t) = x^*, \quad v(t) = v^*, \quad q(t) = 1,$$

$$u(t) = u^*, \quad s(t) = s^*.$$

The path $(x(t), v(t), q(t), u(t), s(t))$, defined by (46), is the only path satisfying all the necessary conditions (28)–(34) in Lemma 2 when the initial capital-labor ratio $x(0)$ is higher than the balanced ratio x^*.

Phase II: $q(t) > 1$. In this phase, we have

$$p(t) \equiv q(t), \quad s(t) \equiv 1.$$

Hence, conditions (28)–(31) in Lemma 1 are reduced to the following:

$$\frac{\dot{x}}{x} = \frac{f\left(\frac{x}{u}\right)}{\frac{x}{u}} - \lambda - \phi(1-u), \tag{47}$$

with initial conditions $x(0)$,

$$\frac{\dot{q}}{q} = \delta + \lambda - f'\left(\frac{x}{u}\right), \tag{48}$$

$$\frac{\dot{w}}{w} \leqq f'\left(\frac{x}{u}\right) - \phi(1-u) - u\phi'(1-u) - \lambda, \tag{49}$$

with equality whenever $u < 1$, where

$$w = \frac{v}{p}, \quad u = \psi(x, w).$$

Differential equations (47) and (49) determine the solution paths of (x, w), independent of the values of q. Let us introduce the function $\alpha(x, w)$

$$\alpha(x, w) = \frac{f\left(\frac{x}{u}\right)}{\frac{x}{u}} - \lambda - \phi(1-u), \tag{50}$$

where $u = \psi(x, \omega)$; i.e., (26) is satisfied with $v/p = w$.

Differentiating (50) partially with respect to w, we get

$$\frac{\partial \alpha}{\partial w} = \left\{ \frac{f\left(\frac{x}{u}\right) - \frac{x}{u} f'\left(\frac{x}{u}\right)}{x} + \phi'(1-u) \right\} \frac{\partial u}{\partial w} < 0. \tag{51}$$

On the other hand, let

$$\gamma(x, w) = f'\left(\frac{x}{u}\right) - \phi(1-u) - u\phi'(1-u) - \lambda; \tag{52}$$

then

$$\frac{\partial \gamma}{\partial x} = f''\left(\frac{x}{u}\right) \frac{\partial\left(\frac{x}{u}\right)}{\partial x} + u\phi''(1-u)\frac{\partial u}{\partial x} < 0. \tag{53}$$

Subtracting (52) from (50), we get

$$\alpha(x, w) - \gamma(x, w) = \frac{f\left(\frac{x}{u}\right) - \frac{x}{u} f'\left(\frac{x}{u}\right)}{\frac{x}{u}} + u\phi'(1-u) > 0. \tag{54}$$

Relations (51), (53), and (54) imply that the solution paths of the

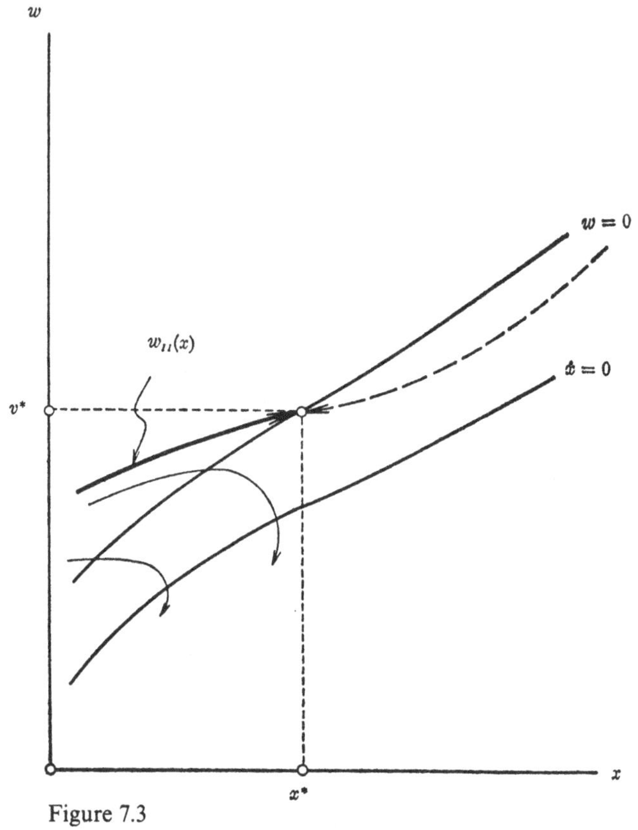

Figure 7.3

differential equations (47) and (49) are those typically illustrated by arrow curves in Figure 7.3.

Point (x^*, v^*) lies on the $\gamma(x, v) = 0$ curve, and for any $x < x^*$ there exists a uniquely determined $w = w_{II}(x)$ such that the solution to the differential equations (47) and (49) reaches the point (x^*, v^*). This path is indicated by the heavy arrow curve in Figure 7.3.

In connection with $x < x^*$, there also exists a uniquely determined value $q = q_{II}(x)$, such that the solution $(x(t), w(t), q(t))$ to the differential equations (47)–(49) with initial condition $(c, w_{II}(x),\ q_{II}(t))$ actually reaches point $(x^*, v^*,\ q^*)$.

Let the initial capital-labor ratio $x(0)$ be less than the balanced ratio x^*, and define

$$w_{II}(0) = w_{II}(x(0)), \quad q_{II}(0) = q_{II}(x(0)).$$

Let t_{II} be the time when the solution $(x_{II}(t),\ w_{II}(t),\ q_{II}(t))$ to the differential equations (47)–(49), with initial condition $(x(0), w_{II}(0), q_{II}(0))$, reaches point $(x^*, v^*, 1)$; i.e.

$$x_{II}(t_{II}) = x^*, \quad w_{II}(t_{II}) = v^*, \quad q_{II}(t_{II}) = 1.$$

It is easily seen that $q_{II}(t) > 1$, for all $0 \leqq t < t_{II}$, and the time path $(x(t), v(t), q(t), u(t), s(t))$ defined as follows satisfies all necessary conditions in Lemma 1:

For $0 \leqq t \leqq t_{II}$:

$$\begin{aligned} &x(t) = x_{II}(t), \quad v(t) = w_{II}(t)q_{II}(t), \quad q(t) = q_{II}(t), \\ &u(t) = \psi(x_{II}(t), w_{II}(t)), \quad s(t) = 1. \end{aligned} \tag{55}$$

For $t > t_{II}$:

$$\begin{aligned} &x(t) = x^*, \quad v(t) = v^*, \quad q(t) = 1, \\ &u(t) = u^*, \quad s(t) = s^*. \end{aligned}$$

A simple calculation again shows that the path defined by (55) is the only one which satisfies all the conditions (28)–(34) for the initial $x(0)$ less than x^*; hence it is optimum.

The analysis above may be summarized as follows:[4]

For any rate of discount, δ satisfying conditions (12), there exists a uniquely balanced capital-labor ratio in terms of the efficiency unit which is obtained by solving equations (35) and (36). If the initial capital-labor ratio in the efficiency unit, $x(0) = K(0)/A(0)L(0)$, is equal to x^*, optimal growth is achieved by allocating labor and annual output such that the rate of increase in labor efficiency, $\dot{A}/A$, equals the rate of increase in the capital-labor ratio, $\dot{k}/k$. The allocation of labor to the productive sector, u^*, is determined by relation (35), while the investment ratio, s^*, is given by (38).

If the initial capital-labor ratio in the efficiency unit, $x(0)$, is greater than the balanced ratio, x^*, then all annual output is consumed until $x(t)$ becomes equal to the balanced ratio, x^*, when the economy is switched to the balanced state. The allocation of labor between the productive and educational sectors during the transient period is precisely determined by (46).

[4] One implication of our results is that the pattern of optimal growth is characterized only in terms of the capital-labor ratio in the efficiency unit. Thus, let us consider two economies, one of which has a higher capital-labor ratio and a higher labor efficiency such that the capital-labor ratios in terms of efficiency are identical. The two economies have otherwise identical structures. Then the optimal patterns of labor allocation and investment are identical in the two economies. This is closely related to the proposition advanced by T. W. Schultz in [4, (2–3)].

If the initial capital-labor ratio in the efficiency unit, $x(0)$, is less than the balanced ratio, x^*, then all annual output is invested unitl $x(t)$ reaches the balanced ratio, x^*, when the economy is switched to the balanced state. The precise allocation of labor during the transient period is determined by (55).

The paths described by either (46) or (55) are the only optimum paths.

References

[1] Harrod, R. F., *Towards a Dynamic Economics* (London: Macmillan, 1948).

[2] Pontryagin, L. S., V. G. Boltyanskii, R. V. Gamkrelidze and E. F. Mishchenko, *The Mathematical Thoery of Optimal Processes* (New York and London: Interscience Publishers, 1962).

[3] Schultz, T. W., "Investment in Human Capital," *American Economic Review*, LI (March, 1961), 5–6.

[4] ———, "Reflections on Investment in Man," *Journal of Political Economy*, LXX (Supplement, 1962), 1–8.

[5] Srinivasan, T. N., "Optimum Savings in a Two-Sector Model of Growth," *Econometrica*, XXXII (July, 1964), 358–74.

[6] Solow, R. M., "A Contribution to the Theory of Economic Growth," *Quarterly Journal of Economics*, XXXII (February, 1956), 65–94.

[7] ———, 'Technical Change and the Aggregate Production Function," *Review of Economics and Statistics*, XXXIX (August, 1957), 312–20.

[8] Swan, T. W., "Economic Growth and Capital Accumulation," *Economic Record*, LXVI (November, 1956), 334–61.

[9] Uzawa, H., "Natural Inventions and the Stability of Growth Equilibrium," *Review of Economic Studies*, XXVIII (February, 1961), 117–24.

[10] ———, "Optimal Growth in a Two-Sector Model of Capital Accumulation," *Review of Economic Studies*, XXXI (January, 1964), 1–24.

PART III

Concave programming

CHAPTER 8

The Kuhn-Tucker Theorem in concave programming

1 Introduction

In order to solve problems of constrained extrema, it is customary in the calculus to use the method of the Lagrangian multiplier. Let us, for example, consider a problem: maximize $f(x_1,\ldots,x_n)$ subject to the restriction $g_k(x_1,\ldots,x_n)=0$ $(k=1,\ldots,m)$. First, formulate the so-called Lagrangian form

$$\varphi(x,y)=f(x_1,\ldots,x_n)+\sum_{k=1}^{m} y_k g_k(x_1,\ldots,x_n),$$

where unknown $y_1,\ldots,y_m$ are called the Lagrangian multipliers. Then solutions $x_1,\ldots x_n$ are found among extreme points of $\varphi(x,y)$, with unrestricted x and y, which in turn are characterized as the solutions of

$$\varphi_{x_i}(x,y)=\frac{\partial f}{\partial x_i}+\sum_k y_k\frac{\partial g_k}{\partial x_i}=0, \qquad i=1,\ldots,n,$$

$$\varphi_{y_k}(x,y)=g_k(x_1,\ldots,x_n)=0, \qquad k=1,\ldots,m.$$

This method, although not necessarily valid without certain qualifications, has been found to be useful in many particular problems of constrained extrema.

The method is with a suitable modification applied to solve the programming problems also where we are concerned with maximizing a function $f(x_1,\ldots,x_n)$ subject to the restrictions $x_i\geqq 0$ $(i=1,\ldots,n)$ and $g_k(x_1,\ldots,x_n)\geqq 0$ $(k=1,\ldots,m)$. Kuhn and Tucker [2] first proved that under some qualifications, concave programming is reduced to finding a saddle-point of the Lagrangian form $\varphi(x,y)$. This Kuhn-Tucker Theorem was further elaborated by Arrow and Hurwicz [1] so that nonconcave

From *Studies in Linear and Non-Linear Programming*, edited by K. Arrow, L. Hurwicz, and H. Uzawa, Stanford University Press, 1958, pp. 32–37; reprinted with permission.

programming may be handled. In the present chapter we shall, under different qualifications, prove the Kuhn-Tucker Theorem for concave programming.

2 Maximum problem and saddle-point problem

Let $g(x) = (g_1(x), \dots, g_m(x))$ be an m-dimensional vector-value function and $f(x)$ be a real-valued function, both defined for non-negative vectors $x = (x_1, \dots, x_n)$.

Consider the following

Maximum problem. Find a vector $\bar{x}$ that maximizes

$$f(x) \tag{1}$$

subject to the restrictions

$$x \geqq 0, \qquad g(x) \geqq 0. \tag{2}$$

A vector x will be called *feasible* if it satisfies (2), and a feasible vector $\bar{x}$ maximizing $f(x)$ subject to (2) will be called an *optimum vector of, or a solution* to, the problem.

Associated with the Maximum Problem, the *Lagrangian form* is defined by

$$\varphi(x, y) = f(x) + y \cdot g(x), \tag{3}$$

where[1]

$$x = (x_1, \dots, x_n) \geqq 0 \quad \text{and} \quad y = (y_1, \dots, y_m) \geqq 0.$$

A pair of vectors $(\bar{x}, \bar{y})$ is called a *saddle-point* of $\varphi(x, y)$ in $x \geqq 0$, $y \geqq 0$, if

$$\bar{x} \geqq 0, \qquad \bar{y} \geqq 0, \tag{4}$$

$$\varphi(x, \bar{y}) \leqq \varphi(\bar{x}, \bar{y}) \leqq \varphi(\bar{x}, y), \quad \text{for all } x \geqq 0 \text{ and } y \geqq 0, \tag{5}$$

[1] For two vectors $x = (x_1, \dots, x_n)$ and $u = (u_1, \dots, u_n)$, we shall, as usual, define

$$x \geqq u \quad \text{if} \quad x_i \geqq u_i \qquad (i = 1, \dots, n),$$

$$x \geq u \quad \text{if} \quad x \geqq u \quad \text{and} \quad x \neq u,$$

$$x > u \quad \text{if} \quad x_i > u_i, \qquad (i = 1, \dots, n),$$

and $x \cdot u$ stands for the inner product

$$x \cdot u = \sum_{i=1}^{n} x_i u_i.$$

which may be written as follows:

$$\varphi(\bar{x}, \bar{y}) = \min_{y \geqq 0} \max_{x \geqq 0} \varphi(x, y) = \max_{x \geqq 0} \min_{y \geqq 0} \varphi(x, y). \tag{6}$$

Saddle-point problem. Find a saddle-point $(\bar{x}, \bar{y})$ of $\varphi(x, y) = f(x) + y \cdot g(x)$.

3 Saddle-point implies the optimality

We are interested in the reduction of a maximum problem to the saddle-point problem of the associated Lagrangian form. First, a proposition will be noted which is true without any qualification on f and g, whenever there exists a saddle-point.

Theorem 1. If $(\bar{x}, \bar{y})$ is a saddle-point of $\varphi(x, y)$ in $x \geqq 0, y \geqq 0$, then $\bar{x}$ is an optimum vector of the maximum problem.

Proof. Substituting (3) into (5), we have

$$f(x) + \bar{y} \cdot g(x) \leqq f(\bar{x}) + \bar{y} \cdot g(\bar{x}) \leqq f(\bar{x}) + y \cdot g(\bar{x}) \quad \text{for all } x \geqq 0,\ y \geqq 0. \tag{7}$$

Since the right-hand inequality holds for any $y \geqq 0$, it follows that $g(\bar{x})$ cannot have a negative component, and $\bar{y} \cdot g(\bar{x})$ must be zero:

$$g(\bar{x}) \geqq 0, \qquad \bar{y} \cdot g(\bar{x}) = 0.$$

Thus the left-hand inequality of (7) may be written as

$$f(x) + \bar{y} \cdot g(x) \leqq f(\bar{x}) \quad \text{for all } x \geqq 0. \tag{8}$$

Since, for any feasible vector x we have $\bar{y} \cdot g(x) \geqq 0$, it follows that $f(x) \leqq f(x) + \bar{y} \cdot g(x) \leqq f(\bar{x})$, which shows that $\bar{x}$ is optimum. ■

4 The Kuhn-Tucker Theorem

Now a question naturally arises whether, given an optimum vector $\bar{x}$, it is possible to find a vector $\bar{y}$ for which $(\bar{x}, \bar{y})$ is a saddle-point of $\varphi(x, y)$. This, of course, is not true in general, e.g., for convex programming (i.e., where the maximand is a convex function). The following simple example shows that it does not hold even for concave programming:

$$f(x) = x, \qquad g(x) = -x^2.$$

Regarding concave programming, however, the reduction is shown to be possible provided f and g satisfy certain regularity conditions, e.g., the Kuhn-Tucker Constraint Qualification.[2] We shall give sufficient conditions which make the reduction possible.

Theorem 2. Suppose that $f(x)$ and $g(x)$ are concave functions on $x \geqq 0$, and $g(x)$ satisfies the following condition (due to M. Slater [3]):[3]

$$\text{There exists an } x^0 \geqq 0 \quad \text{such that } g(x^0) > 0. \tag{9}$$

Then a vector $\bar{x}$ is optimum if, and only if, there is a vector $\bar{y} \geqq 0$ such that $(\bar{x}, \bar{y})$ is a saddle-point of $\varphi(x, y)$.

Proof. Let $\bar{x}$ be optimum. We shall, in the $(m+1)$-dimensional vector space, define A and B by

$$A = \{(z_0, z);\ (z_0, z) \leqq (f(x), g(x)) \quad \text{for some } x \geqq 0\},$$
$$B = \{(z_0, z);\ (z_0, z) > (f(\bar{x}), 0)\}.$$

Since $f(x)$ and $g(x)$ are concave, the set A is convex. Since $\bar{x}$ is optimum, A and B have no vector in common. Therefore, by the lemma on the separation of convex sets, there is a non-zero vector $(v_0, v) \neq 0$ such that

$$v_0 z_0 + v \cdot z \leqq v_0 u_0 + v \cdot u \quad \text{for all } (z_0, z) \in A, \quad (u_0, u) \in B. \tag{10}$$

By the definition of B, (10) implies $(v_0, v) \geqq 0$. Since $(f(\bar{x}), 0)$ is on the boundary of B, we also have, by the definition of A,

$$v_0 f(x) + v \cdot g(x) \leqq v_0 f(\bar{x}) \quad \text{for all } x \geqq 0. \tag{11}$$

We have $v_0 > 0$. Otherwise, we have $v \geq 0$ and $v \cdot g(x) \leqq 0$ for all $x \geqq 0$, which contradicts (9).

Let $\bar{y} = v / v_0$. Then

$$\bar{y} \geqq 0, \tag{12}$$

$$f(x) + \bar{y} \cdot g(x) \leqq f(\bar{x}) \quad \text{for all } x \geqq 0. \tag{13}$$

Putting $x = \bar{x}$ in (13), we have $\bar{y} \cdot g(\bar{x}) \leqq 0$. On the other hand, we have

$$g(\bar{x}) \geqq 0. \tag{14}$$

Hence

$$\bar{y} \cdot g(\bar{x}) = 0. \tag{15}$$

[2] See Kuhn and Tucker [2], p. 483.

[3] A seemingly weaker condition: (9′) for any $u > 0$, there exists a vector $x \geqq 0$ such that $u \cdot g(x) > 0$ is due to S. Karlin. The condition, however, is equivalent to Slater's condition (9).

Relations (13), (14), (15) show that $(\bar{x}, \bar{y})$ is a saddle-point of $\varphi(x, y)$ in $x \geqq 0$, $y \geqq 0$. ∎

5 A modification of the Kuhn-Tucker Theorem

Slater's condition (9), however, excludes the case where part of the second half of restriction (2) is

$$h(x) \geqq 0 \quad \text{and} \quad -h(x) \geqq 0,$$

for linear $h(x)$. In order to make the reduction possible for such cases, we have to modify the Kuhn-Tucker Theorem.

Let sub-sets I and II of $\{1, \ldots, m\}$ be defined by

$$\mathrm{I} = \{k;\ g_k(x) = 0 \quad \text{for all feasible } x\}, \tag{16}$$

$$\mathrm{II} = \{1, \ldots, m\} - \mathrm{I}. \tag{17}$$

We shall assume that

$g_k(x)$ *is linear in* x, *for* $k \in \mathrm{I}$. (18)

For any i, *there is a feasible vector* x^i *such that*

$$x_i^i > 0. \tag{19}$$

Then we have as a modification of Theorem 2 the following:

Theorem 3. Suppose that $f(x)$, $g(x)$ are concave, and $g(x)$ satisfies (18) and (19). Then a vector $\bar{x}$ is optimum if, and only if, there is a vector $\bar{y}$ such that $(\bar{x}, \bar{y})$ is a saddle-point of $\varphi(x, y)$ in $x \geqq 0$ and $y \geqq 0$ (II).[4]

Proof. It is obvious that, if $(\bar{x}, \bar{y})$ is a saddle-point of $\varphi(x, y)$ in $x \geqq 0$ and $y \geqq 0$ (II), then $\bar{x}$ is optimum.

In order to prove the converse we may assume that

$$\frac{\mathrm{d}g_k}{\mathrm{d}x},\ k \in I, \text{ are linear independent.} \tag{20}$$

Let $\bar{x}$ be optimum. We consider two sets A and B defined by

$$A = \{(z_0, z, u);\ z_0 \leqq f(x), \quad z_{\mathrm{I}} = g_{\mathrm{I}}(x), \quad z_{\mathrm{II}} \leqq g_{\mathrm{II}}(x), \quad u \leqq x, \quad \text{for some } x\},$$

$$B = \{(z_0, z, 0);\ z_0 > f(\bar{x}), \quad z = 0(\mathrm{I}), \quad z > 0(\mathrm{II})\}.$$

[4] The notation $y \geqq 0$ (II) means $y_k \geqq 0$ for all $k \in \mathrm{II}$. The point $(\bar{x}, \bar{y})$ is said to be a saddle-point of $\varphi(x, y)$ in $x \geqq 0$ and $y \geqq 0$ (II) if $\bar{x} \geqq 0$, $\bar{y} \geqq 0$ (II) and (5) holds for any $x \geqq 0$ and $y \geqq 0$ (II).

Then A and B are convex, and have no point in common. Therefore, there is a vector $(v_0, v, w) \neq 0$ such that

$$v_0 \geqq 0, \quad v \geqq 0(\mathrm{II}), \quad w \geqq 0, \tag{21}$$

and

$$v_0 f(x) + v \cdot g(x) + w \cdot x \leqq v_0 f(\bar{x}) \quad \text{for all } x. \tag{22}$$

It now suffices to prove that $v_0 > 0$. If we had assumed that $v_0 = 0$, then

$$v \cdot g(x) + w \cdot x \leqq 0 \quad \text{for all } x. \tag{23}$$

For any $k \in \mathrm{II}$, there is a feasible vector x^k such that $g_k(x^k) > 0$. Hence

$$v_k = 0 \quad \text{for } k \in \mathrm{II}. \tag{24}$$

By (19) and (23),

$$w = 0. \tag{25}$$

Using (24) and (25), the inequality (23) may be written as follows:

$$v_{\mathrm{I}} \cdot g_{\mathrm{I}}(x) \leqq 0 \quad \text{for all } x, \quad \text{where } v_{\mathrm{I}} \neq 0. \tag{26}$$

Since we have assumed that $g_{\mathrm{I}}(x)$ is linear, (26) implies

$$v_{\mathrm{I}} \cdot \frac{\partial g_{\mathrm{I}}}{\partial x} = 0, \quad \text{where } v_{\mathrm{I}} \neq 0, \tag{27}$$

which contradicts (20). ■

References

[1] K. J. Arrow and L. Hurwicz, "Reduction of Constrained Maxima to Saddle-Point Problems," in J. Neymen (ed.), *Proceedings of the Third Berkeley Symposium on Mathematical Statistics and Probability*. Berkeley and Los Angeles: University of California Press, 1956, Vol. V, pp. 1–20.

[2] H. W. Kuhn and A. W. Tucker, "Nonlinear Programming," in J. Neyman (ed.), *Proceedings of the Second Berkeley Symposium on Mathematical Statistics and Probability*. Berkeley and Los Angeles: University of California Press, 1951, pp. 481–92.

[3] M. Slater, "Lagrange Multipliers Revisited: A Contribution to Non-Linear Programming," Cowles Commission Discussion Paper, Math. 403, November 1950.

CHAPTER 9

Iterative methods for concave programming

1 Introduction

In order to approach saddle-points of the Lagrangian of the concave programming problem, we have, in Arrow, Hurwicz, and Uzawa [1], considered a system of differential equations—the so-called gradient method. In the present chapter we shall formulate the gradient method in a system of difference equations and investigate the stability of the solution. It will first be shown that the solution monotonically converges to any given neighborhood of a saddle-point provided the rate of change is sufficiently small. Then the method will be slightly modified so that the system consists of the Lagrangian multipliers, and the approximate stability of the modified system will be shown. Especially, for the case where the restrictions are linear, the system is proved to be stable provided the rate of change is small. Finally, linear programming will be reduced to strictly concave quadratic programming and the above iterative methods will be applied to solve linear programming.

2 Concave programming and saddle-point problem

Let $f(x)$ and $g(x) = (g_1(x), \dots, g_m(x))$ be functions defined for $x = (x_1, \dots, x_n) \geqq 0$, and consider

Problem A. Find a vector $\bar{x}$ that maximizes $f(x)$ subject to the restrictions

$$x \geqq 0, \qquad g(x) \geqq 0. \tag{1}$$

It will be assumed that

From *Studies in Linear and Non-Linear Programming*, edited by K. Arrow, L. Hurwicz, and H. Uzawa, Stanford University Press, 1958, 155–165; reprinted with permission.

(a) *$f(x)$ and $g_1(x),\ldots,g_m(x)$ are concave functions in $x \geqq 0$ and have continuous partial derivatives*, and

(b) *there exists a vector x^0 such that*

$$x^0 \geqq 0, \qquad g(x^0) > 0. \tag{2}$$

Then the Kuhn-Tucker Theorem on concave programming (Chapter 8, Theorem 2) may be applied: a vector $\bar{x}$ is an optimum solution to the problem if, and only if, there is an m-vector $\bar{u}$ such that $(\bar{x},\bar{u})$ is a saddle-point of the Lagrangian

$$\varphi(x,u) = f(x) + u \cdot g(x) \tag{3}$$

in $x \geqq 0$ and $u \geqq 0$; i.e.,

$$\varphi(\bar{x},\bar{u}) = \max_{x \geqq 0} \varphi(x,\bar{u}) = \min_{u \geqq 0} \varphi(\bar{x},u). \tag{4}$$

Therefore, solving concave programming is reduced to finding a saddle-point of the Lagrangian $\varphi(x,u)$.

We shall denote by $\bar{X}$ and $\bar{U}$ the sets of the x-components and the u-components of saddle-points of $\varphi(x,u)$; i.e.,

$$\bar{X} = \{\bar{x} \mid (\bar{x},\bar{u}) \text{ is a saddle-point of } \varphi(x,u) \text{ for some } \bar{u}\},$$
$$\bar{U} = \{\bar{u} \mid (\bar{x},\bar{u}) \text{ is a saddle-point of } \varphi(x,u) \text{ for some } \bar{x}\}.$$

It will be noted that *the set $\bar{U}$ is compact* (i.e., closed and bounded). Let $\bar{x} \in \bar{X}$, $\bar{u} \in \bar{U}$. Then

$$\bar{u} \cdot g(\bar{x}) = 0, \tag{5}$$

$$f(x) + \bar{u} \cdot g(x) \leqq f(\bar{x}), \quad \text{for all } x \geqq 0. \tag{6}$$

Take the vector x^0 for which (2) is satisfied. Then (6) implies that

$$0 \leqq \bar{u}_k \leqq \frac{f(\bar{x}) - f(x^0)}{g_k(x^0)} \qquad (k = 1,\ldots,m),$$

which shows that $\bar{U}$ is bounded. Since $\bar{u} \in \bar{U}$ is characterized by (5) and (6), $\bar{U}$ is closed.

In the following sections it will be assumed that

(c) *$f(x)$ is strictly concave in x.*

The optimum solution $\bar{x}$ is then uniquely determined.

3 The Arrow-Hurwicz gradient method

Consider a system of difference equations defined by

$$\begin{cases} x(t+1) = \max\{0, x(t) + \rho\varphi_x(x(t), u(t))\}, \\ u(t+1) = \max\{0, u(t) - \rho\varphi_u(x(t), u(t))\}, \end{cases} \tag{I}$$

with an initial position $(x(0), u(0))$ such that

$$x(0) \geqq 0, \qquad u(0) \geqq 0,$$

where ρ is a given positive number, φ_x and φ_u stand for the partial derivatives of φ with respect to x and u, respectively:

$$\varphi_x(x, u) = f_x(x) + u \cdot g_x(x),$$
$$\varphi_u(x, u) = g(x).$$

We shall define the system (I) as **-stable* if the following condition is satisfied:

(*) *For any initial position* $(x(0), u(0)) \geqq 0$ *and any positive number* $\varepsilon > 0$, *there exists a positive number* $\rho_0 > 0$ *such that, for the solution* $(x(t), u(t))$ *of the system* (I) *with* $\rho \leqq \rho_0$, *there is an integer* t_0 *with the properties*

$$V[x(t+1), u(t+1)] \leqq V[x(t), u(t)], \quad \textit{for } 0 \leqq t < t_0, \tag{7}$$

and

$$V[x(t), u(t)] \leqq \varepsilon, \quad \textit{for } t \geqq t_0, \tag{8}$$

where

$$V(x, u) = \min_{\bar{u} \in \bar{U}} \{|x - \bar{x}|^2 + |u - \bar{u}|^2\}.$$

Now we prove

Theorem 1. Let Problem A satisfy (a), (b), and (c). Then the system (I) is *-stable.

Proof. It is first noted that, by concavity of $\varphi(x, u)$ in x,

$$(\bar{x} - x) \cdot \varphi_x - (\bar{u} - u) \cdot \varphi_u > 0, \quad \text{for } x \neq \bar{x} \text{ or } u \notin \bar{U}. \tag{9}$$

Now from the first equation of (I) we have

$$|x(t+1)|^2 \leqq |x(t)|^2 + 2\rho x(t) \cdot \varphi_x(x(t), u(t)) + \rho^2 |\varphi_x(x(t), u(t))|^2,$$
$$-2\bar{x} \cdot x(t+1) \leqq -2\bar{x} \cdot x(t) - 2\rho\bar{x} \cdot \varphi_x(x(t), u(t)).$$

Hence, we get

$$|x(t+1) - \bar{x}|^2 \leqq |x(t) - \bar{x}|^2 - 2\rho(\bar{x} - x(t)) \cdot \varphi_x(x(t), u(t)) + \rho^2 |\varphi_x(x(t), u(t))|^2. \tag{10}$$

Similarly, from the second equation of (I) we have

$$|u(t+1)|^2 \leqq |u(t)|^2 - 2\rho u(t) \cdot \varphi_u(x(t), u(t)) + \rho^2 |\varphi_u(x(t), u(t))|^2,$$
$$-2\bar{u} \cdot u(t+1) \leqq -2\bar{u} \cdot u(t) + 2\rho\bar{u} \cdot \varphi_u(x(t), u(t)).$$

Hence, we get

$$|u(t+1)-\bar{u}|^2 \leqq |u(t)-\bar{u}|^2 + 2\rho(\bar{u}-u(t))\cdot\varphi_u(x(t),u(t)) + \rho^2|\varphi_u(x(t),u(t))|^2. \tag{11}$$

From (10) and (11),

$$\begin{aligned}[|x(t+1)-\bar{x}|^2 + |u(t+1)-\bar{u}|^2] &\leqq [|x(t)-\bar{x}|^2 + |u(t)-\bar{u}|^2] \\ &- \rho\{2[(\bar{x}-x(t))\cdot\varphi_x(x(t),u(t)) - (\bar{u}-u(t))\cdot\varphi_u(x(t),u(t))] \\ &- \rho[|\varphi_x(x(t),u(t))|^2 + |\varphi_u(x(t),u(t))|^2]\}.\end{aligned} \tag{12}$$

Let ε be a given positive number. We define ρ_0 as the minimum of the following two numbers:

$$\min\left\{\sqrt{\frac{(\varepsilon/2)}{|\varphi_x|^2+|\varphi_u|^2}}\;\middle|\; V(x,u)\leqq\frac{\varepsilon}{2}\right\}$$

and

$$\min\left\{\frac{(\bar{x}-x)\cdot\varphi_x-(\bar{u}-u)\cdot\varphi_u}{|\varphi_x|^2+|\varphi_u|^2}\;\middle|\;\frac{\varepsilon}{2}\leqq V(x,u)\leqq K, \bar{u}\in\bar{U}\right\},$$

where

$$K = \max\{\varepsilon, V(x(0),u(0))\} > 0.$$

By (9) and compactness of $\bar{U}$, $\{(x,u)|\,V(x,u)\leqq\varepsilon/2\}$ and $\{(x,u)|\,\varepsilon/2 \leqq V(x,u)\leqq K\}$, ρ_0 is *positive*.

Let $(x(t),u(t))$ be the solution of (I) with $\rho\leqq\rho_0$. Then (12) and the definition of ρ_0 imply that, for any $\bar{u}\in\bar{U}$,

$$|x(t+1)-\bar{x}|^2 + |u(t+1)-\bar{u}|^2 < |x(t)-\bar{x}|^2 + |u(t)-\bar{u}|^2, \quad \text{if } \varepsilon/2\leqq V(x(t),u(t))\leqq K, \tag{13}$$

and

$$|x(t+1)-\bar{x}|^2 + |u(t+1)-\bar{u}|^2 \leqq \varepsilon, \quad \text{if } V(x(t),u(t))\leqq\varepsilon/2. \tag{14}$$

Since $V(x(0),u(0))\leqq K$, we have

$$V(x(t),u(t))\leqq K \qquad (t=0,1,2,\dots).$$

Hence, the sequence $\{(x(t),u(t))\}$ is bounded. Let (x^*,u^*) be a limiting point of $\{(x(t),u(t))\}$ such that $V(x^*,u^*)$ is the minimum among the limiting points, i.e.,

$$V(x^*,u^*)\leqq V(x^{**},u^{**}), \tag{15}$$

for any limiting point (x^{**},u^{**}) of $\{(x(t),u(t))\}$.

Then we have

$$V(x^*,u^*)\leqq\varepsilon/2. \tag{16}$$

In order to show (16), we may without loss of generality assume that

$$(x^*, u^*) = \lim_{\nu \to \infty} (x(t_\nu), u(t_\nu))$$

such that $(x(t_\nu + 1), u(t_\nu + 1))$ will converge, say to (x^{**}, u^{**}). Then

$$x^{**} = \max\{0, x^* + \rho\varphi_x(x^*, u^*)\},$$
$$u^{**} = \max\{0, u^* - \rho\varphi_u(x^*, u^*)\}.$$

If we had assumed $V(x^*, u^*) > \varepsilon/2$, then, by a formula similar to (13),

$$V(x^{**}, u^{**}) < V(x^*, u^*),$$

which would contradict (15). By (13), (14), and (16), there is an integer t_0 for which (7) and (8) are satisfied. ■

4 A modified Arrow-Hurwicz gradient method

In this section we consider an iterative method, which is a modification of the one described in Section 3.

Here the maximum problem may be formulated as follows:

> **Problem B.** To find a vector x that maximizes $f(x)$ subject to the restriction
>
> $$g(x) \geqq 0. \tag{17}$$

The non-negativity restriction on x, if there is any, may be included in (17), so that Problem A can be reduced to the problem in this section.

It will be assumed that Problem B satisfies (a), (b), (c), and

(d) *for any* $u \geqq 0$, $\varphi(x, u)$ *has a finite maximum with respect to* x.

In this case, a vector $\bar{x}$ is an optimum solution to the problem if and only if there is a vector $\bar{u}$ such that $(\bar{x}, \bar{u})$ is a saddle-point of the Lagrangian $\varphi(x, u)$ in x unrestricted and $u \geqq 0$; i.e.,

$$\varphi(x, \bar{u}) \leqq \varphi(\bar{x}, \bar{u}) \leqq \varphi(\bar{x}, u) \quad \text{for all } x \text{ unrestricted and } u \geqq 0. \tag{18}$$

Now, for any given $u \geqq 0$, the vector that maximizes $\varphi(x, u)$ with respect to unrestricted x is uniquely determined by u. We shall denote it by $x(u)$:

$$\varphi(x(u), u) = \max_x \varphi(x, u). \tag{19}$$

The vector $x(u)$ is characterized as the solution of $\varphi_x = 0$, i.e.,

$$f_x(x(u), u) + u \cdot g_x(x(u)) = 0. \tag{20}$$

We may consider the kth component u_k of u as an imputed price of the kth factor, and $x(u)$ as the optimal level of production that maximizes the net profit

$$f(x) + u \cdot g(x),$$

supposing there be no factor limitations. Then $g_k(x(u))$ represents the excess of supply over demand of the kth factor for the price system u. Therefore in setting the u_k in the next stage, it may be reasonable to determine u_k higher if there is an excess demand, i.e., $g_k(x(u)) < 0$, and lower if there is an excess supply, i.e., $g_k(x(u)) > 0$; the rates of increase and decrease are proportional to the amounts of the excess demand and excess supply, respectively. Furthermore, we have to take into consideration that the imputed price u_k should not be negative.

The above consideration leads us to the following formulation of an iterative method:

$$u(t+1) = \max\{0, u(t) - \rho g(x(t))\}, \qquad t = 0, 1, 2, \ldots, \tag{II}$$

with an initial position $u(0) \geqq 0$, and a given rate of change $\rho > 0$, where

$$x(t) = x(u(t)), \qquad t = 0, 1, 2, \ldots. \tag{21}$$

We define the system (II) as **-stable with respect to* $u(t)$ if, for any initial position $u(0) \geqq 0$ and any positive number $\varepsilon > 0$, there exists a positive number $\rho_0 > 0$ such that, for the solution $u(t)$ of the system (II) with $\rho \leqq \rho_0$, there exists an integer t_0 with the properties:

$$V(u(t+1)) < V(u(t)), \quad \text{for } 0 \leqq t < t_0, \tag{22}$$

and

$$V(u(t)) \leqq \varepsilon, \quad \text{for } t \geqq t_0, \tag{23}$$

where

$$V(u) = \min_{\bar{u} \in \bar{U}} |u - \bar{u}|^2.$$

Theorem 2. Let Problem B satisfy (a), (b), (c), and (d). Then the system (II) is **-stable* with respect to $u(t)$.

Consequently, $x(t)$ converges to an arbitrary small neighborhood of $\bar{x}$ provided the rate of change ρ is sufficiently small.

Proof. Since $x(u)$ uniquely maximizes $\varphi(x, u) = f(x) + u \cdot g(x)$ with respect to x, we have

$$f(x) + u \cdot g(x) < f(x(u)) + u \cdot g(x(u)) \quad \text{for } x \neq x(u). \tag{24}$$

Let $u \notin \bar{U}$ and $\bar{u} \in \bar{U}$. If $x(u) \neq \bar{x} = x(\bar{u})$, then

$$f(\bar{x}) + u \cdot g(\bar{x}) < f(x(u)) + u \cdot g(x(u)), \tag{25}$$

$$f(x(u)) + \bar{u}\cdot g(x(u)) < f(\bar{x}) + \bar{u}\cdot g(\bar{x}). \tag{26}$$

Summing (25) and (26), and noting that $g(\bar{x}) \geqq 0, \bar{u}\cdot g(\bar{x}) = 0$, we have

$$(u - \bar{u})\cdot g(x(u)) > 0, \quad \text{for any } u \notin \bar{U} \text{ and } \bar{u} \in \bar{U}. \tag{27}$$

If $x(u) = \bar{x}$, then $u\cdot g(x(u)) > 0$ and $\bar{u}\cdot g(x(u)) = 0$. Therefore, the relation (27) is also valid.

Now, from (II),

$$|u(t+1)|^2 \leqq |u(t)|^2 - 2\rho u(t)\cdot g(x(t)) + \rho^2 |g(x(t))|^2,$$
$$-2\bar{u}\cdot u(t+1) \leqq -2\bar{u}\cdot u(t) + 2\rho\bar{u}\cdot g(x(t)).$$

Then we have

$$|u(t+1) - \bar{u}|^2 \leqq |u(t) - \bar{u}|^2 - \rho\{2(u(t) - \bar{u})\cdot g(x(t)) - \rho |g(x(t))|^2\}. \tag{28}$$

Let ρ_0 be a number defined by

$$\rho_0 = \min\left\{ \min_{V(u) \leqq \varepsilon/2} \frac{\sqrt{\varepsilon/2}}{|g(x(u))|}, \min_{\substack{\varepsilon/2 \leqq V(u) \leqq K \\ \bar{u} \in \bar{U}}} \frac{(u - \bar{u})\cdot g(x(u))}{|g(x(u))|^2} \right\}, \tag{29}$$

where

$$K = \max\{\varepsilon, V(u(0))\}.$$

By (27), ρ_0 is *positive*.

Then, (28) and the definition of ρ_0 imply that, for the solution $u(t)$ of (II) with $\rho \leqq \rho_0$,

$$|u(t+1) - \bar{u}|^2 < |u(t) - \bar{u}|^2, \quad \text{if } \varepsilon/2 \leqq V(u(t)) \leqq K, \bar{u} \in \bar{U}, \tag{30}$$

and

$$|u(t+1) - \bar{u}|^2 \leqq \varepsilon, \quad \text{if } V(u(t)) \leqq \varepsilon/2, \bar{u} \in \bar{U}. \tag{31}$$

Similar to the proof of Theorem 1, (30) and (31) imply the monotonic convergence of $u(t)$ to the ε-neighborhood of $\bar{U}$. ■

A careful examination of the proof of Theorem 2 shows that the system (II) is *-stable for a broader class of the problems; namely, we can easily prove the following theorem.

Theorem 3. Let the Lagrangian

$$\varphi(x, u) = f(x) + u\cdot g(x)$$

satisfy the following conditions:

(i) There exists a closed set A of n-vectors such that, for any $u \geqq 0$,

$\varphi(x, u)$ has a finite maximum with respect to $x \in A$ and the vector $x_A(u)$ maximizing $\varphi(x, u)$ in A is uniquely determined.

(ii) There is a saddle-point $(\bar{x}_A, \bar{u}_A)$ of $\varphi(x, u)$ in $x \in A$ and $u \geqq 0$.

Then the system

$$u_A(t+1) = \max\{0, u_A(t) - \rho g(x_A(t))\}, \qquad t = 0, 1, 2, \ldots, \qquad \text{(II)}'$$

with $x_A(0) \in A$, is **-stable.*

It will be noted that, in Theorem 3, we do not assume concavity of functions $f(x)$ and $g(x)$.

5 Concave programming with linear restrictions

We shall now consider the case where the restrictions are linear, i.e.,

$$g(x) = b - Bx,$$

and show that the method explained in Section 4 converges to $\bar{U}$, provided ρ is sufficiently small.

It is again assumed that

(b) *there is* x^0 *such that* $b - Bx^0 > 0$,
(c) $f(x)$ *is strictly concave and has continuous partial derivatives* f_{xx},
(d) *for any* $u \geqq 0$, $\max_x \varphi(x, u)$ *is finite.*

The Lagrangian $\varphi(x, u)$ in the present case becomes

$$\varphi(x, u) = f(x) + u \cdot (b - Bx). \qquad (32)$$

For any $u \geqq 0$, the vector $x(u)$ that maximizes $\varphi(x, u)$ in x is characterized by the solution of the following equation:

$$f_x(x(u)) - B'u = 0. \qquad (33)$$

The system (II) in this case will be written as follows:

$$u(t+1) = \max\{0, u(t) - \rho(b - Bx(t))\} \qquad (t = 0, 1, 2, \ldots). \qquad \text{(III)}$$

Theorem 4. Suppose $f(x)$ and $g(x) = b - Bx$ satisfy the conditions (b), (c), and (d). Then there exists a positive number $\rho_0 > 0$ such that solution $u(t)$ of (III) with $\rho \leqq \rho_0$ monotonically converges to a vector $\bar{u} \in \bar{U}$. Consequently the corresponding $x(t)$ converges to the optimum vector $\bar{x}$.

Proof. Let $\bar{x}$ be the unique optimum vector for the problem and II be the set of corner indices; i.e., $II = \{k \mid g_k(\bar{x}) > 0\}$, and $I = \{1, \ldots, m\} - II$.

Then, for any $\bar{u}\in\bar{U}$, we have

$$\bar{u}_{II}=0. \tag{34}$$

By (33) and (c), $x(u)$ is a continuous function of u, so that *there exists a positive number* $\varepsilon>0$ *such that*

$$V(u)\leqq\varepsilon \textit{ implies } g_{II}(x(u))>0. \tag{35}$$

For this ε, let $\rho_0(u(0),\varepsilon)$ be the positive number defined by (29).

Since $f(x)$ is *strictly* concave, the matrix (f_{xx}) is negative definite. Let us denote by $\lambda(x)$ the maximum value of characteristic roots of $B(-f_{xx})^{-1}B'$ at x. Then

$$\lambda(x)\geqq 0. \tag{36}$$

Let

$$\rho_0=\min\left\{\rho_0(u(0),\varepsilon),\ \min_{V(u)\leqq\varepsilon}\frac{1}{\lambda(x(u))}\right\}. \tag{37}$$

By (36) and compactness of the set $\{x(u)|\,V(u)\leqq\varepsilon\}$, ρ_0 is *positive.*

We shall now show that, for any $\rho\leqq\rho_0$, the solution $u(t)$ of (III) converges to a $\bar{u}\in\bar{U}$. We may, by Theorem 3, suppose that

$$V(t)\leqq\varepsilon,\quad \text{for } t=0,1,2,\ldots. \tag{38}$$

It will be first noted that *there is an integer* $\bar{t}$ *such that*

$$u_{II}(t)=0,\quad \text{for } t\geqq\bar{t}. \tag{39}$$

In fact, (35), (38), and compactness of the set $\{u|\,V(u)\leqq\varepsilon\}$ imply that

$$\min g_k(x(t))>0,\quad \text{for } k\in II \qquad (t=0,1,2,\ldots).$$

Therefore there is an integer $\bar{t}$ such that

$$u_{II}(\bar{t}-1)-\rho g_{II}(x(\bar{t}-1))\leqq 0.$$

Then

$$u_{II}(\bar{t})=0,$$

and (39) is satisfied.

Now, from (III), we have

$$|u_I(t+1)|^2\leqq|u_I(t)|^2-2\rho u_I(t)\cdot(b_I-B_Ix_I(t))+\rho^2|b_I-B_Ix_I(t)|^2,$$
$$-2\bar{u}_I\cdot u_I(t+1)\leqq-2\bar{u}_I\cdot u_I(t)+2\rho\bar{u}_I\cdot(b_I-B_Ix_I(t)),$$

where

$$u(t)=\begin{pmatrix}u_I(t)\\ u_{II}(t)\end{pmatrix},\quad b=\begin{pmatrix}b_I\\ b_{II}\end{pmatrix},\quad B=\begin{pmatrix}B_I\\ B_{II}\end{pmatrix}.$$

Then we have

$$|u_I(t+1)-\bar{u}_I|^2 \leqq |u_I(t)-\bar{u}_I|^2 - \rho\{2(u_I(t)-\bar{u}_I)\cdot(b_I - B_I x(t)) - \rho|b_I - B_I x(t)|^2\}. \tag{40}$$

Now, by the definition of I, we have

$$b_I - B_I\bar{x} = 0. \tag{41}$$

Hence,

$$b_I - B_I\cdot x(t) = B_I(\bar{x} - x(t)). \tag{42}$$

Now the relations (33) and (39) imply, for $t \geqq \bar{t}$,

$$\left(\frac{df}{dx}\right)_{x(t)} - B_I' u_I(t) = 0, \tag{43}$$

$$\left(\frac{df}{dx}\right)_{\bar{x}} - B_I'\bar{u}_I = 0. \tag{44}$$

On the other hand, we have

$$\left(\frac{df}{dx}\right)_{x(t)} = \left(\frac{df}{dx}\right)_{\bar{x}} + (f_{xx}^{\theta})(x(t)-\bar{x}), \tag{45}$$

where

$$f_{xx}^{\theta} = (f_{xx})_{x^{\theta}}, \quad x^{\theta} = \bar{x} + \theta(x(t)-\bar{x}), \quad 0 \leqq \theta \leqq 1.$$

Equations (43), (44), and (45) imply

$$B_I'(u_I(t)-\bar{u}_I) = (-f_{xx}^{\theta})\cdot(\bar{x}-x(t)). \tag{46}$$

Since (f_{xx}^{θ}) is non-singular,

$$\bar{x} - x(t) = (-f_{xx}^{\theta})^{-1} B_I'\cdot(u_I(t)-\bar{u}_I). \tag{47}$$

Substituting (47) into (42), we get

$$b_I - B_I\cdot x(t) = B_I(-f_{xx}^{\theta})^{-1} B_I'\cdot(u_I(t)-\bar{u}_I), \qquad t \geqq t_1. \tag{48}$$

Therefore, by (37), (47), and (48), we have

$$\begin{aligned} &2(u_I(t)-\bar{u}_I)\cdot(b_I - B_I x(t)) - \rho|b_I - B_I x(t)|^2 \\ &\quad = (\bar{x}-x(t))\cdot(-f_{xx}^{\theta})\cdot(\bar{x}-x(t)) \\ &\qquad + (u_I(t)-\bar{u}_I)\cdot B_I(-f_{xx}^{\theta})^{-1} B_I'\cdot(u_I(t)-\bar{u}_I) \\ &\qquad - \rho(u_I(t)-\bar{u}_I)\cdot(B_I(-f_{xx}^{\theta})^{-1} B_1')^2\cdot(u_I(t)-\bar{u}_I) \\ &\quad \geqq (\bar{x}-x(t))\cdot(-f_{xx}^{\theta})\cdot(\bar{x}-x(t)) \begin{cases} > 0, & \text{if } x(t) \neq \bar{x}, \\ \geqq 0, & \text{otherwise.} \end{cases} \end{aligned} \tag{49}$$

Hence, by (40), we have, for any $\bar{u} \in \bar{U}$,

$$|u_I(t+1) - \bar{u}_I| \leqq |u_I(t) - \bar{u}_I|, \tag{50}$$

with the strict inequality for $x(t) \neq \bar{x}$.

For $\bar{u} \in \bar{U}$, let u^* be a limiting point of the sequence $u(t)$ such that

$$|u^* - \bar{u}| \leqq |u^{**} - \bar{u}| \tag{51}$$

for any limiting point u^{**} of $u(t)$. Take a subsequence $\{u(t_\nu)\}$ such that

$$\lim_{\nu} u(t_\nu) = u^*.$$

We may, without loss of generality, assume that $u(t_\nu + 1)$ also converges, say to u^{**}.

Then

$$u^{**} = \max\{0, u^* - \rho g(x(u^*))\}.$$

By a formula similar to (50), we have

$$|u^{**} - \bar{u}| \leqq |u^* - \bar{u}|,$$

which, by (51), implies

$$|u^{**} - \bar{u}| = |u^* - \bar{u}|.$$

Hence, by (50),

$$x(u^*) = \bar{x} \quad \text{and} \quad u^* \in \bar{U}.$$

Since the inequality (50) holds for any $\bar{u} \in \bar{U}$, we may put $\bar{u} = u^*$ in (50). Then we know that the sequence $\{u(t)\}$ itself converges to u^*. Consequently,

$$\lim_{t \to \infty} x(t) = \bar{x}.$$ ■

The modified gradient method will be applied to solve concave *quadratic programming: find a vector $\bar{x}$ that maximizes $a'x - x'Ax/2$ subject to $Bx \leqq b$*, where A is positive definite.

The Lagrangian is given by

$$\varphi(x, u) = a'x - \tfrac{1}{2}x'Ax + u'(b - Bx). \tag{52}$$

For $u \geqq 0$, the vector $x(u)$ that maximizes $\varphi(x, u)$ with respect to unrestricted x is characterized by

$$a - Ax(u) - B'u = 0.$$

Therefore,

$$x(u) = A^{-1}(a - B'u). \tag{53}$$

The modified gradient method may be written as follows:

$$\begin{cases} x(t) = A^{-1}a - A^{-1}B'u(t) \\ u(t+1) = \max\{0, (I - \rho BA^{-1}B')u(t) - \rho(b - BA^{-1}a)\} \end{cases} \qquad \text{(IV)}$$

$$(t = 0, 1, 2, \ldots).$$

Since we can beforehand compute $I - \rho BA^{-1}B'$ and $\rho(b - BA^{-1}a)$, the computation of $u(t)$ by (IV) will be easily performed.

Theorem 5. The solution $x(t)$ of the system (IV) converges to the optimum solution provided ρ is a sufficiently small positive number.

6 Linear programming

In the maximum problem with which we have been concerned so far, the maximand has been assumed to be strictly concave. We shall in this section treat linear programming problems and show how the above method can be applied.

Linear programming is formulated as follows:

Problem C. To find a vector $\bar{x}$ that maximizes $a'x$ subject to $Bx \leqq b$. The following conditions will be assumed to be satisfied:

(b) There is a vector x^0 such that $Bx^0 < b$.
(e) The feasible set is bounded.

Lemma. Consider Problem C′: Maximize $c'x$ subject to $Bx \leqq b$. Then there exists a positive number $\delta > 0$ such that, if $|c - a| \leqq \delta$, then every optimum vector $\bar{x}$ for Problem C′ is also optimum to Problem C.

Proof. Since the feasible set is a bounded convex polyhedral set, there exists a matrix

$$K = (k^1 \cdots k^N) = \begin{pmatrix} k_{11} \cdots k_{1N} \\ \cdots \\ k_{n1} \cdots k_{nN} \end{pmatrix}$$

such that a vector x satisfies $Bx \leqq b$ if and only if

$$x = Kw, \qquad w = \begin{pmatrix} w_1 \\ \vdots \\ w_N \end{pmatrix} \geqq 0, \qquad \sum_{\nu=1}^{N} w_\nu = 1.$$

We may without loss of generality assume that

$$a\cdot k^1 = \cdots = a\cdot k^r > a\cdot k^{r+1} \geqq \cdots \geqq a\cdot k^N.$$

Let

$$\delta = \min\left\{\frac{a\cdot(k^\nu - k^\mu)}{2|k^\nu - k^\mu|}\,\middle|\, 1 \leqq \nu \leqq r < \mu \leqq N\right\} > 0$$

and $|a - c| \leqq \delta$. Then

$$|a\cdot(k^\nu - k^\mu) - c\cdot(k^\nu - k^\mu)| \leqq |a - c|\,|k^\nu - k^\mu| < a\cdot(k^\nu - k^\mu),$$

$$\text{for any } 1 \leqq \nu \leqq r < \mu \leqq N.$$

Therefore,

$$c\cdot(k^\nu - k^\mu) > 0, \quad \text{for } 1 \leqq \nu \leqq r < \mu \leqq N.$$

Hence, if a vector $\bar{x}$ is optimum for Problem C′, then

$$\bar{x} = \sum_{\nu=1}^{r} w_\nu k^\nu, \qquad w_\nu \geqq 0, \qquad \sum_{\nu=1}^{r} w_\nu = 1.$$

Therefore, $\bar{x}$ is optimum for Problem C. ■

Now we shall consider the following strictly concave quadratic programming problem:

> **Problem C_ε.** Find a vector x that maximizes $a'x - \varepsilon x'x/2$ subject to $Bx \leqq b$, where ε is a given positive number.

Since the optimum vector for Problem C_ε is unique, we denote it by x_ε. We shall prove the following:

> **Theorem 6.** There exists a positive number ε_0 such that the optimum solution x_ε of Problem C_ε with $\varepsilon \leqq \varepsilon_0$ is optimum for Problem C.

Proof. According to the Kuhn-Tucker Theorem, a vector $\bar{x}$ is optimum for Problem C_ε if and only if there exists a vector $\bar{u}$ such that $(\bar{x}, \bar{u})$ is a saddle-point of the Lagrangian form $\varphi_\varepsilon(x, u) = (a'x - \varepsilon x'x/2) + u\cdot(b - Bx)$ with x unrestricted and $u \geqq 0$. Any saddle-point $(x_\varepsilon, \bar{u})$ is characterized as the solution of

$$\begin{cases} a - \varepsilon x_\varepsilon - B'\bar{u} = 0 \\ b - Bx_\varepsilon \geqq 0 \\ \bar{u} \geqq 0, \quad \bar{u}\cdot(b - Bx_\varepsilon) = 0. \end{cases} \tag{54}$$

But (54) shows that $(x_\varepsilon, \bar{u})$ is also a saddle-point of

$$\varphi(x, u) = (a - \varepsilon x_\varepsilon)'x + u'(b - Bx)$$

with x unrestricted, $u \geqq 0$.

Therefore x_ε maximizes $(a - \varepsilon x_\varepsilon)'x$ subject to $Bx \leqq b$.

Let

$$\varepsilon_0 = \frac{\delta}{K}$$

where δ is the positive number in the Lemma, and

$$K = \max_{x:\text{feasible}} |x|.$$

Since the feasible set is compact, K is finite, and ε_0 is *positive*. Then, by the Lemma, if $0 < \varepsilon \leqq \varepsilon_0$, x_ε is optimum for Problem C. ∎

By Theorem 6, solving linear programming Problem C is reduced to solving the strictly concave programming Problem C_ε with $0 < \varepsilon \leqq \varepsilon_0$, to which the modified gradient method will be applied. The modified gradient method for Problem C_ε is now written as follows:

$$\begin{cases} u(t+1) = \max\left\{0, \left(I - \dfrac{\rho}{\varepsilon}BB'\right)u(t) - \left(\rho b - \dfrac{\rho}{\varepsilon}Ba\right)\right\} \\ x(t) = \dfrac{1}{\varepsilon}a - \dfrac{1}{\varepsilon}B'u(t) \end{cases} \tag{V}$$

$$(t = 0, 1, 2, \ldots, u(0) \geqq 0).$$

The above method can be applied to the case where A is only positive semi-definite. In this case, the iterative method (IV) will be modified as follows:

$$\begin{cases} x(t) = (A + \varepsilon I)^{-1}(a - B'u(t)), \\ u(t+1) = \max\{0, [I - B(A + \varepsilon I)^{-1}B']u(t) - \rho[b - B(A + \varepsilon I)^{-1}a]\}, \end{cases}$$

$$t = 0, 1, 2, \ldots. \qquad \text{(IV)}'$$

The system is stable provided ρ and ε are sufficiently small positive numbers.

Reference

[1] Arrow, Hurwicz, and Uzawa (eds.), *Studies in Linear and Non-Linear Programming*, Stanford: Stanford University Press, 1958, Chapters 6, 7, and 8.

CHAPTER 10

Prices of the factors of production in international trade

The problem of international factor-price equalization is studied by using a technique which combines the Walrasian theory of general equilibrium with the theory of welfare economics. The principle of the complete or partial equalization was first enunciated by Eli Heckscher in his 1919 paper and was later elaborated by Bertil Ohlin, Paul A. Samuelson, and others. The present study shows in particular that the complete factor-price equalization occurs only in the cases in which the factor endowments in the countries are precisely the ones that arise in an equilibrium position of world trade where the factors of production as well as the commodities can move internationally.

1 Introduction

In analyzing the effect of international trade on the prices of the factors of production, E. Heckscher [4] found that the equalization of the absolute as well as the relative prices of factors of production is an inescapable consequence of international trade, provided that the same techniques of production are used in both countries and the supplies of the factors of production are fixed. Differences in techniques, however, lead to differences in factor prices ([4, p. 291]). (Following the tradition of the theory of international trade, he considers the two-commodity, two-factor, two-country case in which finished goods are traded between countries without any transport costs and in which factors of production are completely immobile.)

The results obtained by B. Ohlin [9] are rather different from the Heckscher principle of complete equalization of the absolute prices of

From *Econometrica*, Vol. 27 (1959), pp. 448–68; reprinted with permission.

This work was begun during the summer of 1957 when the writer was a member of the workshop on International Trade and Taxation of the Summer Institute on Application of Mathematics in Social Sciences, and part of the work was read at the Philadelphia meeting of the Econometric Society on December 28, 1957. He wishes to express his gratitude to Professors Kenneth J. Arrow and Martin J. Bailey, to the members of the workshop, and especially to Professor L. W. McKenzie, for their kind criticisms and suggestions.

factors of production. According to Ohlin, international trade has a tendency towards only a *partial* equalization of the prices of factors of production even if all countries have the same techniques of production ([9, pp. 37–42]).

The Heckscher-Ohlin theory of factor price equalization was further investigated by P. A. Samuelson in a series of papers [10, 11, 12]. In the last paper [12], he considers the general n-commodity, r-factor, N-country model of international trade, and proves that if all countries have the same homogeneous production functions of the first order with a nonsingular matrix of the factor intensities, and if complete specialization does not occur in any country, then the prices of the factors of production are completely equalized by international trade, regardless of the factor endowments and the demand structures of the countries.

L. W. McKenzie [8] adapts the activity analysis approach to the factor price equalization problem and also proves the Samuelson proposition on complete equalization of factor prices.

It should be noted also that A. P. Lerner in [7], originally written in 1933, established the same results, essentially, in the two-commodity, two-factor two-country case. Lerner's paper uses a beautiful geometrical approach.

Among many criticisms of the Samuelson theory of complete factor price equalization, the one given by G. Haberler seems to me of some interest. He writes that

> We must thus conclude that the Lerner-Samuelson theory, though formally correct, rests on such restrictive and unrealistic assumptions that it can hardly be regarded as a valuable contribution to economic theory. Its elegance and pedagogic value, as well as its importance as a precise presentation of all the implied assumptions, are, however, in no way affected by this fact. Ohlin's more modest and somewhat unprecise contention, of which he himself admitted the possibility of exceptions, to the effect that trade will tend to bring about a partial equalization of factor prices, would seem to be valid as an empirical proposition. (Haberler [3, p. 20].)

In the present article, we investigate the factor price equalization problem from the viewpoint of welfare economics, and show that the complete equalization of the prices of the factors of production is rather unlikely to occur.

We consider a general model of international trade in which goods are traded without any transport costs while the factors of production are completely immobile. Each country may have different techniques of production and different preference patterns, but supplies of the factors of production are fixed.

We first define a world welfare function so that an equilibrium position of international trade is obtained as a solution to the following problem:

Maximize the world welfare function subject to the restrictions that for each country the use of the factors of production should not exceed the factor endowment of the country.

In order to give a criterion for complete factor price equalization in terms of this welfare function, it is found convenient to develop our argument for three different cases. In the first case we assume there is no trade between countries; the second is the case of international trade, i.e., the case in which finished goods (commodities) are freely traded while factors of production are completely immobile; in the third case we assume there is no barrier to the international movement either of factors of production or of finished goods.

In the first case, equilibrium prices of commodities as well as factors of production are not necessarily the same among countries; in the second, commodity prices are the same among countries, while factor prices are not the same; in the third case, equilibrium factor, as well as commodity, prices are the same among countries. World welfare is clearly greater in the second than in the first, and greater in the third case than in the second.

Then we will show that:

I Equilibrium commodity prices in the first case are the same among countries if and only if world welfare is not greater in the second case than it is in the first.

II Equilibrium factor prices in the second case are the same among countries if and only if world welfare is not greater in the third case than in the second.

The latter proposition may be restated as follows:

II′ Prices of the factors of production are completely equalized by the trade of commodities if and only if the initial factor endowments in the several countries have the same distribution as those which will arise in an equilibrium position in the third case.

In view of these criteria, non-complete equalization of factor prices is more naturally expected than complete equalization. In later sections, we shall consider the two-commodity, two-factor, two-country model with the same Cobb-Douglas production functions and the same exponential utility function, and give an exact condition for complete factor price equalization. In this special situation, it is noted that factor prices are completely equalized by trade if and only if trade does not occur at all or if the volume of trade in each commodity is small.

Finally, in the last section we shall consider the situation in which each country has a definite demand-and-supply schedule, once the prices of commodities and factors of production are given, and show that, under certain linearity conditions, the Ohlin principle of partial equalization of factor prices is valid, while complete factor price equalization occurs only if the factor endowments in all countries are the same.

It may be noted that in the present article we do not consider the costs of transport or tariffs. If we take such possibilities into consideration, most of our results no longer remain valid.

2 A model of general equilibrium: one country

Consider a country where n commodities (consumption goods) are produced by using r factors of production, and consumed according to the preference of the country. Consumption goods are represented by $i = 1, \ldots, n$, and factors of production by $k = 1, \ldots, r$. The processes of production which are possible with the technology of the country will be explained in terms of "activity analysis."[1]

An *activity level* of the economy specifies the techniques used by various firms in the economy and the levels at which these techniques are operated. Let the activities be denoted by $j = 1, \ldots, m$, so that each activity level may be represented by an m-vector $y = (y_1, \ldots, y_m)$, where y_j denotes the level of activity j for $j = 1, \ldots, m$. The technological possibilities open to the economy will be characterized by a pair of functions: an *output* function $f(y) = (f_1(y), \ldots, f_n(y))$ and an *input* function $g(y) = (g_1(y), \ldots, g_r(y))$. Activity level y produces commodity i in the amount $f_i(y)$, $i = 1, \ldots, n$, and uses factor of production k in the amount $g_k(y)$, $k = 1, \ldots, r$.

It will be assumed that *the technology is subject to constant returns to scale and to the law of the nonincreasing marginal rates of transformation*; i.e., the following conditions are satisfied:

(a) $f_1(y), \ldots, f_m(y)$ *are concave, homogeneous of order* 1, *and differentiable for* $y \geqq 0$;[2]

(b) $g_1(y), \ldots, g_r(y)$ *are convex, homogeneous of order* 1, *and differentiable for* $y \geqq 0$.

The produnction side of the economy is concerned with the optimum selection of activity levels, assuming the available quantities of factors of production are given and products are evaluated at market prices.

Let us assume that the available quantity of factor k is v_k, $k = 1, \ldots, r$, and the price of commodity i is $p_i \geqq 0$, $i = 1, \ldots, n$. Then optimum production requires *an activity level y that maximizes*

[1] Detailed explanation is found in Koopmans [5].

[2] As usual, we write, for two vectors $x = (x_1, \ldots, x_m)$ and $y = (y_1, \ldots, y_m)$, $x \geqq y$ if $x_j \geqq y_j$, $j = 1, \ldots, m$, $x \geq y$ if $x \geqq y$ and $x \neq y$, $x > y$ if $x_j > y_j$, $j = 1, \ldots, m$.

$$p \cdot f(y) = \sum_{i=1}^{n} p_i f_i(y),^3 \tag{1}$$

subject to the restrictions

$$y \geqq 0, \tag{2}$$

$$g(y) \leqq v, \tag{3}$$

where

$$p = (p_1, \ldots, p_n), \qquad f(y) = (f_1(y), \ldots, f_n(y)),$$
$$g(y) = (g_1(y), \ldots, g_r(y)), \qquad v = (v_1, \ldots, v_r).$$

We further assume that the following mathematical regularity condition is satisfied:

(c) $g(y) = (g_1(y), \ldots, g_r(y))$ *satisfies the constraint qualification of Kuhn and Tucker* [6, p. 483].

Under assumptions (a–c), an activity level y is optimum if and only if there is an r-vector $\bar{w} = (\bar{w}_1, \ldots, \bar{w}_1)$ such that $(\bar{y}, \bar{w})$ is a saddle-point of the Lagrangean form

$$\phi(y, w) = p \cdot f(y) + w \cdot [v - g(y)].^4 \tag{4}$$

That is,

$$\phi(y, \bar{w}) \leqq \phi(\bar{y}, \bar{w}) \leqq \phi(\bar{y}, w) \quad \text{for all } y \geqq 0, w \geqq 0. \tag{5}$$

On the other hand, $(\bar{y}, \bar{w})$ is a saddle-point of $\phi(y, w)$ if and only if

$$\bar{y} \geqq 0, \qquad \bar{w} \geqq 0, \tag{6}$$

$$\sum_{i=1}^{n} p_i \left(\frac{\partial f_i}{\partial y_j} \right)_{\bar{y}} \leqq \sum_{k=1}^{r} \bar{w}_k \left(\frac{\partial g_k}{\partial y_j} \right)_{\bar{y}}, \qquad j = 1, \ldots, m, \tag{7}$$

with the equality for j such that $\bar{y}_j > 0$, and

$$g_k(\bar{y}) \leqq v_k, \qquad k = 1, \ldots, r, \tag{8}$$

with the equality for k such that $\bar{w}_k > 0$.

Condition (7) states that the marginal value of the product should not exceed the marginal cost and should be equal if the activity is operated at a positive level.

The $\bar{w}_k$ satisfying (6)–(8) will be called *the imputed price* of factor k, $k = 1, \ldots, r$.

[3] For two vectors p and x, $p \cdot x$ will stand for the inner product, $p \cdot x = \sum_{i=1}^{n} p_i x_i$.

[4] Cf. Kuhn and Tucker [6].

It will be noted that as a consequence of conditions (7) and (8), the product, $p \cdot f(\bar{y})$, is equal to the value of the factors of production evaluated by the imputed prices, $\bar{w} \cdot v$:

$$p \cdot f(\bar{y}) = \bar{w} \cdot v. \tag{9}$$

In fact, multiplying (7) by $\bar{y}_j$ and summing over $j = 1, \ldots, m$ we have

$$\sum_j \sum_i p_i \frac{\partial f_i}{\partial y_j} \bar{y}_j = \sum_j \sum_k \bar{w}_k \frac{\partial g_k}{\partial y_j} \bar{y}_j. \tag{10}$$

By the homogeneity of f_i and g_k,

$$\sum_j \frac{\partial f_i}{\partial y_j} \bar{y}_j = f_i(\bar{y}), \qquad \sum_j \frac{\partial g_k}{\partial y_j} \bar{y}_j = g_k(\bar{y}).$$

Therefore, (10) may be written as

$$\sum_i p_i f_i(\bar{y}) = \sum_k \bar{w}_k g_k(\bar{y}). \tag{11}$$

Multiplying (8) by $\bar{w}_k$ and summing over $k = 1, \ldots, r$, we have

$$\sum_k \bar{w}_k g_k(\bar{y}) = \sum_k \bar{w}_k v_k. \tag{12}$$

(11) and (12) prove (9). ■

The consumption side of the economy will now be concerned with obtaining the most preferred position. It will be assumed that preferences are represented by a numerical function $u(x)$, where $x = (x_1, \ldots, x_n)$ is a vector of consumption, with the following property:

(d) *$u(x)$ is strictly concave, strictly increasing, and differentiable for $x \geqq 0$.*

Then the country *maximizes*

$$u(x)$$

subject to the restrictions

$$x \geqq 0, \tag{13}$$

$$p \cdot x \leqq w \cdot v, \tag{14}$$

where p is the vector of the market prices of goods and w is that of the imputed prices of factors.

The market price system $\bar{p}$ will be said to be *in equilibrium*[5] if

$$\bar{x} \leqq f(\bar{y}), \tag{15}$$

[5] The model of general equilibrium explained in this note is a special case of the Arrow-Debreu model [1].

where $\bar{x}$ is an optimum consumption vector and $\bar{y}$ is an optimum activity level for the market price system $\bar{p}$. Now we shall prove

Theorem 1. $\bar{p}$ is an equilibrium price system if and only if the corresponding optimum consumption vector $\bar{x}$ maximizes $u(x)$ subject to the restrictions

$$x \leqq f(y)$$
$$g(y) \leqq v,$$
$$x \geqq 0,\ y \geqq 0.$$

By the Kuhn-Tucker theorem, Theorem 1 is equivalent to

Theorem 1′. $(\bar{x}, \bar{y}; \bar{p}, \bar{w})$ is in equilibrium if and only if it is a saddle-point of

$$\phi(x, y; p, w) = \lambda u(x) + p\cdot[f(y) - x] + w\cdot[v - g(y)] \tag{16}$$

for some $\lambda > 0$.

Proof of Theorem 1′. By definition, $(\bar{x}, \bar{y}; \bar{p}, \bar{w})$ is in equilibrium if

$$\bar{x} \geqq 0, \qquad \bar{y} \geqq 0, \qquad \bar{p} \geqq 0, \qquad \bar{w} \geqq 0; \tag{17}$$

$$\lambda\left(\frac{\partial u}{\partial x_i}\right)_{\bar{x}} \leqq \bar{p}_i, \qquad i = 1, \ldots, n, \tag{18}$$

with the equality for i such that $\bar{x}_i > 0$;

$$\bar{x}_i \leqq f_i(\bar{y}), \qquad i = 1, \ldots, n, \tag{19}$$

with the equality for i such that $\bar{p}_i > 0$;

$$\sum_i \bar{p}_i\left(\frac{\partial f_i}{\partial y_j}\right)_{\bar{y}} \leqq \sum_k \bar{w}_k\left(\frac{\partial g_k}{\partial y_j}\right)_{\bar{y}}, \qquad j = 1, \ldots, m, \tag{20}$$

with the equality for j such that $\bar{y}_j > 0$, and

$$g_k(\bar{y}) \leqq v_k, \qquad k = 1, \ldots, r, \tag{21}$$

with the equality for k such that $\bar{w}_k > 0$.

By the Kuhn-Tucker theorem [5], conditions (17)–(21) are satisfied if and only if $(\bar{x}, \bar{y}; \bar{p}, \bar{w})$ is a saddle-point of $\phi(x, y; p, w)$. ∎

3 Imputation to the factors of production

Before proceeding to deal with the many-country model, a few remarks about the determination of factor prices will be stated in this section.

Prices imputed to factors of production usually have been defined by means of marginality conditions (7) and (8). The imputed price $\bar{w}_k$ of factor k, however, may be interpreted also as the opportunity cost of that factor. The opportunity cost is defined as the maximum value of the product that could be obtained by using the marginal unit of factor k. Mathematically, let $\varphi(v)$ be the maximal value of the product when factor availability is v, i.e.,

$$\varphi(v) = \max\{p\cdot f(y) \mid y \geqq 0, g(y) \leqq v\}. \tag{22}$$

By (a) and (b), $\varphi(v)$ is a convex function of v. Therefore, there exist both derivatives,

$$\left(\frac{\partial \varphi}{\partial v_k}\right)^- = \lim_{\substack{\Delta v_k \to 0 \\ \Delta v_k < 0}} \frac{\varphi(v + \Delta v_k) - \varphi(v)}{\Delta v_k}$$

and

$$\left(\frac{\partial \varphi}{\partial v_k}\right)^+ = \lim_{\substack{\Delta v_k \to 0 \\ \Delta v_k > 0}} \frac{\varphi(v + \Delta v_k) - \varphi(v)}{\Delta v_k},$$

where

$$\Delta v_k = (0, \ldots, 0, \Delta v_k, 0, \ldots, 0) \quad \text{(the } k\text{th component).}$$

By the convexity of $\varphi(v)$, we have

$$\left(\frac{\partial \varphi}{\partial v_k}\right)^- \geqq \left(\frac{\partial \varphi}{\partial v_k}\right)^+, \quad k = 1, \ldots, r. \tag{23}$$

If $(\partial\varphi/\partial v_k)^- = (\partial\varphi/\partial v_k)^+$, which is the case almost everywhere,[6] $\partial\varphi/\partial v_k$ is the opportunity cost of factor k at v.

If $(\partial\varphi/\partial v_k)^{-1} > (\partial\varphi/\partial v_k)^+$, any value between $(\partial\varphi/\partial v_k)^-$ and $(\partial\varphi/\partial v_k)^+$ may be defined as the opportunity cost. Therefore, the imputed price $\bar{w}_k$ should lie between these two derivatives:

$$(\partial\varphi/\partial v_k)^- \geqq \bar{w}_k \geqq (\partial\varphi/\partial v_k)^+, \qquad k = 1, \ldots, r. \tag{24}$$

Since $(\partial\varphi/\partial v_k)^-$ and $(\partial\varphi/\partial v_k)^+$ have the same value, $(\partial\varphi/\partial v_k)$, almost everywhere,[7] the imputed price $\bar{w}_k$ should be uniquely determined almost everywhere and be equal to $(\partial\varphi/\partial v_k)$ wherever it exists.[8]

Thus, given a market price system p, an imputed price system $\bar{w}$ is determined uniquely (up to a certain range). This unique determination holds regardless of whether the activities used are independent or not. The dependency of the imputed price system $\bar{w}$ upon p, however, is relative to the

[6] Cf. Fenchel [2], pp. 103–104.

[7] Cf. Samuelson [13] and Uzawa [14].

[8] The equations (7) combined with (8) determine r unknowns $\bar{w}_k$ and m unknowns $\bar{y}_j$. Since the number of equations $m + r$ is equal to the number of unknowns, the unique determination of $\bar{w}_k$ is not an exceptional case.

factor endowment v. Therefore we must write

$$\bar{w} = \pi(p, v),$$

where the function π is determined solely by the technology of the system, i.e., by f and g.

The functional dependency of factor prices on commodity prices and factor endowment will be more clearly understood when we consider a simple example: the two-commodity, two-factor model with Cobb-Douglas production functions.

Let two commodities, 1 and 2, be produced by two factors of production: labor, L, and capital, C, with the Cobb-Douglas production functions:

$$y_1 = v_{1L}^{\alpha} v_{1C}^{1-\alpha},$$
$$y_2 = v_{2L}^{\beta} v_{2C}^{1-\beta},$$

where v_{iL}, v_{iC} denote the amounts used in industry i of labor and capital respectively.

Given prices of goods, p_1, p_2, and factor endowment, v_L, v_C, the problem is stated as follows:

To maximize the value of product

$$p_1 y_1 + p_2 y_2$$

subject to

$$y_1 = v_{1L}^{\alpha} v_{1C}^{1-\alpha},$$
$$y_2 = v_{2L}^{\beta} v_{2C}^{1-\beta},$$
$$v_{1L} + v_{2L} \leqq v_L,$$
$$v_{1C} + v_{2C} \leqq v_C,$$
$$v_{1L}, v_{2L}, v_{1C}, v_{2C} \geqq 0.$$

The optimum distribution of factors $(v_{1L}, v_{2L}; v_{1C}, v_{2C})$ and the prices of capital and labor, w_C, w_L, are determined as the solution to the following system of inequalities:

$$\alpha p_1 \left(\frac{v_{1C}}{v_{1L}}\right)^{1-\alpha} \leqq w_L, \qquad (1-\alpha) p_1 \left(\frac{v_{1C}}{v_{1L}}\right)^{-\alpha} \leqq w_C,$$

$$\beta p_2 \left(\frac{v_{2C}}{v_{2L}}\right)^{1-\beta} \leqq w_L, \qquad (1-\beta) p_2 \left(\frac{v_{2C}}{v_{2L}}\right)^{-\beta} \leqq w_C,$$

with the equality holding for positive $v_{1L}, v_{1C}, v_{2L}, v_{2C}$, respectively, and

$$v_{1L} + v_{2L} \leqq v_L,$$
$$v_{1C} + v_{2C} \leqq v_C,$$

with the equality holding for positive w_L, w_C, respectively.

Table 10.1. *Situation $\alpha < \beta$*

Relative Endowment of Capital	Relative Price of Labor	Optimum Capital-Labor Ratio	
$r = \dfrac{v_C}{v_L}$	$w = \dfrac{w_L}{w_C}$	Industry 1 $r_1 = v_{1C}/v_{1L}$	Industry 2 $r_2 = v_{2C}/v_{2L}$
$0 \leqq r \leqq Bp^{\frac{1}{\alpha-\beta}}$	$\dfrac{\beta}{1-\beta}r$	Completely specialized to Industry 2	r
$Bp^{\frac{1}{\alpha-\beta}} < r < Ap^{\frac{1}{\alpha-\beta}}$	$\dfrac{\beta}{1-\beta}Bp^{\frac{1}{\alpha-\beta}} = \dfrac{\alpha}{1-\alpha}Ap^{\frac{1}{\alpha-\beta}}$	$Ap^{\frac{1}{\alpha-\beta}}$	$Bp^{\frac{1}{\alpha-\beta}}$
$Ap^{\frac{1}{\alpha-\beta}} \leqq r$	$\dfrac{\alpha}{1-\alpha}r$	r	Completely specialized to Industry 1

Since the production functions are homogeneous, we may speak in terms of the commodity price ratio p, the relative price of labor in terms of capital w, and the optimum capital-labor ratios in the two industries, r_1 and r_2:

$$p = \frac{p_1}{p_2}, \qquad w = \frac{w_L}{w_C},$$

$$r_1 = \frac{v_{1C}}{v_{1L}}, \qquad r_2 = \frac{v_{2C}}{v_{2L}}.$$

The solution may be summarized as follows:

Let A and B be two positive numbers defined by

$$A = \left[\left(\frac{\alpha}{\beta}\right)^{\beta}\left(\frac{1-\alpha}{1-\beta}\right)^{1-\beta}\right]^{1/(\alpha-\beta)}, \quad B = \left[\left(\frac{\alpha}{\beta}\right)^{\alpha}\left(\frac{1-\alpha}{1-\beta}\right)^{1-\alpha}\right]^{1/(\alpha-\beta)}.$$

Since

$$\frac{\alpha}{1-\alpha}A = \frac{\beta}{1-\beta}B,$$

we have

$$A \gtreqless B \text{ if and only if } \alpha \lesseqgtr \beta.$$

First, we are concerned with the situation in which commodity 1 is more capital-intensive than commodity 2: $\alpha < \beta$. Then $A > B$, and the solution will be as shown in Table 10.1 and Figure 10.1.

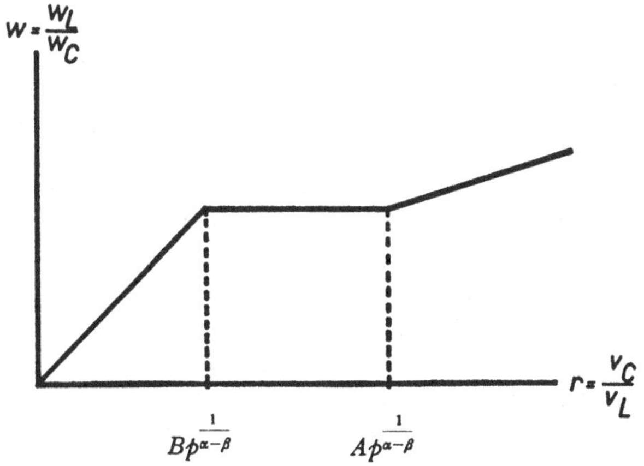

Figure 10.1 Situation $\alpha < \beta$ ($A > B$).

Table 10.2. *Situation* $\alpha = \beta$

Relative Price of Commodity 1	Relative Price of Labor	Optimum Capital-Labor Ratio	
		Industry 1	Industry 2
$p = \frac{p_1}{p_2}$	$w = \frac{w_L}{w_C}$	$r_1 = \frac{v_{1C}}{v_{1L}}$	$r_2 = \frac{v_{2C}}{v_{2L}}$
$0 < p < 1$	$\frac{\alpha}{1-\alpha} r$	Not Produced	r
$p = 1$		r	r
$p > 1$		r	Not Produced

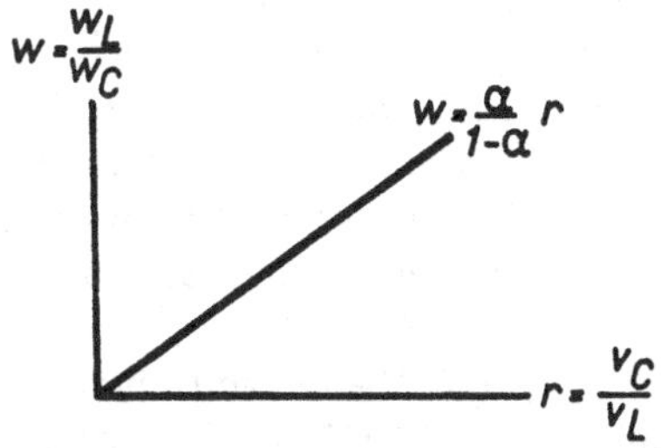

Figure 10.2 Situation $\alpha = \beta$ ($A = B$).

Next we consider the situation where both commodities have the same labor-intensities, $\alpha = \beta$. Then optimum production is either specialized to the industry with the higher price (if $p_1 \neq p_2$), or the factors of production are proportionally distributed to the two industries (if $p_1 = p_2$), as indicated by Table 10.2 and Figure 10.2.

In the event of Cobb-Douglas production functions, whatever the relative factor-intensities may be, the prices of labor and capital, w_L, w_C, are determined by the prices of the two commodities, p_1, p_2, and the factor endowment, v_L, v_C. If the factor intensities in both industries are distinct $(\alpha \neq \beta)$, the prices of the factors are determined independently of the factor endowments, when $r = (v_C/v_L)$ is between $A(p_1/p_2)^{-1/|\alpha-\beta|}$ and $B(p_1/p_2)^{-11/|\alpha-\beta|}$. Stated in another way, if the optimum production is not completely specialized to either industry, then prices of the factors of production are uniquely determined by the prices of the commodities, independently of the factor endowments.

These propositions are easily extended to the general n-commodity, r-factor model with Cobb-Douglas production functions and with a nonsingular matrix of factor intensities. Specifically, when the optimum production is not completely specialized, the unique determination of the prices of the factors of production is independent of the factor endowments.

The propositions we have established so far about the model with homogeneous production functions may now be summarized: The prices of the factors of production are uniquely (or at least up to a certain range) determined by the commodity price system p and the factor endowment v, without any regard for the independency of the factor-intensities of the various industries; changing the factor endowment will not leave the prices of the factors of production unchanged, unless the factor endowment is in an appropriate region.

4 A model of general equilibrium: many countries

We shall now investigate the interrelations among many countries, each of which is a competitive economy of the type discussed in Section 2. As is customary in the theory of international trade, we assume that each country consumes the same commodities and uses the same factors of production, that the factors of production are perfectly immobile, and that commodities are traded without any tariff or any cost of transport. The production functions as well as the utility functions are not assumed to be identical for all countries.

Consider N countries and let u^ν, (f^ν, g^ν), and v^ν be respectively the utility function, the technological possibilities, and the factor endowment of country $\nu, \nu = 1, \ldots, N$.

A set $(\bar{x}^1,\ldots,\bar{x}^N,\bar{y}^1,\ldots,\bar{y}^N,\bar{p},\bar{w}^1,\ldots,\bar{w}^N)$[9] will be in competitive equilibrium if, for $v=1,\ldots,N$,

Optimum consumption: for some $\lambda_v>0$,

$$\lambda_v\left(\frac{\partial u^v}{\partial x_i^v}\right)_{\bar{x}^v}\leqq \bar{p}_i, \qquad i=1,\ldots,n, \tag{25}$$

with the equality for i such that $\bar{x}_i^v>0$.

Optimum production:

$$\sum_i \bar{p}_i\left(\frac{\partial f_i^v}{\partial y_j^v}\right)_{\bar{y}^v}\leqq \sum_k \bar{w}_k^v\left(\frac{\partial g_k^v}{\partial y_j^v}\right)_{\bar{y}^v}, \qquad j=1,\ldots,m, \tag{26}$$

with the equality for j such that $\bar{y}_j^v>0$.

Factor limitation:

$$g_k^v(\bar{y}^v)\leqq v_k^v, \qquad k=1,\ldots,-, \tag{27}$$

with the equality for k such that $\bar{w}_k^v>0$.

No excess demand:

$$\sum_v \bar{x}_i^v\leqq \sum_v f_i^v(\bar{y}^v), \quad i=1,\ldots,n, \tag{28}$$

with the equality for i such that $\bar{p}_i>0$.

Balance of payment:

$$\bar{p}\cdot\bar{x}^v=\bar{p}\cdot f^v(\bar{y}^v), \qquad v=1,\ldots,N. \tag{29}$$

Conditions (25)–(28) are satisfied if and only if $(\bar{x}^v,\bar{y}^v;\bar{p},\bar{w})$ is a saddle-point of

$$\phi_\lambda(x^v,y^v;p,w^v)=\sum_v \lambda_v u^v(x^v)+p\cdot\sum_v[f^v(y^v)-x^v] + \sum_v w^v\cdot[v^v-g^v(y^v)]. \tag{30}$$

Therefore, we have

Theorem 2. For any equilibrium output $(\bar{x}^1,\ldots,\bar{x}^N)$, there exists a set of positive numbers $\lambda_1,\ldots,\lambda_N$ such that $(\bar{x}^1,\ldots,\bar{x}^N)$ is the solution to the following problem:

To find $(x^1,\ldots,x^N)$ that maximizes

$$\sum_v \lambda_v u^v(x^v) \tag{31}$$

[9] For the sake of simplicity, $(\bar{x}^1,\ldots,\bar{x}^N,\ \bar{y}^1,\ldots,\bar{y}^N;\ \bar{p},\ w^1,\ldots,\bar{w}^N)$ will be written as $(\bar{x}^v,\bar{y}^v;\bar{p},\bar{w}^v)$ without causing any ambiguity.

subject to the restrictions

$$x^\nu \geqq 0, \qquad y^\nu \geqq 0, \tag{32}$$

$$\sum_\nu x^\nu \leqq \sum_\nu f^\nu(y^\nu), \tag{33}$$

$$g^\nu(y^\nu) \leqq v^\nu, \qquad \nu = 1, \ldots, N. \tag{34}$$

The weighted sum $\sum \lambda_\nu u^\nu(x^\nu)$ may be considered as a world utility index. Maximizing this world utility index, an equilibrium may be obtained. λ_ν is the inverse of the marginal utility of national income of country ν and will be referred to as the *weight* of country ν, $\nu = 1, \ldots, N$.

Since the $u^\nu(x^\nu)$ are strictly concave, the solution $(\bar{x}^1, \ldots, \bar{x}^N)$ to the above problem is uniquely determined. It will be noticed also that any saddle-point $(\tilde{x}^\nu, \tilde{y}^\nu; \tilde{p}, \tilde{w}^\nu)$ of ϕ_λ is in equilibrium. For this purpose we have only to prove that the balance of payment condition (29) holds.

From $\tilde{x}^\nu = \bar{x}^\nu$, $\nu = 1, \ldots, N$, and condition (25), $\tilde{p}_i = \bar{p}_i$ for i such that

$$\sum_\nu \bar{x}_i^\nu > 0.$$

Hence

$$\tilde{p} \cdot \bar{x}^\nu = \sum \tilde{p}_i \bar{x}_i^\nu = \sum \bar{p}_i \bar{x}_i^\nu = \bar{p} \cdot \bar{x}^\nu. \tag{35}$$

Similarly,

$$\tilde{p} \cdot f^\nu(\bar{y}^\nu) = \bar{p} \cdot f^\nu(\bar{y}^\nu). \tag{36}$$

On the other hand, $(\bar{x}^\nu, \bar{y}^\nu; \tilde{p}, \tilde{w}^\nu)$ is also a saddle-point of ϕ_λ, so that

$$\tilde{p} \cdot f^\nu(\bar{y}^\nu) = \tilde{w}^\nu \cdot g^\nu(\bar{y}^\nu) = \tilde{w}^\nu \cdot v^\nu. \tag{37}$$

Therefore, by (35), (36), and (37),

$$\tilde{p} \cdot \tilde{x}^\nu = \bar{p} \cdot \bar{x}^\nu = \bar{p} \cdot f^\nu(\bar{y}^\nu) = \tilde{p} \cdot f^\nu(\bar{y}^\nu) = \tilde{w}^\nu \cdot v^\nu = \tilde{w}^\nu \cdot g^\nu(\tilde{y}^\nu) = \tilde{p} \cdot f^\nu(\tilde{y}^\nu).$$

■

For the N-country model of international trade, we shall investigate whether the prices of the factors of production in the N countries are equalized or not. In order to deal with this problem, it is most convenient to compare the model with the one in which factors of production, in addition to commodities, are internationally traded. We shall therefore consider the latter case first.

An equilibrium for this model will be described by a set of nonnegative vectors $(\bar{\bar{x}}^\nu \bar{\bar{y}}^\nu; \bar{\bar{p}}, \bar{\bar{w}})$ such that

Optimum consumption: for some $\bar{\bar{\lambda}}^\nu > 0$,

$$\bar{\bar{\lambda}}^\nu \left(\frac{\partial u^\nu}{\partial x_i^\nu} \right)_{\bar{\bar{x}}^\nu} \leqq \bar{\bar{p}}_i, \qquad i = 1, \ldots, n, \tag{38}$$

with the equality for i such that $\bar{\bar{x}}_i^\nu > 0$;

Optimum production:

$$\sum_i \bar{p}_i \left(\frac{\partial f_i^\nu}{\partial y_i^\nu}\right)_{\bar{y}^\nu} \leqq \sum_k \bar{w}_k \left(\frac{\partial g_k^\nu}{\partial y_j^\nu}\right)_{\bar{y}^\nu}, \qquad j = 1, \ldots, m, \tag{39}$$

with the equality for j such that $\bar{y}_j^\nu > 0$;

Non-excess demand:

$$\sum_\nu \bar{x}_i^\nu \leqq \sum_\nu f_i^\nu(\bar{y}^\nu), \qquad i = 1, \ldots, n, \tag{40}$$

with the equality for i such that $\bar{p}_i > 0$,

Factor limitation in the world:

$$\sum g_k^\nu(\bar{y}^\nu) \leqq \sum_l v_k^\nu, \qquad k = 1, \ldots, r, \tag{41}$$

with the equality for k such that $\bar{w}_k > 0$; and

Balance of payment:

$$\bar{p}\cdot\bar{x}^\nu = \bar{p}\cdot f^\nu(\bar{y}^\nu), \qquad \nu = 1, \ldots, N. \tag{42}$$

Again by the Kuhn-Tucker Theorem, conditions (38)–(41) are satisfied if and only if $(\bar{x}^\nu, \bar{y}^\nu; \bar{p}, \bar{w})$ is a saddle-point of

$$\phi_{\bar{\lambda}}^*(x^\nu, y^\nu; p, w) = \sum_\nu \bar{\lambda}_\nu u^\nu(x^\nu) + p\cdot\sum_\nu [f^\nu(y^\nu) - x^\nu] + w\cdot\sum_\nu [v^\nu - g^\nu(y^\nu)].$$

Therefore, if $(\bar{x}^1, \ldots, \bar{x}^N)$ is in equilibrium, then there exists a set of positive numbers $(\bar{\bar{\lambda}}_1, \ldots, \bar{\bar{\lambda}}_N)$ such that $(\bar{x}^1, \ldots, \bar{x}^N)$ maximizes

$$\sum_\nu \bar{\bar{\lambda}}_\nu u^\nu(x^\nu) \tag{43}$$

subject to the restrictions

$$x^\nu \geqq 0, y^\nu \geqq 0 \qquad (\nu = 1, \ldots, N), \tag{44}$$

$$\sum_\nu x^\nu \leqq \sum_\nu f^\nu(y^\nu), \tag{45}$$

$$\sum_\nu g^\nu(y^\nu) \leqq \sum_\nu v^\nu. \tag{46}$$

5 Welfare criteria for factor price equalization

In Section 4, we have seen that an equilibrium for the N-country model, where commodities are freely traded, is an optimal position with respect to the world utility index $u(x) = \sum_{\nu=1}^N \lambda_\nu u^\nu(x^\nu)$, the weights λ_ν being positive numbers. In terms of the world utility function $u(x)$, which by Theorem 2 is defined relatively to an equilibrium output $(\bar{x}^1, \ldots, \bar{x}^N)$, we shall investigate in this section the problem of whether international trade equalizes prices of the productive factors.

Let us consider levels of world utility $\sum_\nu \lambda_\nu u^\nu(x^\nu)$ corresponding to the various cases of international trade. The first case, case I, is one in which neither commodities nor factors of production are internationally traded, and the level of world utility attained here will be denoted by u. u is obtained by summing up, with weights λ_ν, the level of each country's utility at an equilibrium level of consumption. In view of Theorem 1, u is equal to the maximum of $\sum_\nu \lambda_\nu u^\nu(x^\nu)$ subject to the restrictions:

$$\begin{aligned} &x^\nu \leqq f^\nu(y^\nu), \\ &g(y^\nu) \leqq v^\nu, \\ &x^\nu \geqq 0, y^\nu \geqq 0, \qquad \nu = 1,\ldots,N. \end{aligned} \tag{I}$$

In other words, u is the value, at a saddle-point, of

$$\begin{aligned} \phi^{\mathrm{I}}(x^\nu, y^\nu; p^\nu, w^\nu) = \sum_\nu \lambda_\nu u^\nu(x^\nu) + \sum_\nu p^\nu \cdot [f^\nu(y^\nu) - x] \\ + \sum_\nu w^\nu \cdot [v^\nu - g^\nu(y^\nu)]. \end{aligned} \tag{47}$$

The p^ν- and w^ν-components of a saddle-point of $\phi(x^\nu, y^\nu; p^\nu, w^\nu)$ are equilibrium prices of commodities and factors of production in country ν, $\nu = 1,\ldots,N$. Equilibrium prices of commodities as well as of factors of production are not necessarily equal among the N countries.

Case II arises when only commodities are freely traded and factors of production are immobile. The level of world utility, which will be denoted by $\bar{u}$, is then equal to the maximum of $\sum_\nu \lambda_\nu u^\nu(x^\nu)$ subject to the restrictions:

$$\begin{cases} \sum_\nu x^\nu \leqq \sum_\nu f^\nu(y^\nu), \\ g^\nu(y^\nu) \leqq v^\nu, \\ x^\nu \geqq 0, y^\nu \geqq 0, \qquad \nu = 1,\ldots,N. \end{cases} \tag{II}$$

u is also the value at a saddle-point of

$$\begin{aligned} \phi^{\mathrm{II}}(x^\nu, y^\nu; p, w^\nu) = \sum_\nu \lambda_\nu u^\nu(x^\nu) + p \cdot \sum_\nu [f^\nu(y^\nu) - x^\nu] \\ + \sum_\nu w^\nu \cdot [v^\nu - g^\nu(y^\nu)]. \end{aligned} \tag{48}$$

By definition of the weight $\lambda_1,\ldots,\lambda_N$ and by Theorem 2, any saddle-point $(\bar{x}^\nu, \bar{y}^\nu; \bar{p}, \bar{w}^\nu)$ of ϕ^{II} is in equilibrium for this case since the balance of payment condition, $\bar{p}^\nu \cdot \bar{x}^\nu = \bar{p}^\nu \cdot f^\nu(\bar{y}^\nu)$, is satisfied for each country, $\nu = 1,\ldots,N$.

In all countries, the same equilibrium commodity prices prevail, while equilibrium prices of the factors of production do not generally coincide.

As case III, we assume there are no barriers to the international movement either of factors of production or of commodities. The level of world utility is denoted by $\bar{\bar{u}}$, which is equal to the maximum of $\sum_\nu \lambda_\nu u^\nu(x^\nu)$ subject to the restrictions:

$$\begin{cases} \sum_\nu x^\nu \leqq \sum_\nu f^\nu(y^\nu), \\ \sum_\nu g^\nu(y^\nu) \leqq v, \\ x^\nu \geqq 0, y^\nu \geqq 0, \qquad \nu = 1, \ldots, N, \end{cases} \tag{III}$$

where $v = \sum_\nu v^\nu$.

Let $(\bar{\bar{x}}^\nu, \bar{\bar{y}}^\nu; \bar{\bar{p}}, \bar{\bar{w}})$ be a saddle-point of

$$\phi^{\text{III}}(x^\nu, y^\nu; p, w) = \sum \lambda_\nu u^\nu(x^\nu) + p \cdot \sum_\nu [f^\nu(y^\nu) - x^\nu] + w \cdot \left[v - \sum_\nu g^\nu(y^\nu) \right]. \tag{49}$$

Then

$$\bar{\bar{u}} = \phi^{\text{III}}(\bar{\bar{x}}^\nu, \bar{\bar{y}}^\nu; \bar{\bar{p}}, \bar{\bar{w}}) = \sum_\nu \lambda_\nu u^\nu(\bar{\bar{x}}^\nu).$$

Equilibrium factor prices, $\bar{\bar{w}}$, as well as equilibrium commodity prices, $\bar{\bar{p}}$, are the same among the N countries.

It is evident that the levels of world utility for these three cases of international trade are ordered by

$$u \leqq \bar{u} \leqq \bar{\bar{u}}. \tag{50}$$

The relationships of the equilibrium prices of commodities and productive factors for cases I–III, with the increase of the level of world utility, will now be formulated in Theorems 3 and 4.

> **Theorem 3.** The level of world utility remains the same from case I (no international trade) to case II (international trade in commodities) if and only if equilibrium commodity prices in case I are the same among all countries; i.e., $p^1 = \cdots = p^N$ if and only if $u = \bar{u}$, where $p^1, \ldots, p^N$ are the equilibrium commodity prices in case I.

Similarly,

> **Theorem 4.** The level of world utility remains the same from case II (international trade in commodities) to case III (international trade in all commodities and free distribution of factors of production) if and only if equilibrium factor prices in case II are the same among all countries; i.e., $\bar{w}^1 = \cdots = \bar{w}^N$ if and only if $\bar{u} = \bar{\bar{u}}$, where $\bar{w}^1, \ldots, \bar{w}^N$ are the equilibrium factor prices in case II.

Since Theorems 3 and 4 are proved similarly, we shall give only the proof of Theorem 4.

Proof of Theorem 4: First it will be shown that $\bar{u} = \bar{\bar{u}}$ implies $\bar{w}^1 = \cdots = \bar{w}^N$.

Let $(\bar{x}^\nu, \bar{y}^\nu; \bar{p}, \bar{w})$ be a saddle-point of ϕ^{III}. By

$$\sum_\nu \lambda_\nu u^\nu(\bar{x}^\nu) = \sum_\nu \lambda_\nu u^\nu(\bar{\bar{x}}^\nu),$$

we have

$$\varphi^{\mathrm{III}}(x^\nu, y^\nu; \bar{p}, w) \leqq \sum \lambda_\nu u^\nu(\bar{x}^\nu) = \sum \lambda_\nu u^\nu(\bar{x}).$$

Since

$$v^\nu - g^\nu(\bar{y}^\nu) \geqq 0.$$

we have

$$\bar{p}\cdot\sum_\nu [f^\nu(\bar{y}^\nu) - \bar{x}^\nu] = 0,$$

$$\bar{w}\cdot[v^\nu - g^\nu(\bar{y}^\nu)] = 0.$$

Therefore, $(\bar{x}^\nu, \bar{y}^\nu; \bar{p}, \bar{w})$ is a saddle-point of ϕ^{II}. Then $w^\nu = \bar{w}$, $\nu = 1, \ldots, N$ will be the imputed prices of the factors of production.

On the other hand, let us assume $\bar{w}^1 = \cdots = \bar{w}^N = \bar{w}$. Then

$$\varphi^{\mathrm{III}}(x^\nu, y^\nu; \bar{p}, \bar{w}) = \sum_\nu \lambda_\nu u^\nu(x^\nu) + \bar{p}\cdot\sum_\nu [f^\nu(y^\nu) - x^\nu] + \bar{w}\cdot\sum_\nu [v^\nu - g^\nu(y^\nu)]$$

$$\leqq \sum_\nu \lambda_\nu u^\nu(\bar{x}^\nu) = \bar{u}.$$

Putting $x^\nu = \bar{x}^\nu, y^\nu = \bar{y}^\nu$, we have

$$\bar{\bar{u}} \leqq \varphi^{\mathrm{III}}(\bar{x}^\nu, \bar{y}^\nu; \bar{p}, \bar{w}) \leqq \bar{u},$$

while $\bar{\bar{u}} \geqq \bar{u}$ is trivial. ∎

Theorem 4 may be restated more conveniently as follows:

Prices of the factors of production are equalized by international trade in commodities if and only if an equilibrium consumption for this case, $(\bar{x}^1, \ldots, \bar{x}^N)$, is also an equilibrium consumption for the case where the factors of production as well as the commodities are freely traded among countries.

In view of this proposition, factor price equalization in international trade will occur only if the distribution of the factors of production among countries is appropriate so that it coincides with the equilibrium distribution of the factors of production for case III. The concept, "equilibrium distribution" of the factors of production, may be rigorously formulated as follows:

Let the world factor endowment be v. Then the set of *equilibrium distributions* of v among the countries is defined by

$$K_0(v) = \{(v^1, \ldots, v^N) | v^\nu \geqq g^\nu(\bar{y}^\nu), \sum_\nu v^\nu = v, \nu = 1, \ldots, N,$$
$$\text{for some } (\bar{\bar{x}}^\nu, \bar{\bar{y}}^\nu; \bar{\bar{p}}, \bar{\bar{w}}) \text{ satisfying (44)–(46)}\}.$$

By this definition, we have

Theorem 5. Prices of the factors of production are equalized by international trade if and only if the distribution of the factor endowment among countries, $(v^1, \ldots, v^N)$, is an equilibrium distribution of the world factor endowment:

$$(v^1, \ldots, v^N) \in K_0(v),$$

where

$$v = v^1 + \cdots + v^N.$$

If we suppose the set $K_0(v)$ of equilibrium distributions for world factor endowment v consists of only one distribution $(v_0^1, \ldots, v_0^N)$ and all factors of production are imputed positive prices, then prices of the factors of production are equalized by international trade if and only if the distribution of the factor endowments of the countries is exactly $(v_0^1, \ldots, v_0^N)$. The set $K_0(v)$, however, in general consists of two or more distributions. As a simple example, we shall consider a two-commodity, two-factor, two-country model where both countries have the same Cobb-Douglas production functions and the same exponential utility function.

Let the production functions be

$$y_1 = v_{1L}^\alpha v_{1C}^{1-\alpha}, \qquad y_2 = v_{2L}^\beta v_{2C}^{1-\beta}, \qquad 0 < \alpha < \beta < 1,$$

and the utility function

$$u(x_1, x_2) = x_1^\gamma x_2^{1-\gamma}, \qquad 0 < \gamma < 1.$$

We use the same notation as in Section 3, while v_L and v_C stand for the world endowment of labor and capital, respectively, and $v = v_C/v_L$.

Then the optimum capital-labor ratio in industry i in case III becomes

$$r_i = \rho_i r, \qquad i = 1, 2,$$

where

$$\rho_1 = \frac{(1-\gamma)A^{1-\alpha} + \gamma B^{1-\beta}}{(1-\gamma)A^{1-\alpha}B + \gamma B^{1-\beta}A} A,$$

$$\rho_2 = \frac{(1-\gamma)A^{1-\alpha} + \gamma B^{1-\beta}}{(1-\gamma)A^{1-\alpha}B + \gamma B^{1-\beta}A} B.$$

A distribution $(v^{(1)}, v^{(2)})$ belongs to the set $K_0(v)$ if and only if

$$v^{(1)} + v^{(2)} = v, \tag{51}$$

$$\rho_2 r < r^{(i)} = v_C^{(i)}/v_L^{(i)} < \rho_1 r, \qquad i = 1, 2. \tag{52}$$

In other words, the Samuelson assumptions are satisfied in this special case if and only if the distribution of the factor endowments, $(v^{(1)}, v^{(2)})$, is the one for which the conditions (51) and (52) are satisfied. It may be noted that in this case the volumes of trade are in small quantities in both commodities; namely, the complete equalization of prices of the factors of production occurs only if neither of both countries has great comparative advantages in any commodity.

6 Partial equalization (linear excess demand)

In this section we shall prove the Ohlin theorem on the partial equalization of prices of the factors of production if each country has the same (definite) demand-and-supply schedule for any given commodity and the same factor prices.

The excess demand function of a country describes the relation between the amount of the excess demand and prices of commodities and factors of production. Let a commodity, say the nth, be taken as the numéraire, its price being fixed at 1. We assume that each country has the same excess demand function $x(p, w) = (x_1(p, w), \ldots, x_{n-1}(p, w))$ which is linear with respect to the normalized price system $(p, w) = (p_1, \ldots, p_{n-1}, w_1, \ldots, w_r)$:

$$x(p, w) = \begin{pmatrix} A & B \\ C & D \end{pmatrix} \begin{pmatrix} p \\ w \end{pmatrix} - \begin{pmatrix} b \\ a \end{pmatrix}.$$

We shall assume that the excess demand for a commodity (or for a factor of production) decreases if the price of the commodity (or of the factor of production) rises, and that the effects of changes in the price of a commodity or a factor of production upon other commodities are small; more precisely, it will be assumed that $a_{ii} = \partial x_i/\partial p_i$ and $d_{kk} = \partial x_k/\partial w_k$ are negative and in absolute value relatively large with respect to other $a_{ij} = \partial x_i/\partial p_j$, $b_{ik} = \partial x_i/\partial w_k$, $c_{kj} = \partial x_k/\partial p_j$, $d_{kl} = \partial x_k/\partial w_l$, where i, j refer to commodities, and k, l to factors of production, so that A, D, and $(I - D^{-1}A^{-1}B)$ are nonsingular and all characteristic roots of $(I - D^{-1}CA^{-1}B)$ $(I - D^{-1}CA^{-1}B)'$ are less than 1 in absolute value.

We may further suppose, without loss of generality, that $a = 0$.

Let us assume that (p^ν, w^ν), $\nu = 1, \ldots, N$, are price systems before the advent of international trade. These price systems are determined as the solutions to the following equations:

$$\begin{pmatrix} A & B \\ C & D \end{pmatrix}\begin{pmatrix} p^\nu \\ w^\nu \end{pmatrix} = \begin{pmatrix} b \\ v^\nu \end{pmatrix}, \qquad \nu = 1,\ldots,N,$$

where v^ν denotes the vector of the factor endowment for country ν. This gives

$$Ap^\nu + Bw^\nu = b \tag{53}$$

and

$$Cp^\nu + Dw^\nu = v^\nu. \tag{54}$$

From (53) and (54), we have

$$p^\nu = A^{-1}(b - Bw^\nu), \tag{55}$$

and

$$w^\nu = (D - CA^{-1}B)^{-1}(v^\nu - CA^{-1}b). \tag{56}$$

Given international trade, prices $(\bar{p}, \bar{w}^1),\ldots,(\bar{p}, \bar{w}^N)$ are determined by the following equation:

$$\begin{pmatrix} A & \frac{1}{N}B & \cdots & \frac{1}{N}B \\ C & D & \cdots & 0 \\ \vdots & \vdots & & \vdots \\ C & 0 & \cdots & D \end{pmatrix}\begin{pmatrix} \bar{p} \\ \bar{w}^1 \\ \vdots \\ \bar{w}^N \end{pmatrix} = \begin{pmatrix} b \\ v^1 \\ \vdots \\ v^N \end{pmatrix}$$

which may be written as

$$A\bar{p} + B\bar{w} = b, \tag{57}$$

and

$$C\bar{p} + D\bar{w}^\nu = v^\nu, \tag{58}$$

where $\bar{w} = (\bar{w}^1 + \cdots + \bar{w}^N)/N$.

From (57),

$$\bar{p} = A^{-1}(b - B\bar{w}). \tag{59}$$

Substituting (59) for (58),

$$CA^{-1}b - CA^{-1}B\bar{w} + D\bar{w}^\nu = v^\nu. \tag{60}$$

Summing over $\nu = 1,\ldots,N$ and dividing by N,

$$(D - CA^{-1}B)\bar{w} = \bar{v} - CA^{-1}b, \tag{61}$$

where $\bar{v} = (v^1 + \cdots + v^N)/N$.

From (61), we have

$$\bar{w} = (D - CA^{-1}B)^{-1}(\bar{v} - CA^{-1}b). \tag{62}$$

Substituting (62) for (60) and rearranging, we get

$$\bar{w}^{\nu} = D^{-1}(v^{\nu} - CA^{-1}b + CA^{-1}B\bar{w}) = D^{-1}(v^{\nu} - CA^{-1}b) + D^{-1}CA^{-1}B(D - CA^{-1}B)^{-1}(\bar{v} - CA^{-1}b). \tag{63}$$

Therefore,

$$\bar{w}^{\nu} - \bar{w}^{\mu} = D^{-1}(v^{\nu} - v^{\mu}).$$

Hence,

$$(\bar{w}^{\nu} - \bar{w}^{\mu})^2 = (v^{\nu} - v^{\mu})D'^{-1}D^{-1}(v^{\nu} - v^{\mu}). \tag{64}$$

Now, by (56),

$$w^{\nu} - w^{\mu} = (I - D^{-1}CA^{-1}B)^{-1}D^{-1}(v^{\nu} - v^{\mu}).$$

Therefore,

$$(w^{\nu} - w^{\mu})^2 = (v^{\nu} - v^{\mu})D'^{-1}(I - D^{-1}CA^{-1}B)'^{-1} \times (I - D^{-1}CA^{-1}B)^{-1}D^{-1}(v^{\nu} - v^{\mu}). \tag{65}$$

By assumption, the characteristic roots of $(I - D^{-1}CA^{-1}B)$ are less than 1 in absolute value, so that (64) and (65) imply

$$(\bar{w}^{\nu} - \bar{w}^{\mu})^2 \leqq (w^{\nu} - w^{\mu})^2, \tag{66}$$

with strict inequality for $w^{\nu} \neq w^{\mu}$.

Equation (66) shows that a partial equalization of factor prices $(\bar{w}^1, \ldots, \bar{w}^N)$ is the effect of international trade.

By (64) and the nonsingularity of D, we also have the conclusion that $\bar{w}^1 = \cdots = \bar{w}^N$ if and only if $v^1 = \cdots = v^N$.

That is, complete factor price equalization will occur if and only if the initial factor endowment in all countries is the same.

References

[1] Arrow, K. J., and G. Debreu: "Existence of an Equilibrium for a Competitive Economy," *Econometrica*, vol. 22 (1954), pp. 265–90.

[2] Fenchel, W.: *Convex Cones, Sets, and Functions*. Princeton University, 1953 (hectographed).

[3] Haberler, G.: *A Survey of International Trade Theory*, Special Papers in International Economics No. 1, Princeton University, 1955.

[4] Hekscher, E., "The Effect of Foreign Trade on the Distribution of Income," *Ekonomist Tidskrift*, vol. 21 (1919), pp. 497–512. (Reprinted in *Readings in the Theory of International Trade*, 1950, pp. 272–300.)

[5] Koopmans, T. C.: "Analysis of Production as an Efficient Combination of Activities," *Activity Analysis of Production and Allocation*, ed. by T. C. Koopmans, 1951, pp. 33–97.
[6] Kuhn, H. W., and A. W. Tucker: "Nonlinear Programming," *Proceedings of the Second Berkeley Symposium on Mathematical Statistics and Probability*, ed. by J. Neyman, 1951, pp. 481–92.
[7] Lerner, A. P.: "Factor Prices and International Trade," *Economica*, Vol. XIX (N.S.), 1952, pp. 1–15.
[8] McKenzie, L. W.: "Equality of Factor Prices in World Trade," *Econometrica*, vol. 23 (1955), pp. 239–87.
[9] Ohlin, B.: *Interregional and International Trade*. Cambridge: Harvard University Press, 1952, 617 pp.
[10] Samuelson, P. A.: "Frank Knight's Theorem in Linear Programming," *Zeitschrift für Nationalökonomie*, Vol. XVIII (1958), pp. 310–17.
[11] Samuelson, P. A.: "International Trade and the Equalization of Factor Prices," *Economic Journal*, Vol. LVIII (1948), pp. 163–84.
[12] Samuelson, P. A.: "International Factor-price Equalization Once Again," *Economic Journal*, Vol. LIX (1949), pp. 181–97.
[13] Samuelson, P. A.: "Prices of Factors and Goods in General Equilibrium," *Review of Economic Studies*, Vol. 21 (1953–54), pp. 1–20.
[14] Uzawa, H.: "A Note on the Menger-Wieser Theory of Imputation," *Zeitschrift für Nationalökonomie*, Vol. XVIII (1958), pp. 318–34.

PART IV

Equilibrium and stability

CHAPTER 11

Walras's Existence Theorem and Brouwer's Fixed-Point Theorem

1 Introduction

The purpose of this note is to show the equivalence of two fundamental theorems – Walras's Existence Theorem on the one hand and Brouwer's Fixed-Point Theorem on the other.

Walras's theorem[1] is concerned with the existence of an equilibrium in the Walrasian system of general equilibrium and has been a problem of some importance in formal economic analysis since his work [12] appeared in 1874–7. It was, however, not until Wald's contributions, [10] and [11], that the existence problem was rigorously treated. Recent contributions, in particular those of Arrow and Debreu [2], McKenzie [6], Nikaidô [7], and Gale [4], have shown that Walras's theorem is essentially a necessary consequence of Brouwer's Fixed-Point Theorem. The latter theorem,[2] first proved by Brouwer [3] in 1911, also bears a fundamental importance in mathematics. It may be hence of some interest to see that Brouwer's theorem is in fact implied by Walras's theorem. It would indicate the reason that the general treatment of the existence problem in the Walrasian system had to wait for the development of the twentieth century mathematics.

2 Walras's Existence Theorem

According to Gale [4] and Nikaidô [7], Walras's theorem may be formulated as follows.

Let there be n commodities, labeled $1,\ldots,n$, $p=(p_1,\ldots,p_n)$ and $x=$

From *Economic Studies Quarterly*, Vol. 13 (1962), pp. 59–62; reprinted with permission.

I am indebted to Frank H. Hahn for discussions and for suggesting the writing of this note.

[1] The reader is referred to Schumpeter [8], Part IV, especially Chapter 7, for an appraisal of Walras's theory of general equilibrium.

[2] See, for example, Alexandroff and Hopf [1], pp. 376–8 and p. 480, and Lefschetz [5], p. 117.

$(x_1,\ldots,x_n)$ be a price vector and a commodity bundle, respectively. Price vectors are assumed to be nonzero and nonnegative; commodity bundles are arbitrary n-vectors. Let P and X be the sets of all price vectors and of all commodity bundles:

$$P = \{p = (p_1,\ldots,p_n): p_i \geq 0,\ i = 1,\ldots,n, \text{ but } p \neq 0\}$$
$$X = \{x = (x_1,\ldots,x_n)\}.$$

The excess demand function $x(p) = [x_1(p),\ldots,x_n(p)]$ is a mapping from P into X.

A price vector $\bar{p}$ is called an *equilibrium* if

$$x_i(\bar{p}) \leq 0, \qquad (i = 1,\ldots,n)$$

with equality unless $\bar{p}_i = 0$, $(i = 1,\ldots,n)$.

Walras's Existence Theorem. Let an excess demand function $x(p)$ satisfy the following conditions:
(A) $x(p)$ is a continuous mapping from P into X.
(B) $x(p)$ is homogeneous of order 0; i.e., $x(tp) = x(p)$, for all $t > 0$ and $p \in P$.
(C) Walras's law holds:

$$\sum_{i=1}^{n} p_i x_i(p) = 0, \quad \text{for all } p \in P.$$

Then there exists at least an equilibrium price vector $\bar{p}$ for $x(p)$.

3 Brouwer's Fixed-Point Theorem

Brouwer's theorem, on the other hand, is concerned with a continuous mapping on the simplex.

The fundamental $(n-1)$–simplex Π is the set of all nonnegative n-vectors whose component sums are one:

$$\Pi = \left\{\pi = (\pi_1,\ldots,\pi_n); \pi \geqq 0, \sum_{i=1}^{n} \pi_i = 1\right\}.$$

Brouwer's Fixed-Point Theorem. Let $\varphi(\pi)$ be a continuous mapping from Π into itself. Then there is at least a fixed-point $\bar{\pi}$ in Π:

$$\bar{\pi} = \varphi(\bar{\pi}).$$

4 Equivalence theorem

Equivalence theorem. Walras's Existence Theorem and Brouwer's Fixed-Point Theorem are equivalent.

Proof. It is well established[3] that Brouwer's theorem implies Walras's theorem of the form above. We shall therefore prove that Walras's theorem implies Brouwer's theorem.

Let $\varphi(\pi)$ be any continuous mapping from Π into itself. We construct an excess demand function $x(p) = [x_1(p), \ldots, x_n(p)]$ by

$$x_i(p) = \varphi_i\left(\frac{p}{\lambda(p)}\right) - p_i\mu(p), \qquad i = 1, \ldots, n, p \in P, \tag{1}$$

where

$$\lambda(p) = \sum_{i=1}^{n} p_i$$

$$\mu(p) = \frac{\sum_{i=1}^{n} p_i \varphi_i\left[\frac{p}{\lambda(p)}\right]}{\sum_{i=1}^{n} p_i^2}.$$

It may be noted that $\varphi_i(p/\lambda(p))$ and $p_i\mu(p)$ are both positively homogeneous of order 0.

It is evident that the excess demand function thus defined satisfies conditions (A), (B), and (C). Hence, applying Walras's theorem, there is an equilibrium $\bar{p}$. Then, by (1), we have

$$\varphi_i\left(\frac{\bar{p}}{\lambda(p)}\right) \leq \bar{p}_i\mu(\bar{p}), \qquad i = 1, \ldots, n \tag{2}$$

with equality unless $\bar{p}_i = 0$.

Letting

$$\bar{\pi} = \frac{\bar{p}}{\lambda(\bar{p})}, \qquad \beta = \lambda(\bar{p})\mu(\bar{p})$$

the relation (2) may be written

$$\varphi_i(\bar{\pi}) \leq \beta\bar{\pi}_i, \tag{3}$$

with equality unless $\bar{\pi}_i = 0$.

Summing (3) over $i = 1, \ldots, n$, and noticing that $\bar{\pi}, \varphi(\bar{\pi}) \in \Pi$, we have $\beta = 1$; hence,

$$\varphi_i(\bar{\pi}) \leq \bar{\pi}_i, \tag{4}$$

with equality unless $\bar{\pi}_i = 0$.

[3] See Nikaidô [7], Gale [4], and Uzawa [9], Appendix.

The relation (4), again together with $\bar{\pi}$, $\varphi(\bar{\pi}) \in \Pi$, implies that

$$\varphi_i(\bar{\pi}) = \bar{\pi}_i, \qquad i = 1, \ldots, n$$

i.e., $\bar{\pi}$ is a fixed-point for the mapping $\varphi(\bar{\pi})$. ■

References

[1] Alexandroff, P. and H. Hopf, *Topologie*, I, Berlin: Springer, 1935.
[2] Arrow, K. J. and G. Debreu, "Existence of an Equilibrium for a Competitive Economy," *Econometrica*, Vol. 22 (1945), pp. 256–90.
[3] Brouwer, L. E. J., "Über Abbildung von Mannigfaltigkeiten," *Mathematische Annalen*, Vol. 71 (1911–12), pp. 97–115.
[4] Gale, D., "The Law of Supply and Demand," *Mathematica Scandinavica*, Vol. 3 (1955), pp. 155–69.
[5] Lefschetz, S., *Introduction to Topology*, Princeton: Princeton University Press (1949).
[6] McKenzie, L. W., "On Equilibrium in Graham's Model of World Trade and Other Competitive Systems," *Econometrica*, Vol. 22 (1954), pp. 146–61.
[7] Nikaidô, H., "On the Classical Multilateral Exchange Problem," *Metroeconomica*, Vol. 8 (1956), pp. 135–45.
[8] Schumpeter, J. A., *History of Economic Analysis*, New York: Oxford University Press (1945).
[9] Uzawa, H., "Walras's Tâtonnement in the Theory of Exchange," *Review of Economic Studies*, Vol. 27 (1960), pp. 182–94.
[10] Wald, A., "Über die eindeutige positive Lösbarkeit der neuen Produktionsgleichungen," *Ergebnissen eines mathematischen Kolloquiums*, Vol. 6 (1933–4), pp. 12–20.
[11] Wald, A., "Über die Produktionsgleichungen der ökonomischen Wertlehre," *Ergebnisse eines mathematischen Kolloquiums*, Vol. 7 (1934–5), pp. 1–6.
[12] Walras, L., *Elements of Pure Economics*, translated by W. Jaffé, Homewood: Richard D. Irwin (1954).

CHAPTER 12

On the stability of Edgeworth's barter process

1 Introduction

In his discussion on the Marshallian theory of barter,[1] Edgeworth had a precise formulation of barter process for the simple two-good economy.[2] The process of barter dealt with by Marshall and Edgeworth consisted of successive bartering between individuals until the position was reached at which no barter was possible for each individual to become better off. Edgeworth graphically showed that the equilibrium reached by the process depended upon the path of bartering as well as the amount of goods initially held by each individual. The process of barter, therefore, constitutes a strong contrast to Walras's tâtonnement process.[3] Walras's process is a provisional market process by which competitive equilibria are attained, and the equilibrium reached by it is determined solely by the initial holdings, independently of the path of the process. (It is customary in economic literature to say that a market process is *determinate* if the equilibrium reached by that process is determined only by the initial holdings.[4]) However, the markets, of which the tâtonnement process represents the working of exchange, are restricted to those in which either

From *International Economic Review*, Vol. 3 (1962), pp. 218–32; reprinted with permission.

Professor H. Nikaidô of Osaka University pointed out various errors and ambiguities in earlier versions of the paper, particularly in connection with the proof of Theorem 2 below. I owe much to him for his valuable suggestions in writing the present version. I also acknowledge the benefit I have received from Kenneth Arrow, Frank Hahn, Leonid Hurwicz, Michio Morishima, and Takashi Negishi.

[1] Marshall devotes Book V, Chapter II, pp. 276–80, and Appendix F, pp. 652–54 [10], to the discussion of the theory of exchange based on barter.

[2] See Edgeworth [**6**, (316–19)]. Edgeworth's article was written in 1891 just after the second edition of Marshall's *Principles* was published. Mathematical Appendix, Note XII *bis*, pp. 695–96, in Marshall [10] deals with Edgeworth's formulation.

[3] See e.g., Walras [**12**, (37–44)].

[4] See e.g., Kaldor [9].

Edgeworth's *recontracting* is permitted or Walras's device of *bons* is introduced.[5]

In a recent work [8], Hurwicz has attempted to formulate the process of barter in a more general model, and various optimality criteria have been discussed. However, the problem of whether or not the process of barter thus formulated actually reaches (or asymptotically approaches) equilibrium states has not been handled.

The stability problem of adjustment processes in those markets in which transactions may take place during the process of adjustment has been handled by Hahn [7] and Negishi [11]. Hahn [7] has considered an adjustment process in which each individual has a positive excess demand whenever the aggregate demand exceeds the aggregate supply and has shown the stability of such a process under fairly general conditions. The barter process discussed by Negishi [11], on the other hand, does not necessarily belong to such a restricted class as the one discussed by Hahn [7], while the stability of the process has been proved under rather severe conditions such as the gross substitutability assumption.

In this paper we are concerned with precisely formulating Edgeworth's barter process in a more general model of exchange. Edgeworth's barter process consists of successive barters between individuals according to their preferences and budgetary restraints. At each stage of the barter process, each individual transacts whenever he becomes better off by trading; and, in the competitive case, the quantity of a commodity in exchange for the unit quantity of a standard commodity rises or falls according to whether or not the aggregate demand for that commodity exceeds the aggregate supply. In the present article, we show in particular that Edgeworth's barter process is always globally stable, provided the process has a positive solution starting with an arbitrary positive initial distribution.

2 Transaction rules

We consider a model of exchange in which S individuals, labeled $s = 1, \ldots, S$, exchange $n + 1$ commodities, labeled $i = 0, 1, \ldots, n$. Commodity bundles will be represented by vectors with $n + 1$ components, and superscripts to vectors will refer to individuals. We may without loss of generality assume that all commodity bundles are represented by nonnegative vectors.[6]

[5] See Edgeworth [**5**, (18–19)], [**6**, (311–12)], and Walras [**12**, (37)].

[6] The conventional notation is used. For any vectors $x = (x_1, \ldots, x_m)$, $y = (y_1, \ldots, y_m)$,

$$x \geqq y \text{ means } x_i \geqq y_i, \quad i = 1, \ldots, m;$$
$$x \geq y \text{ means } x \geqq y, \quad \text{but } x \neq y;$$
$$x > y \text{ means } x_i > y_i, \quad i = 1, \ldots, m;$$

and

$$xy = \sum_{i=1}^{m} x_i y_i.$$

Each individual has a preference relation over all conceivable commodity bundles (in the present case, over all nonnegative $(n+1)$-dimensional vectors). It is assumed that each individual's preference relation can be represented by a utility function, $u^s(x^s)$, satisfying the following conditions:

$u^s(x^s)$ is defined and differentiable for all nonnegative commodity bundles, $x^s = (x_0^s, x_1^s, \ldots, x_n^s)$. (1)

Marginal utilities, $u_i^s(x^s) = \partial u^s(x^s)/\partial x_i^s, i = 0, 1, \ldots, n$, are positive for all positive commodity bundles. (2)

$u^s(x^s)$ is strictly concave; i.e.,

$$u^s[(1-t)x^s + ty^s] > (1-t)u^s(x^s) + tu^s(y^s),$$

$$\text{for all } x^s \neq y^s, 0 < t < 1. \quad (3)$$

Let $y^s = (y_0^s, y_1^s, \ldots, y_n^s)$ be the commodity bundle initially held by individual s, and let $p = (p_0, p_1, \ldots, p_n)$ be a vector of exchange rates.[7] The optimum commodity bundle, $x^s = (x_0^s, x_1^s, \ldots, x_n^s)$, for individual s is, by conditions (1) and (3), uniquely determined by p and y^s. It will be denoted by $x^s = f^s(p, y^s)$. By condition (2), $x^s = f^s(p, y^s)$ is characterized by

$$px^s = py^s, x^s \geqq 0, \quad (4)$$

and

$$u^s(x^s) \geqq u^s(w^s) \text{ for all } w^s \text{ such that } pw^s \leqq py^s, w^s \geqq 0. \quad (5)$$

The function $f^s(p, y^s)$ is continuous at all (p, y^s) for which

$$py^s > 0, \qquad y^s \geqq 0.$$

In order to describe the path of bartering, we have to specify the rule by which the transaction between individuals takes place at each time. Such a rule will be referred to as the *transaction rule.*

Let y^s be the commodity bundle initially held by individual s, $s = 1, \ldots, S$, and p a price vector prevailing in the economy during this period of the transaction. We denote $Y = (y^1, \ldots, y^s)$ and call it the *initial distribution.* In general, an S-tuple of commodity bundles $W = (w^1, \ldots, w^s)$, of which the s-th commodity bundle w^s specifies the one obtained by individual s, will be referred to as a *distribution (matrix).* A *transaction rule* specifies the distribution matrix $Z = (z^1, \ldots, z^s)$, of which the s-th commodity bundle z^s represents the one held by individual s after the transaction takes place. Each commodity bundle z^s is a function of the price vector p and initial distribution $Y = (y^1, \ldots, y^s)$, and will be denoted by $z^s = g^s(p, Y)$, $s = 1, \ldots, S$. The transaction rule then will be denoted by $G = (g^1, \ldots, g^s)$.

[7] For any commodities i and j, p_i/p_j stands for the quantity of the jth commodity given in exchange for the unit quantity of the ith commodity.

Since the transaction rule $G = (g^1, \ldots, g^s)$ represents a barter, the total quantities of commodities in the economy as a whole remains constant (thus ruling out consumption during barter); i.e.,

(I) $\sum_{s=1}^{S} z^s = \sum_{s=1}^{S} y^s,$

and for each individual, the budget requirement should be satisfied; i.e.,

(II) $pz^s = py^s, \qquad s = 1, \ldots, S.$

An individual will not transact if his position, in terms of his preference relation, becomes worse off. We must have

(III) $u^s(z^s) \geqq u^s(y^s), \qquad s = 1, \ldots, S,$

with the transaction taking place only if at least one individual becomes better off, thus ruling out speculative transactions. Thus

(IV) $u^s(z^s) = u^s(y^s)$ for all s imply $(z^1, \ldots, z^S) = (y^1, \ldots, y^S)$.

Furthermore, if it is feasible for all individuals to obtain their optimum commodity bundles, then the transaction coincides with the optimum ones; i.e.,

(V) $\sum_{s=1}^{S} x^s = \sum_{s=1}^{S} y^s$ implies $(z^1, \ldots, z^S) = (x^1, \ldots, x^S)$.

Finally, we need the following mathematical conditions:

(VI) $z^s = g^s(p, Y)$ is continuous with respect to p and Y.

In order to see that the above hypotheses (I)–(VI) are consistent, we shall give a class of transaction rules for which (I)–(VI) are satisfied. Let all the utility functions $u^1, \ldots, u^S$ satisfy (1)–(3), and $c = (c_1, \ldots, c_S)$ be a positive vector. We define the social utility function, $U_c(W) = U_c(w^1, \ldots, w^S)$, by

$$U_c(W) = \sum_{s=1}^{S} c_s u^s(w^s).$$

For any price vector p and initial distribution, $Y = (y^1, \ldots, y^S)$, consider the following maximization problem:

Maximize $U_c(W)$ subject to the restrictions that

$$\sum_{s=1}^{S} w^s = \sum_{s=1}^{S} y^s, \tag{6}$$

$$pw^s \leqq py^s, w^s \geqq 0, \qquad s = 1, \ldots, S, \tag{7}$$

and

$$u^s(w^s) \geqq u^s(y^s), \qquad s = 1, \ldots, S. \tag{8}$$

Since the set of all W satisfying restrictions (6)–(8) is a nonempty compact convex set and the maximand $U_c(W)$ is strictly concave, the distribution $Z = (z^1, \ldots, z^S)$ which maximizes $U_c(W)$ subject to the above restrictions always exists and is uniquely determined. Let $Z = (z^1, \ldots, z^S)$ be denoted by $G_c(p, Y) = (g_c^1(p, Y), \ldots, g_c^S(p, Y))$. As is easily shown, the transaction rule G_c satisfies all conditions (I)–(VI).

The transaction rule G_c furthermore satisfies the following condition:

(VII) $(z^1, \ldots, z^S) = (y^1, \ldots, y^S)$ if and only if there is no distribution matrix $W = (w^1, \ldots, w^S)$ other than $Y = (y^1, \ldots, y^S)$ for which

$$\sum_{s=1}^{S} w^s = \sum_{s=1}^{S} y^s,$$

$$pw^s = py^s, \qquad s = 1, \ldots, S,$$

and

$$u^s(w^s) \geqq u^s(y^s), \qquad s = 1, \ldots, S.$$

A distribution matrix $Y = (y^1, \ldots, y^S)$ will be referred to as a *Pareto-optimum* if there is no distribution $W = (w^1, \ldots, w^S)$ for which

$$\sum_{s=1}^{S} w^s = \sum_{s=1}^{S} y^s,$$

and

$$u^s(w^s) \geqq u^s(y^s), \qquad s = 1, \ldots, S,$$

with strict inequality for at least one s.

If $Y = (y^1, \ldots, y^S)$ is a Pareto-optimum, then we have

$$g^s(p, Y) = y^s, \qquad s = 1, \ldots, S$$

for all price vectors p.

Lemma 1. Let $Y = (y^1, \ldots, y^S)$ be a Pareto-optimum, and $\alpha_1, \ldots, \alpha_S$ be corresponding utility levels:

$$\alpha_s = u^s(y^s), \qquad s = 1, \ldots, S.$$

Then there is no distribution matrix $W = (w^1, \ldots, w^S)$ other than Y for which

$$\sum_{s=1}^{S} w^s = \sum_{s=1}^{S} y^s \tag{9}$$

and

$$\alpha_s = u^s(w^s), \qquad s = 1, \ldots, S. \tag{10}$$

Proof. Suppose there exists a distribution matrix $W \neq Y$ for which (9) and (10) are satisfied. Let the distribution matrix $V = (v^1, \ldots, v^S)$ be defined by

$$v^s = \frac{w^s + y^s}{2}, \quad \text{for } s = 1, \ldots, S.$$

Then

$$\sum_{s=1}^{S} v^s = \sum_{s=1}^{S} y^s,$$

$$u^s(v^s) \geqq u^s(y^s), \qquad s = 1, \ldots, S,$$

with strict inequality for at least one s, contradicting the Pareto-optimality of Y. ∎

A pair of price vector $\bar{p}$ and distribution matrix $\bar{Y} = (\bar{y}^1, \ldots, \bar{y}^S)$ is called an *equilibrium* if

$$(\bar{x}^1, \ldots, \bar{x}^S) = (\bar{y}^1, \ldots, \bar{y}^S),$$

where

$$\bar{x}^s = f^s(\bar{p}, \bar{y}^s), \qquad s = 1, \ldots, S.$$

3 Edgeworth's barter process

The process of barter introduced by Edgeworth consists of successive bartering between individuals according to their preferences, represented by $u^1, \ldots, u^S$, and according to a given transaction rule, $G = (g^1, \ldots, g^S)$. It is assumed that a uniform price vector prevails in the whole economy at each barter and that it varies from one barter to another. Edgeworth's process may be formulated by the following system of difference equations:

$$\begin{aligned} p_i(t+1) &= h_i[p(t), Y(t)], \qquad i = 1, \ldots, n;\ s = 1, \ldots, S; \\ y^s(t+1) &= g^s[p(t), Y(t)], \qquad t = 0, 1, 2, \ldots, \text{ad inf.}, \end{aligned} \tag{E}$$

with initial position p_0 and $Y_0 = (y_0^1, \ldots, y_0^S)$, where $p(t) = (p_1(t), \ldots, p_n(t))$ is the price vector, and $Y(t) = [y^1(t), \ldots, y^S(t)]$ is the distribution matrix, both at time t. The functions $h_1, \ldots, h_n$ are continuous price adjustment functions.

It may be noted, by condition (I), that

$$y(t) = \sum_{s=1}^{S} y^s(t) = \sum_{s=1}^{S} y_0^s, \quad \text{for all } t \geqq 0. \tag{11}$$

For any initial position (p_0, Y_0), the solution $[p(t; p_0, Y_0), Y(t; p_0, Y_0)]$ to the process (E) uniquely exists and is continuous with respect to initial position (p_0, Y_0).

Theorem 1. Let the transaction rule $G=(g^1,\ldots,g^S)$ satisfy conditions (I)–(VII), and let the price adjustment function $H=(h_1,\ldots,h_n)$ satisfy the following:

(VIII) $\pi=H(p,Y)$ is continuous and bounded for all $p\geq 0$ and $Y=(y^1,\ldots,y^S)\geqq 0$; and

(IX) If Y is not a Pareto-optimum, then there is a distribution matrix $W=(w^1,\ldots,w^S)$ such that

$$\sum_{s=1}^{S} w^s = \sum_{s=1}^{S} y^s,$$

$$\pi w^s = \pi y^s, \qquad s=1,\ldots,S,$$

$$u^s(w^s)\geqq u^s(y^s), \qquad s=1,\ldots,S,$$

with strict inequality for at least one s.

Then, for any nonnegative initial position (p_0, Y_0), the solution $Y(t;p_0,Y_0)$ to Edgeworth's barter process (E) converges to a Pareto-optimum.

Proof. Let $[p(t), Y(t)]=[p(t;p_0,Y_0), Y(t;p_0,Y_0)]$ be the solution to the process (E) with initial position (P_0, Y_0). By condition (III), $p(t)$ is bounded. Since $y^s(t)$ are nonnegative, (11) implies the boundedness of $y^s(t)$, for each s.

Let the function $U^s(t)$ be defined by

$$U^s(t)=u^s[y^s(t)], \qquad t\geqq 0. \tag{12}$$

Then by condition (III)

$$U^s(t+1)\geqq U^s(t), \qquad t\geqq 0. \tag{13}$$

Hence, for each s, $U^s(t)$ converges as, t tends to infinity, say to α_s:

$$\alpha_s=\lim_{t\to\infty} U^s(t), \qquad s=1,\ldots,S. \tag{14}$$

Let the functions $\varphi(Y)$ and $\phi(t)$ be defined by

$$\varphi(Y)=\sum_{s=1}^{S} u^s(y^s), \tag{15}$$

$$\phi(t)=\varphi[Y(t)], \qquad t\geqq 0. \tag{16}$$

The function $\varphi(Y)$ is continuous with respect to Y; and in view of (13), we have

$$\phi(t+1)\geqq\phi(t), \quad \text{for all } t\geqq 0. \tag{17}$$

Relation (17) holds with strict inequality unless

$$Y(t+1) = Y(t).$$

In fact, suppose that relation (17) holds with equality. Then from (13) and (15),

$$u^s[y^s(t+1)] = u^s[y^s(t)], \qquad s = 1, \ldots, S.$$

Since $y^s(t+1) = g^s[p(t), Y(t)]$, we have by Condition (IV)

$$y^s(t+1) = y^s(t), \qquad s = 1, \ldots, S.$$

We now show that $Y(t)$ converges to a Pareto-optimum. Let Y_* be any limiting distribution of $Y(t)$ as t tends to infinity; i.e., for some sequence $\{t_\nu\}$, $t_\nu \to \infty (\nu \to \infty)$,

$$y^s_* = \lim_{\nu \to \infty} y^s(t_\nu), \qquad s = 1, \ldots, S. \tag{18}$$

Since $p(t)$ is bounded, we may, without loss of generality, assume that $p(t_\nu)$ also converges, say to p_*,

$$p_* = \lim_{\nu \to \infty} p(t_\nu). \tag{19}$$

From (14) and (18) we have

$$u^s(y^s_*) = \alpha_s, \qquad s = 1, \ldots, S. \tag{20}$$

Let $[p_*(t), Y_*(t)]$ be the solution to the process (E) with initial position (p_*, Y_*). By uniqueness and continuity with respect to the initial position of the solution to the process (E), we have by (18) and (19)

$$\begin{aligned} y^s_*(t) = y^s[t; p_*, Y_*] &= \lim_{\nu \to \infty} y^s[t; p(t_\nu), Y(t_\nu)] \\ &= \lim_{\nu \to \infty} y^*(t + t_\nu), \qquad s = 1, \ldots, S. \end{aligned}$$

Hence, from (14),

$$\begin{aligned} u^s[y^s_*(t)] &= \lim_{\nu \to \infty} u^s[y^s(t + t_\nu)] \\ &= \lim_{\nu \to \infty} U^s(t + t_\nu) \\ &= \alpha_s, \qquad s = 1, \ldots, S. \end{aligned} \tag{21}$$

The relations (20) and (21) may be written

$$u^s[y^s_*(t)] = u^s(y^s_*), \quad \text{for all } s, \text{ and } t \geqq 0,$$

which together with (IV) implies that

$$Y_*(t) = Y_*, \quad \text{for all } t \geqq 0.$$

Hence, Y_* is a Pareto-optimum. Otherwise, by conditions (IX) and (VII), $Y_*(2) = G[p_*(1), Y_*] \neq Y_*$.

Now any limiting distribution $Y_* = (y_*^1, \ldots, y_*^S)$ of $Y(t)$, as t tends to infinity, is a Pareto-optimum and satisfies (20), where $\alpha_1, \ldots, \alpha_S$ are uniquely determined. Therefore, by Lemma 1, any limiting distribution Y_* is uniquely determined, and $Y(t)$ itself converges to Y_*. ∎

4 A continuous barter process

In this section we are concerned with a barter process in which the rates of exchange and the distribution of commodities among individuals vary continuously over time. Let $p(t) = (p_0(t), \ldots, p_n(t))$ be the price vector and $Y(t) = (y^1(t), \ldots, y^S(t))$ the distribution matrix, both at time t. It will be assumed that:

(I′) There exists a path, $(p(t), Y(t))$, starting from any positive initial position $(p(0), Y(0))$. The rates of change in price vector $p(t)$ and in distribution matrix $Y(t)$ are solely determined by the prevailing price vector $p(t)$ and distribution $Y(t)$, and the path of $(p(t), Y(t))$ remains strictly positive, continuously changing with respect to the positive initial condition $(p(0), Y(0))$.[8]

(II′) There is no consumption during the barter process; i.e., the aggregate commodity bundle $\sum_{s=1}^{S} y^s(t)$ remains constant for all $t \geqq 0$.

(III′) There is no speculative transaction; i.e., for every individual s, the utility level $U^s(t) = u^s(y^s(t))$ does not decrease as t increases.

(IV′) The rate of increase in each individual's utility is zero if and only if the distribution $Y(t)$ is the only distribution $W(t) = (w^1(t), \ldots, w^S(t))$ which satisfies the following conditions:

Budgetary restraints:

$$p(t)w^s(t) = p(t)y^s(t), \qquad s = 1, \ldots, S,$$

Resource restraints:

$$\sum_{s=1}^{S} w^s(t) = \sum_{s=1}^{S} y^s(t),$$

Preference restraints:

$$u^s(w^s(t)) \geqq u^s(y^s(t)), \qquad s = 1, \ldots, S.$$

[8] The solution $[p(t), Y(t)]$ is called *strictly positive* if there exists a positive number $\delta > 0$ for which

$$p_i(t) > \delta, \quad y_i^s(t) > \delta, \quad \text{for all } t > 0,\ i, \text{ and } s.$$

(V′) The rate of change in the price vector $p(t)$ depends continuously on the current excess demand $\sum_{s=1}^{S} x^s(t) - \sum_{s=1}^{S} y^s(t)$, where $x^s(t)$ is the optimum commodity bundle associated with $(p(t), y^s(t))$. Furthermore, $\dot{p}(t) = 0$ if and only if the current excess demand vanishes.

Such a barter process, e.g., may be generated by the following system of differential equations:

$$\dot{p}_i = \rho_i(x_i - y_i), \qquad i = 1, \ldots, n,$$
$$\dot{y}^s = \sigma(z^s - y^s), \qquad s = 1, \ldots, S,$$

with initial position (p_0, Y_0), positive rates of adjustment ρ_i, σ, and

$$x = \sum_{s=1}^{S} x^s, \qquad x^s = f^s(p, y^s),$$

$$y = \sum_{s=1}^{S} y^s,$$

$$z^s = g^s(p, Y), \qquad s = 1, \ldots, S.$$

Theorem 2. Let the model of exchange satisfy the conditions (I′)–(V′) and the price vector $p(t)$ remain bounded and strictly positive, while $Y(t)$ remains strictly positive. Then for any positive initial position $[p(0), Y(0)]$, the distribution matrix $Y(t)$ converges to a Pareto-optimum distribution $\bar{Y}$, and the price vector $p(t)$ has a subsequence converging to an equilibrium price vector corresponding to $\bar{Y}$.

For any positive vector of exchange rates p and the s-th individual's commodity bundle y^s, we define

$$\psi^s(p, y^s) = [\psi_1^s(p, y^s), \ldots, \psi_n^s(p, y^s)], \tag{22}$$

$$\psi_i^s(p, y^s) = \frac{u_i^s(y^s)/p_i}{u_0^s(y^s)/p_0} - 1, \qquad i = 1, \ldots, n, \tag{23}$$

where

$$u_i^s(y^s) = \partial u^s / \partial y_i^s, \qquad i = 0, 1, \ldots, n.$$

If $\psi^s(p, y^s)$ is positive, an exchange of the 0-th commodity for the i-th commodity in a sufficiently small quantity will increase the s-th utility; if $\psi^s(p, y^s)$ is negative, it will decrease the s-th utility. For positive commodity bundle $y^s > 0$, the s-th utility $u^s(w^s)$ is maximized at $w^s = y^s$, subject to

$pw^s \leqq py^s$, if and only if $\psi^s(p, y^s) = 0$. Define

$$B(p, Y) = \left\{ W = (w^1, \ldots, w^S): \sum_{s=1}^{S} w^s = \sum_{s=1}^{S} y^s, w^s \geqq 0, \right.$$

$$\left. pw^s = py^s, \text{ and } u^s(w^s) \geqq u^s(y^s), s = 1, \ldots, S \right\}. \quad (24)$$

Lemma 2. Let $p = (p_0, p_1, \ldots, p_n)$ be a positive vector of exchange rates and $Y = (y^1, \ldots, y^S)$ be a positive distribution matrix; i.e.,

$$y^s > 0, \qquad s = 1, \ldots, S.$$

Then the set $B(p, Y)$ consists of Y alone if and only if there are S nonnegative numbers $\xi_1, \ldots, \xi_S$ and a vector $b = (b_1, \ldots, b_n)$ for which

$$\psi^s(p, y^s) = \xi_s b, \qquad s = 1, \ldots, S. \quad (25)$$

Proof. By definition (24), $B(p, Y) = \{Y\}$ if and only if y^r maximizes $u^r(w^r)$ for each r, subject to the restraints that

$$\sum_{s=1}^{S} w^s \leqq \sum_{s=1}^{S} y^s, \quad (26)$$

$$w^s \geqq 0, \qquad pw^s \leqq py^s, \qquad s = 1, \ldots, S, \quad (27)$$

and

$$u^s(w^s) \geqq u^s(y^s), \quad \text{for } s \neq r. \quad (28)$$

We may, without loss of generality, assume that

$$\psi^s(p, y^s) \neq 0, \qquad s = 1, \ldots, S; \quad (29)$$

otherwise, it may suffice to consider the subset of $\{1, \ldots, S\}$ consisting of all s for which $\psi^s(p, y^s) \neq 0$.

The restraints (28) are the only nonlinear restraints in (26)–(28), and from (29) there exist $w^s (s \neq r)$ satisfying (26)–(28), with strict inequality for (28). Hence, applying Corollary 3 to Theorem 3 in Arrow, Hurwicz, and Uzawa [4][9], the above maximization problem may be reduced to the saddle-point problem; therefore, $B(p, Y) = \{Y\}$ if and only if there exist nonnegative $\lambda'_s (s \neq r)$, positive μ_s, and ν_i, for which we have

$$\lambda'_s u^s_i(y^s) - \mu_s p_i - \nu_i = 0, \quad s = 1, \ldots, S; \ i = 0, 1, \ldots, n, \qquad \lambda'_r = 1. \quad (30)$$

[9] Corollary 3 to Theorem 3 in [4] is concerned with validity of the Kuhn-Tucker theorem on nonlinear programming under slightly weaker conditions than the so-called Kuhn-Tucker Constraints Qualification. It is shown that the Lagrangian method may be applied to the case in which the restraints are concave functions and there exists a feasible vector satisfying all the nonlinear constraints with strict inequality.

Condition (30) may be reduced to

$$\lambda_s' u_i^s(y^s) - \mu_s p_i = \lambda_r' u_i^r(y^r) - \mu_r p_i, \quad s = 1, \ldots, S;\ i = 0, 1, \ldots, n. \tag{31}$$

Dividing (31) by p_i, we get

$$\lambda_s' \frac{u_i^s(y^s)}{p_i} - \mu_s = \lambda_r' \frac{u_i^r(y^r)}{p_i} - \mu_r, \quad s = 1, \ldots, S;\ i = 0, 1, \ldots, n. \tag{32}$$

Condition (32) is equivalent to

$$\lambda_s' \left[\frac{u_i^s(y^s)}{p_i} - \frac{u_0^s(y^s)}{p_0} \right] = \lambda_r' \left[\frac{u_i^r(y^r)}{p_i} - \frac{u_0^r(y^r)}{p_0} \right],$$

i.e.,

$$\lambda_s \psi^s(y^s) = \lambda_r \psi^r(y^r), \qquad s = 1, \ldots, S,$$

with

$$\lambda_s = \lambda_s' \frac{u_0^s(y^s)}{p_0}.$$

It is noted that since $\lambda_r' = 1$ and $\psi^r(y^r) \neq 0$, no λ_s' appearing in the above equations can vanish. This implies, in the general case where not all of $\psi^s(y^s)$ are different from zero, that all nonzero $\psi^s(y^s)$ are mutually positive multiples of each other. Therefore, if we let $b = \sum_{s=1}^{S} \psi^s(p, y^s)$, we have

$$\psi^s(y^s) = \xi_s b, \quad \xi_s \geqq 0, \quad s = 1, 2, \ldots, S. \qquad ■$$

Lemma 3. Let $[p(0), Y(0)]$ be a positive initial position and $[p(t), Y(t)]$ be the solution to the continuous barter process. If $p(t)$ remains strictly positive and bounded for all $t \geqq 0$, and if the distribution matrix $Y(t)$ remains identical with $Y(0)$ for all $t \geqq 0$, then $Y(0)$ is a Pareto-optimum, and there exists a subsequence of $p(t)$ that converges to an equilibrium price vector.[10]

Proof. Since $Y(t) = Y(0)$ for all $t > 0$ and (IV′) is satisfied for any transaction rule, we have

$$B[p(t), Y(t)] = \{Y(0)\}, \quad \text{for all } t \geqq 0. \tag{33}$$

Lemma 2, together with (33) and the positiveness of $Y(t)$, implies that for

[10] The Walras tâtonnement process starting with a Pareto-optimum is shown in Arrow and Hurwicz [3] to be globally stable if the adjustment functions ϕ are linear. For the stability problem of the Walrasian tâtonnement process, see, e.g., Arrow and Hurwicz [3] and Arrow, Block, and Hurwicz [2].

each $t \geqq 0$

$$b(t) = \sum_{s=1}^{S} \psi^s(p(t), y^s),$$

$$\psi^s(t) = \xi_s(t)b(t), \qquad \xi_s(t) \geqq 0, \qquad s = 1, \ldots, S, \tag{34}$$

where

$$\psi_i^s(t) = \psi_i^s[p(t), y^s(t)] = \frac{c_i^s}{p_i(t)} - 1, \qquad s = 1, \ldots, S, \ i = 1, \ldots, n, \tag{35}$$

$$c_i^s = u_i^s(y^s)/u_0^s(y^s)p_0. \tag{36}$$

In what follows we may assume that $b(t)$ never vanishes. For, if $b(t) = 0$ at some t_0, all $\psi^s(t)$ vanish simultaneously at t_0 so that $Y(0) = Y(t_0)$ coincides with $X(t_0)$ which is a Pareto-optimum, as was to be shown. Since $b(t) \neq 0$ over time, the coefficients $\xi_s(t)$ in (34) are uniquely determined. To be explicit, we have

$$\xi_s(t) = \psi^s(t)b(t)/b(t)b(t), \qquad s = 1, 2, \ldots, S.$$

This implies, in view of the special way that $\psi_i^s(t)$ depend on $p_i(t)$ in (35), that $\xi_s(t)$ as well as $b(t)$ in (34) are continuously differentiable with respect to t.

Now if

$$c_i^r = c_i^s, \quad \text{for all } r, s, \text{ and } i = 1, \ldots, n, \tag{37}$$

then the distribution $Y(0)$ is a Pareto-optimum; in fact, the vector $(1, c_1^s, \ldots, c_n^s)$ is an equilibrium price vector corresponding to $Y(0)$, and, by Theorem 5 in Arrow [1], $Y(0)$ is a Pareto-optimum.

Hence, we consider the case in which

$$c_i^r \neq c_i^s, \quad \text{for some } r, s, \text{ and } i. \tag{38}$$

From (34) and (35) we have

$$c_i^r - c_i^s = (\xi_r(t) - \xi_s(t))q_i(t), \qquad i = 1, \ldots, n; \ t \geqq 0, \tag{39}$$

where

$$q_i(t) = b_i(t)p_i(t).$$

We first note that in the present case $\xi_r(t) - \xi_s(t) \neq 0$ at every period t. For, if otherwise, (39) would imply $c_i^r = c_i^s$ for all i, which is a contradiction.

Now substituting (34) into (35), and differentiating with respect to t, we get

$$-\dot{p}_i(t) = \dot{\xi}_s(t)q_i(t) + \xi_s(t)\dot{q}_i(t), \qquad s = 1, \ldots, S, \ i = 1, \ldots, n. \tag{40}$$

Summing (40) over $s = 1, \ldots, S$, and noting that $\sum_{s=1}^{S} \xi_s(t) = 1$ for all t, we get

$$-S\dot{p}_i(t) = \dot{q}_i(t), \qquad i = 1, \ldots, n. \tag{41}$$

Differentiating (39) and substituting (41), we have

$$\dot{p}_i(t) = \frac{c_i^r - c_i^s}{S}\,\omega(t), \qquad i = 1, \ldots, n, \tag{42}$$

where

$$\omega(t) = (\dot{\xi}_r(t) - \dot{\xi}_s(t))/(\xi_r(t) - \xi_s(t))^2.$$

The final course of the proof proceeds as follows: First, under our basic assumption that $b(t) \neq 0$ over time, the function $\omega(t)$ does not vanish either. Indeed, if $\omega(t_0) = 0$ at some t_0, (42) would give $\dot{p}_i(t_0) = 0, i = 1, 2, \ldots, n$, which implies, in view of the latter part of condition (V'), that $p(t_0)$ is an equilibrium price vector and therefore that $b(t_0) = 0$, yielding a contradiction. As $\omega(t)$ is continuous and does not vanish, it is either always positive or always negative, so that, by (42), the $p_i(t)$ vary monotonically in time. Since $p_0(t)$ is strictly positive and bounded above, $p(t)$ must converge to a limit p^*. This p^* is an equilibrium price vector. For, if otherwise, the excess demand $\sum_{s=1}^{S} x^s(p^*, y^s) - \sum_{s=1}^{S} y^s$ does not vanish. As $\lim_{t\to\infty} p(t) = p^*$, we have, by continuity,

$$\lim_{t\to\infty}\left(\sum_{s=1}^{S} x^s(t) - \sum_{s=1}^{S} y^s\right) = \sum_{s=1}^{S} x^s(p^*, y^s) - \sum_{s=1}^{S} y^s \neq 0,$$

and hence, by the former part of (V'), we have $|\dot{p}_i(t)| \geqq \delta > 0$ for some commodity i onwards from some period. T. This implies, however, that either $\lim_{t\to\infty} p_i(t) = +\infty$ or $-\infty$ for this commodity, arriving at a contradiction. Therefore $\sum_{s=1}^{S} x^s(p^*, Y^s) = \sum_{s=1}^{S} y^s$, and $Y(0)$ is a Pareto-optimum. ■

Proof of Theorem 2. Let (p_*, Y_*) be any limiting point of $[p(t), Y(t)]$ as t tends to infinity. By hypothesis in the theorem, both p_* and Y_* are *positive*. By an argument similar to the one in the proof of Theorem 1, we have for the solution $[p_*(t), Y_*(t)]$ with initial position (p_*, Y_*),

$$Y_*(t) = Y_*, \quad \text{for all } t \geqq 0;$$

hence, by Lemma 3, the distribution Y_* is a Pareto-optimum such that

$$u^s(y_*^s) = \alpha^s, \qquad s = 1, \ldots, S,$$

where

$$\alpha^s = \lim_{t\to\infty} u^s[y^s(t)].$$

Since, for each s, $u^s[y^s(t)]$ is nondecreasing with respect to t, the limit exists and is uniquely determined. By applying Lemma 1, therefore, the limiting distribution Y_* is uniquely determined. Any limiting point p_{**} of $p_*(t)$, as t

tends to infinity, is an equilibrium price vector corresponding to Y_*. Since p_{**} is a limiting point of $p(t)$ itself, the existence of a subsequence of $p(t)$ converging to an equilibrium price vector has been established. ■

References

[1] Arrow, K. J., "An Extension of the Basic Theorems of Classical Welfare Economics," *Proceedings of the Second Berkeley Symposium on Mathematical Statistics and Probability* (Berkeley and Los Angeles: University of California Press, 1951), 507–52.

[2] Arrow, K. J., H. D. Block, and L. Hurwicz, "On the Stability of the Competitive Equilibrium, II," *Econometrica*, XXVII (January, 1959), 82–109.

[3] Arrow, K. J., and L. Hurwicz, "On the Stability of the Competitive Equilibrium," *Econometrica*, XXVI (October, 1958), 522–52.

[4] Arrow, K. J., H. Hurwicz, and H. Uzawa, "Constraint Qualifications in Maximization Problems," *Naval Research Logistics Quarterly*, VIII (1961), 175–91.

[5] Edgeworth, F. Y., *Mathematical Psychics* (London: Kegan Paul, 1981).

[6] ———, *Papers Relating to Political Economy*, Vol. II (London: Macmillan, 1925).

[7] Hahn, F. H., "On the Stability of Competitive Equilibrium," Working Paper No. 6, Committee on Econometrics and Mathematical Economics, University of California, Berkeley, 1960.

[8] Hurwicz, L., "Optimality and Informational Efficiency in Resource Allocation Processes," *Mathematical Methods in the Social Sciences, 1959* (Stanford: Stanford University Press, 1960), 27–46.

[9] Kaldor, N., "A Classificatory Note on the Determinateness of Equilibrium," *Review of Economic Studies*, I (1933–34), 122–36.

[10] Marshall, A., *Principles of Economics* (8th ed.) (London: Macmillan, 1952).

[11] Negishi, T., "On the Formation of Prices," *International Economic Review*, II (January, 1961), 122–26.

[12] Walras, L., *Elements of Pure Economics*, trans. by W. Jaffé (Homewood: Richard Irwin, 1954).

PART V

Theory of economic growth

CHAPTER 13

On a two-sector model of economic growth, I

1 Introduction

In the present paper we are interested in the growth process in a two-sector model of capital accumulation and show that balanced growth equilibria are globally stable under the neoclassical hypotheses.

The neoclassical model of economic growth, as it has been developed by Solow [5] and Swan [6], is formulated in terms of the aggregate production function. The aggregate production function specifies the relationship between output and factors of production, and output is assumed to be composed of homogeneous quantities identical with capital, or at least price ratios between output and capital are assumed constant. The economy we are concerned with in this paper, on the other hand, consists of two types of goods, investment-goods and consumption-goods, to be produced by two factors of production, capital and labor; prices of investment-goods and consumption-goods are determined so as to satisfy the demand requirements.[1] It will be assumed that capital depreciates at a fixed rate, the rate of growth in labor is constant and exogenously determined, capitalists' income is solely spent on investment-goods, that of laborers on consumption-goods, and production is subject to the neoclassical conditions. Under such hypotheses, then, it will be shown that the state of steady growth exists and the growth process, starting at an arbitrary capital and labor composition, approaches some steady growth. If the consumption-goods sector is always more capital-intensive than the investment-goods sector, then the steady growth is uniquely determined and it is stable in the small as well as in the large.

From *Review of Economic Studies*, Vol. 14 (1962), pp. 40–47; reprinted with permission.

I owe much to Professor Robert M. Solow and the referees for their valuable comments and suggestions.

[1] Shinkai [4] has investigated the structure of growth equilibria in a two-sector model of growth in which technical coefficients are all constant. Our two-sector model presented here is a neoclassical version of Shinkai's model.

2 Neoclassical production functions

We consider an economic system consisting of investment-goods and consumption-goods sectors, labeled 1 and 2, respectively. It is assumed that in both sectors production is subject to constant returns to scale, marginal rates of substitution are positive and diminishing, and there exist neither joint products nor external (dis-)economies.

The production processes in each sector are summarized by specifying each sector's production function; let $F_1(K_1, L_1)$ be the production function for the investment-goods sector, and $F_2(K_2, L_2)$ for the consumption-goods sector. $F_1(K_1, L_1)$ represents the quantity of the investment-goods, Y_1, produced by employing capital and labor by the quantities K_1 and L_1; and similarly for the consumption-goods sector's production function, $F_2(K_2, L_2)$.

In terms of production functions, the assumptions indicated above may be formulated

$$F_i(\lambda K_i, \lambda L_i) = \lambda F_i(K_i, L_i),\ F_i(K_i, L_i) > 0, \quad \text{for all } K_i, L_i > 0, \text{ and } \lambda > 0; \tag{1}$$

$$F_i(K_i, L_i) \text{ is twice continuously differentiable;} \tag{2}$$

$$\partial F_i/\partial K_i > 0,\ \partial F_i/\partial L_i > 0,\ \partial^2 F_i/\partial K_i^2 < 0,\ \partial^2 F_i/\partial L_i^2 < 0 \quad \text{for all } K_i, L_i > 0. \tag{3}$$

In view of the constant-returns-to-scale hypothesis (1), the output-labor ratio y_i is a function of the capital-labor ratio k_i:

$$y_i = f_i(k_i), \tag{4}$$

where

$$y_i = Y_i/L_i, \quad k_i = K_i/L_i, \quad f_i(k_i) = F_i(k_i, 1), \ . \ i = 1, 2.$$

The assumptions (2–3) are then equivalent to:

$$f_i(k_i) \text{ is twice continuously differentiable;} \tag{5}$$

$$f_i(k_i) > 0, \quad f_i'(k_i) > 0, \quad f_i''(k_i) < 0, \quad \text{for all } k_i > 0. \tag{6}$$

3 A two-sector model

Let K and L be the aggregate quantities of capital and labor at time t; these quantities of the two factors of production are allocated competitively among the two sectors, and prices of goods are determined so as to satisfy the demand conditions. In what follows, we assume that both capital and labor are always fully employed and both goods are produced in positive quantities.

Let K_i and L_i be the quantities of capital and labor allocated to the i-th sector, P_1 and P_2 the price of investment-goods and of consumption goods, and r and w the returns to capital and the wage rate, respectively. Then we have,

$$Y_i = F_i(K_i, L_i), \tag{7}$$

$$P_i \frac{\partial F_i}{\partial K_i} = r, \quad P_i \frac{\partial F_i}{\partial L_i} = w, \quad i = 1, 2. \tag{8}$$

$$K_1 + K_2 = K, \quad L_1 + L_2 = L, \tag{9}$$

$$P_1 Y_1 = rK, \quad P_2 Y_2 = wL. \tag{10}$$

The condition (8) is familiar marginal productivity conditions, and (10) formulates the hypothesis that labor does not save and capital does not consume.

Let

$$k = K/L,$$
$$k_i = K_i/L_i, \quad y_i = Y_i/L_i, \quad \rho_i = L_i/L, \quad i = 1, 2.$$
$$\omega = w/r.$$

Then conditions (7–10) may be reduced to:

$$y_i = f_i(k_i), \quad i = 1, 2. \tag{11}$$

$$\omega = \frac{f_i(k_i)}{f'_i(k_i)} - k_i, \quad i = 1, 2. \tag{12}$$

$$\rho_1 k_1 + \rho_2 k_2 = k, \tag{13}$$

$$\rho_1 + \rho_2 = 1, \tag{14}$$

$$\rho_1 f_1(k_1) = f'_1(k_1) k. \tag{15}$$

Differentiating (12) with respect to k_i, we have:

$$\frac{d\omega}{dk_i} = \frac{-f(k_i) f''_i(k_i)}{[f'_i(k_i)]^2}, \tag{16}$$

which is always positive in view of (6). Hence: *For any wage-rentals ratio ω, the optimum capital-labor ratio k_i in each sector is uniquely determined by the relation* (12), *provided*:

$$\underline{\omega}_i = \lim_{k_i \to 0} \left[\frac{f_i(k_i)}{f'_i(k_i)} - k_i \right] < \omega < \bar{\omega}_i = \lim_{k_i \to \infty} \left[\frac{f_i(k_i)}{f'_i(k_i)} - k_i \right]. \tag{17}$$

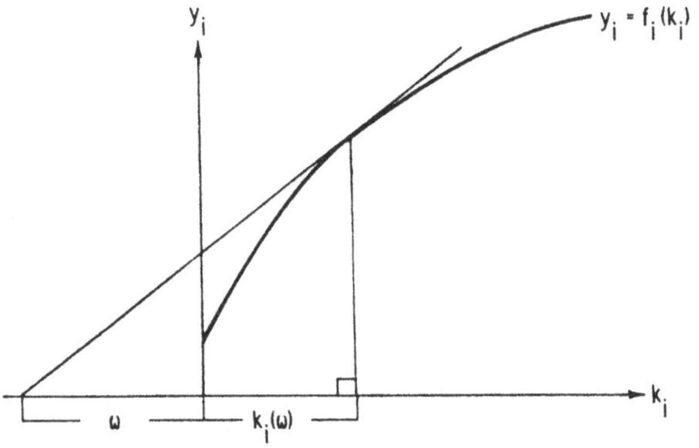

Figure 13.1

The optimum capital-labor ratio k_i corresponding to the wage-rentals ratio ω, uniquely determined by (12), will then be denoted by $k_i = k_i(\omega)$, $i = 1, 2$. The determination of the optimum capital-labor ratio $k_i(\omega)$ may be illustrated by Figure 13.1.

We have from (16) that:

$$\frac{dk_i}{d\omega} = \frac{[f_i'(k_i)]^2}{-f_i(k_i)f_i''(k_i)} > 0, \tag{18}$$

with $k_i = k_i(\omega)$, $i = 1, 2$.

In view of (12), the labor allocation ρ_1 to the investment-goods sector, determined by (15), may be written as:

$$\rho_1 = \frac{k}{\omega + k_1(\omega)}. \tag{19}$$

Substituting (14) and (19) into (13) and rearranging, we have

$$k = \frac{\omega + k_1(\omega)}{\omega + k_2(\omega)} k_2(\omega). \tag{20}$$

The equilibrium wage-rentals ratio ω is obtained by solving the equation (20).

4 Growth process in the two-sector model

Let the rate of growth in labor be a positive constant, say ν, and μ be the instantaneous rate of depreciation in capital. Then the growth process in the two-sector model we have described is formulated by the following differential equations:

$$\frac{\dot{K}}{K} = \frac{r}{P_1} - \mu, \tag{21}$$

and

$$\frac{\dot{L}}{L} = \nu, \tag{22}$$

where r is the equilibrium return to capital and P_1 the equilibrium price of the investment-goods, both at time t.

The equations (21) and (22), together with the equilibrium condition (8), imply that:

$$\frac{\dot{k}}{k} = f'_1(k_1) - \nu - \mu, \tag{23}$$

where $k_1 = k_1(\omega)$ and ω is an equilibrium wage-rentals ratio corresponding to the aggregate capital-labor ratio.

An aggeregate capital-labor ratio k^* may be termed a *balanced capital-labor ratio* if

$$f'_1(k_1^*) = \nu + \mu, \tag{24}$$

where $k_1^* = k_1(\omega^*)$ and ω^* is an equilibrium wage-rentals ratio corresponding to the aggregate capital-ratio k^*.

It is easily shown that at the growth process starting at a balanced capital-labor ratio k^*, the aggregate capital-labor ratio $k(t)$ and equilibrium wage-rentals ratio $\omega(t)$ both remain constant.

5 Capital-intensity hypothesis and the stability of growth equilibrium

Suppose that the consumption-goods sector is always more capital-intensive than the investment-goods sector;[2] namely,

$$k_1(\omega) < k_2(\omega), \quad \text{for all } \omega \text{ such that } \max[\underline{\omega}_1, \underline{\omega}_2] < \omega < \min[\bar{\omega}_1, \bar{\omega}_2]. \tag{25}$$

Let

$$\Psi(\omega) = \frac{\omega + k_1(\omega)}{\omega + k_2(\omega)} k_2(\omega).$$

[2] The concept of relative factor intensities was introduced by Samuelson in the context of international trade theory; see, e.g., [3], p. 9.

Differentiating $\log \Psi(\omega)$ with respect to ω, we have

$$\frac{1}{\Psi(\omega)}\frac{d\Psi}{d\omega} = \frac{1+\frac{dk_1}{d\omega}}{\omega + k_1(\omega)} - \frac{1+\frac{dk_2}{d\omega}}{\omega + k_2(\omega)} + \frac{\frac{dk_2}{d\omega}}{k_2(\omega)}$$

$$= \left[\frac{1}{\omega + k_1(\omega)} - \frac{1}{\omega + k_2(\omega)}\right] + \frac{\frac{dk_1}{d\omega}}{\omega + k_1(\omega)}$$

$$+ \frac{dk_2}{d\omega}\left[\frac{1}{k_2(\omega)} - \frac{1}{\omega + k_2(\omega)}\right],$$

which, by (18) and (25), is always *positive*.

Therefore, we have

$$\frac{d\Psi}{d\omega} > 0, \quad \text{for all } \omega \text{ satisfying } \max[\underline{\omega}_1, \underline{\omega}_2] < \omega < \min[\bar{\omega}_1, \bar{\omega}_2]. \tag{26}$$

The equation (20) has a positive solution ω if and only if:

$$\Psi(0) < k < \Psi(\infty), \tag{27}$$

and the solution ω is uniquely determined by k. The equilibrium factor-price ratio ω may be denoted by $\omega = \omega(k)$.

From (20) and (26), we have

$$\frac{d\omega}{dk} > 0, \quad \text{for all } k \text{ satisfying (27).} \tag{28}$$

In view of conditions (6), (18), and (28), the function $f_1'[k_1(\omega(k))]$ is a strictly decreasing function of the aggregate capital-labor ratio k.

Hence, the balanced capital-labor ratio k^* always exists and is uniquely determined if the following condition is satisfied:

$$\lim_{k_1 \to 0} f_1'(k_1) > \nu + \mu > \lim_{k_1 \to \infty} f_1'(k_1). \tag{29}$$

It is easily shown that, for the growth process starting at an arbitrary initial capital-labor composition, the capital-labor ratio $k(t)$ approaches the balanced capital-labor ratio k^*.[3]

The results in this section may be summarized as:

> **Existence theorem:** Let the consumption-goods sector be more capital-intensive than the investment-goods sector for all relevant

[3] See, e.g., Arrow and Hurwicz [2], p. 540.

factor-price ratios ω. Then for any given aggregate capital-labor ratio k, the equilibrium factor-price ratio $\omega = \omega(k)$, the optimum capital-labor ratios $k_1 = k_1(\omega)$ and $k_2 = k_2(\omega)$ in both sectors, and the equilibrium outputs per head for investment-goods and consumption-goods, $y_1 = y_1(k)$ and $y_2 = y_2(k)$, are all uniquely determined, provided the aggregate capital-labor ratio k satisfies the relation (27).

Stability theorem: Let ν and μ be respectively the growth rate in labor and the instantaneous depreciation in capital; and the balanced capital-labor ratio k^* exist. Then, for the growth process starting at an arbitrary initial position, the capital-labor ratio $k(t)$ approaches the balanced capital-labor ratio k^* as t tend to infinity.

6 Concluding remarks

The uniqueness of the balanced capital-labor ratio and its stability crucially hinge on the hypothesis that the consumption-goods sector be more capital-intensive than the investment-goods sector. In this section, we shall construct an example of the two-sector growth model in which the capital-intensity hypothesis above is not satisfied and there is an unstable balanced capital-labor ratio.

Let the production functions be:

$$y_1 = f_1(k_1) = \tfrac{1}{1000}(k_1^{-3} + 7^{-4})^{1/3}, \quad y_2 = f_2(k_2) = (k_1^{-3} + 1)^{1/3}.$$

The optimum capital-labor ratios are then given by:

$$k_1 = k_1(\omega) = 7\omega^{1/4}, \quad k_2 = k_2(\omega) = \omega^{1/4};$$

hence

$$k_1(\omega) > k_2(\omega), \quad \text{for all } \omega > 0.$$

For aggregate capital-labor ratio k the equilibrium factor-price ratio ω is determined by:

$$k = \frac{\omega + 7\omega^{1/4}}{\omega + \omega^{1/4}}\,\omega^{1/4};$$

hence,

$$\frac{1}{k}\frac{d\omega}{dk} = \frac{1 + \frac{7}{4}\omega^{-3/4}}{\omega + 7\omega^{1/4}} - \frac{1 + \frac{7}{4}\omega^{-3/4}}{\omega + \omega^{1/4}} + \frac{\omega}{\frac{1}{4}}.$$

Let us consider the case in which the sum $\nu + \mu$ of the rate of growth in labor and the rate of depreciation is

$$\frac{7^3\sqrt{7}}{1600} \doteqdot .8\%.$$

Then $k^* = 4$ is a balanced capital-labor ratio and $\omega^* = 1$ is the corresponding wage-rentals ratio.

But

$$\left(\frac{1}{k}\ \frac{dk}{d\omega}\right)_{\omega=1} = -\tfrac{1}{32} < 0;$$

hence, the balanced capital-labor ratio $k^* = 4$ is not stable.

Let us now consider the general case in which the capital-intensity hypothesis is not necessarily satisfied.[4] In this case, the balanced capital-labor ratio may be no longer uniquely determined for given rates of labor growth and of depreciation; hence, there may exist unstable balanced capital-labor ratios, as was discussed in the previous section.

If, however, the conditions (29) and

$$f_1(0) = 0, \quad f_2(0) = 0 \tag{30}$$

are satisfied, then it is possible to show that the growth process represented by (21) and (22) is *globally stable* in the sense introduced by Arrow, Block, and Hurwicz ([2], p. 85); namely, given any initial condition, the aggregate capital-labor ratio $k(t)$ converges to some balanced capital-labor ratio.

To see the global stability of the process (23), it suffices to show that[5]

$$\lim_{k\to\infty} [f'_1(k_1) - \nu - \mu] < 0, \tag{31}$$

$$\lim_{k\to 0} [f'_1(k_1) - \nu - \mu] > 0. \tag{32}$$

The relation (31) may be seen from the assumption (29) and the inequality:

$$k < \omega + k_1$$

which is derived from (20). On the other hand, to see the relation (32), let k tend to zero. Then the corresponding wage-rentals ratio ω converges to zero also; otherwise, the relation (20) would imply

$$0 = \frac{\bar{\omega} + k_1(\bar{\omega})}{\bar{\omega} + k_2(\bar{\omega})}\, k_2(\bar{\omega})$$

[4] This section was written after I read Professor Solow's note which suggests that the stability property of the growth equilibrium as discussed in the present paper may not depend on the capital-intensity hypothesis.

[5] See, e.g., Arrow and Hurwicz [2], p. 540.

for some positive wage-rentals ratio $\bar{\omega}$, contradicting the assumption (30). Hence the corresponding capital-labor ratio $k_1 = k_1(\omega)$ converges to zero, again in view of (30). The relation (32) is then implied by the condition (29).

We may summarize our results as:

> Let the growth rate in labor ν and the depreciation rate in capital μ satisfy the conditions (29) and (30). Then there exists at least one balanced capital-labor ratio, and, for the growth process starting an arbitrary initial capital-labor composition, the aggregate capital-labor ratio $k(t)$ converges to some balanced capital-labor ratio.

References

[1] Arrow, K. J., H. D. Block, and L. Hurwicz. "On the Stability of the Competitive Equilibrium, II," *Econometrica*, Vol. 27 (1959), pp. 82–109.

[2] Arrow, K. J., and L. Hurwicz. "On the Stability of the Competitive Equilibrium, I," *Econometrica*, Vol. 27 (1958), pp. 522–52.

[3] Samuelson, P. A. "Prices of Factors and Goods in General Equilibrium," *Review of Economic Studies*, Vol. 21 (1953–54), pp. 1–20.

[4] Shinkai, Y. "On the Equilibrium Growth of Capital and Labor," *International Economic Review*, Vol. 1 (1960), pp. 107–11.

[5] Solow, R. M. "A Contribution to the Theory of Economic Growth," *Quarterly Journal of Economics*, Vol. 70 (1956), pp. 65–94.

[6] Swan, T. W. "Economic Growth and Capital Accumulation," *Economic Record*, Vol. 32 (1956), pp. 334–61.

CHAPTER 14

On a two-sector model of economic growth, II

1 Introduction

In a previous paper [9], I have analyzed the structure of a two-sector model of neoclassical growth, in which it has been assumed that labor consumes all, while capital only saves. The present paper is concerned with replacing this hypothesis with one which postulates that the propensity to save depends upon the rate of interest and the gross income per capita currently received.[1] The fundamental character of the model remains the same as in [9], except for the determination of investment and of rate of interest. At any moment of time, capital goods will be newly-produced at the rate at which the marginal efficiency of that capital is equated to the prevailing rate of interest. The prospective rentals to capital goods, which together with expected rates of discount determine the marginal efficiency of capital, are assumed to depend upon current rentals and quantities of newly produced and existing capital goods. The rate of interest, on the other hand, is determined at the level which equates the value, at the current market price, of newly-produced capital goods to the amount of savings forthcoming at that level of the rate of interest.

It is assumed that prospective rentals to capital are positively correlated with current rentals, while they decrease as the quantity of new capital goods increases (with the elasticity less than unity). The average propensity

From *Review of Economic Studies*, Vol. 19 (1963), pp. 105–18; reprinted with permission.

I have benefited from Robert M. Solow's comments, appearing as [7], on which the present version of the two-sector model is largely based. I also wish to acknowledge valuable comments and criticism by Ken-ichi Inada and Mordecai Kurz of Stanford University.

[1] Thus, the model presented here is an extension of the aggregate models of Solow and Swan ([6] and [8]) to the two-sector economy. It is a slightly different version of Meade's two-product economy without technical progress (see [5], Appendix II, pp. 83–133). The structure of a similar two-sector growth model has been analyzed by Kurz [4], where the elasticities of substitution in both sectors are assumed unity and the perfect foresight hypothesis is postulated.

to save is assumed to increase as rate of interest or current income per capita increases, and the marginal propensity to save is assumed less than or equal to unity.

Section 2 below investigates the structure of such a two-sector growth model when the average propensity to save is fixed at a certain level. It will be shown in particular that for arbitrarily given quantities of capital and labor, equilibrium quantities of consumption and capital goods currently produced, equilibrium prices of factors and goods, and rate of interest are all uniquely determined, and capital and labor both are fully employed. Any path of growth equilibrium will also be shown to approach a certain long-run steady state of balanced growth.

In later sections, the simple two-sector growth model will be extended to allow for a variably propensity to save, being dependent upon rate of interest and gross income per capita, and then to have the amount of new investment determined by the schedule of marginal efficiency of capital. The model preserves the main conclusions concerning the existence of short-run equilibrium and stability of the long-run growth equilibrium after such modification.

Finally, we shall briefly analyze the structure of growth equilibrium in a model in which factor prices are not instantaneously adjusted to marginal products and "involuntary" unemployment of either labor or capital may result at each moment of time. It will be shown that if the investment goods are more capital-intensive than the consumption goods, then the path of growth equilibrium approaches the state of balanced growth. On the other hand, if the consumption goods are more capital-intensive than the investment goods, the stability of growth equilibrium is not necessarily guaranteed, but the case of limit cycles may be observed.

2 A neoclassical model of economic growth

At the risk of repetition, the basic structure of the model will be described briefly. We consider an economy in which there exist two productive sectors, one producing consumption goods and another producing capital goods, respectively labeled C and I. Both consumption goods and capital goods are assumed to be composed of homogeneous quantities and to be produced by two homogeneous factors of production: labor and capital. Consumption goods are instantaneously consumed, while capital goods depreciate at a fixed rate μ. Let $L(t)$ be the total supply of labor at time t, and $K(t)$ the quantity of capital goods existing at time t. If we assume that labor forces grow at a constant rate, ν, and new capital goods are produced by the rate $Y_I(t)$ at the moment of time t, then the path of $K(t)$

and $L(t)$ is described by the following dynamic equations:

$$\dot{L}(t)/L(t) = \nu, \tag{1}$$

$$\dot{K}(t) = Y_I(t) - \mu K(t). \tag{2}$$

In each sector, production is subject to constant returns-to-scale and diminishing marginal rates of substitution. Joint products are excluded and external (dis-) economies do not exist. The quantity of consumption goods, $Y_C(t)$, produced at time t is then related to the quantities of labor and capital employed in the C-sector, $L_C(t)$ and $K_C(t)$, respectively:

$$Y_C(t) = F_C(K_C(t), L_C(t)), \tag{3}$$

where F_C is the C-sector's production function. Similarly, for the quantity of capital goods, $Y_I(t)$, produced at time t:

$$Y_I(t) = F_I(K_I(t), L_I(t)). \tag{4}$$

The gross national product in terms of consumption goods, $Y(t)$, is measured by

$$Y(t) = Y_C(t) + p(t)\,Y_I(t), \tag{5}$$

where $p(t)$ is the ratio of the price of the new capital good over that of the consumption good at time t. In what follows, prices are all measured in terms of the consumption good.

We assume that labor and capital are freely transferred from one sector to another[2] and both are fully employed;[3] namely,

$$K_I(t) + K_C(t) = K(t), \tag{6}$$

$$L_I(t) + L_C(t) = L(t). \tag{7}$$

The allocation of the two factors of production existing at any moment of time is assumed perfectly competitive, so that in each sector the wage $w(t)$ is equal to the marginal product of labor and the rentals $r(t)$ of capital goods to the marginal product of capital:

$$w(t) = \frac{\partial F_C}{\partial L_C} = p(t)\frac{\partial F_I}{\partial L_I}, \tag{8}$$

and

$$r(t) = \frac{\partial F_C}{\partial K_C} = p(t)\frac{\partial F_I}{\partial K_I}, \tag{9}$$

where partial derivatives are evaluated at $(K_C(t), L_C(t))$ or $(K_I(t), L_I(t))$.

[2] Namely, capital goods are perfectly malleable in Meade's terminology (see [5], e.g., p. 45).

[3] Under the hypotheses made on the production functions, (21) and (22), it is possible to show that both labor and capital are always fully employed.

The price, $p(t)$, of the new capital good, satisfying equations (8) and (9), is considered as the supply price of capital; i.e., $p(t)$ is equal to the price of the new capital good which is just enough to induce each manufacturer in the I-sector to produce an additional unit of such a capital good.

Let us now assume that at any moment of time a constant fraction is saved out of the current gross national product.[4] If s stands for the average propensity to save $(0 < s < 1)$, we have an equation which determines the quantity of new capital goods:

$$p(t)Y_I(t) = sY(t). \tag{10}$$

The model above completely describes the path of growth equilibrium. At any moment of time t, the existing capital stock $K(t)$ is a result of past accumulation, and labor forces $L(t)$ are exogenously given. The equilibrium amount of new capital goods, $Y_I(t)$, is determined by solving equilibrium equations (3–10), and the dynamic equations (1) and (2) prescribe the path of growth equilibrium. The model will be conveniently referred to as *a neoclassical model of economic growth.*

3 The determination of short-run equilibrium

We shall first discuss the determination of equilibrium quantities and prices at each moment of time, given capital stock, $K(t)$, and available labor forces, $L(t)$. For brevity, all variables are denoted without explicitly referring to time t.

Let k and y be, respectively, the capital-labor ratio and the gross national product per head at time t:

$$k = K/L, \quad y = Y/L.$$

We also define:

$$k_i = K_i/L_i, \quad y_i = Y_i/L, \quad l_i = L_i/L, \quad i = I, C,$$
$$\omega = w/r.$$

The relations (3) and (4) are reduced to:

$$y_i = f_i(k_i)l_i, \quad i = I, C, \tag{11}$$

[4] Throughout the paper, the propensity to save refers to that including depreciation, thus making its constancy or a variable version discussed below somewhat out of traditional formulation. The main reason for adopting gross instead of net propensity is due to the separation of entrepreneurs and owners of factors of production in my model. The interest of entrepreneurs is in maximizing their profits net of factor payments, while owners of productive factors are concerned not with keeping intact the means of production they own, but instead with achieving the highest level in their intertemporal preference scale. To analyze such a model fully would require the introduction of a new commodity, namely a bond, through which the saving behavior of the economy would be explicitly formulated.

where

$$f_i(k_i) = F_i(k_i, 1), \quad i = I, C.$$

It is assumed that, for each i, the function $f_i(k_i)$ is continuously twice differentiable for all $k_i > 0$, and

$$f_i(k_i) > 0, \quad f'_i(k_i) > 0, \quad f''_i(k_i) < 0, \quad \text{for all } k_i > 0, \tag{12}$$

$$f_i(0) = 0, \quad f_i(\infty) = \infty, \tag{13}$$

$$f'_i(0) = \infty, \quad f'_i(\infty) = 0. \tag{14}$$

A procedure similar to one used in [9] reduces the equilibrium conditions (3–10) to the following:

$$\omega = \frac{f_i(k_i)}{f'_i(k_i)} - k_i, \qquad i = C, I, \tag{15}$$

$$p = \frac{f'_C(k_C)}{f'_I(k_I)}, \tag{16}$$

$$y = y_C + p y_I, \tag{17}$$

$$y_I = f_I(k_I)\frac{k_C - k}{k_C - k_I}, \qquad y_C = f_C(k_C)\frac{k - k_I}{k_C - k_I}, \tag{18}$$

$$p y_I = s y. \tag{19}$$

Given an arbitrary wage-rentals ratio ω, the optimum capital-labor ratio $k_i = k_i(\omega)$ in each setor is uniquely determined from equation (15). Differentiate (15) with respect to ω to get:

$$\frac{dk_i}{d\omega} = \frac{-[f'_i(k_i)]^2}{f_i(k_i) f''_i(k_i)} > 0, \qquad i = C, I. \tag{20}$$

Substituting (15–18) into (19), we have:

$$[k + \omega] = \frac{[k_C(\omega) + \omega][k_I(\omega) + \omega]}{s[k_C(\omega) + \omega] + (1 - s)[k_I(\omega) + \omega]}. \tag{21}$$

Equation (21) uniquely determines the wage-rentals ratio ω. To see this, let us introduce new variables:

$$Z = k + \omega, \quad Z_i = k_i(\omega) + \omega, \quad i = C, I. \tag{22}$$

Equation (21) then becomes

$$Z = \frac{Z_C Z_I}{s Z_C + (1 - s) Z_I}. \tag{23}$$

The right-hand side of equation (23) is a function of ω, which will be denoted by $g(\omega)$.

Differentiate $g(\omega)$ to get:

$$g'(\omega) = \frac{sZ_C^2 Z_I' + (1-s)Z_I^2 Z_C'}{[sZ_C + (1-s)Z_I]^2},$$

which, in view of (20), yields:

$$g'(\omega) > \frac{sZ_C^2 + (1-s)Z_I^2}{[sZ_C + (1-s)Z_I]^2} \geqq 1.$$

The function $g(\omega)$ takes all positive values and has a derivative greater than unity everywhere. Therefore, for any given positive k, equation (23) is uniquely solvable for ω, and ω increases as k increases. Thus we have:

> Let us consider a neoclassical model of economic growth where the average propensity to save s remains constant, $0 < s < 1$. Then, for any positive capital-labor ratio, k, the equilibrium wage-rentals ratio $\omega = \omega(k)$ is uniquely determined by solving the fundamental equation (21). The higher the capital-labor ratio k, the higher the equilibrium wage-rentals ratio ω.

Let us now, in more detail, analyze the determination of short-run equilibrium in a neoclassical model. In most subsequent discussions we shall assume that the C-sector is always more capital-intensive than the I-sector; namely,

$$k_C(\omega) > k_I(\omega), \quad \text{for all positive wage-rentals ratio } \omega, \tag{24}$$

which is required mainly for reasons of a mathematical nature and for which it seems to be difficult to give any economic justification (see [7]). Such a hypothesis was made in its extreme form by Wicksell in his analysis of Åkerman's problem ([10, pp. 274–99]), and an empirical evidence in the case of the United States economy was suggested by Professor Gordon in his recent paper ([2, p. 948]).

Let us first observe that *if the capital-intensity hypothesis* (24) *is satisfied, the supply price p of the capital good increases as the wage-rentals ratio ω increases.* In fact, differentiating (16) logarithmically with respect to ω and substituting (20) and (15), we obtain:

$$\frac{1}{p}\frac{dp}{d\omega} = \frac{1}{\omega + k_I(\omega)} - \frac{1}{\omega + k_C(\omega)}. \tag{25}$$

Hence, by the hypothesis (24), $dp/d\omega$ is positive for an arbitrary wage-rentals ratio ω. In other words, as labor becomes relatively more expensive than capital, the capital good, in the production of which relatively more labor is employed than the consumption good, becomes relatively more expensive.

We next analyze the effect of a change in the wage-rentals ratio upon the gross national product. The gross national product per capita, y, defined by (17) with (16), (18), and (19), represents the level of the gross national product that corresponds to the full employment of labor and capital at a given wage-rentals ratio ω.

Substituting (16) and (18) into (17), and using (15), we get Walras's law:

$$y = f'_C(k_C)(\omega + k). \tag{26}$$

Differentiating (26) logarithmically with respect to ω, we get

$$\frac{1}{y}\frac{dy}{d\omega} = \frac{f''_C(k_C)}{f'_C(k_C)}\frac{dk_C}{d\omega} + \frac{1}{\omega + k},$$

which, together with (20) and (15), yields:

$$\frac{1}{y}\frac{dy}{d\omega} = \frac{1}{\omega + k} - \frac{1}{\omega + k_C(\omega)}. \tag{27}$$

The right-hand side of equation (27) is positive if and only if the hypothesis (24) is satisfied at ω; namely, we have shown that *the gross national product per capita is an increasing function of the wage-rentals ratio if and only if the capital-intensity hypothesis* (24) *is satisfied.*

A similar method may be used, e.g., to see the effect of a change in the wage-rentals ratio on the quantity of capital goods corresponding to full employment of labor and capital. Differentiating the first equation in (18) logarithmically and noting (15), we have:

$$\frac{1}{y_I}\frac{dy_I}{d\omega} = \left(\frac{1}{\omega + k_I(\omega)} + \frac{1}{k_C(\omega) - k_I(\omega)}\right)\frac{dk_I}{d\omega} + \left(\frac{1}{k_C(\omega) - k} - \frac{1}{k_C(\omega) - k_I(\omega)}\right)\frac{dk_C}{d\omega}. \tag{28}$$

which has a positive value if $k_C(\omega) > k > k_I(\omega)$. Hence,

> if the capital-intensity hypothesis is satisfied, the higher the wage-rentals ratio ω, the larger the amount of new capital goods y_I.

Let us see, finally, how the short-run equilibrium is related to the average propensity to save. We start with the following equation which is derived from the fundamental equation (21):

$$\frac{1}{Z} = \frac{s}{Z_I} + \frac{1-s}{Z_C}, \tag{29}$$

where Z, Z_I, Z_C are defined by (22).

Differentiating (29) with respect s and noting that $\partial Z/\partial\omega = 1$, we get

$$\frac{\partial\omega}{\partial s} = \frac{\dfrac{1}{Z_I} - \dfrac{1}{Z_C}}{\dfrac{sZ'_1}{Z_I^2} + \dfrac{(1-s)Z'_C}{Z_C^2} - \dfrac{1}{Z^2}}. \tag{30}$$

Then under the capital-intensity hypothesis (24), both the numerator and the denominator in the right-hand side of (30) are positive. Hence, *the equilibrium wage-rentals ratio $\omega(s)$ increases as the average propensity to save s increases.*

We have from (30) and (20) that

$$\frac{\partial\omega}{\partial s} < \frac{\dfrac{1}{Z_I} - \dfrac{1}{Z_C}}{\dfrac{s}{Z_I^2} + \dfrac{1-s}{Z_C^2} - \dfrac{1}{Z^2}}. \tag{31}$$

4 The determination of long-run equilibrium

The dynamic equations (1) and (2) are reduced to

$$\frac{\dot{k}}{k} = \frac{y_I}{k} - \nu - \mu, \tag{32}$$

where $k = K(t)/L(t)$ and $y_I = Y(t)/L(t)$.

Since

$$y = rk + w = r(k+\omega) = pf'_I(k_I)(k+\omega),$$

we have from (19) that

$$y_I = s\frac{y}{p} = sf'_1(k_I)(k+\omega),$$

where ω is the equilibrium wage-rentals ratio and k_I is the corresponding optimum capital-labor ratio in the I-sector.

Equation (32) then becomes

$$\frac{\dot{k}}{k} = sf'_I(k_I)\frac{k+\omega}{k} - \nu - \mu, \tag{33}$$

where the right-hand side is a continuous function of ω. It is assumed that the differential equation (33) with any positive initial condition possesses a solution continuous with respect to the initial condition.

Let k^* be a capital-labor ratio such that

$$sf_I'(k_I^*)\frac{k^*+\omega^*}{k^*}=\nu+\mu, \tag{34}$$

where ω^* is the equilibrium wage-rentals ratio for k^* and k_I is the optimum capital-labor ratio in the I-sector. Such a k^* may be referred to as a *balanced capital-labor ratio.*

Let us first observe that *if the capital-intensity hypothesis* (24) *is satisfied, there always exists a uniquely determined balanced capital-labor ratio* k^*, *corresponding to each level of the average propensity to save* s. To see this, define

$$\phi(\omega)=f_I'(k_I(\omega))\frac{k(\omega)+\omega}{k(\omega)}, \tag{35}$$

where $k(\omega)$ satisfies

$$k(\omega)+\omega=\frac{[k_C(\omega)+\omega][k_I(\omega)+\omega]}{s[k_C(\omega)+\omega]+(1-s)[k_I(\omega)+\omega]}. \tag{36}$$

Differentiate (35) logarithmically and substitute (20) to get

$$\frac{1}{\phi(\omega)}\frac{\partial\phi}{\partial\omega}=-\frac{1}{\omega+k_I(\omega)}+\frac{1}{k(\omega)+\omega}+\left(\frac{1}{k(\omega)+\omega}-\frac{1}{k(\omega)}\right)\frac{dk(\omega)}{d\omega},$$

which, together with (24) and $dk(\omega)/d\omega>0$, implies that

$$\frac{\partial\phi(\omega)}{\partial\omega}<0, \quad \text{for all } \omega. \tag{37}$$

Hence, for any λ and μ, there exists one and only one wage-rentals ratio ω^* for which

$$\phi(\omega^*)=\nu+\mu.$$

The corresponding capital-labor ratio $k^*=k(\omega^*)$ is a balanced capital-labor ratio, which is uniquely determined by $\nu+\mu$.

The relation (37) and $dk(\omega)/d\omega>0$ yield the following stability theorem:

> Let the capital-intensity hypothesis (24) be satisfied, and let the propensity to save be kept constant at a certain positive level $s(0<s<1)$. Then, along an arbitrary path of growth equilibrium

$(K(t), L(t))$, the capital-labor ratio $k(t) = K(t)/L(t)$ asymptotically approaches the uniquely determined balanced capital-labor ratio k^*. The convergence of the growth equilibrium $k(t)$ is monotone; i.e., if $k(0)$ is greater than k^*, $k(t)$ decreasingly approaches k^* and if $k(0)$ is less than k^*, $k(t)$ increasingly approaches k^*, and similarly all the other equilibrium variables.

In the general case where the capital-intensity hypothesis (24) is not necessarily satisfied, the balanced growth capital-labor ratio may be no longer uniquely determined, but there may be multiple balanced capital-labor ratios. However, *the growth path described by* (1–2), *or by* (32), *is globally stable; namely, the capital-labor ratio k(t) satisfying* (32) *converges monotonically to some balanced capital-labour ratio.* This is proved as follows.[5]

In view of the Arrow-Block-Hurwicz theorem,[6] it suffices to show that the right-hand side of the equation (33) tends to infinity as k goes to zero, and to zero as k goes to infinity. But k lies between $k_C(\omega)$ and $k_I(\omega)$, both of which tend to infinity (or zero) as k tends to infinity (or zero). Hence, it may suffice to show the following:

$$\lim_{\omega \to 0} \phi(\omega) = \infty, \quad \lim_{\omega \to \infty} \phi(\omega) = 0, \tag{38}$$

where $\phi(\omega)$ is defined by (35).

The first relation in (38) is easily derived from (14). To see the second relation, substitute (15) and (36) into (35) to get:

$$\phi(\omega) = \frac{f_I[k_I(\omega)]}{(1-s)\omega + k_I(\omega) - \dfrac{(1-s)\omega[\omega + k_I(\omega)]}{\omega + k_C(\omega)}} < \frac{1}{s}\frac{f_I[k_I(\omega)]}{k_I(\omega)},$$

which implies the second relation in (38).

[5] In Section 7 of [9], I have stated that the equilibrium growth is globally stable, as derived by the Arrow-Block-Hurwicz theorem. However, as Ken-ichi Inada pointed out to me, the steady state of balanced growth in the model of [9] is uniquely determined, but the differential equation describing the path of growth equilibrium may not have a continuous solution unless the capital-intensity hypothesis is satisfied. The Arrow-Block-Hurwicz theorem is not applicable to such a differential equation, which has no continuous solution. Hence, the original two-sector model as introduced in [9] may have a uniquely determined *unstable* steady state of growth equilibrium, and such is in fact the case with the example given in Section 6 of [9].

[6] The theorem referred to here is concerned with the global stability of a differentiable equation; namely, any solution to a differential equation $\dot{k} = \phi(k)$ converges to *some* equilibrium if $\lim_{k \to 0} \phi(k) > 0$ and $\lim_{k \to \infty} \phi(k) < 0$. See Arrow, Block, and Hurwicz [1, *p.* 108].

5 The propensity to save and the inducement to invest

The neoclassical growth model as described in the previous sections will now be refined to allow for a variable propensity to save and for an adjustment in the amount of new capital goods to equate the rate of interest to the marginal efficiency of capital.

It will be assumed that the average propensity to save, $s(t)$, is dependent upon the current rate of interest, $\rho(t)$, as well as upon the gross national product per capita, $y(t)$:

$$s(t) = g(\rho(t), y(t)). \tag{39}$$

The function $g(\rho, y)$ is assumed to be continuously differentiable, and

$$0 < \underline{g} < g(\rho, y) < \bar{g} < 1, \tag{40}$$

with some $\underline{g}$ and $\bar{g}$,

$$\frac{\partial g}{\partial \rho} \geqq 0, \quad \frac{\partial g}{\partial y} \geqq 0. \tag{41}$$

It is assumed that the marginal propensity to save does not exceed unity, which may be in terms of function $g(\rho, y)$ formulated as:

$$\frac{\partial g}{\partial y} \leqq \frac{1-s}{y} \quad \text{for all } \rho \text{ and } y > 0. \tag{42}$$

At each moment of time, new capital goods are produced up to the rate at which the marginal efficiency of that capital is equal to the prevailing rate of interest. The prospective rentals, which together with the expected rates of discount determine the marginal efficiency of capital, are assumed to be dependent on the current rentals, on the existing capital stock, and on the rate at which capital goods are newly-produced.

Let $\hat{r}(t, \tau)$ be the prospective returns v years ahead to the capital good newly-produced at time t. The prospective returns $\hat{r}(t, \tau)$, $0 < \tau < \infty$, are assumed to be dependent only on the current returns $r(t)$, the amounts of current capital stock $K(t)$, and of newly-produced capital goods $Y_I(t)$, and the existing labor forces $L(t)$. Let us assume that

$$\hat{r}(t, \tau) = \varphi(t, \tau; r(t), k(t), y_t(t)), \tag{43}$$

where $k(t) = K(t)/L(t)$ is the aggregate capital-labor ratio and $y_I(t) = Y_I(t)/L(t)$ is the investment per head.

The function φ, which relates prospective returns of the newly-produced capital goods to current conditions of the economy, summarizes the state of long-term expectation[7] and will be assumed to satisfy:

$$\frac{\partial \varphi}{\partial r} > 0, \quad \frac{\partial \varphi}{\partial y_I} < 0. \tag{44}$$

If for the sake of simplicity we assume that the expectation on future rates of interest is stationary, i.e., the current rate of interest, $\rho(t)$, is expected to prevail indefinitely, then the present value, $p_D(t)$ of prospective returns to newly-produced capital goods is given by

$$p_D(t) = \int_0^\infty \hat{r}(t, \tau) e^{-(\mu + \rho(t))\tau} \, d\tau. \tag{45}$$

The quantity $Y_I(t)$ of capital goods to be produced at time t is determined so as to satisfy the equation:

$$p(t) = p_D(t), \tag{46}$$

where $p(t)$ is the supply price of capital and $p_D(t)$ the demand price of capital defined by (45).

As for the determination of the current rate of interest, $\rho(t)$, let us postulate that the rate of interest is so determined as to equate the value, evaluated at the prevailing market price, of the newly-produced capital goods to the savings.

For any given amounts of capital stock $K(t)$ and labor forces $L(t)$, equations (3–10) and (46), together with (39), (43), and (45), determine the equilibrium prices and quantities, in particular the rate at which capital goods are constructed, $Y_I(t)$. The dynamic equations (1) and (2) then characterize the path of growth equilibrium $(K(t), L(t))$ in the enlarged growth model.

The method used in section 3 may be slightly modified to discuss the determination of the short-run equilibrium in the enlarged growth model. For any given aggregate capital ratio $k(t) = K(t)/L(t)$, the equilibrium conditions are reduced to (15–18), (21), (39), and (46). Let the propensity to save be temporarily fixed at an arbitrary level s $(0 < s < 1)$; then the fundamental equation (21) uniquely solves the wage-rentals ratio $\omega = \omega(s)$ corresponding to the arbitrary fixed propensity to save s. The equations (16–18) then determine equilibrium price ratio $p = p(s)$, rentals $r = r(s)$, gross national product $y = y(s)$, and the new capital construction $y_I = y_I(s)$, both per capita. The expected rentals $\hat{r}(t, \tau)$ are also determinate. The equilibrium rate of interest, $\rho = \rho(s)$, is hence uniquely solved by the equation (46).

[7] Chapter 12, pp. 147–64, in Keynes [3] is devoted to a discussion of the state of long-term expectation. Conditions (44) are based on Chapter 11, in particular Section II [3, pp. 141–44].

Let the function $\psi(s)$ be defined by

$$\psi(s) = s - g(\rho(s), y(s)), \qquad 0 < s < 1, \tag{47}$$

where $\rho(s)$ and $y(s)$ are the equilibrium rate of interest and gross national product corresponding to the level s of the propensity to save. We shall show that *the function $\psi(s)$ thus defined is an increasing function of s, provided the capital intensity hypothesis* (24) *is satisfied.*

We have seen in Section 3 that $\omega(s)$ is an increasing function of s and $d\omega/ds$ satisfies the inequality (31). The supply price $p(s)$ and the quantity $y_I(s)$ of capital goods are then both increasing functions of s, as seen from (25) and (28), while current rentals $r(s)$ is a decreasing function. Hence, in view of the assumptions (44) and (45), *the rate of interest $\rho(s)$ satisfying equation* (46) *is a decreasing function of s.* Now let us differentiate (47) with respect to s:

$$\frac{d\psi}{ds} = 1 - \frac{\partial g}{\partial \rho}\frac{d\rho}{ds} - \frac{\partial g}{\partial y}\frac{dy}{d\omega}\frac{d\omega}{ds}. \tag{48}$$

Substituting (27), (31) into (48) and using (41), we get:

$$\frac{d\psi}{ds} \geqq 1 - \frac{1}{y}\frac{\partial g}{\partial y}\left(\frac{1}{Z} - \frac{1}{Z_C}\right)\frac{\dfrac{1}{Z_I} - \dfrac{1}{Z_C}}{\dfrac{s}{Z_I^2} + \dfrac{1-s}{Z_C^2} - \dfrac{1}{Z^2}},$$

which, together with (29) and (42), yields

$$\frac{d\psi}{ds} > 1 - \frac{(1-s)s\left(\dfrac{1}{Z_I} - \dfrac{1}{Z_C}\right)^2}{\dfrac{s}{Z_I^2} + \dfrac{1-s}{Z_C^2} - \dfrac{1}{Z^2}} = 0. \tag{49}$$

The value of the function $\psi(s)$ becomes negative as s approaches zero, and positive as s approaches unity. Hence, there exists a uniquely determined level s of the propensity to save at which $\psi(s) = 0$. Such a level of the propensity to save and the corresponding equilibrium prices and quantities satisfy the equilibrium conditions (15–18), (21), (39), and (46). We have thus proved the following existence theorem:

> Let the capital-intensity hypothesis (24) be satisfied in the extended neoclassical model of economic growth, in which the average propensity to save depends on the rate of interest and gross income, while the marginal efficiency of capital is equated to the prevailing rate of interest. Then, for any arbitrary given

capital-labor ratio k, the average propensity to save, $s = s(k)$, is uniquely determined, and the equilibrium prices and quantities are accordingly determined,

The equations (1) and (2), as discussed in Section 4, may be reduced to equation (3) with s equal to the equilibrium average propensity to save corresponding to the capital-labor ratio k:

$$s = s(k).$$

An argument similar to the one given in Section 4 yields the following stability theorem:

> In the extended neoclassical model of economic growth, for given rates of labor growth ν and of capital depreciation μ, there exists at least one balanced capital-labor ratio k^*. If the capital-intensity hypothesis (24) is satisfied, the dynamic equations (1) and (2) describe a continuous path, and along any path of growth equilibrium $(K(t), L(t))$, the capital-labor ratio $k(t) = K(t)/L(t)$ converges to some balanced capital-labor ratio k^*.

6 Inflexibility of factor prices and "involuntary" unemployment

The method we have developed in the previous sections may be extended without much difficulty to analyze the impact of the factor price inflexibility upon the behavior of growth equilibrium. In this section, we shall consider the two-sector model in which the rate of adjustment in real wage is inversely related to the quantity of "involuntary" unemployment, and the stability of growth equilibrium will be investigated.

At each moment of time, the quantities we take as given are the amounts of capital and labor available to the economy as a whole and the real wage prevailing in the economy at that moment. For the sake of simplicity, the average propensity to save, s, is assumed to be constant, and the basic premises of the model are identical with those described in the previous sections. We may then, without loss of generality, take as independent variables the aggregate capital-labor ratio $k = K/L$, and the wage-rentals ratio $\omega = w/r$. The full employment conditions (6) and (7), however, are not necessarily satisfied; instead, they are replaced by the following inequalities:

$$K_I(t) + K_C(t) \leqq K(t), \tag{50}$$

$$L_I(t) + L_C(t) \leqq L(t), \tag{51}$$

where either one is satisfied with equality. The remaining equilibrium conditions (3–5) and (8–10) are preserved without change.

The method discussed in Section 3 above may be slightly modified to determine the short-run equilibrium in such a model; namely, let the optimum aggregate capital-labor ratio $k(\omega)$, corresponding to given wage-rentals ratio ω, be defined by the equation:

$$\frac{1}{k(\omega)+\omega}=\frac{s}{k_I(\omega)+\omega}+\frac{1-s}{k_C(\omega)+\omega}. \tag{52}$$

It is easily seen that, if $k \geqq k(\omega)$, labor is fully employed and the equilibrium quantity of newly-produced capital goods per capita, y_I, is determined by:

$$y_I = sf'_I[k_I(\omega)]\ (k(\omega)+\omega). \tag{53}$$

On the other hand, if $k < k(\omega)$, labor is not fully employed and y_I is given by:

$$y_I = sf'_I[k_I(\omega)]\ (k(\omega)+\omega)\frac{k}{k(\omega)}. \tag{54}$$

The dynamic path of $k(t)$ and $\omega(t)$ is then described by the following differential equations:

$$\dot{k} = y_I - (v+\mu)k, \tag{55}$$

$$\dot{\omega} = H[k - k(\omega)], \tag{56}$$

where H is a continuous sign-preserving function. In what follows, it will be assumed that, for any positive initial condition (k_0, ω_0), the pair of differential equations (55) and (56) has a positive solution $(k(t), \omega(t))$, for all $t > 0$, which is unique and continuous with respect to initial condition (k_0, ω_0).

Let us first consider the case where investment goods are more capital-intensive than consumption goods; i.e.,

$$k_I(\omega) > k_C(\omega), \quad \text{for all } \omega > 0.$$

Then, differentiating (53) logarithmically with respect to ω, we get

$$\frac{1}{y_I}\frac{dy_I}{d\omega} = -\frac{1}{k_I(\omega)+\omega}+\frac{\frac{dk(\omega)}{d\omega}+1}{k(\omega)+\omega} > 0;$$

hence, if $k \geqq k(\omega)$, y_I is an increasing function of ω. The optimum aggregate capital-labor ratio $k(\omega)$ is also an increasing function of ω, but

$$y_I < k(\omega) \quad \text{for sufficiently small } \omega,$$

and

$$y_I < k(\omega) \quad \text{for sufficiently large } \omega,$$

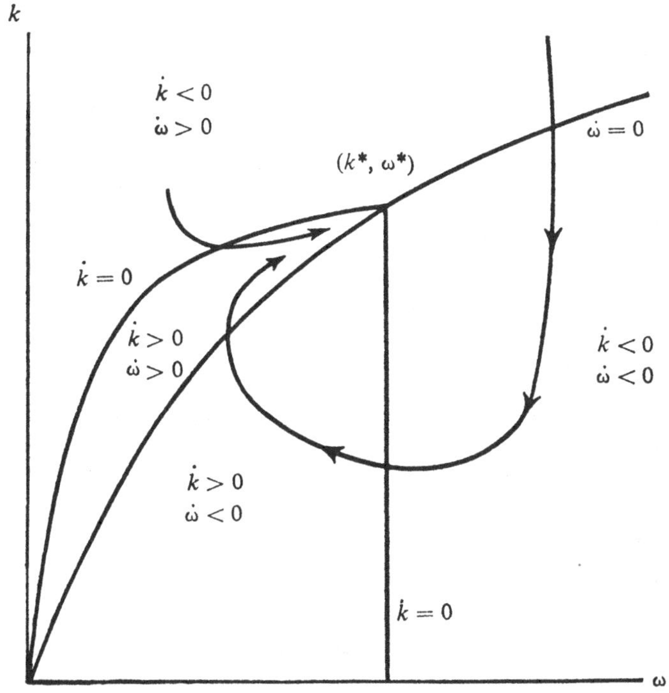

Figure 14.1

therefore, the path described by the differential equations (55) and (56) behaves as those illustrated in Fig. 14.1, and any solution $(k(t), \omega(t))$ approaches the state of balanced growth (k^*, ω^*); or, in the case of multiple balanced growth equilibria, $(k(t), \omega(t))$ approaches *a* state of balanced growth (k^*, ω^*).

If consumption goods are always more capital-intensive, i.e.,

$$k_I(\omega) < k_C(\omega), \quad \text{for all } \omega > 0,$$

then the investment per capita, y_I, may not be an increasing function of ω, although the state of balanced growth equilibrium is uniquely determined. In this case, it is easily established (by using the Poincaré-Bendixon Theory) that the solution $(k(t), \omega(t))$ of differential equations (55) and (56) approaches either the state of balanced growth equilibrium or a periodic orbit. The case of limit cycles may be illustrated by Fig. 14.2.

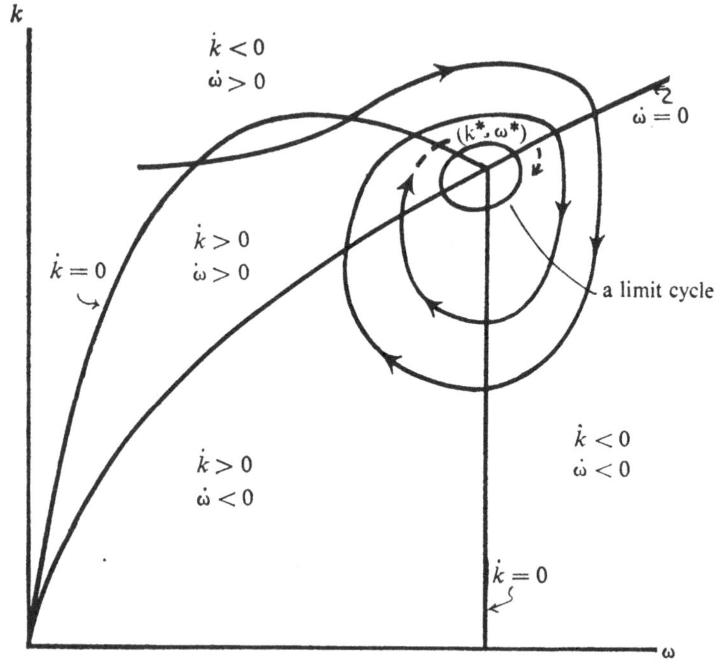

Figure 14.2

References

[1] Arrow, K. J., H. D. Block, and L. Hurwicz, "On the Stability of Competitive Equilibrium, II," *Econometrica*, Vol. 27 (1959), 82–109.

[2] Gordon, R. A., "Differential Changes in the Prices of Consumers' and Capital Goods," *American Economic Review*, Vol. 51 (1961), 937–57.

[3] Keynes, J. M., *The General Theory of Employment, Interest and Money*, London: Macmillan, 1936.

[4] Kurz, M., "Patterns of Growth and Valuation in a Two-Sector Model," *Yale Economic Essays*, Vol. 2 (1962), 403–73.

[5] Meade, J. E., *A Neo-Classical Theory of Economic Growth*, New York: Oxford University Press, 1961.

[6] Solow, R. M., "A Contribution to the Theory of Economic Growth," *Quarterly Journal of Economics*, Vol. 32 (1956), 65–94.

[7] Solow, R. M., "Note on Uzawa's Two-Sector Model of Economic Growth," *Review of Economic Studies*, Vol. 29 (1961–62), 48–50.

[8] Swan, T., "Economic Growth and Capital Accumulation," *Economic Record*, Vol. 66 (1956), 334–61.

[9] Uzawa, H., "On a Two-Sector Model of Economic Growth," *Review of Economic Studies*, Vol. 29 (1961–62), 40–47.

[10] Wicksell, K., *Lectures on Political Economy, I: General Theory*, London: Routledge and Kegan Paul, 1934.

CHAPTER 15

Time preference and the Penrose effect in a two-class model of economic growth

1 Introduction

In the theory of economic growth, we are concerned with the analysis of those economic factors which crucially determine the process of growth for a national economy. Our primary interest is in the mechanisms by which aggregate variables such as national income, aggregate stock of capital, and others are interrelated and in how they change as time passes. Since Harrod (1948) first laid down the fundamental theorems for a dynamic economics, we have seen the emergence of an increasing number of aggregate growth models to clarify and extend these theorems, as aptly described in Hahn and Matthews's (1964) survey article. These growth models, however, have been mostly built upon premises directly involving aggregate variables, without specifying the postulates which govern the behavior of individual units comprising the national economy. In particular, the specifications of aggregate savings are seldom based upon analysis of individual behavior concerning savings and consumption; instead, they have been merely hypothesized in terms of historical and statistical observations. Similarly, the aggregative behavior of investment has been either entirely neglected, as has been typically the case with the so-called neoclassical models, or it has been postulated in terms of somewhat *ad hoc* relations involving market rate of interest, rate of profit, and other variables.

In the present paper, I should like to pay closer attention to the behavior of individual units concerning consumption, saving, and investment, and

From *Journal of Political Economy*, Vol. 77 (1969), pp. 628–52; reprinted with permission.

This paper has been presented at seminars at the University of Chicago and Cambridge University from whose participants I have received a number of valuable comments and suggestions. I should like particularly to acknowledge my indebtedness to Professors Milton Friedman, Arnold Harberger, Joan Robinson, and Lord Kahn.

to build a formal model of economic growth for which the aggregate variables are described in terms of these microeconomic analyses.

A private-enterprise economy, with which the present paper is concerned, may be conveniently divided into two sectors; the household sector and the corporate sector. Decisions regarding the consumption of goods and services produced in the corporate sector are made by households; the households in turn are endowed with labor and possess, as assets, the securities issued by the corporate sector.

The analysis of the behavior of an individual household is carried out in terms of the Böhm-Bawerk-Fisher theory of time preference. My presentation is based upon the mathematical formulation recently developed by Koopmans (1960), with certain modifications, and it may be regarded as an extension of a similar formulation introduced in a previous article of mine (1968*a*).[1] The marginal rate of substitution between current and future consumption is approximated by the schedule of time preference to be referred to as the Fisherian schedule. It relates the rate of time preference to the current level of consumption and to the utility level for all future consumption. Under the hypothesis that intertemporal preference orderings are homothetic, it will be possible to derive the optimum propensities to consume and save – both as functions of the expected market rate of interest alone – independently of the household's income.

To analyze the investment behavior of business firms in the corporate sector, it is necessary to re-examine the concept of real capital which will play a central role in the determination of the levels of output, employment, and investment in general. At each moment of time, a business firm consists of a complex of fixed factors of production, such as factories, machinery, and others, including managerial abilities and technological skills. Real capital is here introduced as an index to measure the productive capacity of such a complex of capital goods endowed within the firm at a particular time. Real capital, as the index of productive capacity of the firm, is then increased as the stock of fixed factors of production is accumulated. The relationships between the real value of investment and the resulting increase in the index of real capital will be described by the Penrose curve, discussed below in detail. It is assumed that the business firm plans the levels of employment and investment in order to maximize the present value of expected future net cash flows, which will be discounted by the market rate of interest. The desired level of investment per unit of real capital will be shown to depend upon the expected rate of profit and the market rate of interest.

[1] The paper referred to here contains a number of ambiguities both in its exposition and in its basic assumptions, particularly with respect to the shape of what I have called the Fisherian schedule of time preference.

Finally, these analyses are put together to formulate an aggregative model of capital accumulation and to briefly analyze the structure of short-run and long-run equilibrium processes.

2 Intertemporal utility and the rate of time preference

Let us consider a consumer unit which knows with certainty the stream of consumption over its lifetime. For the sake of simplicity, we assume that there is one kind of consumption good, remaining invariant over time, and the time horizon of the consumer unit is infinite.[2] It is assumed that the unit possesses an intertemporal preference ordering between any pair of consumption streams (subject to certain mathematical regularity conditions) and that indifference surfaces for such an intertemporal preference ordering are homothetic. In what follows, we restrict our attention to those intertemporal preference orderings which it is possible to represent by a utility functional of the following type:

$$U(0) = \int_0^\infty c(s)e^{-\Delta(s)}\,ds, \tag{1}$$

where $c(t)$ is the time path of the consumption stream over time ($0 \leqq t < \infty$), and $\Delta(t)$ is the accumulated rate of time preference associated with the consumption path $c(t)$. In general, the utility functional is defined for any truncated part of the original consumption path:

$$U(t) = \int_t^\infty c(s)e^{-\Delta(s,t)}\,ds, \tag{2}$$

where $\Delta(s,t)$ is the accumulated rate of time preference between t and s. The rate of time preference $\Delta(s,t)$ depends upon the whole path of the consumption stream $c(\tau)$, $t \leqq \tau < \infty$, and the meaning of the definition (2) may be easily seen by differentiating it with respect to t:

$$\dot{U}(t) = \delta(t)U(t) - c(t), \tag{3}$$

where the (marginal) rate of time preference $\delta(t)$ is given by

$$\delta(t) = \left(\frac{\partial\Delta(t,t')}{\partial t'}\right)_{t'=t}. \tag{4}$$

At each moment of time $t, c(t)$ represents the level of current consumption at time t, while $U(t)$ may be regarded as the index measuring the utility of the consumption stream $c(t)$ in the future. Suppose the time

[2] The consumer unit in consideration here is a perpetual institution of which each individual is responsible for the management during his lifetime.

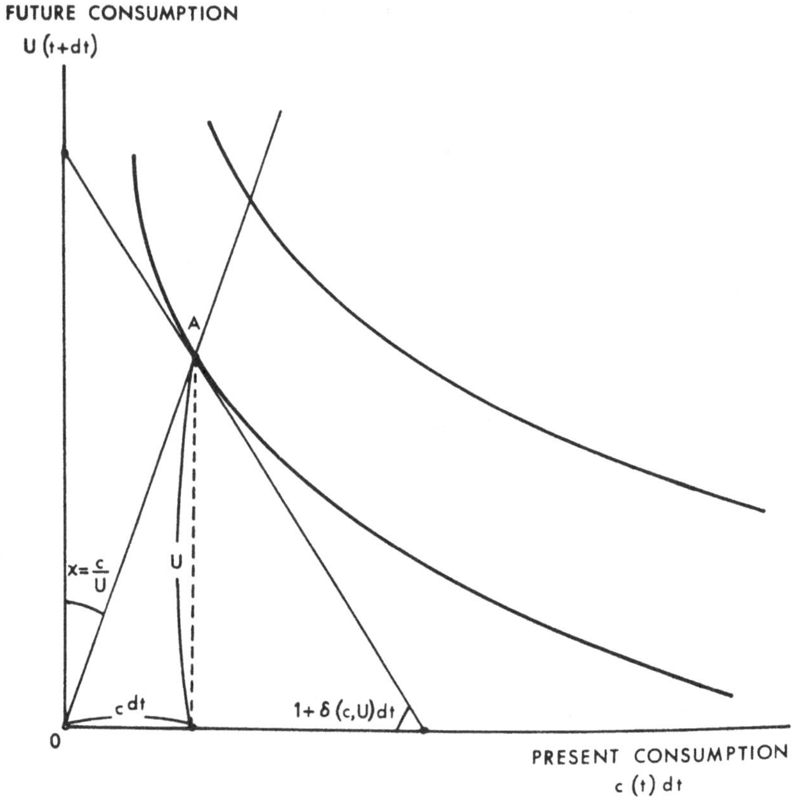

Figure 15.1

preference ordering of the consumer unit in question is represented by indifference curves on the (c, U) plane, as indicated in Figure 15.1, where the horizontal axis measures the current consumption $c(t)dt$ and the utility of the future consumption $U(t + dt)$ is measured along the vertical axis. For any combination of current consumption $c(t)dt$ and future consumption $U(t + dt)$, to be represented by the point A, the marginal rate of substitution between present consumption and future consumption (that is, the negative of the slope of the tangent line at A to the indifference curve) is equal to unity plus the rate of time preference, $1 + \delta(t)dt$. If we assume the intertemporal preference structure of the consumer unit remains identical over time, the schedule relating the rate of time preference $\delta(t)$ to the combination of current consumption $c(t)$ and the utility of future consumption $U(t)$ remains invariant, namely, $\delta(t) = \delta[c(t), U(t)]$ with a certain function $\delta(c, U)$.

Since we have assumed that the intertemporal preference ordering is homothetic, we may assume that indifference curves for c and U are also homothetic, so the schedule of the rate of time preference (c, U) is homogeneous of order zero with respect to c and U; namely,

$$\delta(c, U) = \delta(x), \quad x = c/U. \tag{5}$$

The differential equation (3) may be written as

$$\frac{\dot{U}(t)}{U(t)} = \delta[x(t)] - x(t), \quad x(t) = \frac{c(t)}{U(t)}. \tag{6}$$

The intertemporal preference ordering is subject to a diminishing marginal rate of substitution between current and future consumption if the time preference function $\delta(x)$ is convex. On the other hand, as is seen from Figure 15.1, an increase in the consumption-utility ratio, $x = c/U$, results in a decrease in $\delta(x)$. We may therefore assume that

$$\delta(x) > 0, \quad \delta'(x) < 0, \quad \delta''(x) > 0, \quad \text{for all } x > 0 \tag{7}$$

as is typically illustrated in Figure 15.2, where x is measured along the horizontal axis and the rate of time preference δ along the vertical axis.

In general, it is difficult to find the level of the intertemporal utility functional for an arbitrary stream of consumption. However, if the rate of increase in the level of consumption $\dot{c}(t)/c(t)$ is constant over time, the intertemporal utility function $U(t)$ for the stream of consumption $c(s)$, $t \leqq s < \infty$, is easily derived. Let $U(0)$ be the utility of the consumption stream $c(s)$, $0 \leqq s < \infty$, for which the rate of increase in consumption $\dot{c}(t)/c(t)$ is constant over time, say

$$\dot{c}(t)/c(t) = \lambda. \tag{8}$$

The level of the intertemporal utility $U(0)$ now depends upon the initial level of consumption $c(0)$ and the rate of increase λ in consumption over time. Let us define the relationships by the functional notation:

$$U(0) = h[c(0), \lambda]. \tag{9}$$

Because of the linear homogeneity of the intertemporal utility functional (1), the function $h[c(0), \lambda]$ is linear homogeneous with respect to $c(0)$; namely,

$$h[\alpha c(0), \lambda] = \alpha h[c(0), \lambda]. \tag{10}$$

Since we have assumed that the intertemporal preference ordering remains invariant over time, we have

$$U(t) = h[c(t), \lambda], \tag{11}$$

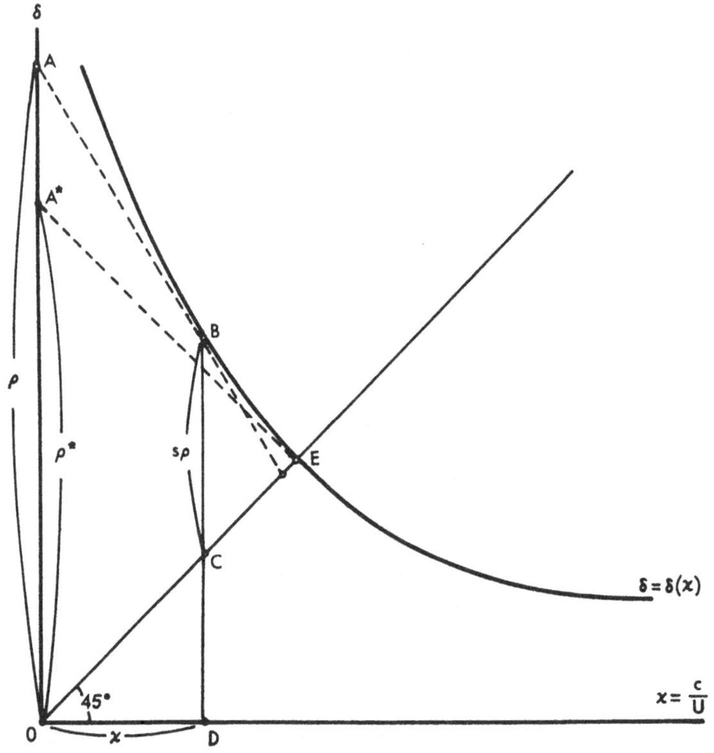

Figure 15.2

where $U(t)$ is by definition the level of the intertemporal utility for the truncated consumption path $c(s)$, for $t \leqq s < \infty$. Hence, from (9), (10), and (11), we get

$$\frac{U(t)}{U(0)} = \frac{c(t)}{c(0)}. \tag{12}$$

Thus the consumption-utility ratio, $x(t) = c(t)/U(t)$, remains constant over time:

$$x(t) = x(0), \qquad \text{for all } t. \tag{13}$$

On the other hand, by differentiating $x(t)$ logarithmically and by taking (6) and (8) into account, we get

$$\frac{\dot{x}(t)}{x(t)} = \lambda + x(t) - \delta[x(t)], \tag{14}$$

which together with the constancy of $x(t)$ yields

$$x(t) = x^*, \tag{15}$$

where x^* is the solution to the following equation:

$$\lambda + x^* = \delta(x^*). \tag{16}$$

Since the schedule of the time preference $\delta(x)$ is negatively sloped, the consumption-utility ratio x^* satisfying (16) is uniquely determined, as illustrated in Figure 15.2. The level of the intertemporal utility $U(0)$ now is given by

$$U(0) = \frac{c(0)}{x^*} = \frac{c(0)}{\delta(x^*) - \lambda}. \tag{17}$$

As is seen from Figure 15.2, an increase in the rate of increase in consumption results with a lower rate of time preference $\delta(x^*)$ but with a higher consumption-utility ratio x^*. An increase in the rate of increase in consumption will lower the current level of consumption $c(0)$ relative to the future levels of future consumption, thus making a marginal increase in future consumption less desirable. It will then result in a higher rate of time preference, but an increase in the rate of increase in consumption, with given current consumption $c(0)$, will make the whole path of consumption more preferable, so the present value of consumption will be increased.

3 Time preference and the optimum propensity to save

The theory of homothetic intertemporal preference orderings may now be applied to examine the structure of each individual unit's consumption and saving functions. Let us consider a consumer unit which, at a certain moment of time 0, possesses an asset whose market value is $a(0)$ in real terms and which expects to receive wages and certain yields (dividends plus capital gains) for the asset it owns. We are interested in the way in which the consumer unit divides its income between current consumption and savings at each moment of time, and in the effects which changes in some of the basic variables exert upon the consumption and saving pattern. For the sake of simplicity, let us assume that the consumer unit's expectations concerning future real wages and interest rates are stationary, kept constant over time, say at w and ρ respectively. The current real income $y(0)$ then becomes

$$y(0) = w + \rho a(0). \tag{18}$$

Future real income is determined by the way real income is divided between consumption and savings; namely, real income $y(t)$ at time t is given by

$$y(t) = w + \rho a(t), \tag{19}$$

where $a(t)$ is the real value of assets held at time t, to be determined by

$$\dot{a}(t) = y(t) - c(t), \tag{20}$$

where $c(t)$ is real consumption planned at time t.

The differential equation (20) may be transformed to one involving real income $y(t)$:

$$\dot{y}(t) = \rho[y(t) - c(t)], \tag{21}$$

with the initial real income $y(0)$ given by (18).

The intertemporal preference ordering associated with the planned path of consumption $c(t)$, $0 \leqq t < \infty$, is represented by the utility functional $U(0)$ defined by (1), and the consumer unit is interested in choosing the time paths of consumption $c(t)$ and asset holdings $a(t)$, $0 \leqq t < \infty$, which satisfy the budget constraints (18–20) and for which the level of the intertemporal utility $U(0)$ is maximized among all feasible consumption paths starting with the initial quantity of assets $a(0)$.

We have assumed that the intertemporal utility functional $U(0)$ is (strictly quasi-) concave and homogeneous of order one, and the consumer unit's expectations concerning real wages and rates of interest are stationary. It is readily observed that, *for any initial real income* y_0, *the optimum paths of real consumption and asset holdings are uniquely determined and that the consumption-income ratio,* $c(t)/y(t)$, *remains constant along the optimum path.* This will be proved rigorously as follows:

First, let us suppose there exist two optimum paths of consumption, $c^0(t)$ and $c^1(t)$, starting with the given initial level of real income y_0. Then the weighted average of these two consumption paths:

$$c^\theta(t) = (1 - \theta)c^0(t) + \theta c^1(t), \quad \text{for some } 0 < \theta < 1,$$

becomes feasible, and, in view of the (strict) convexity of intertemporal indifference surfaces, $c^\theta(t)$ will attain a higher value for the intertemporal utility functional $U(0)$, thus contradicting the optimality of the consumption path $c^0(t)$ or $c^1(t)$.

Second, to see the constancy of the consumption-income ratio $c(t)/y(t)$ along the optimum path, let us introduce the notations $c(t, y_0)$ and $y(t, y_0)$, which are, respectively, the optimum paths of real consumption and real income, starting with the initial level of real income y_0; $y(t, y_0)$ satisfies the differential equation (21) with the initial condition y_0 and consumption $c(t, y_0)$, and the value of the intertemporal utility functional (1) is maximized for the consumption path $c(t, y_0)$ among all feasible paths, starting with the same initial real income y_0. Let us consider another initial level of real income $\bar{y}_0$, and the corresponding optimum paths of consumption and real income, $c(t, \bar{y}_0)$ and $y(t, \bar{y}_0)$. Then the path of real income defined by $by(t, \bar{y}_0)$, where $b = y_0/\bar{y}_0$, becomes a feasible path of real income starting with initial real income y_0 and the consumption path $bc(t, \bar{y}_0)$. It is also seen that the value of the intertemporal utility functional $U(0)$ is maximized at $bc(t, \bar{y}_0)$ among all feasible consumption paths starting with initial income y_0; hence, by the uniqueness property of the optimum paths of consumption and real income, we get $c(t, y_0) = bc(t, \bar{y}_0)$, $y(t, y_0) = by(t, \bar{y}_0)$. That is

$$\frac{c(t, y_0)}{c(t, \bar{y}_0)} = \frac{y(t, y_0)}{y(t, \bar{y}_0)} = \frac{y_0}{\bar{y}_0}, \quad \text{for all } t. \tag{22}$$

Let us now consider the truncated parts $c(s, y_0)$ and $y(s, y_0)$, $t \leqq s < \infty$ of the optimum path, $c(t, y_0)$ and $y(t, y_0)$. The time path $c(t + \tau, y_0)$ and $y(t + \tau, y_0)$, $0 \leqq \tau < \infty$, now becomes the optimum path for the initial real income $y(t, y_0)$; otherwise, it would be possible to find a feasible path of consumption starting with initial real income y_0. Therefore

$$c(t + \tau, y_0) = c[\tau, y(t, y_0)], \qquad y(t + \tau, y_0) = y[\tau, y(t, y_0)]. \tag{23}$$

Hence, by applying (22) to (23), we get

$$c(t, y_0) = c[0, y(t, y_0)] = \frac{y(t, y_0)}{y(0, y_0)} c(0, y_0); \tag{24}$$

making the consumption-income ratio, $c(t)/y(t)$, constant along the optimum path.

The optimum path then may be found among those for which the consumption-income ratio, $c(t)/y(t)$, or equivalently the saving-income ratio, $1 - [c(t)/y(t)]$, remains constant over time. Let us consider a time path, $c(t)$ and $y(t)$, for which the saving-income ratio remains at the constant ratio s over time:

$$1 - s = c(t)/y(t), \tag{25}$$

then,

$$\dot{y}(t) = \rho s y(t), \tag{26}$$

and

$$\frac{\dot{c}(t)}{c(t)} = \frac{\dot{y}(t)}{y(t)} = \rho s. \tag{27}$$

The time path of consumption $c(t)$ then has a constant rate of increase, and the level of the intertemporal utility functional U_0 is determined as has been worked out in detail above. Let the consumption-utility ratio, x, be obtained by

$$\rho s + x = \delta(x). \tag{28}$$

Then,

$$U_0 = \frac{c_0}{x} = \frac{(1-s)y_0}{x}, \tag{29}$$

which, together with (28), may be written as

$$\frac{\rho U_0}{y_0} = \frac{\rho - \delta(x)}{x} + 1. \tag{30}$$

The optimum saving-income ratio s may be obtained by first finding the consumption-utility ratio x which maximizes

$$\frac{\rho - \delta(x)}{x}. \tag{31}$$

Such an x may be obtained by solving the following equation:

$$\frac{\rho - \delta(x)}{x} = \delta'(x). \tag{32}$$

The determination of the optimum x may be easily seen from Figure 15.2, where the vertical axis measures the rate of time preference and the horizontal axis the consumption-utility ratio x. Let OA be equal to the rate of interest ρ and draw the tangent line from A to the schedule of the rate of time preference, intersecting at B. Then the slope of the line AB with the horizontal axis, measured in the negative direction, gives us the maximized value of (31). If C and D are the points which the perpendicular line going through B intersects with the 45° ray and the horizontal axis, respectively, then $BD = \delta(x)$, $BC = s\rho$. Hence, the optimum saving-income ratio s is obtained by the ratio of BC over AO. Since the optimum saving-time ratio s is uniquely determined by the rate of interest alone, we may denote it as $s(\rho)$. Then the saving and consumption functions are given by:

$$\begin{cases} s(\rho, y) = s(\rho)y \\ c(\rho, y) = [1 - s(\rho)]y. \end{cases} \tag{33}$$

It is easily seen from Figure 15.2 that an increase in the rate of interest ρ results in an increase in $\rho s(\rho)$, but not necessarily in an increase in $s(\rho)$.

The elasticity of the average propensity to save with respect to the rate of interest, then, is greater than -1, but not necessarily positive.

Let E = the intersection of the 45° ray with the schedule of the rate of time preference, A^* = the intersection of the tangent line at E with the vertical axis, and $\rho^* = OA^*$. Hence, if the rate of interest is given as ρ^*, then the optimum propensity to save is zero, and $s(\rho)$ is positive or negative, according to whether ρ is higher or lower than ρ^*. Namely, there exists what may be termed the natural rate of interest, ρ^* (uniquely determined by the schedule of the rate of time preference), for which the following conditions are satisfied for the schedule of the optimum propensity to save $s(\rho)$:

$$s(\rho) \gtreqless 0, \quad \text{according to whether } \rho \gtreqless \rho^*. \tag{34}$$

4 Concept of real capital, the production function, and the Penrose curve

The model of economic growth to be constructed in this paper focuses upon the analysis of the investment behavior of business firms, beginning with an examination of the concept of real capital upon which the production function of each individual firm is based.

Any business firm, as a productive agent, consists of a complex of machinery, equipment, tools, and other fixed factors of production, including managerial and administrative abilities, which, when combined with those factors of production readily available in the market, are employed to produce the output of the firm. At each moment of time, the available quantities of variable factors of production are assigned to various types of machinery, equipment, and other fixed means of production in such a way that the value of the resulting output is maximized. The maximum ouput thus obtained may generally depend upon the administrative, managerial, and engineering abilities of the firm, to be summarized by its short-run production function. Since the discussion throughout the present paper may be carried out in terms of a homogeneous output, as typically assumed in the standard neoclassical theory of economic growth, let us suppose that various kinds of output are always produced and consumed in fixed proportions. It will be further assumed that there is only one kind of variable factor of production – services of homogeneous labor – so that the short-run production function may be illustrated in Figure 15.3, where the quantity of output is measured along the vartical axis and that of available labor services along the horizontal axis. Let OQ_t represent the short-run production at a certain moment of time t when the firm possesses a certain quantity of each of the fixed

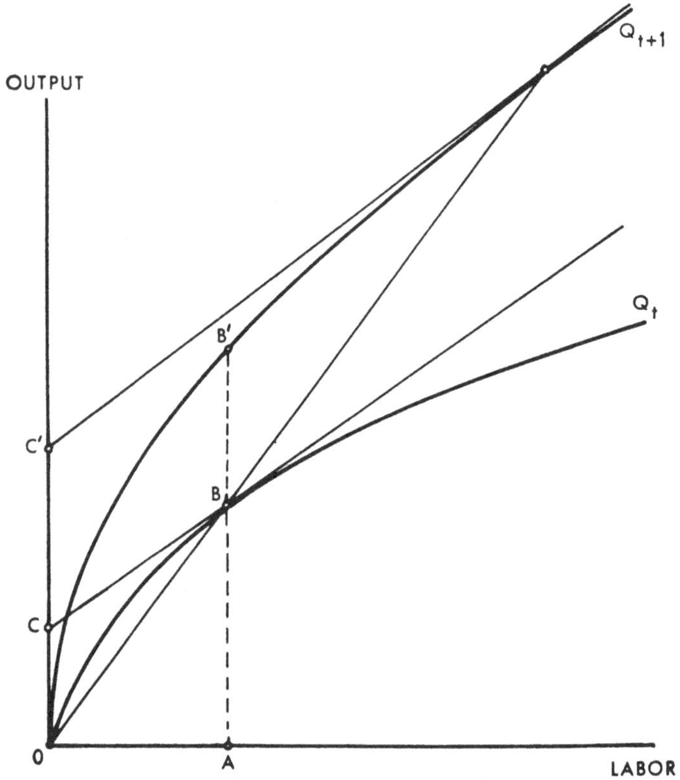

Figure 15.3

factors of production; output AB thus stands for the maximum output which can be produced by the firm by properly allocating the quantity OA of labor services. Let us now consider the short-run production function of the same firm at the next instance, say $t+1$, when the composition of fixed factors of production comprising the firm is different from that at time t. The maximum quantity of output $B'A$ which can be produced at time $t+1$ from the available quantity of labor services OA in general differs from OB, thus resulting in a shift in the short-run production curve from OQ_t to OQ_{t+1}. The change in the composition of fixed factors of production from time t to time $t+1$ involves changes not only in the number of readily measurable machinery, equipment, and so forth, but also in managerial and other abilities generally impossible to quantify. However, the question naturally arises whether it is possible to find an index to measure the extent to which the capacity of the firm as a productive agent has been increased by such changes in the composition of real capital. To examine the circumstances under which such an index may be unambiguously defined, let us consider the amount of the maximum profits the firm can obtain when it is faced with a competitive labor market. For a given real wage rate w, it employs labor services up to the level at which the marginal product of labor is equated to the real wage rate w, and the firm's earning capacity may be measured by the profits to be earned, as indicated by OC or OC' in Figure 15.3. Because of the shift in the short-run production curve, the profits obtained at time $t+1$ would be larger than that at time t; the ratio OC' over OC may be used as an index of real capital at $t+1$ with reference to the base year t; and we may define the index of real capital K_t at time t to satisfy:

$$K_{t+1}/K_t = OC'/OC. \tag{35}$$

The index of real capital thus defined, however, generally depends upon the real wage rate with respect to which total output is obtained. We may assume that *the ratio of profits at time t over that at time t + 1 is defined independently of the real wage rate with respect to which the labor employment is determined.*

The index of real capital at time t, K_t, is then uniquely determined with respect to the base year $t = 0$ when K_0 is assumed to be unity.

It is easily seen, from the way in which the index of real capital K_t is constructed, that the output Q_t at time t is determined by the index of real capital K_t at time t and the quantity of labor services L_t employed at time t.

$$Q_t = F(K_t, L_t), \tag{36}$$

where the production function F remains invariant over time. The above assumption then implies that the production function $F(K, L)$ is *homogeneous of degree one and that the isoquants are all convex toward the origin.*

The per capita output $q_t = Q_t/L_t$ is then a function of the capital-labor ratio $k_t = K_t/L_t$:

$$q_t = f(k_t),$$

for which it is assumed that

$$f(k) > 0, \quad f'(k) > 0, \quad f''(k) < 0, \quad \text{for all } k > 0. \tag{37}$$

The shift in the short-run production function from OQ_t to OQ_{t+1} is primarily due to changes in the composition of real capital which have been induced by an investment of certain quantities of capital good. Let us denote by Φ_t the value of such an investment measured in terms of the output produced by the firm (an increase in real investment Φ_t generally results in an increase in the index of real capital K_t, as defined above).

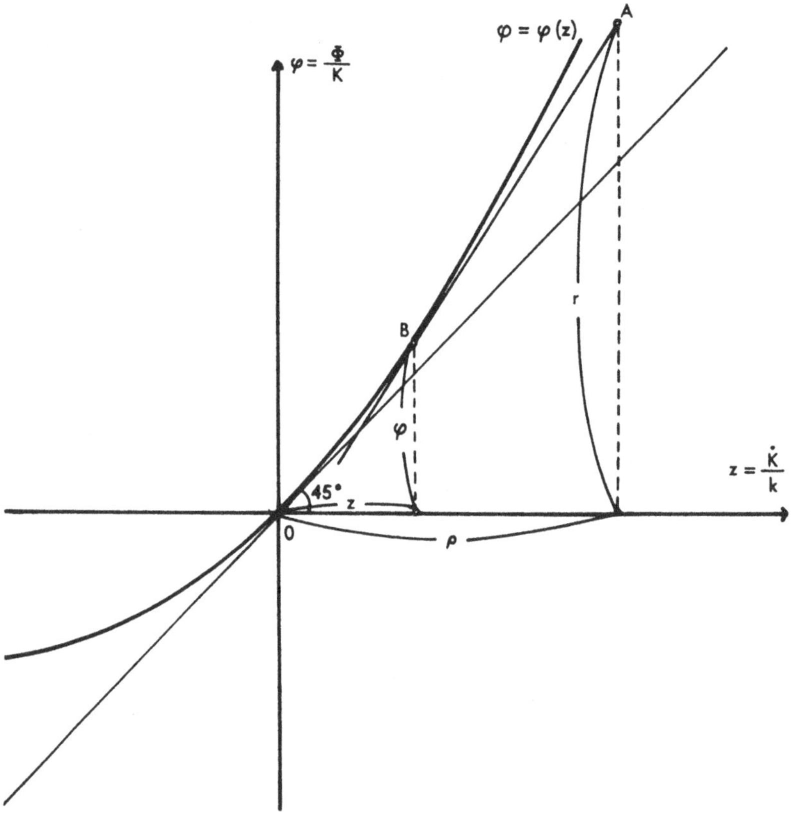

Figure 15.4

The index of real capital K_t reflects the managerial and administrative abilities of the firm as well as the quantities of physical factors of production such as machinery and equipment. The actual increase in the index of real capital K_t due to a certain amount of investment is also constrained by the magnitude and quantities of managerial resources possessed by the firm at that moment. The schedule relating the rate of increase in K_t and the required level of investment will in general shift whenever there is a change in the quantity of real capital. If we suppose that the administrative, managerial, and other abilities which are required by the firm in the process of growth and expansion are present in proportion to the index of real capital K_t, the schedule relating the rate of increase, $z = \dot{K}/K$, in real capital with the investment-capital ratio, $\varphi = \Phi/K$, may be assumed to remain invariant over time, independently of the level of real capital possessed by the firm at each moment of time. Such a schedule is in general described by a convex curve, as in Figure 15.4, where the rate of increase in real capital z and the investment-capital ratio φ are measured along the horizontal and vertical axes, respectively. For the sake of convenience, it will be referred to as the Penrose curve (see Penrose, 1959; and Uzawa, 1968*b*), to be denoted by $\varphi = \varphi(z)$, and it is assumed to satisfy the following conditions:

$$\varphi'(z) > 0, \quad \varphi''(z) > 0, \quad \text{for all } z, \tag{38}$$

particularly reflecting the scarcity of those factors which are indispensable to the firm in the process of growth. The conditions (38) indicate that the higher the rate of increase in real capital, the higher is the level of investment, and that the marginal cost of investment is increasing. We may without loss of generality assume that the Penrose curve has the slope of 45° when the rate of increase in real capital is zero:

$$\varphi(0) = 0, \qquad \varphi'(0) = 1. \tag{39}$$

5 Investment function and marginal efficiency of investment

The concept of real capital and the Penrose effect as developed in section 4 will be used to discuss the investment behavior of a competitive firm. Let us consider a firm for which the index of real capital is measured at K_0 at a certain moment of time 0, and which possesses the production function $q = f(k)$ and the Penrose curve $\varphi = \varphi(z)$, as typically illustrated in Figures 15.3 and 15.4. To simplify the analysis, let us suppose that the firm has stationary expectations concerning future rates of real wages (w) and interest (ρ). Then the present value of future net cash flows becomes

$$\int_0^\infty [Q(t) - wL(t) - \Phi(t)]e^{-\rho t}\, dt, \tag{40}$$

where $Q(t) = F[K(t), L(t)]$ is the quantity of output, $K(t)$ and $L(t)$ are, respectively, the levels of real capital and labor employment, and $\Phi(t)$ is the level of investment, all planned for time t. The index of real capital $K(t)$ is increased by $Z(t)$:

$$\dot{K}(t) = Z(t), \tag{41}$$

where the investment-capital ratio $[\varphi(t) = \Phi(t)/K(t)]$ is related to the rate of increase in real capital $[z(t) = Z(t)/K(t)]$, by the Penrose curve:

$$\varphi(t) = \varphi[z(t)]. \tag{42}$$

The firm then is interested in finding the planned paths of real capital, labor employment, and investment for which the present value (40) of the expected future net cash flow is maximized subject to the constraint (41) with the initial level of real capital K_0.

In view of the assumptions (38), it can be shown that *if an optimum path of capital accumulation exists, then it is uniquely determined.* Indeed, suppose there were to exist two different paths of capital accumulation, $K^0(t)$ and $K^1(t)$, starting with K_0, for both of which the present value (40) is maximized. Let $Q^0(t)$, $L^0(t)$, $Z^0(t)$ and $Q^1(t)$, $L^1(t)$, $Z^1(t)$ be, respectively, the corresponding levels of output, labor employment, and increase in real capital. Define the path of capital accumulation $K^\theta(t)$ by $K^\theta(t) = (1-\theta)K^0(t) + \theta K^1(t)$, $0 < \theta < 1$, and the corresponding levels of employment and capital accumulation by $L^\theta(t) = (1-\theta)L^0(t) + \theta L^1(t)$, $Z^\theta(t) = (1-\theta)Z^0(t) + \theta Z^1(t)$. Then, because of the convexity assumption (38), the required level of investment $\Phi^\theta(t)$ satisfies the inequality, $\Phi^\theta(t) \leqq (1-\theta)\Phi^0(t) + \theta\Phi^1(t)$, for all t, with strict inequality for some time interval. Hence, the new path of capital accumulation $K^\theta(t)$ is also feasible and attains a higher present value, thus contradicting the optimality of $K^0(t)$ or $K^1(t)$.

To see the structure of the optimum path of capital accumulation, let us first observe that the optimum level of labor employment $L(t)$ at each moment of time t is so determined as to equate the marginal product of labor to the expected rate of real wages. Since the production function $F(K, L)$ is assumed to be linear homogeneous, the optimum capital-labor ratio $k = K(t)/L(t)$ at each moment of time t is uniquely determined, independently of time t, at the level satisfying the marginality condition:

$$f(k) - kf'(k) = w. \tag{43}$$

If we denote by $r = f'(k)$ the marginal product of real capital corresponding to the optimum capital-labor ratio k, the present value (40) may be reduced to

$$\int_0^\infty \{r - \varphi[z(t)]\} K(t) e^{-\rho t}\, dt, \tag{44}$$

with

$$\dot{K}(t)/K(t) = z(t), . \qquad K_0 \text{ given.} \tag{45}$$

As we have seen above, the optimum path of capital accumulation is uniquely determined, and the optimum rate of increase in the index of real capital $z(0)$ at time 0 may be regarded as a function of $K(0)$, r, and ρ, to be denoted by

$$z(0) = G[K(0), w, \rho]. \tag{46}$$

Let $z(t)$ be the optimum path of the rate of increase in real capital starting with initial $K(0)$, then the truncated path $z(s)$, $t \leqq s < \infty$, also becomes optimum with respect to the initial level of capital $K(t)$, with respect to the same expected rates of wages w and interest ρ. Hence, we have

$$z(t) = G[K(t), w, \rho]. \tag{47}$$

On the other hand, the present value of net cash flows (44) is a linear homogeneous functional and the function $G(K, w, \rho)$ is homogeneous of order zero, namely,

$$z(t) = g(w, \rho), \quad \text{for all } t, \tag{48}$$

with a certain function $g(w, \rho)$ of w and ρ alone.

Thus, we have shown that, *for any initial level of real capital K_0 and for any expected rates of real wages* w *and interest ρ, if an optimum path of capital accumulation exists, it is uniquely determined and the rate of capital accumulation, $z = \dot{K}(t)/K(t)$, is constant over time.*

The optimum path of capital accumulation now may be found among those paths for which the rate of increase in real capital is constant. If z is a constant rate of increase in K, then the present value (44) per $K(0)$ may be simply reduced to

$$v = \frac{r - \varphi(z)}{\rho - z}. \tag{49}$$

The maximization of the present value v given by (49) is easily done in terms of the Penrose curve in Figure 15.4. Let A be the point whose coordinates are (ρ, r). Then the present value v represents the slope of the line connecting A and the point on the Penrose curve $B = [z, \varphi(z)]$, corresponding to the planned rate of increase z in real capital. Therefore, the maximum value of v is attained when the point B is chosen in such a way that the line AB is tangent to the Penrose curve. Analytically, the optimum rate of increase in real capital z is obtained by solving the following marginality condition:[3]

$$\frac{r - \varphi(z)}{\rho - z} = \varphi'(z). \tag{50}$$

Since the optimum rate of increase in real capital z and the optimum investment-capital ratio φ are uniquely determined by the rate of interest ρ and the rate of profit r, we may use the functional notation:

$$z = z(\rho, r), \qquad \varphi = \varphi(\rho, r). \tag{51}$$

[3] As is seen from (50), the deviation of the investment function is an application of the principle of marginal efficiency of investment of Keynes.

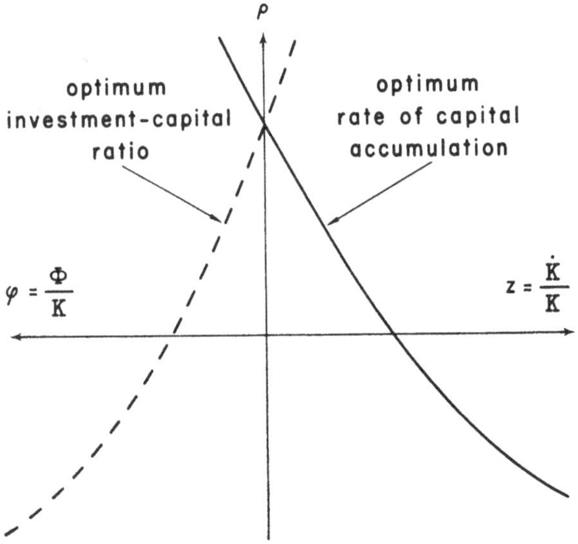

Figure 15.5

As is seen Figure 15.4, an increase in the rate of profit r or a decrease in the rate of interest ρ always increases both the optimum rate of capital accumulation and the optimum investment-capital ratio; namely,

$$\begin{cases} \dfrac{\partial z}{\partial \rho} < 0, & \dfrac{\partial z}{\partial r} > 0, \\ \dfrac{\partial \varphi}{\partial \rho} < 0, & \dfrac{\partial \varphi}{\partial r} > 0. \end{cases} \tag{52}$$

We can also see that the optimum rate of capital accumulation $z(\rho, r)$ is positive or negative according to whether the rate of interest ρ is smaller or larger than the rate of profit r:

$$z(\rho, r) \gtreqless 0, \quad \text{according to } \rho \lesseqgtr r. \tag{53}$$

For the given rate of profit r, the schedule of the optimum investment-capital ratio and the optimum rate of increase in real capital are typically illustrated by the curves in Figures 15.5.

6 An aggregate model of economic growth

The analysis of the saving and investment behaviors of individual economic units as introduced in the previous sections may now be applied to examine the pattern of equilibrium growth for an aggregative economy.

The basic structure of the model presented here is similar to the one discussed in detail in another paper (Uzawa, 1968*b*). At the risk of repetition, however, the premises on which the following model is built are briefly outlined.

The aggregative economy here is visualized as composed of two classes of economic units: households on the one hand, and business firms on the other. Households are the owners of labor and assets; their income consists of wages for the labor they provide and the interest and dividend payments for the assets they hold, and they divide their income between consumption and savings, the latter in the form of an increase in the asset holdings. On the other hand, business firms are engaged in the production of goods and services; they employ labor and other factors of production and determine the levels of output and employment in order to maximize the present value of future profits, to be discounted in terms of expected rates of interest. It is assumed that firms finance their investment through an issuance of shares.

At each moment of time, aggregate demand consists of the value of consumption goods demanded by households and the level of investment planned by business firms. The total output which the corporate sector plans to produce depends upon the level of the aggregate demand which it expects to get for its output, and the quantities of labor and other productive factors which the corporate sector desires to employ are accordingly determined. The rewards for these factors of production then constitute the national income, which in turn determines the actual level of the aggregate demand, together with actual consumption and investment. If we assume that the goods-and-services market, the labor market, and the share market are all perfectly competitive, then the economy attains a short-run equilibrium where the planned aggregate demand is equated to the actual level. The level of investment corresponding to such a short-run equilibrium then determines the rate by which real capital is accumulated.

In order to examine the process of capital accumulation in such an equilibrium system, let us postulate that the aggregate behavior of the household sector and that of the corporate sector are respectively explained in terms of the representative household and business firm, both of which possess the structure described in the previous sections.

It will be further assumed that output and labor are composed of homogeneous quantities, respectively, so it is possible to measure them in unambiguous terms. At each moment of time t, we assume as given the level of real capital K_t accumulated in the corporate sector (capital being defined in the way introduced in the above section), the quantity of labor available N_t, and the outstanding number of shares issued B_t, together with the conditions governing the processes of production and the choice of desirable consumption patterns. The aggregate income Y_t is composed of wages W_t, dividends D_t, and expected capital gains G_t^e:

$$Y_t = W_t + D_t + G_t^e. \tag{54}$$

Let p_t be the market price of a share. Then the value V_t of the share holdings at time t is given by

$$V_t = p_t B_t.$$

Hence, the rate of interest ρ_t prevailing in the securities market is denoted by

$$\rho_t = \frac{D_t + G_t^e}{V_t}, \tag{55}$$

and the national income may be written as

$$Y_t = W_t + \rho_t V_t. \tag{56}$$

The desired levels of consumption C_t and savings S_t are then described in terms of the consumption and saving functions derived in section 3, namely,

$$C_t = [1 - s(\rho_t)]Y_t, \qquad S_t = s(\rho_t)Y_t, \tag{57}$$

where $s(\rho_t)$ is the average propensity to save.

The number of new shares which the household sector as a whole desires to purchase, $\dot{B}_t^D$, is now given by

$$\dot{B}_t^D = \frac{S_t - G_t^e}{p_t}. \tag{58}$$

On the other hand, the desired level of investment Φ_t in the corporate sector is determined in the manner described in section 5. The investment per unit of real capital, $\varphi_t = \Phi_t/K_t$, depends upon the rate of profit, r_t, and the market rate of interest, ρ_t:

$$\Phi_t/K_t = \varphi(\rho_t, r_t), \tag{59}$$

where $\varphi(\rho, r)$ is the investment function derived from the Penrose theory of capital.

The aggregate supply of goods and services, Q_t, is determined in terms of the short-run production function: $Q_t = F(K_t, L_t)$, where labor is employed at the level L_t at which the marginal product of labor is equal to the real wage rate w_t.

The aggregate output Q_t is distributed as:

$$Q_t = W_t + D_t + RP_t, \tag{60}$$

where RP_t is the retained profit.

The number of new shares to be issued by the corporate sector, B_t^s, is then given:

$$\dot{B}_t^s = \frac{\Phi_t - RP_t}{p_t}. \tag{61}$$

The goods-and-services market is then at an equilibrium when the following condition is satisfied:

$$C_t + \Phi_t = Q_t. \tag{62}$$

The equilibrium conditions for the labor market and the share market are, respectively, given by:

$$L_t = N_t, \tag{63}$$

and

$$\dot{B}_t^D = \dot{B}_t^S. \tag{64}$$

The rate of capital accumulation z_t is determined relative to the equilibrium investment ratio φ_t through the Penrose curve, as described in section 5:

$$\dot{K}_t/K_t = z_t, \tag{65}$$

while the supply of labor is assumed to be inelastic and increasing at a certain rate, say n, to be exogenously given:

$$\dot{N}_t/N_t = n. \tag{66}$$

The dynamic structure of the equilibrium growth is now completely determined by the pair of differential equations (65) and (66). To analyze the structure of such a system, let us first reduce the equilibrium conditions (62–64) to those involving per capita quantities only.

7 Analysis of the growth equilibrium

It may be useful first to note that the equilibrium conditions (62) and (64) for the goods-and-services market and the securities market are interrelated in the sense that, if either one of these markets is in equilibrium, the other must automatically be in equilibrium. To verify this Walras's Law, it suffices to rearrange the equations (54), (57), and (60) to obtain

$$p_t\dot{B}_t^s = (C_t + \Phi_t - Q_t) + (S_t - G_t^e),$$

which, together with the relation (58), shows that (62) and (64) are related to each other.

Let us introduce the following per capita variables:

$k_t = K_t/N_t$: the aggregate capital-labor ratio,
$q_t = Q_t/N_t$: per capita real net national product,
$y_t = Y_t/N_t$: per capita real national income.
$b_t = B_t/N_t$: the number of outstanding shares per capita,
$v_t = V_t/N_t$: the market value of shares per capita, $v_t = p_t b_t$.

Then, the real wage rate w_t and the rate of profit r_t under the full-employment condition (63) are determined respectively by

$$w_t = f(k_t) - k_t f'(k_t), \tag{67}$$

and

$$r_t = f'(k_t), \tag{68}$$

where $f(k)$ is the per capita production function.

The per capita net national product q_t and national income y_t are given by:

$$q_t = f(k_t), \tag{69}$$

and

$$y_t = w_t + \rho_t v_t. \tag{70}$$

The concept of real national income y_t which has been adopted here involves the expected capital gains, and it may not necessarily coincide with per capita real national product y_t. However, since we assume that whatever profits retained in the corporate sector are always reflected in capital gains, real income y_t in fact equals net national product q_t:

$$y_t = f(k_t). \tag{71}$$

It may be noted that the following conclusions remain valid for the case in which the expected capital gains are adaptively adjusted to the actual capital gains, provided the familiar qualifications are imposed upon the speed of adjustment.

Then the short-run equilibrium conditions discussed above are reduced to the following single equation:

$$\varphi(\rho_t, r_t) = s(\rho_t)\frac{y_t}{k_t}, \tag{72}$$

which corresponds to what Harrod (1948) termed the fundamental equation. The left-hand side of the equation (72) denotes the desired level of investment per unit of real capital, while the right-hand side indicates the amount of savings per unit of real capital which the community as a whole is willing to make when the market rate of interest is ρ_t. The short-run equilibrium is attained when the market rate of interest ρ_t is adjusted to equate both sides of (72). The dynamic system is then described by

$$\dot{k}_t/k_t = z(\rho_t, r_t) - n, \tag{73}$$

where $z(\rho_t, r_t)$ is the equilibrium rate of capital accumulation.

The analysis of the short-run equilibrium may be done in terms of the Hicksian technique as illustrated in Figure 15.6. Let the rate of interest ρ be measured along the vertical axis and let the investment-capital ratio or the saving-capital ratio be measured along the horizontal axis.

The desired level of investment per unit of capital, $\varphi(\rho, r_t)$, is increased whenever the market rate of interest ρ is increased as shown by curve II in Figure 15.6. In general, $s(\rho)y_t/k_t$ increases as the rate of interest ρ is increased; then it starts to decline, as typically illustrated by curve SS. Hence, the equilibrium rate of interest ρ_t is determined uniquely by the intersection of curves II and SS, leaving a certain possibility of multiple equilibria. In what follows, let us concentrate upon the case in which the equilibrium rate of interest is uniquely determined.

As the aggregate capital-labor ratio k_t is increased, the average output y_t/k_t and the rate of profit r_t are both decreased, thus shifting curve II and curve SS to the left, as indicated by the dashed curves in Figure 15.6. Hence, the new equilibrium rate of investment is definitely decreased. The equilibrium rate of interest may be either increased or decreased depending upon the way these curves shift.

Since the dynamics of such an economy is described by the differential equation (73), it remains at a steady state if, and only if, the aggregate capital-labor ratio is kept at the level k^* for which the equilibrium rate of investment equals the level $\varphi(n)$ corresponding to the rate of labor growth n. Let us draw a vertical line AB in Figure 15.6 for the rate of investment $\varphi(n)$. Then we can easily see from Figure 15.6 that the aggregate capital-labor ratio k_t tends to increase ($\dot{k}_t > 0$) whenever k_t is lower than the long-run equilibrium ratio k^*, and it tends to decrease ($\dot{k}_t < 0$) if k_t is higher than k^*. If the initial aggregate capital-labor ratio k_0 is lower than the long-run ratio k^*, the equilibrium rate of investment is higher than the level which is required to maintain the capital-labor ratio intact, thus the aggregate capital-labor ratio tends to increase while the equilibrium rate of investment continues to decrease. The aggregate capital-labor ratio k_t then approaches the long-run ratio k^*, and the rate of investment continues to fall to approach the long-run equilibrium level $\varphi(n)$.

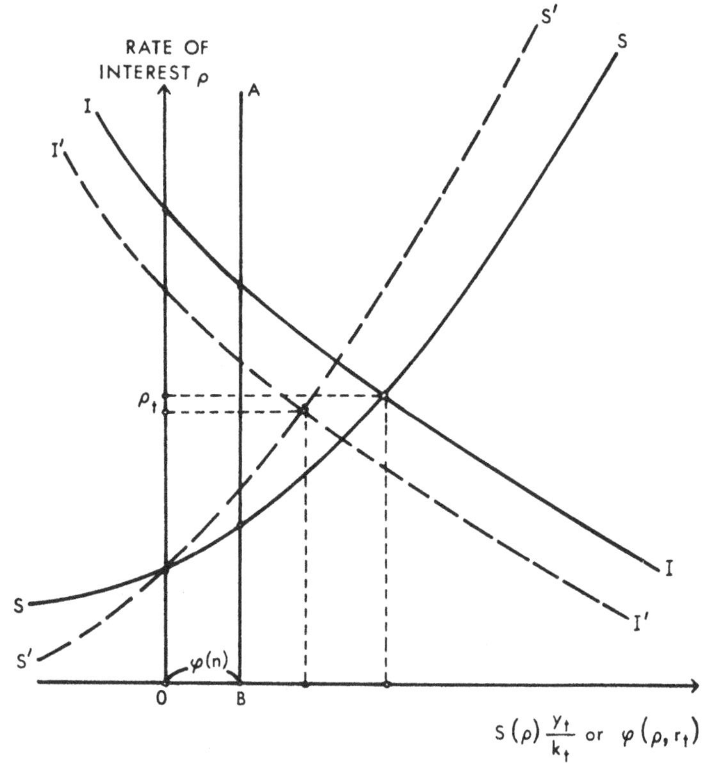

Figure 15.6

The long-run equilibrium capital-labor ratio k^* is determined by the following two equations:

$$\varphi(\rho^*, r^*) = \varphi(n), \tag{74}$$

$$s(\rho^*)\frac{y^*}{k^*} = \varphi(n), \tag{75}$$

when $y^* = f(k^*)$, $r^* = f'(k^*)$, and ρ^* is the long-run equilibrium rate of interest.

Equation (74) requires that the rate of investment the corporate sector desires to make must be equal to $\varphi(n)$. A higher rate of interest ρ^* has to be accompanied by a higher rate of profit r^*, thus by a lower capital-labor ratio k^*, in order to maintain the rate of investment at the level $\varphi(n)$. Therefore, the combinations (ρ^*, k^*) which satisfy (74) are described by a downward sloping curve AA' in Figure 15.7, where the two axes represent the long-run rate of interest and capital-labor ratio,

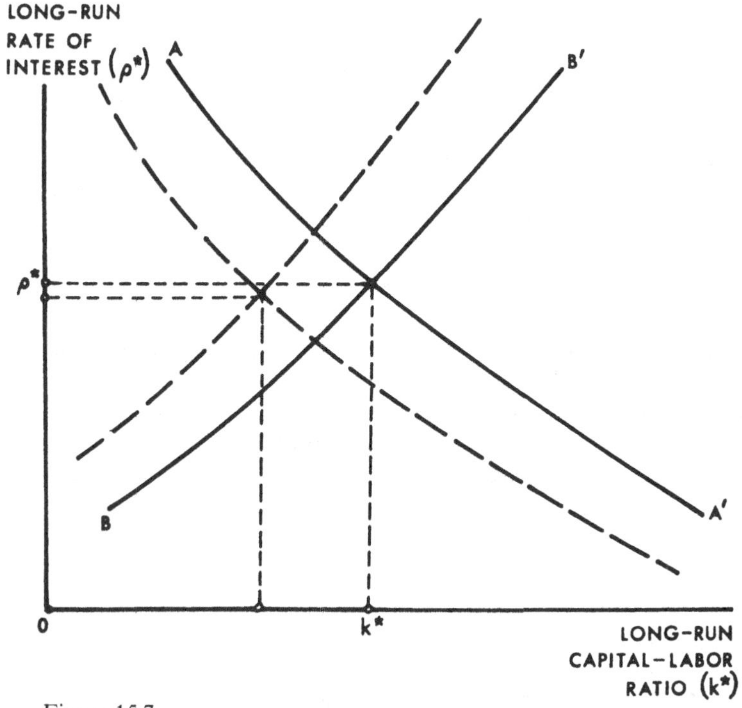

Figure 15.7

respectively. On the other hand, equation (75) denotes that the desired level of savings per unit of capital has to be at $\varphi(n)$. The combinations of (ρ^*, k^*) which meet the requirement (75) are represented by an upward sloping curve such as BB', since a higher rate of interest ρ^* must be accompanied by lowering the average output y^*/k^*, hence in a higher capital-labor ratio k^*, in order to result in the long-run level $\varphi(n)$. The long-run rate of interest ρ^* and capital-labor ratio k^* are then uniquely determined.

In general, the long-run equilibrium is determined once we specify the Penrose curve, the production function, the Fisherian schedule of time preference, and the rate of labor growth n. The effect of a change or shift in one of these factors upon the long-run capital-labor ratio k^* may be analyzed by using curves AA' and BB' in Figure 15.7. For example, suppose the rate of labor growth n has been increased. Then, we can see from the structure of the investment and saving functions that curves AA' and BB' both shift to the left, thus resulting in a decrease in the long-run capital-labor ratio k^*.

8 Concluding remarks

In this paper we have formulated an aggregative model of economic growth for which the postulates concerning investment and savings are derived from those involving the behavior of individual economic units. The saving behavior of the representative household has been examined in terms of the Fisherian theory of time preference along the lines of the Koopmans reformulation. The investment behavior of business firms in the corporate sector has been based upon a concept of real capital which measures the productive capacity of each business firm as an organic entity. The central role in the derivation of the investment function of a firm in a perfectly competitive market has been played by what has been termed the Penrose curve reflecting the amount of endowments within each firm of those productive factors which are limitational to the firm in the process of growth. Then a growth model has been constructed by postulating that the aggregative behavior of the household sector or of the corporate sector may be described by that of the representative household or business firm, each of which possesses the structure thus specified.

The model being constructed here is restricted to the aggregative national economy in which output, labor, and capital are all composed of homogeneous quantities. The nature of the securities market also has been limited to that of a share market in which no attention has been paid to the uncertainties with respect to expected capital gains. However, the most serious limitation of the present analysis is the hypothesis that the aggregative behavior of each of two major sectors of the national economy may be explained in terms of the representative unit which behaves itself in a way similar to each individual unit. It might be less objectionable for a static or stationary analysis, but an economic model which is purportedly analyzing the mechanism of a growing economy would be deemed questionable if enough attention were not paid to the process of aggregation.

References

Fisher, I. *The Theory of Interest*. New York: Macmillan, 1930.

Hahn, F. H., and Matthews, R. C. O. "The Theory of Economic Growth: A Survey," *Economic Journal*, LXXIV (1964), 779–902.

Harrod, R. F. *Towards A Dynamic Economics*. London: Macmillan, 1948.

Koopmans, T. C. "Stationary Ordinary Utility and Impatience," *Econometrica*, XXVIII (1960), 287–309.

Penrose, T. E. *The Theory of the Growth of the Firm*. Oxford: Blackwell, 1959.

Uzawa, H. "Time Preference, the Consumption Function, and Optimum Asset Holdings," in J. N. Wolfe (ed.). *Papers in Honour of Sir John Hicks: Value, Capital, and Growth*. Edinburgh: University Press, 1968, pp. 485–504. (*a*)

Uzawa, H. "The Penrose Effect and Optimum Growth," *Economic Studies Quarterly*, XIX (1968), 1–14. (*b*)

CHAPTER 16

On the dynamic stability of economic growth

The neoclassical versus Keynesian approaches

1 Introduction

Whether or not the dynamic allocation of scarce resources through the market mechanism can achieve stable economic growth is not simply a matter of theoretical interest, but also is indispensable in the consideration of the effects of public policy. However, there are two opposing approaches to the problem of the dynamic stability of the market mechanism. One approach bases its analysis on the neoclassical economic theory, the other considers the problem within the framework developed in Keynes's *General Theory*. The approach based on neoclassical theory concludes that the process of market growth is usually stable, and, but for exceptional situations, prices change stably and full-employment growth obtains. Keynesian theory, on the other hand, comes to the conclusion that the market allocation of scarce resources is an inherent cause of instability in a modern capitalistic system and that maintaining stable economic growth is akin to walking on the edge of a knife.

The primary purpose of this paper is to examine the kind of assumptions on which these two conclusions concerning the stability of the growth process in a market economy are based, and, if possible, to ferret out some of the more fundamental differences between the neoclassical and Keynesian approaches.

2 Basic assumptions of the neoclassical growth theory

The neoclassical theory of economic growth was first formulated in the works of Tobin [32], Solow [28], and Swan [31]. Although the theoretical

From *Trade, Stability, and Macroeconomics: Essays in Honor of Lloyd A. Metzler*, edited by G. Horwich and P. Samuelson, pp. 523–53.

I should like to express my gratitude to Professors George Horwich and Akira Takayama for their comments and criticisms on an earlier version of this paper.

background is much older and may be traced back to the early works of Jevons, Menger, and Walras, the models of Tobin, Solow, and Swan have put neoclassical theory into an even clearer form, and at the same time the limitations of the neoclassical framework have been more explicitly brought out.

Let us first consider the concept of capital which lies at the basis of neoclassical theory. Capital refers to the various factors of production which have been accumulated through refraining from past consumption. Added to capital are the variable factors of production, such as the labor employed through the labor market, and these are combined for the purposes of productive activity. However, the phenomenon of the fixity of capital has been ignored in neoclassical theory. It has been assumed that the market price of the stock of capital which is traded on the market is the same for newly produced capital goods and for existing capital goods which are the result of past investment. Entrepreneurs engage in productive activity either by purchasing capital goods or by renting the services of capital goods, and by employing variable factors of production. However, any individual may similarly engage in productive activity, resulting in the disappearance of the essential difference between consumers and producers.

This assumption has important implications for the portfolio behavior of each economic unit. Namely, various economic units may hold either physical capital or financial assets in whatever way they prefer. In order to examine in more detail the implications of the neoclassical hypothesis concerning the choice of assets, let us consider a simplified case in which physical capital and financial assets are each composed of a homogeneous type. Let us also assume that the goods produced are of one variety, identical with the capital assets.

Financial assets will be defined as fixed-interest bearing short-term securities. The holder of these assets can divide the total real amount A between real capital K and financial assets B:

$$A = K + B.$$

The holders of assets choose their portfolios in such a way as to maximize profits. If the real rate of interest of financial assets is ρ, the real amount of interest income becomes ρB. Physical capital is used as a factor of production and, with the addition of various other factors, goods and services are produced. Assuming that labor is the only other factor besides physical capital, the production function is given by $F(K, N)$, where K and N stand for the amounts of physical capital and labor, respectively. In order to maximize profits, labor is employed at the level where the real wage rate w is equal to the marginal product of labor F_N:

$$F_N(K, N) = w.$$

The net profit then becomes

$$F(K, N) - wN = rK$$

where r is the marginal product of capital F_K.

Assuming a linear homogeneous production function, the marginal products of both labor and capital are determined solely by the labor/capital ratio $n = N/K$. For example, denoting the production function per unit of capital by

$$f(n) = F(1, n),$$

the marginal products of labor and capital become

$$F_N = f'(n), \qquad F_K = f(n) - nf'(n),$$

respectively.

In this way, the profit yielded by portfolio (K, B) becomes

$$rK + \rho B.$$

If the profits from real capital and financial assets possess the same degree of uncertainty, it is easy to choose the portfolio which will maximize profits. When $r > \rho$, $K = A$ and $B = 0$; and when $r < \rho$, $K = 0$ and $B = A$. Both are held in positive amounts only when $r = \rho$.

Let us denote the economic units comprising the national economy by $j = 1, \ldots, J$, and the various physical capital and financial assets held at the beginning point in time by K_j^0, B_j^0. The amount of assets held by unit j, A_j^0, is

$$A_j^0 = K_j^0 + B_j^0.$$

The optimum portfolio (K_j, B_j) is that which maximizes profits $rK_j + \rho B_j$ subject to

$$A_j^0 = K_j + B_j.$$

At the beginning of the period, the total amounts of physical capital and financial assets in the society are, respectively, given by

$$K^0 = \sum_j K_j^0, \qquad B^0 = \sum_j B_j^0.$$

Accordingly, in order for the supply and demand of physical capital and financial assets to be in equilibrium, we must have

$$K^0 = \sum_j K_j, \qquad B^0 = \sum_j B_j.$$

To realize these conditions, the marginal product of capital and the real rate of interest must be equal: $r = \rho$. The labor market attains a state of equilibrium when the real wage rate is at the level where demand equals supply. Hence,

$$w = f'(n^0), \qquad n^0 = N^0/K^0.$$

Now, if the labor possessed by economic unit j at the beginning point of time is N_j^0,

$$N^0 = \sum_j N_j^0,$$

and the income of unit j is given by

$$Y_j = rK_j + \rho B_j + wN_j^0,$$

then, in a state of equilibrium, the above can also be written

$$Y_j = rA_j^0 + wN_j^0.$$

Each economic unit determines consumption and saving not only according to present income, but also according to expectations of future income and future market conditions. If the expectations are static, i.e., if income is expected to remain at current levels and the rate of interest is not expected to change, consumption and saving will be determined by current income Y_j and the current market rate of interest ρ. And if the subjective preference over consumption paths of each economic unit is homothetic, the consumption and saving functions take on the form

$$C_j = [1 - s(\rho)]Y_j, \qquad S_j = s(\rho)Y_j$$

where $s(\rho)$ is the average propensity to save, depending solely on the rate of interest ρ. As shown in Uzawa [36], $s(\rho)$ is in general an increasing function of ρ.

The aggregate consumption C and saving S of the national economy are given by

$$C = \sum_j C_j = [1 - s(\rho)]Y, \qquad S = \sum_j S_j = s(\rho)Y,$$

with Y as the aggregate income:

$$Y = \sum_j Y_j = rK^0 + \rho B^0 + wN^0.$$

Hence,

$$Y = F(K^0, N^0) + \rho B^0.$$

If financial assets possessed and those issued by each economic unit cancel each other out, $B^0 = 0$. Hence,

$$Y = F(K^0, N^0).$$

Summarizing the above analysis, we derive the following prototype of the neoclassical model of economic growth.

The national economy is comprised of economic units $j = 1, \ldots, J$, and these units possess various quantities of physical capital K_j, financial assets B_j, and labor N_j. Aggregating the capital and labor, we get

$$K = \sum_j K_j, \qquad N = \sum_j N_j. \tag{1}$$

If we assume that there are no external assets, then

$$\sum_j B_j = 0. \tag{2}$$

Equilibrium of the assets market is established when the rate of interest and the marginal product of capital are equal:

$$\rho = r. \tag{3}$$

The marginal product of capital and the wage rate of labor are established in response to the conditions of full employment:

$$r = f(n) - nf'(n), \qquad w = f'(n), \tag{4}$$

with n being the labor/capital ratio at the current point in time.

National income Y equals the amount produced:

$$Y = F(K, N) = rK + wN, \tag{5}$$

and the levels of consumption and saving are given by

$$C = [1 - s(\rho)]\,Y, \qquad S = s(\rho)\,Y. \tag{6}$$

The accumulation of capital is determined by

$$\dot{K} = S, \tag{7}$$

while the rate of increase of the labor supply is exogenously given:

$$\dot{N}/N = \nu. \tag{8}$$

As shown in the dynamic equation (7), the saving of each economic unit automatically becomes investment and capital accumulation. This conclusion is derived naturally from the concept of capital in neoclassical theory. Based on the assumption that real capital and financial assets can both be freely traded in the same way on the market, each economic unit can at various points in time continuously put together a desirable portfolio of assets according to income and market conditions. Accordingly, each economic unit is always satisfied with the composition of its assets, and there is no incentive to change them. Saving – that is, the portion of income not consumed – is simply accumulated as capital.

3 Dynamic equilibrium of the neoclassical model

It is easy to prove the stability of the dynamic process of the neoclassical model. Define the variables per unit of real capital as

$n = N/K,$ labor/capital ratio

$y = Y/K,$ income/capital ratio.

The conditions of equilibrium and the dynamic equation can be simplified as

$$y = f(n) \tag{9}$$

$$\rho = r = f(n) - nf'(n), \qquad w = f'(n) \tag{10}$$

$$\dot{n}/n = v - sf(n) \tag{11}$$

where s is the average propensity to save.

The neoclassical assumptions concerning the production functions and the average propensity to save are

$$f(0) = 0, \quad f(\infty) = \infty; \qquad f'(0) = \infty, \quad f'(\infty) = 0 \tag{12}$$

$$f'(n) > 0, \qquad f''(n) < 0 \tag{13}$$

$$s = s(\rho), \qquad s'(\rho) \geqq 0. \tag{14}$$

The right-hand side of the dynamic equation (11) decreases with increases in n. Accordingly, the stability of (11) may easily be shown, as illustrated in Fig. 16.1. The horizontal and vertical axes are the labor/capital ratio and the income/capital ratio, respectively. The production function $f(n)$ and the saving function $sf(n)$ are illustrated by curves OA and OB, respectively. The labor supply is represented by the straight line CC at height v. Taking n^* as the labor/capital ratio corresponding to the intersection of curves OB and CC, n^* represents the state of long-term steady growth.

When n is larger than n^*, the saving curve OB is above the labor supply line CC. Hence, the rate of capital accumulation exceeds the rate of increase of the labor supply, and n tends to decrease. In the same way, when n is less than n^*, there is a tendency for n to increase. That is, the labor/capital ratio tends to appraoch the long-run steady state with the passag of time. In other words, the process of economic growth in the neoclassical system is dynamically stable.

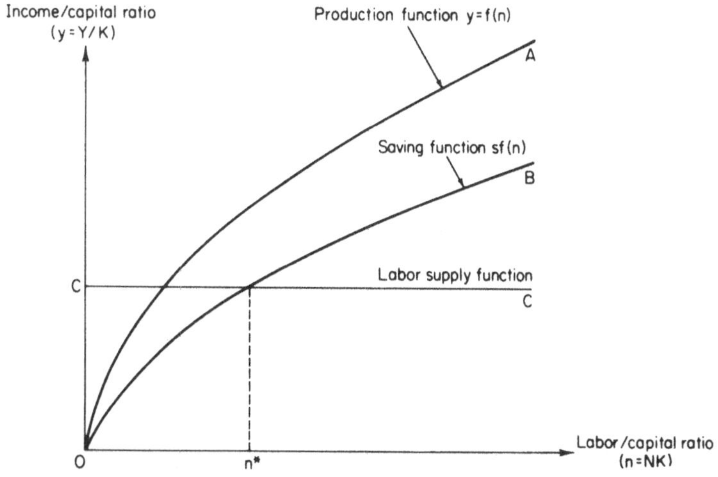

Figure 16.1

4 The neoclassical theory of monetary growth

Attention up to this point has been paid to the real aspect of the neoclassical process of economic growth, in which money has not played any role. How is the process of growth, when money plays an essential role, formulated? Monetary growth in neoclassical theory has been treated by Tobin [32, 33], Sidrauski [27], Johnson [10], Levhari and Patinkin [15], and Uzawa [34], among others. Characteristic of the neoclassical theory of monetary growth is its hypothesis concerning the money supply. It ignores the institutional details of the money supply mechanism. The central bank, through transfer payments, distributes money to the economic units of the national economy. Money supplied in this way supplements each unit's income as transfer payments. In one formulation money performs the function of a consumer good which increases the level of utility for each individual; in another, it is a factor of production which is a substitute for labor and capital. Accordingly, it may be assumed that the demand for money depends on the market rate of interest and the level of income.

At a certain point of time, the physical capital held by each economic unit will be denoted by K_j^0 and the cash balance by M_j^0. If the market price of goods and services is taken as P, the real amount of assets is expressed by

$$A_j^0 = K_j^0 + (M_j^0/P).$$

The profit derived from real capital will be obtained in the same way

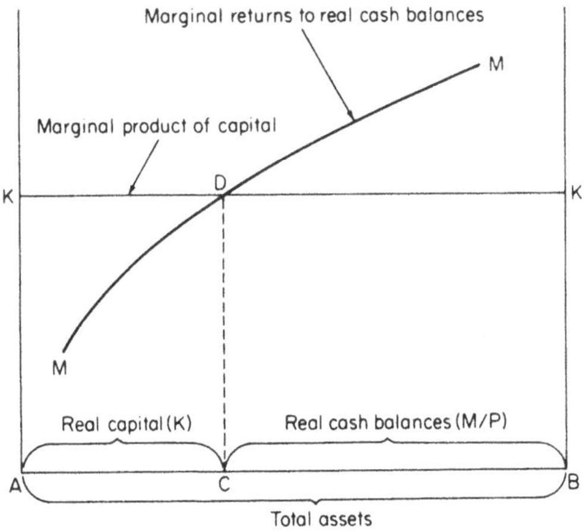

Figure 16.2

as it was previously. When the real wage rate is given, the marginal product of capital which corresponds to it becomes the rate of profit. The gains derived from real cash balances M_j/P, as a consumption good, is in the form of marginal utility, and, as a production good, in the form of marginal product. If the rate of profit from real cash balances is taken as having no relation to capital, labor, and consumption levels, then, as shown in Fig. 16.2, the larger M_j/P is (with quantities increasing to the left), the lower is the marginal product of real balances. In Fig. 16.2, AB represents the real amount of total assets held A_j, $AC = K$ is the quantity of real capital, and $CB = M_j/P$ is the amount of real balances held. The marginal products of real capital KK and of real balances MM are measured along the vertical axis. The optimum composition of capital is at point C, which corresponds to the intersection D of the KK and MM curves.

Thus the optimum asset portfolio $(K_j, M_j/P)$ is related to the marginal product of capital.

The conditions of equilibrium of the stock of capital and money can be stated by

$$K_j = K^0\left(\equiv \sum_j K_j^0\right), \qquad M_j = M^0\left(\equiv \sum_j M_j^0\right).$$

The real wage rate is determined at the level at which demand and supply in the labor market are equal, and the marginal product of capital at full employment is given by

$$r = f(n^0) - n^0 f'(n^0), \qquad n^0 = N^0/K^0.$$

It follows from the preceding analysis that the aggregate demands for real capital and cash balances can both be regarded as being related to the price level P, and that the equilibrium price level is uniquely determined. It is also assumed that the market price P of real capital determined through the process of equilibrium in the assets market can be regarded as the price of goods and services.

The increase in the money supply is included in income as a transfer payment; nominal income becomes

$$PF(K, N) + \dot{M}.$$

Now, if the expected rate of increase of the price level is given by

$$\pi^e = (\dot{P}/P)^e,$$

real income Y is obtained by subtracting the depreciation of real cash balances from nominal income:

$$Y = F(K, N) + (\dot{M}/P) - \pi^e(M/P).$$

If the rate of increase in the money supply is denoted by

$$\mu = \dot{M}/M,$$

real income Y may be expressed by

$$Y = F(K, N) + (\mu - \pi^e)(M/P).$$

Denoting the average propensity to consume by $1 - s$, consumption is $C = (1 - s)Y$, while the nominal amount of saving S is given by

$$S = [PF(K, N) + \dot{M}] - PC$$

or

$$S = s[PF(K, N) + \mu M] + (1 - s)\pi^e M.$$

Saving is used either for the purchase of capital $P\dot{K}$ or for the increase in cash balances. Hence, the amount of new capital purchased may be written as

$$P\dot{K} = S - \mu M = sPF(K, N) - (1 - s)(\mu - \pi^e)M$$

or

$$\dot{K} = sF(K, N) - (1 - s)(\mu - \pi^e)M/P.$$

The rates of increase of the money supply and labor are exogenously given:

$$\dot{M}/M = \mu, \qquad \dot{N}/N = \nu.$$

If the portfolio preference is homothetic, the demand function for real cash balances may be given by

$$M/PK = \lambda(i, Y/K)$$

where i is the nominal (or market) rate of interest, being the sum of the real rate of interest ρ and the expected rate of price increase π^e: $i = \rho + \pi^e$.

It may be assumed that $\lambda(i, Y/K)$ is a decreasing function of i and a increasing function of Y/K:

$$\frac{\partial \lambda}{\partial i} < 0, \qquad \frac{\partial \lambda}{\partial (Y/K)} > 0.$$

In order to analyze the model of neoclassical monetary growth formulated here, the following variables will be introduced:

$m = M/PK$: real cash balances per unit of capital
$y = Y/K$: income per unit of capital
$n = N/K$: labor/capital ratio.

The short-run equilibrium conditions may be stated as

$$y = f(n) + (\mu - \pi^e)m \tag{15}$$

$$m = \lambda(i, y) \tag{16}$$

where

$$i = \rho + \pi^e, \qquad \rho = r = f(n) - nf'(n). \tag{17}$$

The basic dynamic equation becomes

$$\dot{n}/n = v - [f(n) - (1 - s)y]. \tag{18}$$

At each moment of time, n and π^e are given at the levels historically determined, while μ is a policy variable. Then ρ and $m = M/PK$ are established so as to satisfy the equilibrium conditions (15) and (16), together with the equilibrium level of n. Finally $\dot{n}/n$ is simply given by (18).

When the expected rate of price increase is inelastic, namely, π^e is maintained at a fixed level, it can be shown that the dynamic equation (18) is stable. To prove this stability, (15) and (16) may be rewritten as

$$y = (\mu - \pi^e)\lambda(i, y) + f(n). \tag{19}$$

For a given n, the y satisfying (19) may be assumed to be uniquely determined. This is indeed the case if the following condition is satisfied:

$$(\mu - \pi^e)\frac{\partial \lambda}{\partial y} < 1.$$

Moreover, it may be assumed that when n increases, the y satisfying

(19) also increases. This condition is met if either μ is less than π^e or the elasticity of demand for real balances with respect to the rate of interest i is relatively small.

The average propensity to save is in general a function of the expected real rate of interest. However, this dependency will be ignored in the following analysis, so that the average propensity to save is assumed to be constant, taking a value between 0 and 1. It is also easily seen that the right-hand side of the dynamic equation (18) is a decreasing function of the labor/capital ratio, provided the elasticity of demand for real balances with respect to the rate of interest is small relative both to $\mu - \pi^e$ and s. In this case, there is a uniquely determined long-run steady labor/capital ratio n^* for which $\dot{n} = 0$. When the current n is larger than n^*, $\dot{n} < 0$ and n tends to decrease. On the other hand, when n is less than n^*, $\dot{n} > 0$ and n tends to increase. Thus the long-run steady state n^* is dynamically stable.

It is not generally the case that the right-hand side of (18) is a decreasing function of n. However, in the general case the right side of (18) tends to be positive as n tends to 0 and to be negative as n tends to infinity. Hence, it can be shown that there exists at least one long-run steady labor/capital ratio n^* and that any dynamic path satisfying (18) converges to a certain long-run steady state.

The dynamic stability shown above crucially depends on the assumption that the expected rate of price increase is inelastic. Let us assume instead that expectations are adjusted according to the adaptive expectation of the Cagan–Nerlove type ([1, 19]):

$$\dot{\pi}^e = \beta(\pi - \pi^e), \qquad \pi = \dot{P}/P \tag{20}$$

where β is the speed of adjustment in expectations.

Equation (20) has the following meaning. When each economic unit chooses its asset portfolio, it does so not with reference to the current rate of price increase but rather to the expectations of the average rise in prices from now through the future. Moreover, when there is a discrepancy between π and π^e, expectations are adjusted according to the difference between these two rates.

When β is close to 0, the dynamic system (18) and (20) can be shown to be stable. One has only to note that the stability criterion obtained in the previous case remains valid because of a slight perturbation caused by the process of adaptive expectations for which the speed of adjustment is small.

However, β is expected to be generally large within the framework of neoclassical theory. In order to explain why this is the case, let us note that the following reasons are offered to justify the use of the expected rate of price increase in choosing a portfolio. The real value of profits

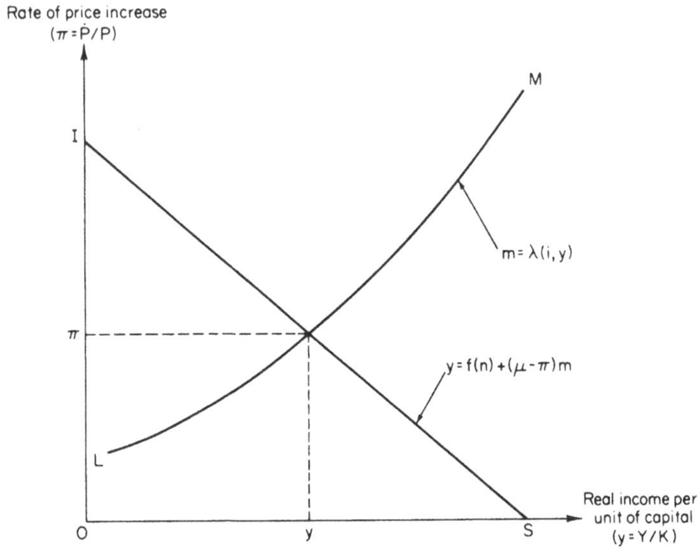

Figure 16.3

from various assets is affected by the rate of price increase; when choosing a portfolio at the current point in time, it is necessary to make choices according to the expectations of the price increase during the period that the portfolio is to be held. In neoclassical theory, it is assumed that the portfolio may be instantaneously and freely changed without incurring any costs of adjustment and without regard to whether the portfolio consists of real capital or financial assets. Hence, the expectation of price increases in the very near future may be regarded as relevant, and there is no need to anticipate the rate of price increase over a longer term because the portfolio can be rechosen at any time in the future. Thus it may be assumed that π^e is either little different from that of the present or, if there is a difference, it is quickly adjusted to the current level. In other words, under the assumption of neoclassical theory, β is expected to be large.

I should like to consider the limiting case in which the speed of adjustment is infinity and it is assumed that the expected rate of price increase coincides with the current rate of price increase:

$$\pi^e = \pi = \dot{P}/P.$$

The equilibrium conditions (15)–(17) may now be written as

$$y = f(n) + (\mu - \pi)m \tag{21}$$

$$m = \lambda(i, y) \tag{22}$$

$$i = \rho + \pi, \qquad \rho = r = f(n) - nf'(n). \tag{23}$$

At each moment of time, n and m are given, together with μ. The level of real income per unit of capital and the rate of price increase are determined in such a way that equilibrium conditions (21) and (22) are both satisfied. Since, under (21), increases in π have to be accompanied by decrease in y, the combinations of π and y for which (21) is satisfied may be described by a downward-sloping curve IS in Fig. 16.3. Similarly, the combinations of π and y for which (22) is satisfied may be described by an upward-sloping curve LM in Fig. 16.3. The equilibrium (y, π) then is uniquely determined by the intersection of the IS and LM curves.

The dynamic path of such a monetary growth model then is described by the differential equations

$$\dot{n}/n = v - [f(n) - (1 - s)y] \tag{24}$$

$$\dot{m}/m = \mu - \pi - [f(n) - (1 - s)y]. \tag{25}$$

The long-run behavior of dynamic paths described by (24) and (25) is not easy to analyze, particularly in view of ambiguities concerning the effects of changes in n and m on π. However, it can be shown that the solution paths to the dynamic system (24) and (25) either converge cyclically to, or approach a limit cycle around, the long-run steady state. This is due to the fact that solution paths are all bounded and that, in view of the Poincaré–Bendixon theorem on a pair of differential equations, any solution path has to converge to a singular point or to a limit cycle. The stability of typical solution paths is illustrated by the curves with arrows in Figs. 16.4 and 16.5. The cases illustrated assumed that the $\dot{m} = 0$ curve (AA) is steeper than the $\dot{n} = 0$ curve (BB). The dynamic stability for other cases may be similarly illustrated.

The preceding was an attempt at considering the basic assumptions underlying neoclassical theory and analyzing the stability of the dynamic process of the neoclassical growth modesl developed by Tobin, Solow, and Swan. The model formulated here does not necessarily incorporate all the characteristic features of their model, but it does seem to describe essential aspects of neoclassical theory. Among them, the lack of a distinction between business firms and households as the basic units of the national economy; the assumption that real capital as a factor of production is simply the accumulation of invested goods; and the assumption that the assets market is perfectly competitive. Further, the assumption is made that the money supply mechanism simply distributes new money to each member as transfer payments. Within this framework,

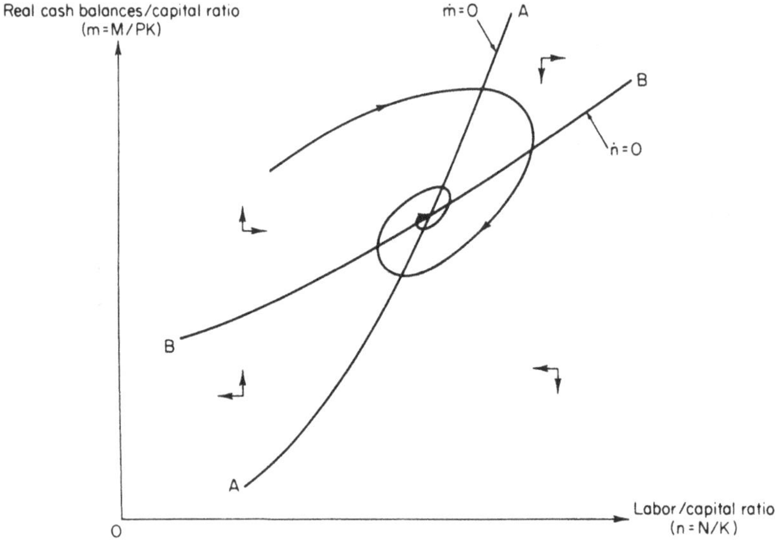

Figure 16.4

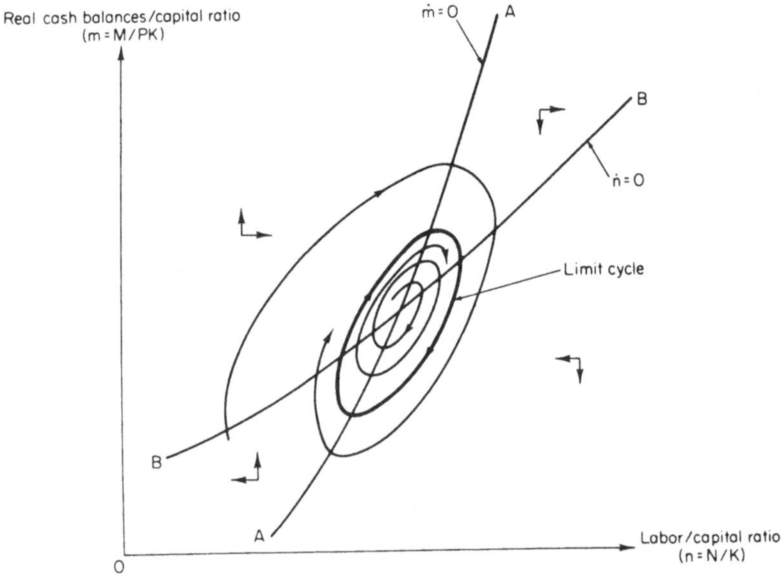

Figure 16.5

it has been shown that both the real and monetary growth processes are dynamically stable, provided certain qualifying constraints are satisfied.

5 A Keynesian theory of economic growth

In the previous sections, I presented a general view of the process of economic growth within the framework of neoclassical theory. Next I should like to consider the problem based on the theoretical framework of Keynes's *General Theory*.

Many economists have constructed what may be termed Keynesian growth models. Examples may be found in the works of Stein [29, 30], Hahn [3, 4], and Rose [21–23]. But these writers seem to have emphasized only certain aspects without touching on what seem to be the central features of the *General Theory*. They are based on the theoretical models developed by Hicks [8], Hansen [5], Lange [13], Modigliani [17, 18], and others, which have slightly different nuances than those originally intended by Keynes. The formulation commonly referred to as the income–expenditure approach seems, for the following reasons, not to be in accord with the theoretical framework of the *General Theory*.

The first point concerns the price mechanism of the goods and services market. The income–expenditure approach presupposes that the price level is fixed as long as there is involuntary unemployment. This assumption is difficult to reconcile with other aspects of the theory of effective demand, as discussed in detail by Sato [26], Saito [24, 25], Fujino [2], and Leijonhufvud [14].

The second point concerns the role of the market rate of interest in the process of investment determination. In the income–expenditure approach the premise is that the current level of investment is determined by the rate of interest and other factors concerning the expectations of future profits and costs. Recent empirical research on whether investment is flexible in relation to the market rate of interest seems to be not entirely consistent with the income–expenditure assumption. It would be more in accord with the *General Theory* to assume that investment behavior is based on expectations formed in the corporate sector concerning future profits and the rate of interest, as discussed by Inada and Uzawa [9] and Uzawa [37, 38], among others.

For purposes of developing a simplified Keynesian model, the national economy is viewed as consisting of business firms and households. Business firms employ labor and other factors of production and engage in production and sales; households own the primary factors of production and possess as assets securities issued by the firms.

Besides households and business firms, which make up the private sector, there is also a governmental sector. The latter provides various public goods and services which are financed through taxes or the issue of new money. New money is provided by the central bank and includes not only increases in the money supply to meet fiscal deficits, but also money issued through open market operations. It is assumed that governmental policies concerning expenditures and revenues, i.e., fiscal policy, and policies concerning the money supply, i.e., monetary policy, can be controlled independently. This assumption, of course, does not obtain in reality, but it is assumed here chiefly to bring out the crucial differences in the effects of the two policies on the working of the national economy.

An abstraction is also made concerning the market system. The market is broken down into three main divisions: the goods and services market, the labor market, and the financial market. The following simplified assumptions will be made about the mechanisms by which these markets are adjusted. First, in the goods and services market it is assumed that prices are always adjusted to equate supply with demand, and in the corporate sector production is always adjusted in response to changes in prices. In the labor market it is assumed that when the demand for labor exceeds supply, money wage rates are immediately increased and equilibrium is restored, but when the supply of labor exceeds demand, wage rate do not decline, resulting in involuntary unemployment. In the core of the financial market lies the money (short-term asset) market, which is highly organized and operates efficiently. It is assumed that money and short-term financial assets are transacted efficiently in the money market, but the price adjustment mechanism for long-term securities is not efficient and there is a time lag in the adjustment of securities prices.

The total amount of goods and services supplied by the whole corporate sector is determined by the scale of the production schedule of individual firms in response to market conditions. The productive capacity of various firms depends on the amounts of fixed factors of production accumulated through past investment. Assuming that labor is the only variable factor of production which can be obtained in the market, the production function of each firm may be expressed as

$$Q_j = F_j(N_j)$$

where Q_j is the amount produced and N_j is the amount of labor employed. It is assumed that only one kind of good is produced so that products of different firms may be measured by the same unit. The amount produced by firm j, Q_j, and the labor employment N_j will be determined so as to maximize profits $PQ_j - WN_j$, where P is the market price of the product and W is the money wage rate. Profits are maximized when the marginal product of labor equals real wages:

$$F_j'(N_j) = W/P.$$

It must be kept in mind that this assumes that labor is a variable factor of production and that the firm can, at any point in time, freely increase or decrease its labor employment.

Now, by aggregating the amount of labor employed by each firm, the total amount of labor employed is

$$N = \sum_j N_j.$$

An increase in W or a decrease in P both increase real wages. The amount produced by firm j is measured in terms of money wages:

$$P_W Q_j = PQ_j/W, \qquad P_W = P/W.$$

In this way the aggregate quantity Z defined as

$$Z = \sum_j P_W Q_j$$

becomes what Keynes referred to as the aggregate supply price.

The aggregate supply price Z corresponds to the goods and services produced by the corporate sector as measured in units of money wages. An increase in market price P induces a decline in real wages W/P, increasing the amount of labor employed N as well as the aggregate supply price Z. The relationship between Z and P is commonly shown in a curve such as OZ in Fig. 16.6. An increase in money wages increases the real wage rate, resulting in a downward shift in the aggregate supply curve and the aggregate labor demand curve.

In this way, the aggregate supply price can be explained by the productive capacity of the corporate sector as expressed by the production function and the maximizing behavior of business firms. On the other hand, aggregate demand is determined by the behavior of households, business firms, and government vis-à-vis consumption and investment.

First, consumption demand is determined by the way in which households choose to divide their income between consumption and saving. Household income consists of wages, dividends, and interest payments. Current consumption is determined by expected real income, which is based on long-term expectations concerning future wages rates and future earnings obtained from currently held financial assets.

Expressing real income measured in money wages as Y_W,

$$Y_W = N + \rho A_W$$

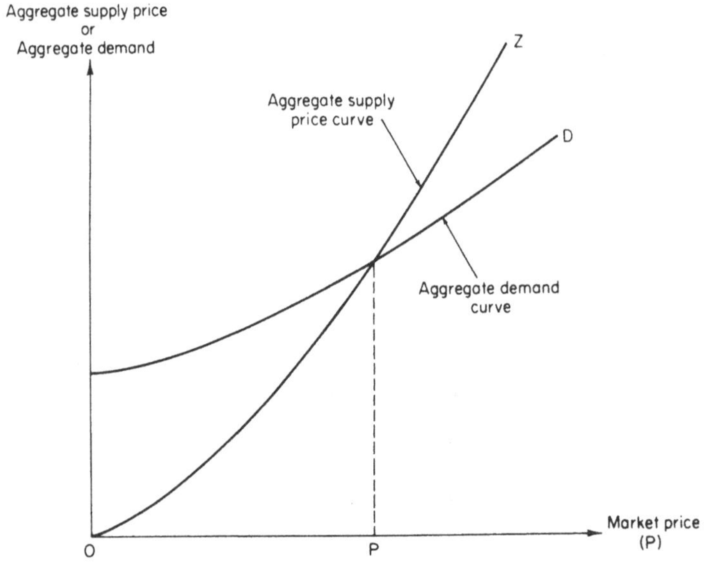

Figure 16.6

where ρ is the real rate of interest (to be obtained by subtracting the rate of price increase π from the market rate of interest i) and A_W is the amount of assets measured in money wage units. Permanent income Y_W^e is based on the expected real rate of interest and the expected increase in the wage rate.

Consumption demand C_W is a function of the expected real rate of interest ρ^e and permanent real income Y_W^e:

$$C_W = C_W(\rho^e, Y_W^e).$$

When the relationship of time preference which expresses subjective value judgments is homothetic, the elasticity of consumption demand with respect to permanent real income is 1 and the consumption function may be written as

$$C_W = [1 - s(\rho^e)]Y_W^e$$

where $s(\rho^e)$ is the average propensity to save (relative to the level of permanent real income). In what follows, the dependency of $s = s(\rho^e)$ on the expected real rate of interest will be mostly ignored.

Since consumption depends on permanent real income, increasing the money supply through open market operations can be seen to have the following effects on consumption demand. Permanent real income is defined as the level of real income which households expect to receive for the entire period of their lifetime, and it has to take into account the effects that fiscal and monetary policies may have on the financial situation of the private sector. Since an open market purchase of privately held securities tends to have a compensating effect on the future earnings of the private sector, it may be assumed that any change in the money supply does not induce private economic units to change their long-term expectations. This is related to the point mentioned by Metzler, [16, p. 109, n. 16]. It will also be assumed that the expected real rate of interest ρ^e is not affected by changes in the market rate of interest which accompany fluctuations in the money supply. However, ρ^e is assumed to be adaptively adjusted over time; namely, ρ^e is assumed to change according to the differential equation

$$\dot{\rho}^e = \beta(\rho - \rho^e), \tag{26}$$

with β being the speed of adjustment.

Next let us consider the factors determining investment demand. First it is necessary to touch on the concept of capital in Keynes's theory. In neoclassical theory, capital has been merely understood as material factors of production, with little attention paid to its fixity. Only the demand and the market for capital goods as a stock are allowed for. Keynes's treatment differs from neoclassical theory on this point concerning the fixity of capital.

The firm carries on production with an assortment of fixed and variable factors of production. The management consists of various scarce resources which are employed for accomplishing certain specific goals. The firm tries to maximize profit by producing and selling goods and services, but to maximize the future flow, as well as the current level, of profits. For that purpose it not only employs variable factors, but accumulates fixed factors in order to produce efficiently in the future. The fixed factors are land, factories, machines, equipment, and other physical inputs, as well as technological, managerial, administrative, and other scarce resources. Moreover, once these scarce resources are accumulated in a firm they cannot be disposed of easily without sustaining a substantial loss. These fixed resources are not accumulated simply by being purchased on the market, but expenditures are needed for their installation as well.

What effect does the system of fixed factors of production have on the activities of the firm at different points in time? Two difficulties arise with respect to this problem. First, the fixed factors of a firm are of many different types and, moreover, they have been accumulated in the past when different market conditions prevailed. Accordingly, it is not always possible to quantify the role they play in the production process. This problem was avoided earlier in this paper by assuming that all goods and services are of one kind. Whether or not a market price exists, the role of scarce resources in the production process is not reflected in the price when the factors are fixed. An evaluation of the accumulated fixed scarce resources of the firm must be related to the role these resources play in the production process. Because profits express the accomplishment of the firm, it is natural to measure its capacity by the ability to create profits. The index of the capacity of the firm at a point in time t, to be denoted by K_t, is defined as the ratio of the real profit $Q_t - wN_t$ at time t over the real profit $Q_0 - wN_0$ at the standard time 0, with w being the real wage rate. However, the index of a firm's capacity thus defined is related to the real wage. When a different real wage rate is used, the profit ratio will differ and the index of the firm's capacity will possibly change as well. Uzawa [35] avoided this difficulty by postulating that the profit ratio is determined independently of w. Based on this postulate, the production relation at time t can be expressed in terms of K_t and N_t:

$$Q_t = K_t f(N_t/K_t) \tag{27}$$

where $f(\cdot)$, the production function, is the same as that prevailing at the standard time 0.

The index of the firm's capacity derived in this manner expresses the role that accumulated fixed resources play in the firm's production process. It corresponds to the concept of real capital in neoclassical theory, and it will be referred to simply as real capital in the present context.

Real capital K_t is increased by investment activity. What is referred to as investment activity means not only the accumulation of physical factors, such as the purchase of capital goods and construction, but also the accumulation of technology through research and development, as well as the accumulation of managerial and administrative resources.

How can the effect of fixed factors accumulated through the purchase of goods and services be measured? The effects of investment are measured by the extent to which the production function shifts as a result of investment. It is assumed that there is a fixed relationship between the real amount of investment Φ_t and the resulting increase in real capital $\dot{K}_t$. This relationship is determined by the scarce resources accumulated by the firm which are required for growth and expansion. Uzawa [35] called this the Penrose effect, associated with the pioneering work of Edith Penrose [20] on the theory of the growth of the firm. For the purposes of considering this problem from a general standpoint, it will simply be called the investment effect. The investment effect depends on the quantity of fixed factors accumulated for the purpose of growth and on the shift which accompanies changes in that quantity. Assuming that the index of a firm's capacity is proportional to the amount of scarce resources, the relationship between the rate of investment Φ_t/K_t and the resulting rate of increase of real capital $\dot{K}_t/K_t$ is expressed as

$$\Phi_t/K_t = \varphi(\dot{K}_t/K_t). \tag{28}$$

The effect of investment is governed by the investment-effect function $\varphi(\cdot)$, which is assumed to exhibit the features of diminishing returns to investment:

$$\varphi'(\alpha) > 0, \qquad \varphi''(\alpha) > 0. \tag{29}$$

As was touched on previously, real investment becomes an increase in real capital in neoclassical theory; namely, in neoclassical theory the investment-effect function is given by

$$\varphi(\alpha) = \alpha \quad \text{or} \quad I = \dot{K}. \tag{30}$$

The long-run behavior of the firm may be assumed to be described by the maximization of the discounted present value of future net cash flows. Let the real net cash flow at time t be denoted by Γ_t, namely,

$$\Gamma_t = Q_t - w_t N_t - \Phi_t \tag{31}$$

where

$$Q_t = K_t f(N_t/K_t) \tag{32}$$

$$\Phi_t = K_t \varphi(\dot{K}_t/K_t). \tag{33}$$

The discount rate to be used to discount future real net cash flows is not simply the market rate of interest, but the real rate of interest expected to prevail in the future. The scarce resources which are accumulated through investment activity will become fixed factors of production not to be disposed of easily during their lifetime. Hence, the firm has to use the rate of discount which is expected to prevail during the period in which invested resources will last. The rate depends on the way in which the firm obtains its funds for investment, but the model being developed here ignores such aspects of the financial market.

It will be assumed that the expectations adjustment mechanisms concerning the real rate of interest are the same for the corporate sector as for the household sector. Accordingly, the discounted present value V_0 is given by

$$V_0 = \int_0^\infty \Gamma_t \exp(-\rho^e t)\, dt, \tag{34}$$

which is to be maximized subject to the investment and employment schedules (31)–(33) of the firm.

If the expectations of the real wage rate are assumed to be constant, the following conditions are established concerning the plan for which V_0 is maximized. First, the labor/capital ratio is a constant depending on the expected real wage rate only:

$$N_t/K_t = n \quad \text{where } f'(n) = w.$$

Moreover, the optimum rate of investment and the rate of growth are both constant over time:

$$\Phi_t/K_t = \varphi(\alpha), \qquad \dot{K}_t/K_t = \alpha.$$

Then the discounted present value simply becomes

$$V_0 = ([r - \varphi(\alpha)]/[\rho^e - \alpha])K_0 \tag{35}$$

where r is the marginal product of capital corresponding to the labor/capital ratio n:

$$r = f(n) - nf'(n).$$

The rate of accumulation for which (35) is maximized is a function of ρ^e and r:

$$\alpha = \alpha(\rho^e, r), \qquad \varphi = \varphi(\rho^e, r).$$

Both α and φ are decreasing functions with respect to ρ^e, and increasing functions with respect to r.

From the preceding argument the investment function can be expressed as

$$\Phi = \varphi(\rho^e, r)K.$$

Government expenditures can be formulated in a variety of ways depending on how policy variables are used. Here, government expenditures are assumed to have a fixed ratio g to national income, and taxation may be ignored. Government expenditures G_W become

$$G_W = gY_W \tag{36}$$

where g is a policy variable.

The aggregate demand for goods and services is the sum of consumption demand, investment demand, and government expenditures:

$$D = C_W + \Phi_W + G_W$$

or

$$D = [1 - s]Y_W{}^e + P_W\varphi(\rho^e, r)K + gY_W. \tag{37}$$

An increase in the price level measured in wage units P_W is always accompanied by an increase in the level of labor employment, which in turn results in an increase in the rate of profit. Hence aggregate demand increases when the price level increases, provided the market rate of interest is kept constant and the expected real rate of interest remains fixed. As shown in Fig. 16.6, aggregate demand can be expressed by a curve having a slope less steep than the schedule of the aggregate supply function, given that the average propensity to save s exceeds the governmental expenditure ratio g and that permanent real income coincides with current income.

Equilibrium in the goods and services market is obtained when aggregate supply Z equals aggregate demand D:

$$D = Z \tag{38}$$

or

$$(1 - s)Y_W^e + P_W\varphi(\rho^e, r)K + gY_W = Y_W. \tag{39}$$

When (39) is measured not in money wage units, but in units of produced goods and services, we get

$$\varphi(\rho^e, r)K = (s - g)Q + (1 - s)(Y_W - Y_W{}^e)/P_W. \tag{40}$$

If expectations concerning the real wage rate are static, then

$$Y_W^e/P_W = wN + \rho^e A/P$$

where A is evaluated according to the market price of assets in the private sector.

The aggregates in real capital are defined as

$$f(n) = Q/K, \qquad \text{output/capital ratio}$$

$$a = A/PK = \frac{[r - \varphi(\alpha)]}{\rho^e - \alpha}, \qquad \text{assets/capital ratio.}$$

The condition of equilibrium for the goods and services market can be expressed by

$$\varphi(\rho^e, r) = (s - g)f(n) + (1 - s)(r - \rho^e a). \tag{41}$$

The price level P and the corresponding labor/capital ratio are uniquely determined by

$$f'(N/K) = w = W/P. \tag{42}$$

The investment function $\varphi(\rho^e, r)$ may be assumed to be a decreasing function of ρ^e and an increasing function of r. As was discussed in detail in Uzawa [36], these assumptions may be justified for a broad class of circumstances in which the schedule of the marginal efficiency of investment is subject to a diminishing rate of return. A simple calculation also shows

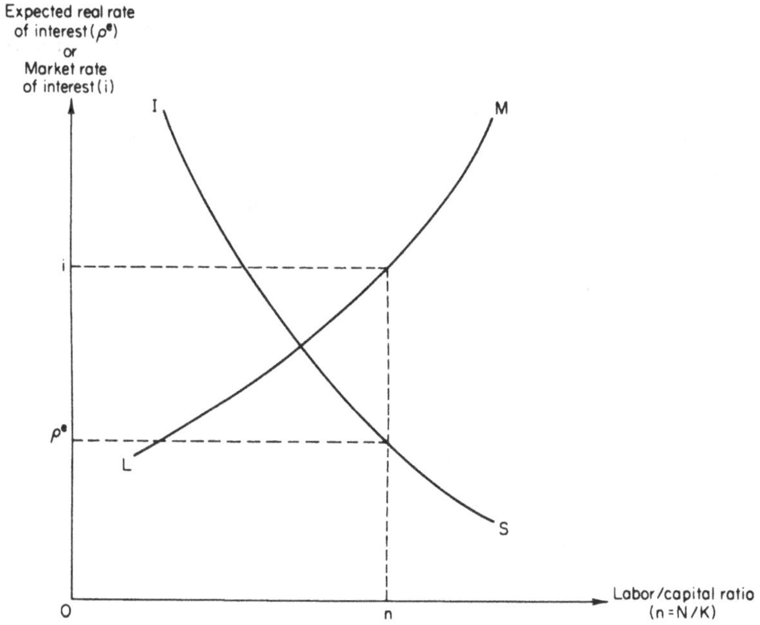

Figure 16.7

that

$$\rho^e a = \rho^e[r - \varphi(\alpha)]/(\rho^e - \alpha)$$

is a decreasing function of ρ^e. Hence, a decrease in ρ^e results in a decrease of the quantity on the left side of (41), while the quantity on the right side is increased. Hence, a decrease in ρ^e (or similarly an increase in r) results in an increase in the demand for both investment and consumption, thus entailing an increase in the effective level of employment. The equilibrium relation between ρ^e and n can be seen in (41) and is plotted as the downward-sloping curve IS in Fig. 16.7.

The market rate of interest is related to the market price of securities, which in turn is related to the condition of portfolio demand. This makes it necessary to consider the factors which go into determining the portfolio of financial assets.

In the *General Theory*, a broad class of money was used including time deposits and short-term securities such as Treasury bills, thus justifying the focus on the analysis of speculative motives (see, e.g., Keynes [11, p. 167]). In this chapter, however, money is used in a narrower sense; it is comprised of cash and demand deposits, so that the motives for holding it are based mainly on transaction purposes, while speculative motives may be ignored.

The demand for money depends first on expectations of the aggregate amount of transactions. If the demand for real cash balances L_W has unit elasticity and we let income stand in for total transactions, we may write

$$L_W = \lambda Y_W \tag{43}$$

where L_W and Y_W are measured in money wage units. The coefficient λ is the demand for real cash balances per unit of income, corresponding to Marshall's k.

The demand for real balances depends not only on real income, but also on the opportunity costs of holding money or on the market rate of interest. When the rate of interest increases, it becomes desirable to possess securities and the demand for money per unit of income falls. Namely, λ is a decreasing function of the market rate of interest:

$$\lambda = \lambda(i), \qquad \lambda'(i) < 0. \tag{44}$$

When the nominal quantity of money is determined by the central bank, the market rate of interest is determined by the equilibrium of the money market:

$$\lambda(i)\,Y_W = M_W(\equiv M/W). \tag{45}$$

If the demand for money is less than the supply, i.e., if $\lambda(i)\,Y_W < M_W$, the demand for securities exceeds the supply and the price of securities increases, resulting in a decrease in the market rate of interest. In the opposite situation, there is an increase in the rate of interest; equilibrium is established in the money market only if (45) is satisfied. The LM curve in Fig. 16.7 expresses the combinations of i and the labor/capital ratio n for which the money market is in equilibrium. An increase in the aggregate level of labor employment or in n shifts the demand schedule for real balances upward, entailing an increase in the equilibrium rate of interest. Hence, the LM curve has an upward-sloping shape as indicated in Fig. 16.7.

The determination of the short-run equilibrium in our model may be illustrated in terms of the IS and LM curves in Fig. 16.7. The level of the expected real rate of interest is historically given at ρ^e. Then the labor/capital ratio n corresponding to the effective level of employment is determined by the IS schedule, as illustrated by a dotted line in Fig. 16.7. The market rate of interest i for which the money market is in equilibrium then is determined by the LM schedule, as indicated again by a dotted line in Fig. 16.7.

A decrease in the expected real rate of interest ρ^e increases effective demand, and the labor/capital ratio corresponding to the effective employment of labor is increased. At the same time, the demand for money shifts upward, resulting in an increase in the market rate of interest.

6 Keynesian growth under full employment

In Section 5 we considered how employment, income, prices, and the market rate of interest are determined in a Keynesian system. Next, let us consider these variables under the conditions of full employment and continuous economic growth.

Let the rates of increase in money supply and labor supply both be exogenously given:

$$\dot{M}/M = \mu, \qquad \dot{N}/N = \nu.$$

When the conditions of full employment are satisfied, real national income per capita $\hat{y}$ becomes

$$\hat{y} = f(n)/n, \quad n = N/K.$$

When economic growth is to continue under the conditions of full employment, the following conditions have to be satisfied. First ρ^e must be at a level where the aggregate demand it engenders is equal to the supply of goods and services. Given ρ^e and the governmental expenditure coefficient g, the labor/capital ratio corresponding to effective demand can be expressed as $n(\rho^e, g)$. The elasticity of the effective labor/capital ratio with respect to ρ^e is denoted by η:

$$\eta = -\frac{1}{n}\frac{\partial n}{\partial \rho^e}.$$

The rate of change in n under conditions of full employment is

$$\dot{n}/n = \nu - \alpha \tag{46}$$

where α is the rate of increase in real capital under the equilibrium conditions:

$$\dot{K}/K = \alpha = \alpha(\rho^e, r). \tag{47}$$

In order to maintain full-employment growth, the changes in ρ^e must fulfill the conditions

$$\dot{\rho}^e = (1/\eta)(\alpha - \nu). \tag{48}$$

On the other hand, ρ^e is assumed to be adaptively adjusted:

$$\dot{\rho}^e = \beta(\rho - \rho^e), \qquad \rho = i - \pi. \tag{49}$$

Hence, in order for changes in ρ^e to satisfy the conditions of full employment, the market rate of interest i and the rate of price increase π simultaneously satisfying (48) and (49) must be realized. Therefore, the following relation exists between i and π:

$$i - \pi = \rho = \rho^e + (1/\beta\eta)(\alpha - v)$$

or

$$\pi = i - \rho^e - (1/\beta\eta)(\alpha - v). \tag{50}$$

A necessary condition for full-employment growth is that the money wage rate change so as to establish the equality of supply and demand in the labor market. Since

$$f'(n) = W/P,$$

the required rate of increase $\omega = \dot{W}/W$ in the money wage rate satisfies the relation

$$\omega = \pi + \varepsilon(\alpha - v)$$

where ε is the elasticity of the marginal product of labor,

$$\varepsilon = s_K/\sigma,$$

and s_K is the relative share of capital and σ is the elasticity of substitution between labor and capital.

Finally, it is necessary to maintain the market rate of interest at a level where the money market is continuously in equilibrium. The equilibrium of the money market was formulated in (45), and putting it into units of real capital we get

$$\lambda(i)f(n) = M/PK.$$

Since the rate of increase in the money supply is exogenously given through monetary policy,

$$\dot{M}/M = \mu,$$

the continuation of the equilibrium of the money market yields the condition

$$-\gamma\frac{di}{dt} + (1 - s_K)\frac{dn}{dt} = \mu - \pi - \alpha \tag{51}$$

where γ is the elasticity of the demand for money with respect to the market rate of interest:

$$\gamma = -\frac{1}{\lambda}\frac{d\lambda}{di} > 0.$$

Equation (51) may be written as

$$\frac{di}{dt} = \frac{1}{\gamma}[\pi - (\mu - \nu) + s_K(\alpha - \nu)] \tag{52}$$

or, using (50),

$$\frac{di}{dt} = \frac{1}{\gamma}\left[i - \rho^e - (\mu - \nu) - \left(\frac{1}{\beta\eta} - s_K\right)(\alpha - \nu)\right]. \tag{53}$$

For the rate of change of per capita real national income, we have

$$\frac{1}{\hat{y}}\frac{d\hat{y}}{dt} = s_K(\alpha - \nu). \tag{54}$$

When full-employment growth continues, the dynamic equations (53) and (54) have to prevail. These are the two basic equations in a Keynesian theory of growth.

To analyze this dynamic system, let us consider the changes in ρ^e and α accompanying changes in $\hat{y}$. As seen from the definition of per capita income $\hat{y}$, an increase in $\hat{y}$ results in a decrease in n. Hence, the value of ρ^e for which n corresponds to equilibrium in the goods and services market has to be increased, entailing a decrease in the rate of capital accumulation α. Thus, an increase in $\hat{y}$ is shown to result in a decrease in α. Moreover, because α is not directly affected by changes in i, changes in $\hat{y}$ can be examined separately. The level $\hat{y}^*$ of per capita real income for which $\dot{\hat{y}} = 0$ is uniquely determined. Namely, there is a level $\hat{y}^*$ which corresponds to the condition of long-term equilibrium and it is easily shown that it is dynamically stable. The long-run steady level $\hat{y}^*$ of per capita real income is determined independently of monetary policy μ and is affected only by the government expenditure coefficient g. In Fig. 16.8, the straight line AA is a distance $\hat{y}^*$ from the vertical axis.

Next let us consider the dynamic equation (53) concerning the market rate of interest i. For the market rate of interest i to be maintained at a constant level, it is necessary for the right side of (53) to equal 0; namely,

$$i = \rho^e + (\mu - \nu) + [(1/\beta\eta) - s_K](\alpha - \nu). \tag{55}$$

The right side of (55) is a function of y, and it can be typically expressed by the upward-sloping curve BB in Fig. 16.8, where the market rate of interest i is measured along the vertical axis and per capita real income $\hat{y}$ along the horizontal axis.

When the combination of i and $\hat{y}$ is such that it lies on the BB curve, the market rate of interest i remains stationary over time. If it lies above the BB curve, then $di/dt > 0$ and i tends to increase. Conversely, if i is

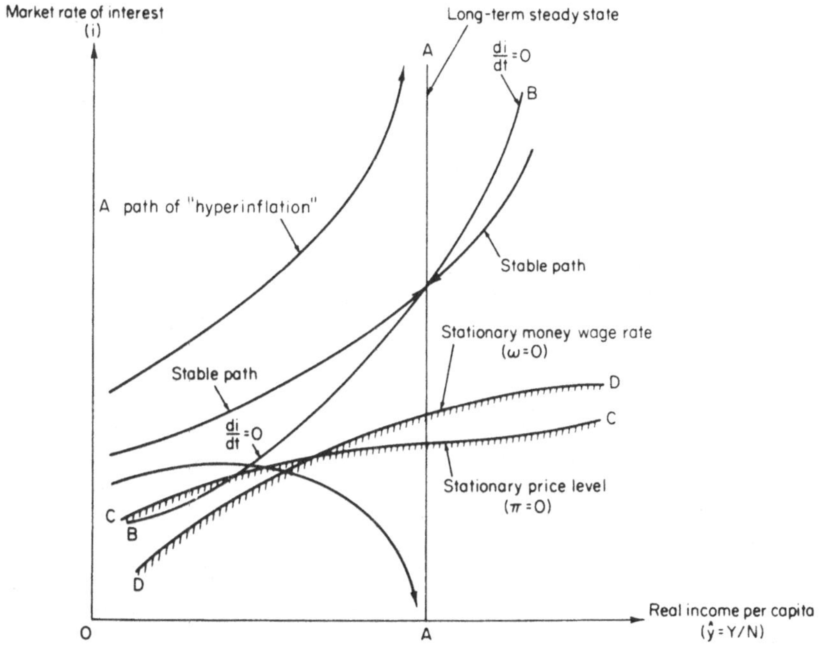

Figure 16.8

lower than the level corresponding to the *BB* curve, then $di/dt < 0$ and i tends to decrease. Accordingly, the dynamic equation (53), which describes changes in the market rate of interest i, is unstable with respect to i.

Since the last term of the quantity on the right side of (55) disappears on the *AA* line, it can be shown that the solution paths of the dynamic equations (53) and (54) may be represented in Fig. 16.8 by the cluster of curves with arrows. As indicated in Fig. 16.8, this system exhibits a kind of knife-edge instability. Namely, there are only two stable paths approaching long-term equilibrium states; for any other path the market rate of interest approaches either 0 or ∞.

In Fig. 16.8 there are two curves *CC* and *DD* which correspond to the conditions of stationary price level and stationary wage level, respectively. The *CC* curve represents the combinations of i and $\hat{y}$ for which the price level remains stationary, i.e., $\pi = 0$. From (50), we can see that an increase in $\hat{y}$ has to be associated with an increase in i in order for π to be 0, thus resulting in the upward-sloping curve *CC*. The rate of price increase is positive above the *CC* curve. On the other hand, the *DD* curve corresponds to the combinations of i and $\hat{y}$ for which the rate of money wage increase is 0, i.e., $\omega = 0$. Again we can show that the *DD* curve has an upward slope, intersecting with the *DD* curve as illustrated in Fig. 16.8. Below the *DD* curve, the money wage rate has to decrease in order to maintain economic growth under the conditions of full employment. Hence, the phenomenon of involuntary unemployment occurs below the *DD* curve.

For the general situation where the *BB* curve is not necessarily rising to the right, it can be shown that the long-run steady state is uniquely determined. However, the saddle-point property of the long-run steady state may not necessarily be valid, and there exists a possibility that there is a class of solution paths to the dynamic system (53) and (54) which converges to the long-run steady state. Outside of such a class of solution paths, the asymptotic behavior of dynamic processes exhibits an unstable feature as already depicted.

Thus, it is very difficult to maintain a stable full-employment growth under the conditions of a constant rate of increase in the money supply. There are either unlimited increases in the rate of price increase, i.e., the state of hyper-inflation, or there comes to be a state of involuntary unemployment. Economic growth displays the kind of knife-edge instability discussed by Harrod [6, 7]. To realize stable economic growth, it is necessary to have a flexible policy concerning the supply of money, e.g., that directed toward stabilization of the market rate of interest or the rate of price increase.

7 Concluding remarks

In this paper I have examined the various implications of the neoclassical and Keynesian approaches to the analysis of economic growth. The phenomenon of economic growth has been analyzed within an extremely simplified framework, and it is difficult to argue the general validity of the conclusions concerning the two approaches. However, the implications for the dynamic stability of the growth process seem to reflect the differences in the basic premises of each framework, suggesting that the implications may be generally applicable to a broader class of circumstances. In the neoclassical growth model, the path of economic growth is dynamically stable under fairly general assumptions, while, in the Keynesian theory, there is an intrinsic tendency for the growth process to be dynamically unstable unless certain stabilizing monetary and fiscal policies are adopted.

The two approaches have been discussed within a framework of dynamic equilibrium in which all markets are in equilibrium at each moment of time. It has not yet been possible to analyze the disequilibrium situation where all or some of the markets are not necessarily in equilibrium and changes in monetary and fiscal policies may bring about additional disequilibrating effects.

References

[1] Cagan, P., "The Monetary Dynamics of Hyperinflation," in *Studies in the Quantity Theory of Money* (M. Friedman, ed.), pp. 25–117. Chicago: Univ. of Chicago Press, 1956.
[2] Fujino, S., "Keynesian Theory and the Determination of National Income," in *Keynes and Modern Economics* (R. Tachi, ed.), pp. 174–93. Tokyo: Univ. of Tokyo Press, 1968 (in Japanese).
[3] Hahn, F. H., "The Stability of Growth Equilibrium," *Quarterly Journal of Economics* **74** (1960), 206–26.
[4] ———"On Money and Growth," *Journal of Money, Credit, and Banking* **1** (1969), 172–87.
[5] Hansen, A. H., *Monetary Theory and Fiscal Policy*. New York: McGraw-Hill, 1949.
[6] Harrod, R. F., "An Essay in Dynamic Theory," *Economic Journal* **64** (1939), 14–33.
[7] ———*Towards a Dynamic Economics*. New York: Macmillan, 1948.
[8] Hicks, J. R., "Mr. Keynes and the 'Classics'; A Suggested Interpretation," *Econometrica* **5** (1937), 147–59..
[9] Inada, K., and Uzawa, H., *Economic Development and Fluctuations*, particularly pp. 245–334. Tokyo: Iwanami, 1972 (in Japanese).
[10] Johnson, H. G., "The Neo-Classical One-Sector Growth Model: A Geometric Exposition and Extension to a Monetary Economy," *Economica* **33** (1966), 265–87.
[11] Keynes, J. M., *The General Theory of Employment, Interest and Money*. New York: Macmillan, 1936.
[12] Klein, L. R., *The Keynesian Revolution*. New York: Macmillan, 1947.
[13] Lange, O., *Price Flexibility and Employment*. Bloomington, Indiana: Principia Press, 1944.
[14] Leijonhufvud, A., *On Keynesian Economics and the Economics of Keynes*. London and New York: Oxford Univ. Press, 1968.
[15] Levhari, D., and Patinkin, D., "The Role of Money in a Simple Growth Model," *American Economic Review* **58** (1968), 713–53.
[16] Metzler, L. A., "Wealth, Saving, and the Rate of Interest," *Journal of Political Economy* **59** (1951), 93–116.
[17] Modigliani, F., "Liquidity Preference and the Theory of Interest and Money," *Econometrica* **12** (1944), 45–88.
[18] ———"The Monetary Mechanism and Its Interaction with Real Variables," *Review of Economics and Statistics* **45** (1963), 79–107.
[19] Nerlove, M., *Dynamics of Supply Estimation of Farmers' Response to Price*. Baltimore: Johns Hopkins Univ. Press, 1958.
[20] Penrose, E. T., *The Theory of the Growth of the Firm*. Oxford: Blackwell, 1959.
[21] Rose, H., "Unemployment in a Theory of Growth," *International Economic Review* **7** (1966), 260–82.
[22] ——— "On the Non-Linear Theory of the Employment Cycle," *Review of Economic Studies* **34** (1967), 153–73.
[23] ———"Real and Monetary Factors in the Business Cycle," *Journal of Money, Credit, and Banking* **1** (1969), 138–52.
[24] Saito, K., "On the Short-Run Mechanism of the Aggregate Income Distribution," *Shogaku Ronshu* **30** (1962), 1–44 (in Japanese).

[25] ———"The Aggregate Supply Function and Macro-Economic Distribution," *Keizai Kenkyu* **13** (1962), 314–21 (in Japanese).
[26] Sato, K., "On the Synthesis of Income Analysis and Price Theory: A Reconstruction of the Multiplier Theory," *Keizaigaku Kenkyu* **8** (1955), 51–88 (in Japanese).
[27] Sidrauski, M., "Rational Choice and Pattern of Growth in a Monetary Economy," *American Economic Review, Proceedings* **57** (1967), 534–44.
[28] Solow, R. M., "A Contribution to the Theory of Economic Growth," *Quarterly Journal of Economics* **70** (1956) , 65–95.
[29] Stein, J. L., "Money and Capacity Growth," *Journal of Political Economy* **74** (1966), 451–65.
[30] ———"'Neoclassical' and 'Keynes-Wicksell' Monetary Growth Models," *Journal of Money, Credit, and Banking* **1** (1969), 153–71.
[31] Swan, T. W., "Economic Growth and Capital Accumulation," *Economic Record* **32** (1956), 334–61.
[32] Tobin, J., "A Dynamic Aggregative Model," *Journal of Political Economy* **63** (1955), 103–15.
[33] ———"Money and Economic Growth," *Econometrica* **33** (1965), 671–84.
[34] Uzawa, H., "On a Neoclassical Model of Economic Growth," *Economic Studies Quarterly* **17** (1966), 1–15.
[35] ———"The Penrose Effect and Optimum Growth," *Economic Studies Quarterly* **19** (1968), 1–14.
[36] ———"Time Preference and the Penrose Effect in a Two-Class Model of Economic Growth," *Journal of Political Economy* **77** (1969), 628–52.
[37] ———"Towards a Keynesian Model of Monetary Growth," *Proceedings of the International Economic Association Conference on the Theory of Economic Growth*, 1973.
[38] ———"Diffusion of Inflationary Processes in a Dynamic Model of International Trade," *Economic Studies Quarterly* **22** (1971), 14–37.

PART VI

Optimum growth

CHAPTER 17

Optimal growth in a two-sector model of capital accumulation

1. Introduction

One of the basic problems in economic planning, in particular in underdeveloped countries, is concerned with the rate at which society should save out of current income to achieve a maximum growth. It is closely related to the problem of how scarce resources at each moment of time should be divided between consumer's goods industries and capital goods industries. In the present paper, we shall analyze the problem in the framework of the two-sector growth model as introduced by Meade [3], Srinivasan [6], and Uzawa [8]. We shall abstract from the complications which would arise by taking into account those factors such as changing technology and structure of demand, the role of foreign trade (in particular, of capital imports), and tax policy that are generally regarded as decisive in the determination of the course of economic development. Instead, we shall focus our attention on evaluating the impact of roundabout methods of production upon the welfare of society, as expressed by a discounted sum of per capita consumption. However, since our primary concern is with economic planning in underdeveloped countries, we shall depart with respect to one important point from the two-sector growth model as formulated in [3, 6, 8] which is, in general, concerned with an economy with fairly advanced technology and relatively abundant capital; namely, we shall postulate that a certain quantity of consumers' goods (per capita) is required to sustain a given rate of population growth. This restraint becomes ineffective for an economy with relatively abundant capital; however, for an economy with a low capital-labor ratio and high rate of population growth, it results in the

From *Review of Economic Studies*, Vol. 31 (1964), pp. 1–24; reprinted with permission.

The author is greatly indebted to Professors Kenneth J. Arrow and Samuel Karlin for their valuable comments and suggestions.

phenomenon frequently referred to as "the vicious circle of poverty".[1] In the course of the discussion below on optimal growth, we shall briefly investigate the existence of such a vicious circle and its implications upon patterns of optimal growth.

Mathematically, our problem is that of finding a growth path over which the criterion function (i.e., the discounted sum of per capita consumption over the whole period) is maximized among all feasible growth paths. It is a problem in concave programming in linear spaces, to use the term of Hurwicz [2], and the techniques developed by him and others, particularly the extensions of the Kuhn-Tucker theorem, may be applicable. In the present case, however, it is possible to solve our problem without recourse to these advanced methods, and the optimal growth paths are instead characterized by a simple extension of the Euler equations in the classical calculus of variations. The mathematical structure of the auxiliary differential equations arising from the Euler equations differs markedly, according to whether consumer's goods are more or less capital-intensive than capital goods, and the detailed structure of the optimal growth path differs in these two cases. Therefore, for the convenience of analysis, we shall first present the discussions for these two cases separately, and then the general case in which no restrictions are imposed on relative capital intensities will be briefly discussed. It will be generally shown that for any economy with a relatively low capital-labor ratio, consumers' goods are produced in the amounts just necessary to satisfy the minimum requirements until a certain critical level is reached, and from then on the rate of production of consumers' goods is gradually increased toward a certain balanced rate. Our results are thus extensions of those obtained by Srinivasan [6] for the case in which the minimum wage rate is zero and for which consumer's goods are always more capital-intensive than capital goods.

2 A two-sector model of capital accumulation

To begin with, let us describe the basic premises of our two-sector model in terms of a mathematical model.[2] We are concerned with an economy in which consumption goods and capital goods are composed of homogeneous quantities. Both goods are produced by combinations of two factors of production, labor and capital, but the possibility of joint products is excluded. The sole aim of the economy is to consume consumption goods, while capital goods are produced only to increase

[1] See, e.g., Nurkse [5, p. 4 f.] and Myrdal [4, p. 11 f.].

[2] Such a model of the two-sector economy was first introduced in Meade [3]. The present formulation modifies slightly that introduced in Uzawa [8].

future production of consumption goods. Consumption goods may be assumed instantaneously consumed and capital goods to depreciate at a certain rate, say μ, which is technologically given. It will be assumed that technological knowledge remains constant in the whole period in question, constant returns to scale and diminishing marginal rate of substitution between capital and labor prevail in each sector, and there exist no external (dis-) economies. The sector producing consumption goods will be referred to as the C-sector, while that producing capital goods as the I-sector.

To make the analysis simpler, it is assumed that the size of the working population and the rate at which it grows are exogeneously given, and that labor is inelastically offered for employment at any moment of time. Let $L(t)$ denote the size of the working population at time t, then

$$\dot{L}(t)/L(t) = v, \tag{1}$$

where v stands for the rate of increase in labor forces.

It is furthermore assumed that the working population is a stationary proportion of the total population and that no external (dis-) economies exist for consumption, so that the minimum amount of consumption goods per capita required to sustain the given labor growth v may be assumed determinate. Let w_{min} denote the minimum wage rate in terms of consumption goods corresponding to the labor growth v.[3] In general, the minimum wage rate w_{min} is assumed positive.[4]

The aggregate quantity of capital $K(t)$ existing at any moment of time is determined by the accumulation of capital goods which have been produced in the past; namely, the rate of change in the aggregate stock of capital at time t, $\dot{K}(t)$, is given by

$$\dot{K}(t) = Y_I(t) - \mu K(t), \tag{2}$$

where $Y_I(t)$ stands for the rate at which new capital goods are produced at time t.

The rate $Y_I(t)$ at which new capital goods are produced, on the other hand, is determined by the quantities of capital and labor allocated to the I-sector, $K_I(t)$ and $L_I(t)$; namely

$$Y_I(t) = F_I(K_I(t), L_I(t)), \tag{3}$$

where F_I is the production function which summarizes the production processes in the I-sector.

[3] Several authors, in particular Buttrick [1] and Tsiang [7], have postulated certain relationships between the rate of labor growth and minimum wages, and have effectively analyzed the characteristics of various stages of economic growth.

[4] The case discussed by Srinivasan [6] and Uzawa [8] may be considered as a limiting case when the minimum wage rate tends to zero, which in the present paper will be discussed only to illustrate the techniques to be used for the general case.

The rate of production of consumption goods at time t, $Y_C(t)$, is similarly determined by

$$Y_C(t) = F_C(K_C(t), L_C(t)), \tag{4}$$

where $K_C(t)$ and $L_C(t)$, respectively, are the quantities of capital and labor employed in the C-sector at time t.

The quantities of capital and labor allocated to the two sectors should remain within the available quantities existing in the economy as a whole; i.e.,[5]

$$K_I(t) + K_C(t) = K(t), \tag{5}$$

$$L_I(t) + L_C(t) = L(t). \tag{6}$$

The conditions (5) and (6) in particular imply that both capital and labor may be transferred from one sector to another without any cost; our capital thus is malleable in Meade's terminology ([3], p. 45).

The quantity of consumption goods, on the other hand, must be sufficient to afford the minimum wage rate w_{min}; hence, we have inequality:

$$Y_C(t) \geqq w_{min} L(t). \tag{7}$$

The quantity of capital available to the economy at the beginning ($t = 0$), $K(0)$, is given as one of the data, together with technological conditions and population growth. A continuous path of consumption $\{Y_C(t); t \geqq 0\}$ is termed *feasible* if it is possible to find allocations of capital and labor at each moment of time such that all the conditions (2–7) are satisfied.

In what follows, it will be assumed that production in each sector is subject to constant returns to scale, the marginal rate of substitution between capital and labor is smooth and diminishing, the marginal physical products of both factors are always positive, and both factors are indispensable. Let $k_j = K_j/L_j$ be the capital stock per unit of employment in the jth sector ($j = C, I$), and the function $f_j(k_j)$ be defined by:

$$f_j(k_j) = F_j(k_j, 1), j = C, I.$$

Then $f_j(k_j)$ is continuously twice differentiable and

$$f_j(k_j) > 0, f'_j(k_j) > 0, f''_j(k_j) < 0, \quad \text{for all } k_j > 0, \tag{8}$$

$$f_j(0) = 0, \quad f_j(\infty) = \infty, \tag{9}$$

$$f'_j(0) = \infty, \quad f'_j(\infty) = 0. \tag{10}$$

[5] In view of the assumptions made below, (8–10), both capital and labor are fully employed at any optimal growth path, and we may without loss of generality postulate the full employment of both capital and labor at any moment of time.

3 Optimal growth in the two-sector model

Since there is only one consumption good in our two-sector economy, the social welfare may be determined, once we specify the rate of discount by which future consumption is weighed against present consumption. It will be assumed that the rate of discount is held at a fixed positive level δ. A feasible path will be termed *optimal* (relative to the rate of discount δ) if it maximizes the discounted sum of per capita consumption

$$\int_0^\infty \frac{Y_C(t)}{L(t)} e^{-\delta t}\, dt \tag{11}$$

among all feasible paths of consumption arising from the given capital stock $K(0)$ initially held in the economy.

In view of the assumptions (8–10), it is easily seen that the quantity (11) is finite for any feasible path, provided that

$$\lambda = \nu + \mu > 0. \tag{12}$$

It may be noted first that *an optimal path, if it exists, is uniquely determined.* Indeed, suppose two growth paths, $(K^0(t), Y_I^0(t), Y_C^0(t))$ and $(K^1(t), Y_I^1(t), Y_C^1(t))$, are both optimal with respect to the initial stock of capital $K(0)$ and labor growth $L(t)$. Let capital and labor allocations at time t be $K_I^j(t)$, $K_C^j(t)$, $L_I^j(t), K_C^j(t)$ for the optimal growth j ($j = 0, 1$). Then we have, for $j = 0, 1$,

$$\int_0^\infty \frac{Y^0(t)}{L(t)} e^{-\delta t}\, dt = \int_0^\infty \frac{Y^1(t)}{L(t)} e^{-\delta t}\, dt, \tag{13}$$

$$\dot{K}^j(t) = Y_I^j(t) + \mu K^j(t), \tag{14}$$

$$Y_I^j(t) = F_I[K_I^j(t), L_I^j(t)], \tag{15}$$

$$Y_C^j(t) = F_C[K_C^j(t), L_C^j(t)], \tag{16}$$

$$K_I^j(t) + K_C^j(t) = K^j(t), \tag{17}$$

$$L_I^j(t) + L_C^j(t) = L(t), \tag{18}$$

where

$$K^j(0) = K(0), j = 0, 1.$$

Let us define, for $0 \leqq \theta \leqq 1$,

$$K^\theta(t) = (1-\theta)K^0(t) + \theta K^1(t),$$
$$K_I^\theta(t) = (1-\theta)K_I^0(t) + \theta K_I^1(t),$$
$$K_C^\theta(t) = (1-\theta)K_C^0(t) + \theta K_C^1(t),$$

$$Y_I^\theta(t) = (1-\theta)Y_I^0(t) + \theta Y_I^1(t),$$
$$Y_C^\theta(t) = (1-\theta)Y_C^0(t) + \theta Y_C^1(t).$$

Then we have

$$\int_0^\infty \frac{Y^\theta(t)}{L(t)} e^{-\delta t}\, dt = \int_0^\infty \frac{Y^0(t)}{L(t)} e^{-\delta t}\, dt, \tag{19}$$

$$\dot K^\theta(t) = Y_I^\theta(t) - \mu K^\theta(t), \tag{20}$$

$$Y_I^\theta(t) \leqq F_I[K_I^\theta(t), L_I^\theta(t)], \tag{21}$$

with strict inequality if $K_I^0(t)/L_I^0(t) \neq K_I^1(t)/L_I^1(t)$,

$$Y_C^\theta(t) \leqq F_C[K_C^\theta(t), L_C^\theta(t)], \tag{22}$$

with strict inequality if $K_C^0(t)/L_C^0(t) \neq K_C^1(t)/L_C^1(t)$,

$$K_I^\theta(t) + K_C^\theta(t) = K^\theta(t), \tag{23}$$

$$L_I^\theta(t) + L_C^\theta(t) = L(t), \tag{24}$$

with $K^\theta(0) = K(0)$.

If $K_C^0(\bar t)/L_C^0(\bar t) \neq K_C^1(\bar t)/L_C^1(\bar t)$ at some time $\bar t$, then, because of (22), $Y_C^\theta(t)$ may be increased in some period around $\bar t$ without violating the feasibility conditions. Hence, there exists a feasible path on which the value of the criterion function (11) is greater than

$$\int_0^\infty \frac{Y_C^0(t)}{L(t)} e^{-\delta t}\, dt,$$

thus contradicting the optimality of the path $(K^0(t),\ Y_I^0(t),\ Y_C^0(t))$. On the other hand, if $K^0(\bar t)/L_I^0(\bar t) \neq K_I^1(\bar t)/L_I^1(\bar t)$ at some time $\bar t$, then, because of (21) and (23), it is possible to increase the value of $Y_C^\theta(t)$ in some period around $\bar t$ by reducing $K_I^\theta(t)$ and increasing $K_C^\theta(t)$ in small quantities. It is again possible to find a feasible path on which (11) is greater than $\int_0^\infty (Y_C^0(t)/L(t))e^{-\delta t}\, dt$, thus contradicting the optimality of the path $(K^0(t), Y_I^0(t), Y_C^0(t))$. Therefore, we must have

$$\frac{K_I^0(t)}{L_I^0(t)} = \frac{K_I^1(t)}{L_I^1(t)}, \tag{25}$$

$$\frac{K_C^0(t)}{L_C^0(t)} = \frac{K_C^1(t)}{L_C^1(t)}, \quad \text{for all } t. \tag{26}$$

Let

$$k_i(t) = \frac{K_i^j(t)}{L_i^j(t)}, \quad j = 0, 1, i = I, C, \tag{27}$$

then we have

$$\frac{K_i^{\theta}(t)}{L_i^{\theta}(t)} = k_i(t), \quad \text{for all } i = I, C, 0 \leqq \theta \leqq 1, t \geqq 0. \tag{28}$$

The relations (23), (24), and (28) together imply that

$$L_I^{\theta}(t) = \frac{k_C(t)L(t) - K^{\theta}(t)}{k_C(t) - k_I(t)}, \quad L_C^{\theta}(t) = \frac{K^{\theta}(t) - k_I(t)L(t)}{k_C(t) - k_I(t)}; \tag{29}$$

since (21) holds with equality and $F_I(K_I, L_I)$ is homogeneous of order one, we have

$$Y_I^{\theta}(t) = f_I(k_I(t)) \frac{k_C(t)L(t) - K^{\theta}(t)}{k_C(t) - k_I(t)}. \tag{30}$$

Hence,

$$\dot{K}^{\theta}(t) = \frac{k_C(t) f_I(k_I(t))}{k_C(t) - k_I(t)} L(t) - \left(\frac{f_I(k_I(t))}{k_C(t) - k_I(t)} + \mu \right) K^{0}(t), \tag{31}$$

with $K^{\theta}(0) = K(0)$, $0 \leqq \theta \leqq 1$. Therefore, $K^0(t)$ and $K^1(t)$ both satisfy the identical differential equation (31) with initial condition $K(0)$; hence, by the uniqueness of the solution to (31), we have

$$K^0(t) = K^1(t), \quad \text{for all } t. \tag{32}$$

From (28), (29), and (32), the two optimal growth paths $(K^0(t), Y_I^0(t), Y_C^0(t))$ and $(K^1(t), Y_I^1(t), Y_C^1(t))$ are necessarily identical.

Let us now introduce auxiliary variables (Lagrange multipliers) $q(t)$, $p_I(t)$, $p_C(t)$, $r(t)$, $w(t)$, and $v(t)$, respectively, corresponding to the restraints (2), (3), (4), (5), (6), and (7), and consider the following quantity:

$$\begin{aligned} \int_0^{\infty} \{ & Y_C(t) + p_C(t)(F_C(K_C(t), L_C(t)) - Y_C(t)) \\ & + p_I(t)(F_I(K_I(t), L_I(t)) - Y_I(t)) + r(t)(K(t) - K_C(t) - K_I(t)) \\ & + w(t)(L(t) - L_C(t) - L_I(t)) + q(t)(Y_I(t) - \mu K(t) - \dot{K}(t)) \\ & + v(t)(Y_C(t) - w_{min}L(t)) \} e^{-(v+\delta)t} dt, \end{aligned} \tag{33}$$

where all variables are non-negative and $K(0)$ is a given quantity.

The expression (33) is concave in $Y_C(t)$, $Y_I(t)$, $K_C(t)$, $K_I(t)$, $K(t)$, $L_C(t)$, and $L_I(t)$. Suppose we have found a set of auxiliary variables $p_C(t)$, $p_I(t)$, $q(t)$, $v(t)$ for which the variables $Y_C(t)$, $Y_I(t)$, $K_C(t)$, $K_I(t)$, $K(t)$, $L_C(t)$, $L_I(t)$, maximizing the quantity (33) without any restraint satisfy the feasibility conditions (2–7). Then the path of the corresponding $Y_C(t)$ is an optimal path. Our optimum problem thus is reduced to that of maximizing the quantity (33) for a given set of auxiliary variables. The latter is a concave problem in the calculus of variations and its solution may be obtained by solving the following Euler equations:

$$\nu(t) \geqq 0, \tag{34}$$

with equality if $Y_C(t) > w_{min}L(t)$;

$$1 + \nu(t) - p_C(t) = 0; \tag{35}$$

$$q(t) - p_I(t) \leqq 0, \tag{36}$$

with equality if $Y_I(t) > 0$;

$$p_C(t)\frac{\partial F_C(t)}{\partial K_C(t)} - r(t) \leqq 0, \tag{37}$$

with equality if $K_C(t) > 0$;

$$p_I(t)\frac{\partial F_I(t)}{\partial K_I(t)} - r(t) \leqq 0, \tag{38}$$

with equality if $K_I(t) > 0$;

$$p_C(t)\frac{\partial F_C(t)}{\partial L_C(t)} - w(t) \leqq 0, \tag{39}$$

with equality if $L_C(t) > 0$;

$$p_I(t)\frac{\partial F_I(t)}{\partial L_I(t)} - w(t) \leqq 0, \tag{40}$$

with equality if $L_I(t) > 0$;

$$r(t) - \mu q(t) = (\nu + \delta)q(t) - \dot{q}(t), \tag{41}$$

where $K(0)$ is a given quantity and all variables are non-negative and bounded.

4 Reduction of optimality conditions

In view of the constant-returns-to-scale assumption, it is possible to reduce the system of Euler equations (34–41) and the feasibility conditions (2–7) to those involving only per capita quantities.

Let ω be an arbitrarily given wage-rentals ratio and define the optimum capital-labor ratio k_j in each sector by solving

$$\omega = \frac{f_j(k_j)}{f'_j(k_j)} - k_j \qquad (j = C, I), \tag{42}$$

in terms of k_j. By assumptions (8–10), such a capital-labor ratio k_j is uniquely determined for any wage-rentals ratio ω and it will be denoted by $k_j(\omega)$. From (42), we have

$$\frac{dk_j(\omega)}{d\omega} = \frac{[f'_j(k_j(\omega))]^2}{-f_j(k_j(\omega))f''_j(k_j(\omega))} > 0. \tag{43}$$

We next introduce the supply price of capital, $p(\omega)$, in terms of consumption goods:

$$p(\omega) = \frac{f'_C(k_C(\omega))}{f'_I(k_I(\omega))}. \tag{44}$$

The supply price thus defined corresponds to the price of capital (in terms of consumers' goods) which would just induce each entrepreneur in a competitive economy to produce an additional unit of new capital goods under the prevailing wage-rentals ratio ω. Logarithmically differentiate (44) and substitute (43) to get

$$\frac{1}{p(\omega)}\frac{dp(\omega)}{d\omega} = \frac{1}{k_I(\omega) + \omega} - \frac{1}{k_C(\omega) + \omega}, \tag{45}$$

which is positive or negative, according to whether consumption goods are more or less capital-intensive than capital goods.

Let us finally introduce:

$$y_j(t) = \frac{Y_j(t)}{L(t)},$$

$$k_j(t) = \frac{K_j(t)}{L_j(t)},$$

$$l_j(t) = \frac{L_j(t)}{L(t)}, \qquad j = I, C$$

$$k(t) = \frac{K(t)}{L(t)}.$$

A simple manipulation shows that the Euler equations (34–41) and the feasibility conditions (2–6) together are reduced to the following system:

$$y_C(t) = f_C(k_C(t))l_C(t), \qquad y_I(t) = f_I(k_I(t))l_I(t), \tag{46}$$

$$k_C(t)l_C(t) + k_I(t)l_I(t) = k(t), \tag{47}$$

$$l_C(t) + l_I(t) = 1, \tag{48}$$

$$y_C(t) \geqq w_{min}, \tag{49}$$

$$p(t) \leqq q(t), \quad \text{if } y_I(t) > 0, \tag{50}$$

$$p(t) \geqq q(t), \quad \text{if } y_C(t) > w_{min}, \tag{51}$$

$$\dot{k}(t) = y_I(t) - \lambda k(t), \tag{52}$$

$$\dot{q}(t) = (\delta + \lambda)q(t) - r(t), \tag{53}$$

where all variables are nonnegative and bounded,

$$k_C(t) = k_C(\omega(t)), \qquad k_I(t) = k_I(\omega(t)),$$
$$p(t) = p(\omega(t)),$$
$$r(t) = f'(k_C(t)),$$
$$\lambda = \mu + \nu > 0$$

and

$$k(0) = K(0)/L(0) \text{ is given.}$$

The auxiliary variable, $q(t)$, may be interpreted as the *demand price of capital* (in terms of consumers' goods) at time t. The relations (50) and (51) then simply mean that no capital goods are produced when the supply price of capital $p(t)$ exceeds the demand price of capital $q(t)$, while consumers' goods are produced just enough to meet the minimum requirement when the demand price $q(t)$ exceeds the supply price $p(t)$.

Our optimum problem now is reduced to solving the system of the optimality conditions (46–53). We shall first discuss the case in which consumption goods are always more capital-intensive than capital goods, and proceed to discuss the case in which consumption goods are always less capital-intensive than capital goods. Finally, the general case will be briefly discussed by using the results obtained for these two special cases.

5 The case when consumption goods are always more capital-intensive than capital goods

Let us first consider the case in which consumption goods are always more capital-intensive than capital goods; namely,

$$k_C(\omega) > k_I(\omega), \quad \text{for all } \omega > 0. \tag{54}$$

To solve the system (46–53), it is found useful to investigate the structure of the differential equations which describe the behavior of the capital-labor ratio k and the wage-rentals ratio ω when capital goods are produced with positive quantities, and consumption goods exceed minimum requirements. In such a case, we have from (46), (47), (48), (50), and (51) that

$$p(t) = q(t) \tag{55}$$

$$y_C(t) = \frac{k(t) - k_I(t)}{k_C(t) - k_I(t)} f_C(k_C(t)), \qquad y_I(t) = \frac{k_C(t) - k(t)}{k_C(t) - k_I(t)} f_I(k_I(t)). \quad (56)$$

The differential equations (52) and (53) are accordingly reduced to:

$$\dot{k} = \frac{k_C(\omega) - k}{k_C(\omega) - k_I(\omega)} f_I(k_I(\omega)) - \lambda k, \quad (57)$$

$$\frac{\dot{p}(\omega)}{p(\omega)} = \lambda + \delta - f'_I(k_I(\omega)), \quad (58)$$

where for the sake of simplicity the variables are described without explicitly referring to the time variable t. The differential equations (57) and (58) will be referred to as the *auxiliary differential equations.*

In view of (45) and (54), the auxiliary differential equations (57) and (58) may be written as:

$$\dot{k} = \left\{ \frac{f_I[k_I(\omega)]}{k_C(\omega) - k_I(\omega)} + \lambda \right\} (\hat{k}(\omega) - k), \quad (59)$$

$$\dot{\omega} = \frac{\lambda + \delta - f'_I(k_I(\omega))}{\dfrac{1}{k_I(\omega) + \omega} - \dfrac{1}{k_C(\omega) + \omega}}, \quad (60)$$

where

$$\hat{k}(\omega) = \frac{f_I[k_I(\omega)]}{f_I[k_I(\omega)] + \lambda[k_C(\omega) - k_I(\omega)]} k_C(\omega). \quad (61)$$

The quantity $\hat{k}(\omega)$ is always smaller than $k_C(\omega)$ and it is larger than $k_I(\omega)$ if and only if

$$\frac{f_I[k_I(\omega)]}{k_I(\omega)} > \lambda.$$

Since the average productivity of capital, $f_I(k_I)/k_I$, is a decreasing function of k_I and $k_I(\omega)$ is an increasing function of ω, we have

$$k_I(\omega) < \hat{k}(\omega) < k_C(\omega) \quad \text{if and only if } \omega < \omega_\lambda,$$

where ω_λ is defined by

$$\frac{f_I(k_I(\omega_\lambda))}{k_I(\omega_\lambda)} = \lambda. \quad (62)$$

Let us now define *the balanced wage-rentals ratio,* ω^*, by

$$f'_I(k_I(\omega^*)) = \lambda + \delta. \quad (63)$$

Define $k^* = \hat{k}(\omega^*)$, $k_I^* = k_I(\omega^*)$, $k_C^* = k_C(\omega^*)$. The determination of ω_λ and

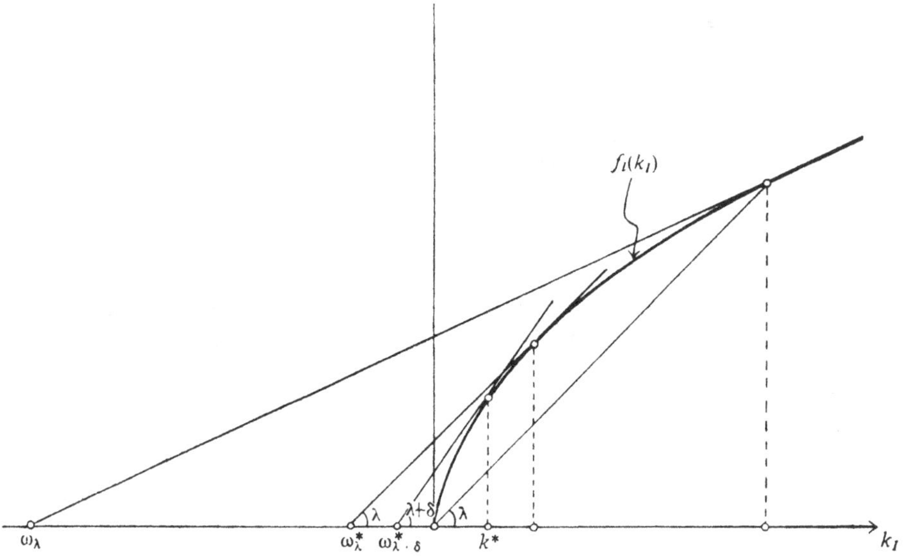

Figure 17.1

ω^* may be illustrated by Figure 17.1. The ratio ω_λ is always greater than the balanced ratio ω^*; in particular,

$$k_I^* < k^* < k_C^*.$$

The relationships between $k_C(\omega)$, $k_I(\omega)$, and $\hat{k}(\omega)$ are illustrated by Figure 17.2.

For any initial condition, the solution to the auxiliary differential equations (57) and (58) will be assumed to exist and to change continuously as the initial condition changes. The rate of change in k is positive, zero, or negative according to whether k is smaller than, equal to, or larger than $\hat{k}(\omega)$, while the rate of change in ω is positive, zero, or negative according to whether ω is larger than, equal to, or smaller than the balanced ratio ω^*. Therefore, the structure of the solution paths to the auxiliary differential equations may be described by the arrow curves as illustrated in Figure 17.2.

The structure of the solution to the auxiliary differential equations described above will be used to solve the system (46–53) of the optimality conditions. To illustrate the method, let us first discuss the limiting case in which the minimum wage rate is zero:

$$w_{min} = 0.$$

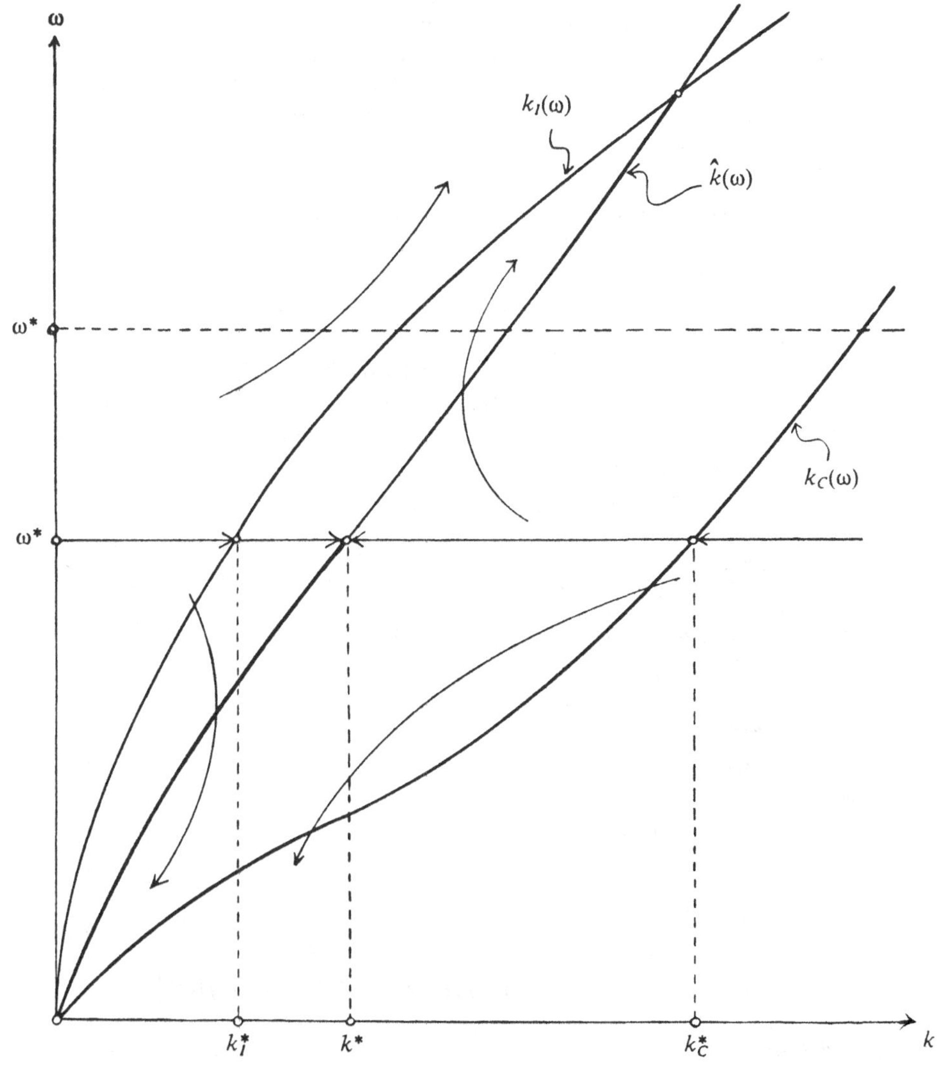

Figure 17.2

It is first noted that if the supply price of capital $p(t)$ is identical with the demand price $q(t)$ at any point on the $k_I(\omega)$ curve below the ω^*-line, and if the economy is specialized to the production of capital goods, then the demand price $q(t)$ satisfying the equation (53) falls while the supply price $p(t)$ rises; therefore, the economy continues the specialization in capital goods. This is easily seen from Figure 17.2, or it may be analytically shown by solving for the case in which the economy is specialized to capital goods.

It is similarly shown that if the supply price $p(t)$ is identical with the demand price $q(t)$ on the $k_C(\omega)$ curve above the ω^*-line, and if the economy is specialized in consumption goods, then the demand price rises while the supply price falls along the optimal path.

These considerations lead us to the following solutions to the optimality conditions (46–53): (a) *If the initial capital-labor ratio $k(0)$ is smaller than k_I^*, then, along the optimal path, the economy is specialized to the production of capital goods until the capital-labor ratio $k(t)$ reaches the critical ratio k_I^*. When the critical ratio k_I^* is reached, both consumption goods and capital goods are produced, keeping the wage-rentals ratio at the level ω^*. The optimal path then approaches asymptotically the balanced ratio k^* along the ω^*-line.* The precise analytical expressions may be given as follows, and it is easily shown that the path characterized by (64–76) satisfies all the optimality criteria (46–53).

Let the critical time t^* be defined by

$$t^* = \int_{k(0)}^{k_I^*} \frac{dk}{f_I(k) - \lambda k}. \tag{64}$$

For $0 \leqq t \leqq t^*$: $k(t)$ and $\omega(t)$ are respectively obtained by solving

$$\int_{k(0)}^{k(t)} \frac{dk}{f_I(k) - \lambda k} = t, \tag{65}$$

$$k(t) = k_I(\omega(t)), \tag{66}$$

and

$$y_I(t) = f_I(k(t)), \tag{67}$$

$$y_C(t) = 0, \tag{68}$$

$$p(t) = p[\omega(t)], \tag{69}$$

$$q(t) = e^{-(\lambda+\delta)(t^*-t)}\left\{\int_t^{t^*} f'_C[k_C(\omega(\tau))]e^{(\lambda+\delta)(t^*-\tau)}d\tau - p(t^*)\right\}. \tag{70}$$

For $t \geqq t^*$:

$$k(t) = k^* - (k^* - k_I^*)e^{-\theta(t-t^*)}, \tag{71}$$

where

$$\theta = \frac{f_I[k_I(\omega^*)]}{k_C(\omega^*) - k_I(\omega^*)} + \lambda, \tag{72}$$

$$\omega(t) = \omega^*, \tag{73}$$

$$y_I(t) = \frac{k_C^* - k(t)}{k_C^* - k_I^*} f_I(k_I^*), \tag{74}$$

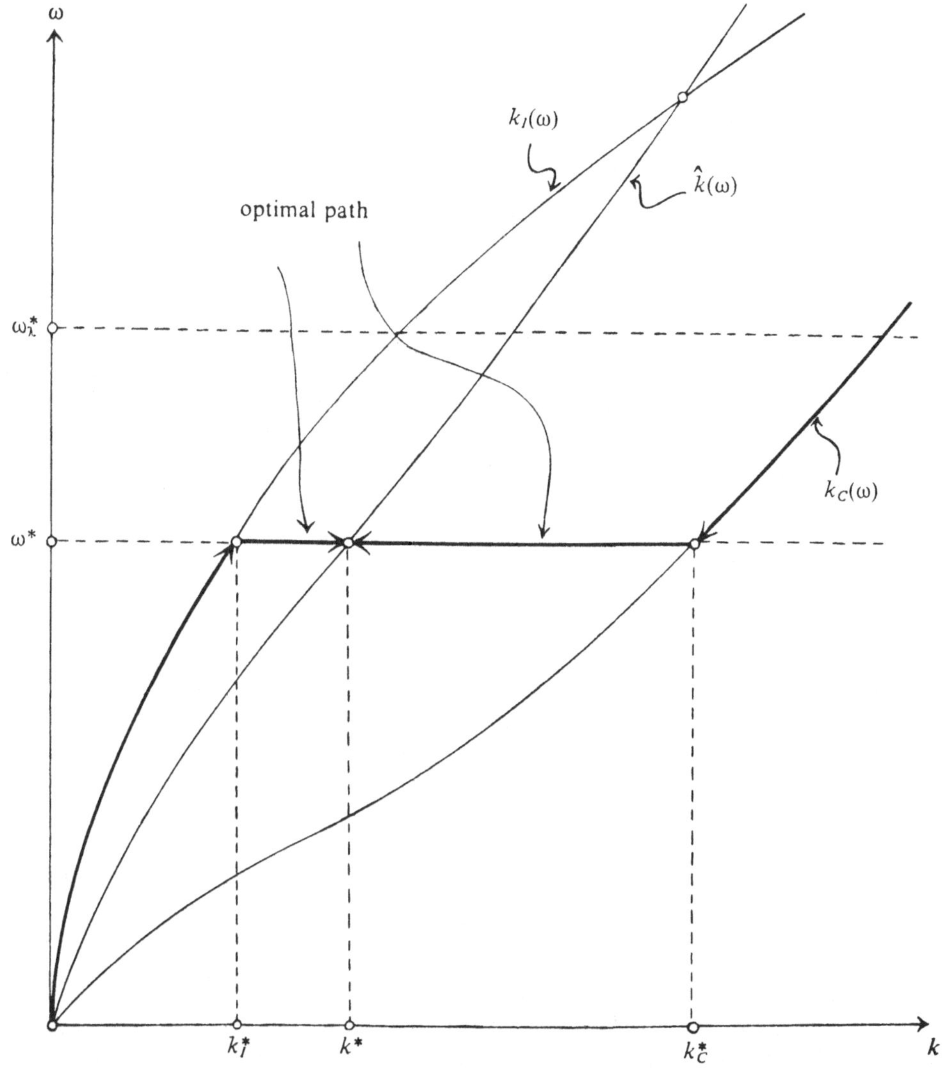

Figure 17.3

$$y_C(t) = \frac{k(t) - k_I^*}{k_C^* - k_I^*} f_C(k_C^*), \tag{75}$$

$$p(t) = q(t) = p(\omega^*). \tag{76}$$

It is easily seen that $k(t)$ increasingly converges to k^*, $y_I(t)$ decreasingly converges to

$$y_I^* = \frac{k_C^* - k^*}{k_C^* - k_I^*} f_I(k_I^*),$$

and $y_C(t)$ increasingly converges to

$$y_C^* = \frac{k^* - k_I^*}{k_C^* - k_I^*} f_C(k_C^*).$$

(b) *If the initial capital-labor ratio $k(0)$ is larger than k_C^*, then along the optimal path the economy is specialized to the production of consumption goods until the capital-labor ratio $k(t)$ is reduced to the ratio k_C^*. When the capital-labor ratio k_C^* is reached, both consumption goods and capital goods are produced, keeping the wage-rentals ratio at the level ω^*. The optimal path then asymptotically approaches the balanced ratio k^*.* The analytical expressions for this case may be given as follows:

The critical time t^* is defined by

$$t^* = \frac{1}{\lambda} \log \frac{k(0)}{k_C^*}. \tag{77}$$

For $0 \leqq t \leqq t^*$:

$$k(t) = k(0)e^{-\lambda t}, \tag{78}$$

and $\omega(t)$ is obtained by solving

$$k(t) = k_C(\omega(t)), \tag{79}$$

and

$$y_I(t) = 0, \tag{80}$$

$$y_C(t) = f_C(k(t)), \tag{81}$$

and $p(t)$, $q(t)$ are given by (69) and (70).

For $t \geqq t^*$:

$$k(t) = k^* + (k_C^* - k^*)e^{-\theta(t-t^*)}, \tag{82}$$

where the parameter θ is defined by (72), and $\omega(t)$, $y_I(t)$, $y_C(t)$, $p(t)$, and $q(t)$ are the same as those given by (73–76).

In this case, $k(t)$ decreasingly converges to k^*, $y_I(t)$ increasingly converges to y_I^*, and $y_C(t)$ decreasingly converges to y_C^*.

The optimal growth paths are indicated by the heavy arrow curves in Figure 17.3.

Let us now extend our analysis to the case in which the minimum wage rate is positive:

$$w_{min} > 0.$$

Then the per capita consumption $y_C(t)$ given by (56) is greater than the minimum wage rate w_{min} if and only if

$$k(t) > k_{min}(\omega(t)), \tag{83}$$

where the function $k_{min}(\omega)$ is defined by

$$k_{min}(\omega) = k_I(\omega) + \frac{k_C(\omega) - k_I(\omega)}{f_C(k_C(\omega))} w_{min}. \tag{84}$$

By assumption (54), $k_{min}(\omega)$ is always larger than $k_I(\omega)$, while it is smaller than $k_C(\omega)$ if and only if $f_C[k_C(\omega)] > w_{min}$.

Let the wage-rentals ratio ω_{min} be defined as the one satisfying

$$f_C[k_C(\omega_{min})] = w_{min}. \tag{85}$$

Then we have that

$$k_I(\omega) < k_{min}(\omega) < k_C(\omega) \quad \text{if and only if } \omega > \omega_{min}. \tag{86}$$

On the other hand, $k_{min}(\omega) < \hat{k}(\omega)$ if and only if

$$\frac{f_I(k_I(\omega)) - \lambda k_I(\omega)}{f_I(k_I(\omega)) - \lambda k_I(\omega) + \lambda k_C(\omega)} f_C(k_C(\omega)) > w_{min}. \tag{87}$$

The left-hand side of the inequality (87) is an increasing function of ω, provided $\omega < \omega_\lambda^*$ where ω_λ^* is the wage-rentals ratio for which the optimum marginal productivity in the I-sector is λ; i.e.,

$$f'_I(k(\omega_\lambda^*)) = \lambda. \tag{88}$$

Hence, by defining the wage-rentals ratio $\hat{\omega}$ by

$$\frac{f_I(k_I(\hat{\omega})) - \lambda k_I(\hat{\omega})}{f_I(k_I(\hat{\omega})) - \lambda k_I(\hat{\omega}) + \lambda k_C(\hat{\omega})} f_C(k_C(\hat{\omega})) = w_{min}, \tag{89}$$

we have that, for $\omega < \omega_\lambda^*$,

$$k_{min}(\omega) < \hat{k}(\omega) \quad \text{if and only if } \omega > \hat{\omega}. \tag{90}$$

The relationships of the $k_{min}(\omega)$ curve to the $k_C(\omega)$, $k_I(\omega)$, and $\hat{k}(\omega)$ curves may be typically illustrated in Figure 17.4.

Let us now define the capital-labor ratios $\hat{k}$ and k_{min} corresponding to the wage-rentals ratios $\hat{\omega}$ and ω_{min}, respectively by

$$\hat{k} = \hat{k}(\hat{\omega}) = k_{min}(\hat{\omega}), \tag{91}$$

$$k_{min} = k_C(\omega_{min}) = k_{min}(\omega_{min}). \tag{92}$$

It is easily established that if the initial capital-labor ratio $k(0)$ is smaller than $\hat{k}$, then the capital-labor ratio $k(t)$ is decreasing over any feasible path

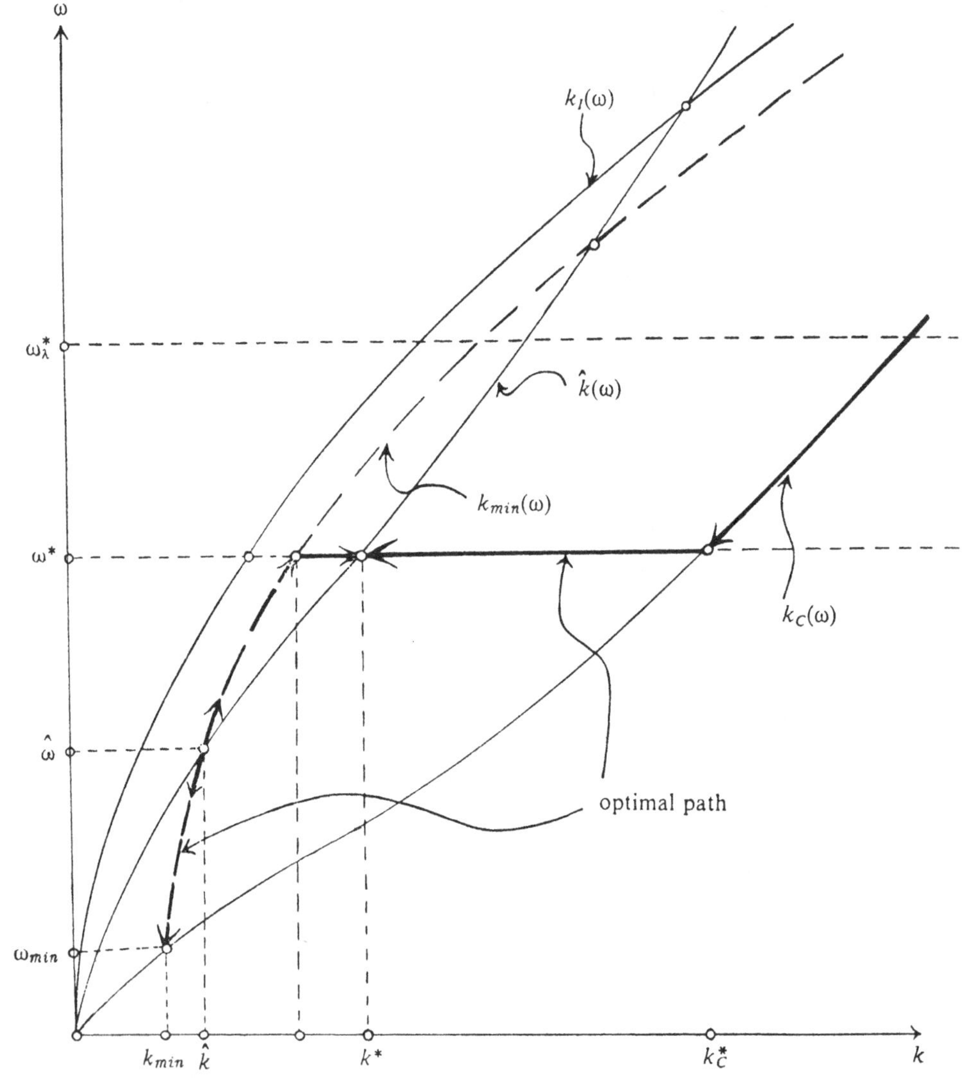

Figure 17.4

and eventually reaches the capital-labor ratio k_{min}. However, if the capital-labor ratio is smaller than the ratio k_{min}, the economy is not able to produce consumption goods to afford the minimum requirement even though all capital and labor are allocated to the C-sector. Therefore, if the capital-labor ratio is smaller than k_{min}, our model is inconsistent in the sense that no feasible solution satisfying the minimum wage requirement may be found.

To explain fully the phenomena would require the introduction of a certain Malthusian function explicitly relating the population growth to the minimum wage rate. In the present paper, however, we assume that the economy has somehow attained a capital-labor ratio larger than the critical capital-labor ratio $\hat{k}$.

The structure of the optimal growth is then analyzed, and is analogous to the previous case; namely, we have that: (a) *If the initial capital-labor ratio $k(0)$ is smaller than k_I^* but larger than the critical ratio $\hat{k}$, then along the optimal path the economy produces just enough consumption goods to meet the minimum requirements, until the time when the capital-labor ratio reaches the level $k_{min}(\omega^*)$, and from then on it proceeds to produce both capital goods and consumption goods for more than the minimum requirements. The optimal path increasingly approaches the balanced capital-labor ratio k^*.*

(b) *If the initial capital-labor ratio $k(0)$ is larger than k_C^*, then the optimal path proceeds exactly as in the case with zero minimum wage rate.*

The analytical expressions are similar to those for the previous case. In Figure 17.4, the structure of the optimal path is depicted with the heavy arrow curves.

6 The case when capital goods are always more capital-intensive than consumption goods

Let us next consider the case where *the capital good is always more capital-intensive than the consumption good*; namely

$$k_I(\omega) > k_C(\omega), \quad \text{for all } \omega > 0. \tag{93}$$

In this case, the auxiliary differential equations (57) and (58) may be rewritten as:

$$\dot{k} = \left\{ \frac{f_I[k_I(\omega)]}{k_I(\omega) - k_C(\omega)} - \lambda \right\} (k - \hat{k}(\omega)), \tag{94}$$

$$\dot{\omega} = \frac{f_I'[k_I(\omega)] - \lambda - \delta}{\dfrac{1}{k_C(\omega) + \omega} - \dfrac{1}{k_I(\omega) + \omega}}, \tag{95}$$

where

$$\hat{k}(\omega) = \frac{f_I[k_I(\omega)]}{f_I[k_I(\omega)] - \lambda[k_I(\omega) - k_C(\omega)]} k_C(\omega). \tag{96}$$

The quantity $\hat{k}(\omega)$ is always larger than $k_C(\omega)$ and smaller than $k_I(\omega)$ if and only if $\omega < \omega_\lambda$, where ω_λ is defined by (62).

The relationships among $k_C(\omega)$, $k_I(\omega)$, and $\hat{k}(\omega)$ are then illustrated by Figure 17.4.

For a wage-rentals ratio ω satisfying

$$\lambda < \frac{f_I[k_I(\omega)]}{k_I(\omega) - k_C(\omega)},$$

the rate of change in k has the same sign as $k - \hat{k}(\omega)$; namely, k is increased or decreased according to whether k is larger or smaller than $\hat{k}(\omega)$. On the other hand, ω is increased or decreased according to whether ω is smaller or larger than ω^*.

The auxiliary differential equations are unstable in k. However, *for any given wage-rentals ratio ω_0, it is possible to find a corresponding k_o such that the solution ($k(t)$, $\omega(t)$) to the auxiliary differential equations* (94) *and* (95) *with initial condition (k_0, ω_0) converges to (k^*, ω^*)*. The existence of such a k_0 may be established simply by taking the supremum of the initial values of k for which the k-component of the solution to the auxiliary differential equation approaches zero. It is explicitly given by the following formula:

$$k_0 = \int_{\omega_0}^{\omega^*} e^{-A(\omega,\omega_0)} \alpha(\omega) \hat{k}(\omega)\, d\omega, \tag{97}$$

where

$$\alpha(\omega) = \frac{\dfrac{f_I[k_I(\omega)]}{k_I(\omega) - k_C(\omega)} - \lambda}{f'_I[k_I(\omega)] - \lambda - \delta} \left(\frac{1}{k_C(\omega) + \omega} - \frac{1}{k_I(\omega) + \omega} \right),$$

$$A(\omega, \omega_0) = \int_{\omega_0}^{\omega} \alpha(\omega)\, d\omega.$$

In fact, the k-component of the solution ($k(t)$, $\omega(t)$) to the auxiliary differential equations with initial condition (k_0, ω_0) is given by:

$$k(t) = e^{A[\omega(t),\omega_0]} \left\{ k_0 - \int_{\omega_0}^{\omega(t)} e^{-A(\omega,\omega_0)} \alpha(\omega) \hat{k}(\omega)\, d\omega \right\}.$$

Now we have that

$$\lim_{t \to \infty} \omega(t) = \omega^*, \ \lim_{\omega \to \omega^*} A(\omega, \omega_0) = \infty;$$

hence, if $k(t)$ converges to k^*, as t tends to infinity, then

$$\begin{aligned} k_0 &= \lim_{t \to \infty} \int_{\omega_0}^{\omega(t)} e^{-A(\omega,\omega_0)} \alpha(\omega) \hat{k}(\omega)\, d\omega \\ &= \int_{\omega_0}^{\omega^*} e^{-A(\omega,\omega_0)} \alpha(\omega) \hat{k}(\omega)\, d\omega. \end{aligned}$$

On the other hand, let k_0 be given by (97). Then, by using l'Hospital's

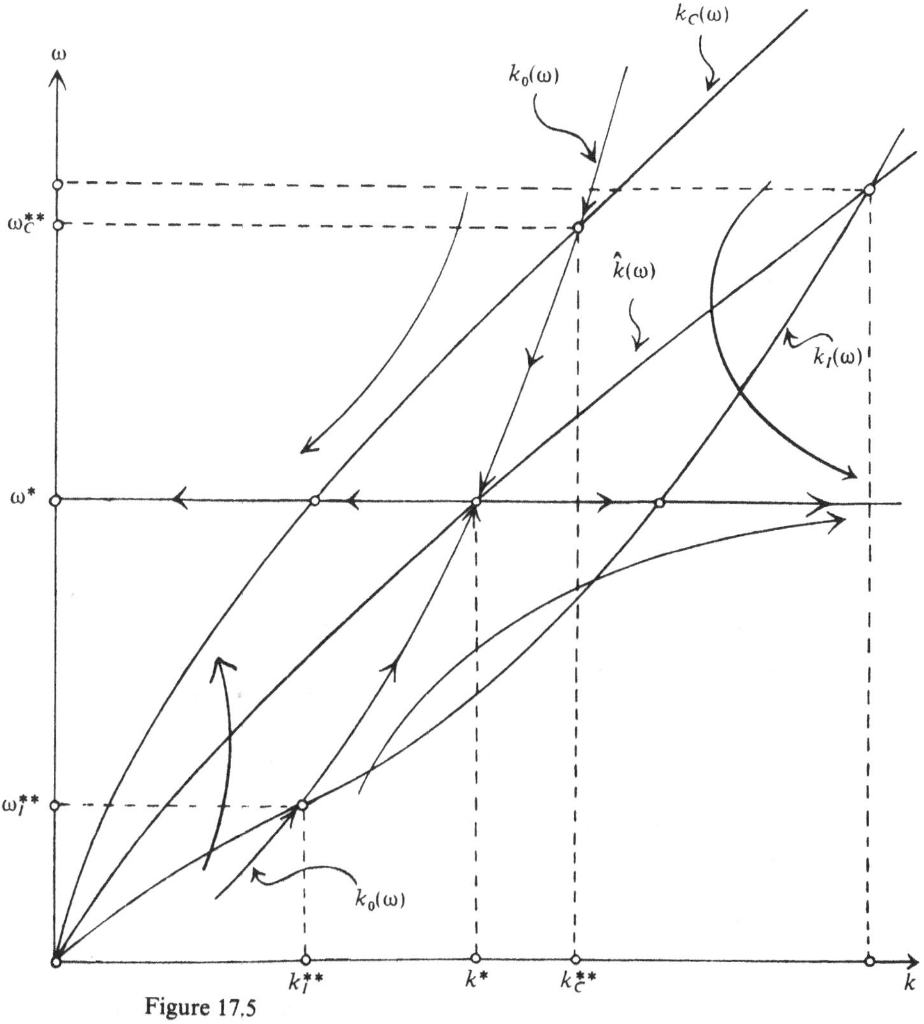

Figure 17.5

rule, we have

$$\lim_{t\to\infty} k(t) = \lim_{\omega\to\omega^*} \frac{k_0 - \int_{\omega_0}^{\omega} e^{-A(\omega',\omega_0)}\alpha(\omega')\hat{k}(\omega')\delta\omega'}{e^{-A(\omega,\omega_0)}}$$

$$= \lim_{\omega\to\omega^*} \frac{-e^{-A(\omega,\omega_0)}\alpha(\omega)\hat{k}(\omega)}{-e^{-A(\omega,\omega_0)}\dfrac{\partial A(\omega,\omega_0)}{\partial\omega}}$$

$$= \lim_{\omega\to\omega^*} \hat{k}(\omega) = \hat{k}(\omega^*).$$

It is easily seen that, for any positive ω_0, the integral in (97) exists and is positive; we may write

$$k_0 = k_0(\omega_0).$$

The relationship of $k_0(\omega_0)$ to $k_C(\omega)$, $k_I(\omega)$, $\hat{k}(\omega)$ may be described by Figure 17.5.

The structure of optimal growth is analyzed by a method similar to one we have used in the previous case. Let us first discuss the limiting case in which the minimum wage rate is zero. Let the two critical points $(k_I^{**}, \omega_I^{**})$ and $(k_C^{**}, \omega_C^{**})$ be defined as the intercepts of the $k_0(\omega)$ curve with the $k_I(\omega)$ curve and the $k_C(\omega)$ curve respectively:

$$k_I^{**} = k_0(\omega_I^{**}) = k_I(\omega_I^{**}),$$
$$k_C^{**} = k_0(\omega_C^{**}) = k_C(\omega_C^{**}).$$

We have

$$k_I^{**} < k^* < k_C^{**}.$$

It is noted that if the supply price of capital $p(t)$ is equal to the demand price of capital $q(t)$ on the $k_I(\omega)$ curve below the critical point $(k_I^{**}, \omega_I^{**})$, and if the economy is specialized in capital goods, then the demand price of capital along the differential equation (33) falls while the supply price rises, and the economy continues the specialization in capital goods along the optimal path. Similarly, if the supply price of capital is equal to the demand price of capital on the $k_C(\omega)$ curve above the critical point $(k_C^{**}, \omega_C^{**})$, and if the economy specializes in consumption goods, then the supply price rises while the demand price falls; thus the economy continues the specialization in consumption goods along the optimal path.

Therefore, the optimal paths are characterized by the following two propositions:

> (a) If the initial capital-labor ratio $k(0)$ is smaller than the critical ratio k_I^{**}, then along the optimal path the economy is specialized to capital goods until the capital-labor ratio $k(t)$ reaches the critical ratio k_I^{**}. Once the critical level k_I^{**} is reached, the economy proceeds along the $k_0(\omega)$ curve toward the balanced state (k^*, ω^*).
>
> (b) if the initial capital-labor ratio $k(0)$ is larger than the critical ratio k_C^{**}, then along the optimal path the economy is specialized to consumption goods until the capital-labor ratio $k(t)$ is reduced to the critical ratio k_C^{**}, and from then on it proceeds along the $k_0(\omega)$ curve toward the balanced state (k^*, ω^*).

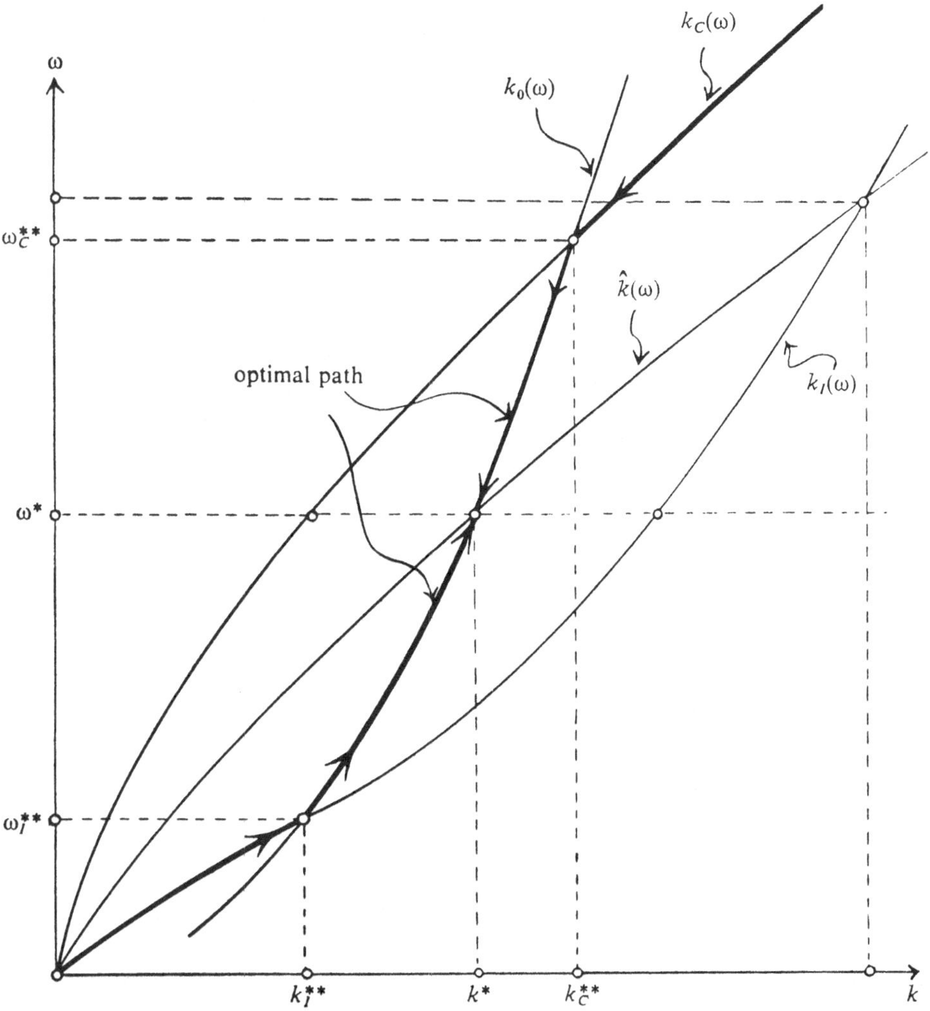

Figure 17.6

The analytical expressions for these two cases are similarly described by those given in (a) and (b) in the previous section.

In Figure 17.6, the optimal paths are indicated by the heavy arrow curves.

To discuss the general case in which the minimum wage rate is positive,

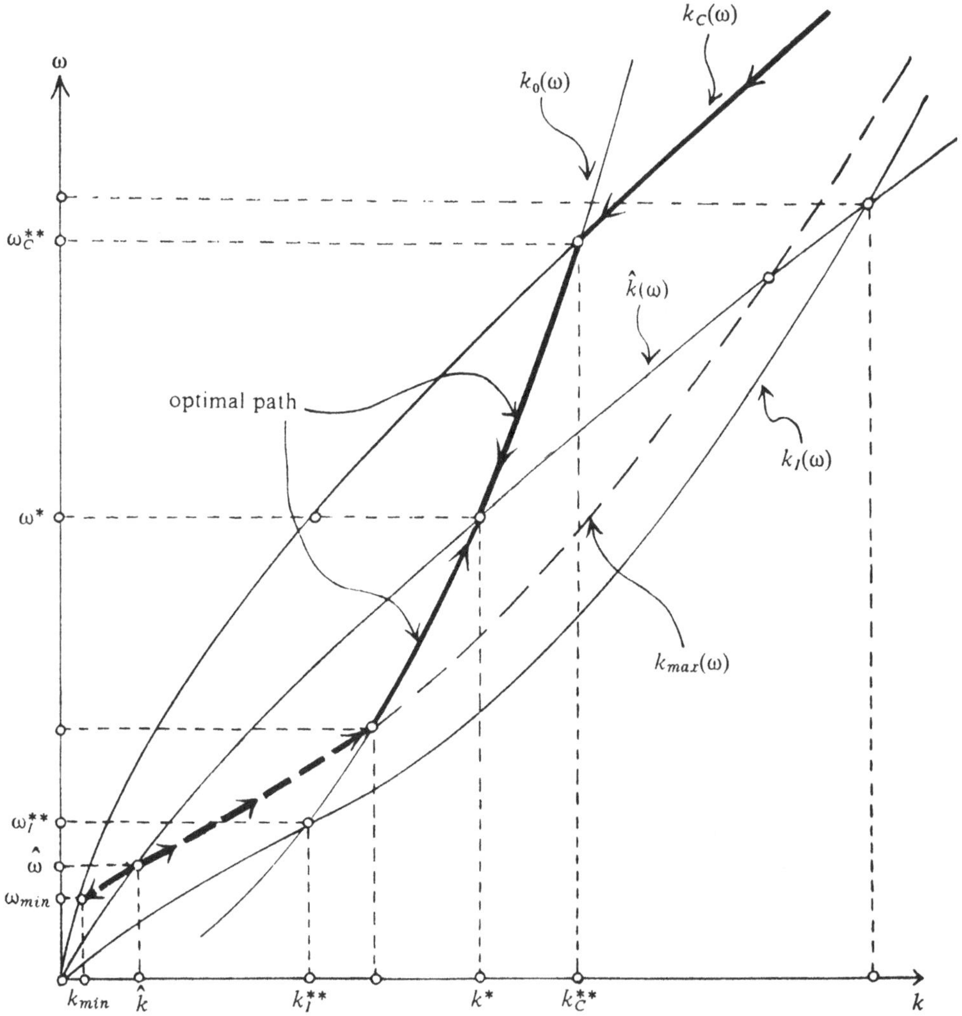

Figure 17.7

let us introduce the function, $k_{max}(\omega)$, by:

$$k_{max}(\omega) = k_I(\omega) - \frac{k_I(\omega) - k_C(\omega)}{f_C(k_C(\omega))} w_{min}.$$

It is then shown that the per capita consumption $y_C(t)$ exceeds the minimum wage rate w_{min} if and only if

$$k(t) < k_{max}(\omega(t)).$$

By assumption (93), $k_{max}(\omega)$ is always less than $k_I(\omega)$, while it is larger than $k_C(\omega)$ if and only if $f_C[k_C(\omega)] > w_{min}$; namely,

$$k_{max}(\omega) > k_C(\omega), \quad \text{if and only if } \omega > \omega_{min}.$$

On the other hand, $k_{max}(\omega) > \hat{k}(\omega)$ if and only if the inequality (87) holds. Reasoning similar to that used in the previous section leads us again to the following conclusion that, for $\omega < \omega^*_\lambda$,

$$k_{max}(\omega) > \hat{k}(\omega) \quad \text{if and only if } \omega > \hat{\omega},$$

where $\hat{w}$ is defined by (89).

The relationship of the $k_{max}(\omega)$ curve to the $k_C(\omega)$, $k_I(\omega)$, and $\hat{k}(\omega)$ curves is illustrated in Figure 17.7.

The critical capital-labor ratios $\hat{k}$ and k_{min} are defined by

$$\hat{k} = \hat{k}(\hat{\omega}) = k_{max}(\hat{\omega}),$$
$$k_{min} = k_C(\omega_{min}) = k_{max}(\omega_{min}).$$

The critical capital-labor ratio, $\hat{k}$, again represents the level of the capital-labor ratio below which the economy suffers from the steadily declining capital-labor ratio, whatever the allocation of the scarce resources may be, while below the minimum ratio, k_{min}, the economy cannot afford production of consumption goods with the minimum requirement even though capital goods are not produced. When the initial capital-labor ratio, $k(0)$, exceeds the critical ratio, $\hat{k}$, the structure of the optimal paths is characterized similarly to those described for the previous cases. In Figure 17.7, the optimal paths are depicted by the heavy arrow curves.

7 Optimal growth for the general case

The foregoing analysis may be, without modification, applied to characterize the optimal paths for the general case in which the relative capital intensity may be reversed; namely, if consumption goods are more capital-intensive than capital goods for the balanced wage-rentals ratio ω^*, then the pattern described in Section 5 prevails for the optimal paths, while the pattern in Section 6 is applied for the optimal paths in the economy in which consumption goods are less capital-intensive than capital goods for the balanced wage-rentals ratio ω^*. The structure of the optimal haths is illustrated in Figures 17.8 and 17.9.

8 Summary

To analyze the patterns of optimum allocations of annual output between consumption and investment, we have employed the two-sector model of

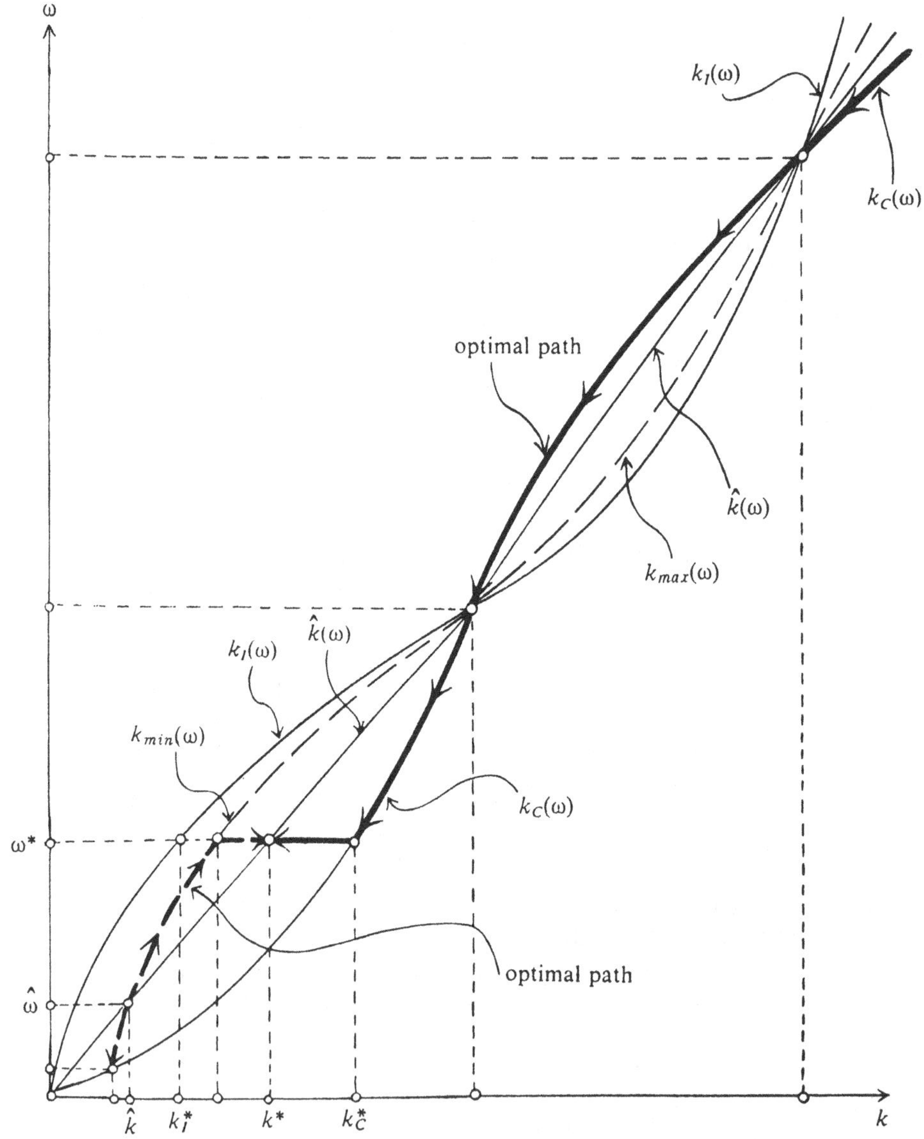

ω
$k_I(\omega)$
$k_C(\omega)$
optimal path
$\hat{k}(\omega)$
$k_{max}(\omega)$
$k_I(\omega)$
$\hat{k}(\omega)$
$k_{min}(\omega)$
$k_C(\omega)$
ω^*
optimal path
$\hat{\omega}$
$\hat{k}$
k_I^*
k^*
k_C^*
k

Figure 17.8

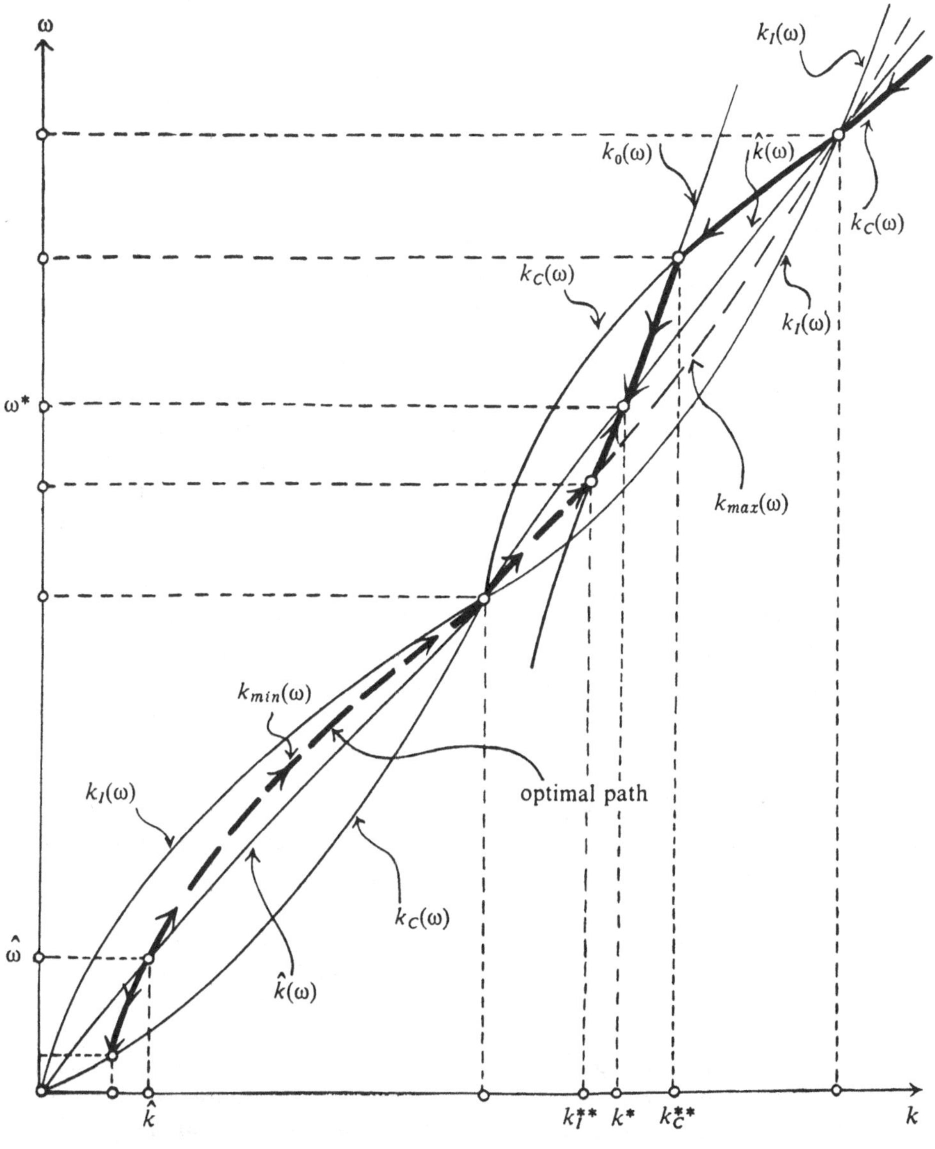

ω
ω*
ω̂
$k_I(\omega)$
$k_0(\omega)$
$\hat{k}(\omega)$
$k_C(\omega)$
$k_C(\omega)$
$k_I(\omega)$
$k_{max}(\omega)$
$k_{min}(\omega)$
optimal path
$k_I(\omega)$
$k_C(\omega)$
$\hat{k}(\omega)$
$\hat{k}$
k_I^{**}
k^*
k_C^{**}
k

Figure 17.9

economic growth of the type introduced by Meade. Consumers' goods and capital goods are both composed of homogeneous quantities and are produced by labor and capital. All the neo-classical hypotheses are assumed for production processes in each sector, together with the malleability of capital. We have adapted the discounted sum of consumption per capita as the criterion by which various paths of capital accumulation are compared. The rate by which future consumption is discounted is assumed to be independent of the level of consumption.

At the beginning of time, we take as given the discount rate, the state of technological knowledge, the state of capital initially held in the economy, and the amount of labor available at each moment of time, to be assumed to grow at a constant rate. The problem is to find a path of capital accumulation over which the criterion function is maximized among all feasible paths. The optimum path always exists and is uniquely determined relative to the data stated above. Associated with a given rate of discount there exists a balanced capital-labor ratio, k^*, and two critical capital-labor ratios, k_I^{**} and k_C^{**}. If the initial capital-labor ratio, $k(0)$, is smaller than the critical ratio k_I^{**}, along the optimal path the economy is specialized to capital goods and consumption goods are produced for the minimum requirements, and when the economy reaches the critical ratio, k_I^{**}, it starts to produce both goods asymptotically to approach the balanced ratio k^*. Similarly, if the initial capital-labor ratio, $k(0)$, is larger than the critical ratio, k_C^{**}, along the optimal path the economy is specialized to consumption goods until the critical ratio, k_C^{**}; at k_C^{**} it starts to produce both goods asymptotically to approach the balanced ratio k^*. The structure of the optimal path is more precisely characterized by specifying the efficient wage-rentals ratio $\omega(t)$, and the efficient price of investment $q(t)$, at each moment of time t.

The optimum capital-labor ratio in each sector is uniquely determined by the wage-rentals ratio $\omega(t)$ so as to minimize the average cost; hence, the supply price $p(t)$ of capital goods in terms of consumption goods is also determined by the wage-rentals ratio $\omega(t)$ alone, as described by the equations (42) and (44). If the supply price $p(t)$ exceeds the efficient price $q(t)$, no investment goods are produced, while if the supply price $p(t)$ is less than the efficient price $q(t)$, the economy is specialized in investment goods. When the supply price $p(t)$ and the efficient price $q(t)$ are identical, both goods are produced, and the allocation of labor and capital between two sectors is simply determined by the conditions that labor and capital are both fully employed, as described by the equations (46) and (47). The rate of capital accumulation is determined by the gross investment and the depreciation, so that the rate of change in the capital-labor ratio $\dot{k}(t)$ satisfies the equation (52). The change in the efficient price $q(t)$, as described by (53), is such that the net capital gain is equated to the interest charges; i.e., the capital market is competitive with perfect foresight.

The balanced capital-labor ratio k^* is determined at the level for which the aggregate capital-labor ratio and the efficient price of investment both remain stationary. The efficient price of investment q^* at such a balanced state must coincide with the supply price p^*, such that the marginal product of capital at the corresponding optimum capital-labor ratio k_I^* in the I-sector is equal to the sum of rates of population growth v, of depreciation μ, and of discount δ. The balanced capital-labor ratio k^* is then determined by the condition that the net rate of capital accumulation is zero; namely, it is given by:

$$k^* = \frac{f_I(k_I^*)}{f_I^*(k_I^*) + \lambda(k_C^* - k_I^*)} k_C^*,$$

where k_C^* is the corresponding optimum capital-labor ratio in the C-sector, and $f_I(k_I^*)$ is output per unit employment of capital goods.

The quantities per capita of consumption goods and capital goods at the balanced state are given by:

$$y_C^* = \frac{k^* - k_I^*}{k_C^* - k_I^*} f_C(k_C^*),$$

$$y_I = \frac{k_C^* - k^*}{k_C^* - k_I^*} f_I(k_I^*).$$

If, at the balanced state, the C-sector is more capital-intensive than the I-sector, i.e., if $k_C^* > k_I^*$, the critical capital-labor ratios k_I^{**} and k_C^{**} are respectively identical with the optimum capital-labor ratios k_I^* and k_C^*, for the case when the minimum wage rate w_{min} is zero. For the case of a positive w_{min}, k_C^{**} is adjusted so that consumption goods are produced for the minimum requirements.

On the other hand, if the C-sector is less capital-intensive than the I-sector at the balanced state ($k_C^* < k_I^*$), the critical capital-labor ratio k_I^{**} may differ from k_I^* but k_C^{**} is identical with k_C^*. The precise value of k_I^{**} is determined as the intersection of the $k_0(\omega)$ curve and the $k_I(\omega)$ curve, as described in Fig. 17.6, or as the intersection of the $k_0(\omega)$ curve and the $k_{max}(\omega)$, as described in Fig. 17.7, depending on whether w_{min} is zero or positive.

Along the optimal path, the capital-labor ratio $k(t)$, the wage-rentals ratio $\omega(t)$, the per capita consumption $y_C(t)$, and the per capita investment $y_I(t)$ all approach monotonically to the balanced capital-labor ratio k^*, wage-rentals ratio $\omega_{\lambda+\delta}^*$, per capita consumption y_C^*, and per capita investment y_I^*. The economy is specialized either in capital goods (consumption goods being produced only for minimum requirements) or in consumption goods until a certain critical level is reached for the capital-labor ratio.

The higher the discount rate δ, the lower the balanced capital-labor ratio k^* and the balanced wage-rentals ratio $\omega^*_{\lambda+\delta}$. As the discount rate δ tends to zero, the balanced wage-rentals ratio $\omega^*_{\lambda+\delta}$ approaches the level ω^*_λ defined by:

$$f'_I[k_I(\omega^*_\lambda)] = \lambda.$$

References

[1] Buttrick, J. A. "A Note on Growth Theory," *Economic Development and Cultural Change*, Vol. 9 (1960), pp. 75–82.

[2] Hurwicz, L. "Programming in Linear Spaces," *Studies in Linear and Nonlinear Programming*, by K. J. Arrow, L. Hurwicz, and H. Uzawa. Stanford: Stanford University Press, 1958, pp. 38–102.

[3] Meade, J. A. *A Neo-Classical Theory of Economic Growth*. New York: Oxford University Press, 1961.

[4] Myrdal, G. *Economic Theory and Under-Developed Regions*. London: Gerald Duckworth, 1957.

[5] Nurkse, R. *Problems of Capital Formation in Underdeveloped Countries*. New York: Oxford University Press, 1953.

[6] Srinivasan, T. N. "On a Two-Sector Model of Growth," *Econometrica*, Vol. 32 (1964), pp. 158–374.

[7] Tsiang, S. C. "A Model of Economic Growth in Rostovian Stages," *Econometrica*, Vol. 32 (1964), pp. 619–48.

[8] Uzawa, H. "On a Two-Sector Model of Economic Growth, II," *Review of Economic Studies*, Vol. 30 (1963), pp. 105–18.

CHAPTER 18

Optimum fiscal policy in an aggregative model of economic growth

In this paper, the problem of optimum fiscal policy is discussed in terms of the techniques of optimum economic growth. The model is a simple extension of the aggregative growth model of the type introduced by Solow [13], Swan [16], and Tobin [17]. It consists of private and public sectors, both employing labor and private capital to produce goods and services. Private goods may be either consumed or accumulated as capital, while public goods are all consumed. The public sector raises revenues by levying income taxes or by issuing money to pay wages and rentals to the labor and capital it hires to produce goods. The private sector decides how much is to be consumed and invested and how to allocate portfolio balances between real capital and money. These decisions are based upon certain behavioristic assumptions and are made in a perfectly competitive institutional setting. It will then be shown that by a proper choice of dynamic fiscal policy, which consists of income tax rates and growth rates of money supply through time, it is possible to achieve an optimal growth path corresponding to any form of social utility function and any rate of discount.

1. Introduction

In the postwar period, many countries, both advanced and less advanced, have come to regard fiscal policy both as an instrument to achieve short-run goals and to implement long-run objectives, such as economic growth. The theoretical analysis of the dynamic implications of fiscal policy has been recently started, in particular by Gurley [3], Brown [1], Smith [12], Musgrave [10], and others. In this paper, we will examine the dynamics of fiscal policy in terms of the theory of optimum economic growth developed in the past few years by Koopmans [6], Srinivasan [14], Cass [2], Kurz [7], Stoleru [15], Mirrlees [9], von Weiszaecker [21], and Inagaki [5].

From *The Theory and Design of Economic Development*, edited by I. Adelman and E. Thorbecke, The Johns Hopkins Press, 1969, pp. 113–39; reprinted with permission.

The basic framework of the theory of optimum economic growth originates in Ramsey's classical paper [11], but only recently has the problem of achieving desired economic growth through optimum allocation of scarce resources between consumption and investment become a central issue in economic analysis. The Ramsey theory, however, is based upon an economic structure similar to that of a centrally planned economy in which a central planning bureau is free to allocate the means of production, labor, and capital, in whatever manner it desires. In most countries, the allocation of the means of production is not directly governed by the state authorities. The Ramsey theory nevertheless is applicable to such economies with proper modifications, and the purpose of the paper is to illustrate with a simple model how an optimum growth can be achieved through limited policy tools, such as income taxes and changes in the money supply.

The basic structure of the model presented below is similar to that of the aggregative dynamic model first introduced by Tobin [17] to discuss the dynamic implications of monetary policies. In the present model, government is engaged in the production of different goods from those produced by private entrepreneurs; for the sake of simplicity they will be referred to as public goods, in contrast to private goods. Each category of goods is composed of homogeneous quantities, which are substitutes for each other. Public goods disappear instantaneously, while private goods may be either consumed or accumulated as capital. Both sectors employ labor and capital, and the production processes are subject to all the neoclassical conditions (constant returns to scale, diminishing marginal rates of substitution, and the like). The public sector pays wages and rentals from the revenues it gets through income taxes and from deficits; the deficits must be met by an increase in the money supply. The policy variables the public sector can control, however, are assumed to be the income tax rate and the rate of change in the money supply. The private sector decides the allocations of output between consumption and investment and the portfolio balance between monetary and real assets.

We shall first examine (by using the methods developed by Hicks [4] and Metzler [8]) the structure of short- and long-run equilibria in such a model when the fiscal policy (the income tax rate and the rate of change in money supply) is exogenously determined and kept constant throughout the period in question. We then postulate a utility function for the representative member of the economy, which is assumed to depend upon the per capita consumption of private goods and the average amount of public goods available at each moment. The structure of capital accumulation which is optimal with respect to the discounted sum of utility levels will be analyzed in terms of mathematical techniques developed by [2, 19].

Finally, we shall discuss the structure of optimum fiscal policy in detail for the special case in which the average propensity to consume (out of disposable income) is constant and the velocity of money is independent of the rate of interest.

2 The model

The analysis will be carried out in terms of the aggregative growth model where a number of simplifying, somewhat unrealistic, assumptions will be postulated to make the analysis possible, although some of them could be relaxed without substantially altering the conclusions.

We consider an economic system composed of public and private sectors. The private sector comprises business firms and households; business firms employ labor and either own or rent capital, while households receive wages for the labor they provide and interest and dividends for the capital they rent to business firms. The output produced in the private sector is assumed to be composed of homogeneous quantities so that any portion of it may be either instantaneously consumed or accumulated as part of the capital stock. The public sector provides the private sector with different goods and services than those it produces. The goods and services produced in the public sector are assumed to be measurable and distributed uniformly to the private sector without cost. The public sector raises revenues through income taxes and increases in the money supply to pay wages and rentals for the private means of production it employs. It is required to employ labor and capital in such a way that total expenditure is minimized for any level of public goods produced. The public sector has two means of raising revenues – taxation and printing money – but is assumed to be able to control only the rate of income tax and the rate of increase in money supply. Capital accumulation takes place only in the private sector, and public goods are not accumulated.[1]

At each moment of time, t, we take as given the amounts of (private) capital $K(t)$, and labor $L(t)$, available in the economy, together with the outstanding amount of money $M(t)$.[2] The public sector is in principle free to choose any fiscal policy it desires characterized by the income tax rate $\tau = \tau(t)$ and the rate of increase in money supply $\theta = \theta(t)$.

The aggregative output $Y_C(t)$ in the private sector is assumed to depend

[1] In another context, I have analyzed the problem of optimum investment in public capital in which all public goods are regarded as social capital to increase productivity of labor and private capital in the private sector; see Uzawa [20].

[2] The concept of money being used here is similar to one adapted by Tobin [17]; it includes all the short-term liabilities of the public sector to the private sector.

only on the amounts of capital $K_C(t)$ and labor $L_C(t)$ employed:

$$Y_C(t) = F_C(K_C(t), L_C(t)), \tag{1}$$

where F_C is the private sector's productive function. Production processes here are assumed to be subject to constant returns to scale and to a positive, diminishing marginal rate of substitution between capital and labor, ranging from infinity to zero as the capital-labor ratio is increased from zero to infinity. These assumptions are stated in terms of the per capita production function, $f_C(k_C) = F_C(K_C, L_C)/L_C, k_C = K_C/L_C$:

$$f_C(k_C) > 0, \qquad f'_C(k_C) > 0, \qquad f''_C(k_C) < 0, \quad \text{for all } k_C > 0; \tag{2}$$

$$f_C(0) = 0, \qquad f_C(\infty) = \infty; \tag{3}$$

$$f'_C(0) = \infty, \qquad f'_C(\infty) = 0. \tag{4}$$

Perfect competition prevails in the private sector, so that the real wage $w(t)$ and the real rental rate $r(t)$ are equated to the marginal products of labor and capital, respectively:

$$w(t) = \frac{\partial F_C}{\partial L_C}, \qquad r(t) = \frac{\partial F_C}{\partial K_C}. \tag{5}$$

The public sector, on the other hand, employs capital and labor in such a combination that the total cost in terms of market prices is always minimized. Let

$$Y_V(t) = F_V(K_V(t), L_V(t)) \tag{6}$$

be the aggregative output in the public sector, where $K_V(t)$ and $L_V(t)$ are respectively the employments of capital and labor. As for the public sector's production function, F_V, it is again assumed that all the neoclassical hypotheses are satisfied, namely, F_V is homogeneous of order one and strictly quasi-concave, with positive marginal products everywhere. In terms of the per capita production function.

$$f_V(k_V) = F_V(K_V, L_V)/L_V, \qquad k_V = K_V/L_V,$$

these neoclassical hypothesis are stated by:

$$f_V(k_V) > 0, \qquad f'_V(k_V) > 0, \qquad f''_V(k_V) < 0, \quad \text{for all } k_V > 0; \tag{7}$$

$$f_V(0) = 0, \qquad f_V(\infty) = \infty; \tag{8}$$

$$f'_V(0) = \infty, \qquad f'_V(\infty) = 0. \tag{9}$$

The cost in the public sector is minimized when the marginal rate of substitution between labor and capital is equated to the wage-rentals ratio

$w(t)/r(t)$ at time t:

$$\frac{\partial F_V/\partial L_V}{\partial F_V/\partial K_V} = \frac{w(t)}{r(t)}. \tag{10}$$

The real gross national income $Y(t)$ is given by

$$Y(t) = r(t)K(t) + w(t)L(t). \tag{11}$$

Hence the tax revenue in the public sector is equal to

$$\tau(t)Y(t) = \tau(t)[r(t)K(t) + w(t)L(t)],$$

while the total expenditure is given by

$$r(t)K_V(t)L_V(t).$$

Since the deficit in the public sector's budget is met by an increase in money supply, we have the balance-of-the-budget equation:

$$[r(t)K_V(t) + w(t)L_V(t)] - \tau(t)Y(t) = \theta(t)M(t)/p(t), \tag{12}$$

where $p(t)$ is the market price of private goods and $\theta(t)$ is the rate at which money increases.

Since the quantities of capital and labor available are $K(t)$ and $L(t)$, we have

$$K_C(t) + K_V(t) = K(t), \tag{13}$$

$$L_C(t) + L_V(t) = L(t). \tag{14}$$

The output of private goods $Y_C(t)$ is divided between consumption $C(t)$ and investment $Z(t)$:

$$C(t) + Z(t) = Y_C(t). \tag{15}$$

To determine the allocation of private output between consumption and investment, we need to examine the behavior of households and business firms. Household's allocation of the aggregative disposable income between consumption and savings is chiefly governed by the level of the disposable income, total assets held, and the rate of interest $\rho(t)$. The disposable income in real terms is given by

$$Y^d(t) = (1 - \tau(t))Y(t), \tag{16}$$

while the total monetary and nonmonetary assets $A(t)$ are evaluated as

$$A(t) = K(t) + M(t)/p(t) \tag{17}$$

in real terms.

Let the consumption function be given by $C(\rho, Y^d, A)$ which relates the level of the consumption the private sector wants to maintain with the rate of interest ρ, the real disposable income Y^d, and the monetary and nonmonetary asset in real terms A. Then we have

$$C(t) = C(\rho(t), Y^d(t), A(t)). \tag{18}$$

It is assumed that C is homogeneous of order one with respect to Y^d and A and that the private sector increases the desired level of consumption whenever disposable income Y^d, or assets A, are increased or the rate of interest ρ is decreased. Namely, we have

$$\frac{\partial C}{\partial \rho} \leqq 0, \qquad \frac{\partial C}{\partial Y^d} > 0, \qquad \frac{\partial C}{\partial A} \geqq 0. \tag{19}$$

As will be more explicitly formulated later, we postulate the existence of a utility function for each member of the society. Each member's utility level is assumed to be related to the amounts of private and public goods available to him, and his intertemporal utility level is determined as the discounted sum of atemporal levels of utilities throughout his time horizon. In terms of the consumption function postulated above, we assume that the level of consumption each member desires to attain is independent of the amount of public goods available, although his utility level may depend upon public as well as upon private goods.

The desired level of investment, on the other hand, is determined by the Keynesian principle of marginal efficiency of investment, as mathematically formulated in [18]. Business firms in the private sector try to increase the level of investment to that at which the supply price of capital is equated with the demand price (defined as the discounted sum of the expected returns). In general, the desired level of investment $Z(t)$ is determined by the current rate of returns $r(t)$, the money price $p(t)$, the rate of interest $\rho(t)$, and the stock of capital $K(t)$. If we assume that the elasticities of expected returns are all unity and that the expected returns depend upon the rate at which the current stock of capital is increased, together with the current level of per capita output, the desired level of investment is described by the following relation:

$$\frac{Z(t)}{K(t)} = Z\left(\rho(t), \frac{Y(t)}{K(t)}\right), \tag{20}$$

where the investment function $Z(\rho, Y/K)$ satisfies the following conditions:

$$\frac{\partial Z}{\partial \rho} < 0, \qquad \frac{\partial Z}{\partial (Y/K)} \geqq 0, \tag{21}$$

$$\phi(0, Y/K) = \infty, \qquad \phi(\infty, Y/K) = 0. \tag{22}$$

As for the portfolio balance between the two types of assets existing in the economy, real capital and money, the private sector as a whole wishes to maintain a certain level of real cash balances to meet transaction, precautionary, or speculative requirements. It will be postulated, as in Tobin [17], that the desired level of real cash balance M/p is determined by the rate of interest ρ, the level of disposable income Y^d, and the amount of real capital K:

$$\frac{M/p}{K} = \lambda\left(\rho, \frac{Y^d}{K}\right). \tag{23}$$

The demand-for-money function, λ, is assumed to satisfy the following conditions:

$$\frac{\partial \lambda}{\partial \rho} < 0, \tag{24}$$

$$0 \leq \frac{\partial \log \lambda}{\partial \log (Y^d/K)} \leq 1. \tag{25}$$

At each moment of time, t, we are given the available stock of capital $K(t)$, the supply of labor $L(t)$, and the outstanding amount of money $M(t)$, together with the rate of income tax $\tau(t)$ and the rate of increase in money supply $\theta(t)$, both of which are set as part of a fiscal policy. Then the equations described above, (1), (5–6), (10–12), (13–18), and (20), together determine the allocations of capital and labor, $K_C(t)$, $K_V(t)$, and $L_C(t)$, $L_V(t)$, outputs of private and public goods, $Y_C(t)$ and $Y_V(t)$, real wage and rental rates, $w(t)$ and $r(t)$, the money price of private goods $p(t)$, consumption $C(t)$, investment $Z(t)$, and rate of interest $\rho(t)$. In the next sections, we shall show that all these variables are uniquely determined.

The accumulation of capital is described by

$$\dot{K}(t) = Z(t) - \mu K(t), \tag{26}$$

where μ is the rate of depreciation, while the growth rate of labor ν is assumed to be exogenously given:

$$\dot{L}(t) = \nu L(t). \tag{27}$$

If the fiscal policy $(\theta(t)), \tau(t))$, is predetermined through time, the differential equation (26) for capital accumulation specifies the time path of capital $K(t)$ throughout time t for any given stock of capital $K(0)$, initially held in the economy. After we examine the determination of short-run equilibrium in such an economy, the long-run structure will be briefly analyzed for a particular case in which the rates of income tax and increase in money supply are held constant through time:

$$\tau(t) = \tau, \qquad \theta(t) = \theta, \quad \text{for all } t.$$

We then analyze the problem of optimum fiscal policy by introducing a social welfare criterion, which will be expressed as a maximization of a discounted sum of instantaneous utility levels.

3 Analysis of the short-run equilibrium

To analyze the workings of the model, we first reduce the model introduced above to one involving per capita quantities only. In defining the following notation, for the sake of simplicity, the time suffix t, will be omitted:

$k = K/L$: the aggregate capital-labor ratio.
$y_j = Y_j/K$: the output of good j per unit of capital ($j = C, V$).
$l_j = L_j/L$: the labor allocation to sector j ($j = C, V$).
$k_j = K_j/L_j$: the capital-labor ratio in sector j ($j = C, V$).
$y = Y/K$: the real national income per unit of capital.
$y^d = Y^d/K$: the real disposable income per unit of capital.
$c = C/K$: the level of consumption per unit of capital.
$z = Z/K$: the investment-capital ratio.
$m = M/pK$: the real cash balance per unit of capital.
$a = A/K$: the assets in real terms per unit of capital.
$\omega = w/r$: the wage-rental ratio.

The marginal productivity conditions in both sectors (5) and (10) are then reduced to the following familiar equations:

$$\omega = \frac{f_j(k_j)}{f'_j(k_j)} - k_j, \qquad j = C, V, \tag{28}$$

which are solved to derive the optimum capital-labor function $k_j = k_j(\omega)$ in each sector. As was discussed in detail in [18 and 19] the optimum capital-labor ratio curve $k_j(\omega)$ is an increasing function of the wage-rental ratio, ω, ranging from 0 to infinity as ω moves from 0 to infinity. For the sake of simplicity, it will be assumed that the optimum capital-labor curves in the two sectors never intersect. Thus the two curves are typically related to each other as illustrated in Figure 18.1.

Conditions (13–14) are then solved in terms of l_C and l_V:

$$l_C = \frac{k - k_V}{k_C - k_V},$$

$$l_V = \frac{k_C - k}{k_C - k_V}, \tag{29}$$

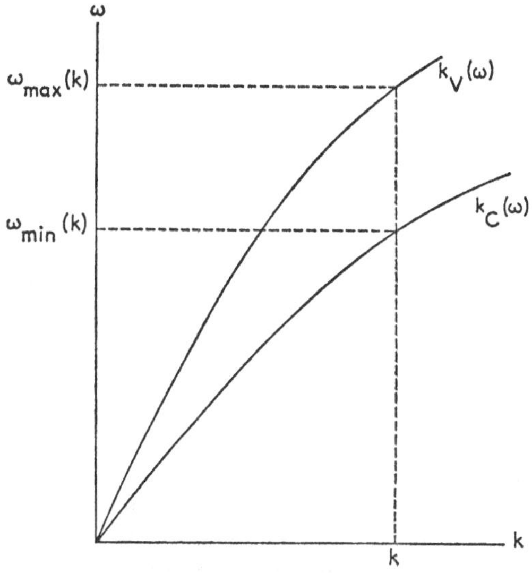

Figure 18.1

where k_C and k_V are respectively optimum capital-labor ratios in the private and public sectors. The output-capital ratios are correspondingly determined:

$$y_C = y_C(\omega, k) = f_C(k_C)l_C/k, \qquad y_V = y_V(\omega, k) = f_V(k_V)l_V/k. \tag{30}$$

For the rest of the paper, the discussion will be carried on only for the case in which the private sector is always relatively more capital-intensive than the public sector:

$$k_V(\omega) < k_C(\omega), \quad \text{for all } \omega > 0. \tag{31}$$

For the labor allocations, l_C and l_V, to be positive, the aggregative capital-labor ratio k has to lie between the two optimum capital-labor ratios:

$$k_V(\omega) < k < k_C(\omega). \tag{32}$$

Then relation (31) or (32) may be written as:

$$\omega_{\min}(k) < \omega < \omega_{\max}(k), \tag{33}$$

where the critical wage-rental ratios, $\omega_{\min}(k)$ and $\omega_{\max}(k)$, are defined by:

$$\omega_{\min}(k) = \omega_C(k), \qquad \omega_{\max}(k) = \omega_V(k), \tag{34}$$

$$k_C(\omega_C(k)) = k, \qquad k_V(\omega_V(k)) = k. \tag{35}$$

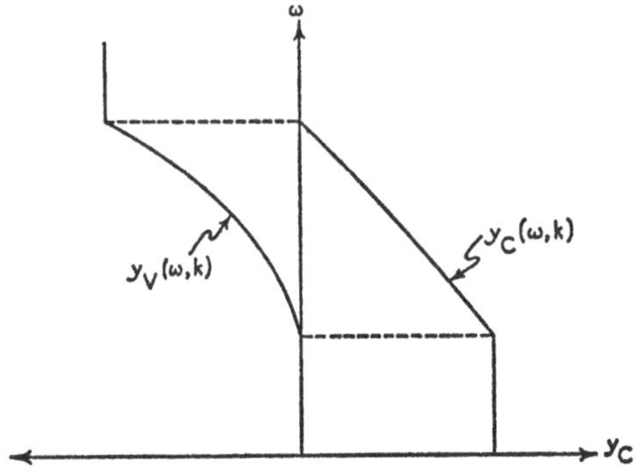

Figure 18.2

It is easily seen that an increase in the wage-rental ratio ω will increase the output of goods whose production is relatively more capital-intensive. Since the private sector is relatively more capital-intensive than the public sector, $y_C(\omega, k)$ is a decreasing function of ω, while $y_V(\omega, k)$ is an increasing function of ω. On the other hand, an increase in k will increase $y_C(\omega, k)$ and decrease $y_V(\omega, k)$. The relationships between the wage-rental ratio and the output of private and public goods are illustrated in Figure 18.2.

Equations (11–12), (15–18), (20), and (23) are now reduced to:

$y = r(k + \omega)/k$: national income in real terms per unit of capital, (36)

$r = f'_C(k_C)$: marginal product of capital, (37)

$y^d = (1 - \tau)y$: disposable income per unit of capital, (38)

$a = 1 + m$: assets per unit of capital, (39)

$c = c(\rho, y^d, a)$: consumption per unit of capital, (40)

$z = z(\rho, y)$: investment per unit of capital, (41)

$c + z = y_C(\omega, k)$: allocation of private goods between consumption and investment, (42)

$m = \lambda(\rho, y^d)$: portfolio balance, (43)

and

$$\frac{r(k_V + \omega)l_V}{k} - \tau y = \theta m: \text{ balance of the budget.} \tag{44}$$

To analyze the balance-of-the-budget equation (44), let us first introduce the imputed price p of public goods:

$$p = f'_C(k_C)/f'_V(k_V), \tag{45}$$

where

$$k_C = k_C(\omega) \text{ and } k_V = k_V(\omega).$$

The imputed price of public goods is solely determined by the wage-rental ratio ω; it may be denoted by $p(\omega)$. Differentiating (45) logarithmically and taking into account the derivative of (28), we get:

$$\frac{1}{p(\omega)}\frac{dp(\omega)}{d\omega} = \frac{1}{k_V(\omega)+\omega} - \frac{1}{k_C(\omega)+\omega} < 0. \tag{46}$$

Since we have

$$y = y_C + py_V = [rl_C(k_C + \omega) + rl_V(k_V + \omega)]/k, \tag{47}$$

the balance-of-the-budget equation (44) may be rewritten as:

$$\theta m = (1-\tau)y(\omega,k) - y_C(\omega,k), \tag{48}$$

where

$$y(\omega,k) = f'_C(k_C)\left(1+\frac{\omega}{k}\right), \tag{49}$$

$$y_C(\omega,k) = \frac{f_C(k_C)}{k_C - k_V}\left(1-\frac{k_V}{k}\right), \tag{50}$$

$$y_V(\omega,k) = \frac{f_C(k_C)}{k_C - k_V}\left(\frac{k_C}{k}-1\right). \tag{51}$$

For fixed values of k and τ, the right-hand side of (48) is an increasing function of the wage-rentals ratio. Therefore, for a positive rate of increase in the money supply θ the real cash balance m satisfying (48) is also given by a curve with a positive slope, as indicated by the FF curve in Figure 18.3. In other words, any point on the FF curve represents a combination of the wage-rental ratio ω and the real cash balance (per unit of capital) m at which the budget in the public sector is in balance for a given fiscal policy (τ, θ). The FF curve shifts to the left when the tax rate τ, the growth rate in money supply θ, or the capital-labor ratio k is increased.

The real cash balance-capital ratio m, on the other hand, must be related to the disposable real income per unit of capital ratio y^d in such a manner that the private sector's portfolio is in balance, so that equation (43) is satisfied. For a given value of the interest rate ρ, the function $\lambda(\rho, y^d)$ is an increasing function of y^d, with an elasticity not greater than unity. The real cash balance m satisfying (43), therefore, is depicted again by a curve with a positive slope, such as the MM curve in Figure 18.3. Since the elasticity of λ

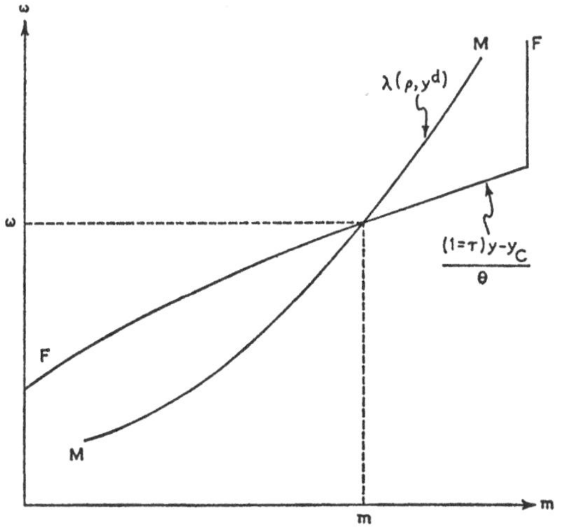

Figure 18.3

with respect to y^d is not greater than unity, the MM curve has a slope steeper than the FF curve at the point (ω, m) where these two curves intersect.

Since an increase in the rate of interest ρ shifts the MM curve to the left, the equilibrium wage-rental ratio ω and the real cash balance m both are decreased whenever the rate of interest ρ is increased. In Figure 18.4 below, the FM curve represents all the combinations of the rates of interest and wage-rental ratios at which the public budget and the private sector's portfolios are in equilibrium. An increase in the tax rate τ, a higher growth rate in money supply θ, or an increase in the capital-labor ratio k will easily be seen to result in a shift to the left of the FM curve in Figure 18.4.

To see the conditions under which the goods-and-services market in the private sector is in equilibrium, let us rewrite the equilibrium condition (42) as follows:

$$z(\rho, y) = y_C(\omega, k) - c(\rho, y^d, 1 + m). \tag{52}$$

For any given level of the rate of interest ρ, the investment function $z(\rho, y)$ is by assumption an increasing function of y, while the income-capital ratio y, defined by (36) is an increasing function of the wage-rental ratio. To see the latter, differentiate (36) and (37) logarithmically and rearrange the result to get:

$$\frac{1}{y}\frac{dy}{d\omega} = \frac{1}{k + \omega} - \frac{1}{k_C + \omega}, \tag{53}$$

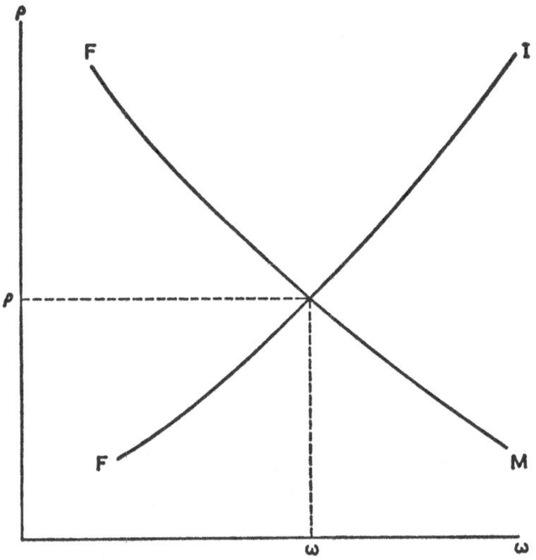

Figure 18.4

which is always positive because of the capital-intensity hypothesis we have made.

The left-hand side of equation (52) is therefore an increasing function of ω, which is described by the II curve in Figure 18.5. The right-hand side of equation (52), on the other hand, is a decreasing function of ω. In Figure 18.5, the SS curve represents the $y_C - c$ function for given levels of the rate of interest and real cash balance. The wage-rental ratio at which the II curve intersects with the SS curve equilibrates the goods-and-services market for given levels of the rate of interest ρ and real cash balances m.

An increase in real cash balances is assumed to increase the desired level of consumption c, thus shifting the SS curve to the left. Hence, the equilibrium wage-rental ratio is decreased as m is increased. In other words, the greater the real cash balances, the smaller must the wage-rental ratio be for the goods-and-services market to be in equilibrium, because an increase in assets would induce the private sector to increase the desired level of consumption. The relationships between the wage-rental ratio and real cash balance for which the goods-and-services market is in equilibrium are described by the IS curve in Figure 18.6.

The intersection of the IS curve with the FF curve represents the combination of the wage-rental ratio and the real cash balance at which the public budget and the goods-and-services market are both in equilibrium for a given level of interest rate. An increase in the rate of interest will decrease

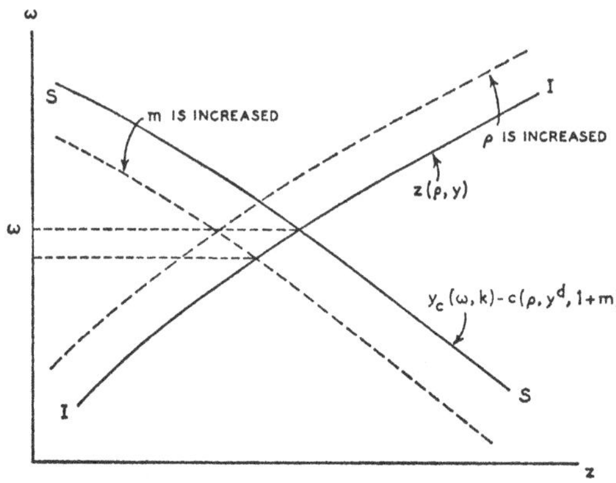

Figure 18.5

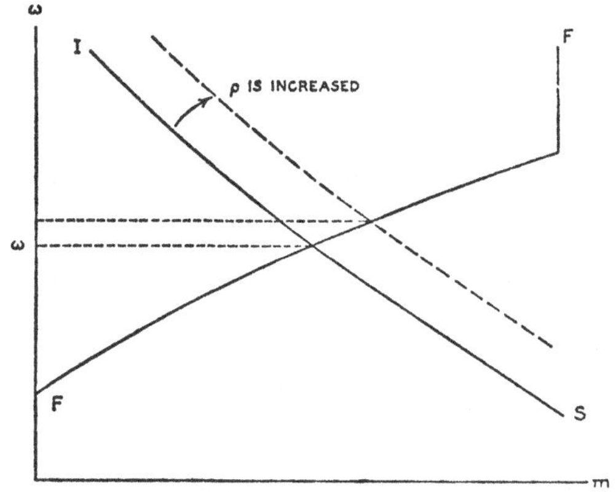

Figure 18.6

the desired levels of both investment $z(\rho, y)$ and consumption $c(\rho, y^d, 1 + m)$, thus shifting the IS curve upward. Therefore, an increase in the rate of interest will result in increases in both the wage-rental ratio and the real cash balance for which the goods-and-services market is in equilibrium.

The combinations of the rates of interest and wage-rental ratios at which the public sector and the goods-and-services market are in equilibrium are represented by the FI curve in Figure 18.4. It has a positive slope, while the FM curve previously derived has a negative slope. Therefore, these two curves have a unique intersection (if one exists). The pair of interest rate ρ and wage-rental ratio ω, at which the FI and FM curves intersect, together with the corresponding real cash balance m, gives the solution to the system of short-run equilibrium conditions (36–44).

4 Constant average propensity to consume and the quantity theory of money

We have seen under fairly general conditions that the short-run equilibrium is uniquely determined at each moment of time t. The process of capital accumulation is simply described by the following differential equation:

$$\frac{\dot{k}}{k} = z - v - \mu, \tag{54}$$

where $z = z(\rho, y)$ is the equilibrium rate of investment per unit of capital, v and μ are respectively the growth rate of labor and the rate of depreciation.

The characteristics of such a dynamic system with respect to the existence and stability of long-run equilibrium may be analyzed with the aid of the techniques developed in the previous section. Here, however, we are interested in a particular case in which the average propensity to consume γ is always constant and the velocity of money λ is independent of the rate of interest.

The equilibrium conditions (41–44) then are reduced to the following system of equations:

$$\theta m = (1 - \tau)y - y_C, \tag{55}$$

$$z(\rho, y) = y_C - \gamma(1 - \tau)y, \tag{56}$$

$$m = \lambda(1 - \tau)y, \tag{57}$$

which are further simplified to:

$$y_C = (1 - s)y, \tag{58}$$

$$z = \beta y_C, \tag{59}$$

where

$$s = 1 - (1 - \tau)(1 - \lambda\theta), \tag{60}$$

$$\beta = 1 - \frac{\gamma}{1 - \lambda\theta}. \tag{61}$$

In order for the short-run equilibrium solution to be meaningful, it is necessary and sufficient that τ and θ must satisfy the following conditions:

$$\theta < \frac{1 - \gamma}{\lambda}, \tag{62}$$

$$\frac{s - \lambda\theta}{1 - \lambda\theta} \leqq \tau \leqq 1. \tag{63}$$

The dynamic equation (54) may be written as

$$\frac{\dot{k}}{k} = \alpha f_C'(k_C) \frac{k + \omega}{k} - \nu - \mu, \tag{64}$$

where ω is the equilibrium wage-rental ratio, $\omega = \omega(k)$, and

$$\alpha = (1 - \tau)(1 - \lambda\theta - \gamma). \tag{65}$$

If the rates of income tax τ and of increase in money supply θ remain constant through time, the mathematical structure of the dynamic system becomes identical with the one introduced in [18], and the stability analysis presented there applies to the present case. In particular, we can show that if the parameters satisfy conditions (62–63), a long-run (quasi-) stationary state exists and the dynamic system defined by (64) is globally stable.

5 Optimum fiscal policies

In the model of fiscal policy introduced above, we have analyzed the dynamic implications of a fiscal policy defined in terms of an exogenously determined income tax rate and a growth rate in the money supply. If the public sector is free to choose any fiscal policy it desires but is also interested in achieving that allocation of private means of production which would maximize certain welfare criteria, the problem of optimum fiscal policy becomes to choose at each moment a combination of income tax rate and rate of money supply increase such that an optimum rate of investment is attained through time. We shall show that the techniques of optimum economic growth recently developed by Koopmans [6], Mirrlees [9], Srinivasan [14], Inagaki [5], von Weiszaecker [21], Cass [2], Kurz [7], and others are readily applicable to the formulation and analysis of the problem of optimum fiscal policy.

As before, the economy we are concerned with produces two types of goods, private and public. Public goods are regarded as consumption goods, while private goods can either the consumed instantaneously or accumulated as capital. For the sake of simplicity, the utility function of the representative member of the society depends upon the amount of private goods to be consumed and upon the average quantity of public goods available at each moment. Public goods are assumed to be distributed equally among the members of the society. Let $u(c, x)$ be the utility function where c and x stand respectively for the quantities of per capita consumption of private and public goods (in this and next few sections notation is slightly different from that in the previous sections). It will be assumed that the social welfare function is represented as the discounted sum of instantaneous utilities through time:

$$\int_0^\infty u(c, x)e^{-\delta t}\,dt, \tag{66}$$

where δ is the rate by which future utilities are compared with the present utilities with a proper modification when the population is not stationary.

A *dynamic fiscal policy* is defined here as a piece-wise continuous time-path $(\tau(t), \theta(t))$ of income tax rates $\tau(t)$ and growth rates of money supply $\theta(t)$. With the structure of the economy introduced in the previous sections, any dynamic fiscal policy uniquely determines the time-paths of capital accumulation, the allocations of capital and labor between the private and public sectors, the allocation of private goods between consumption and investment, and the market prices of output and factors of production. In particular, the time-paths of output of public goods and the consumption of private goods are uniquely determined for a given dynamic fiscal policy $(\tau(t), \theta(t))$.

A dynamic fiscal policy then is defined as *optimal* if, for a feasible path of capital accumulation, it results in that time-path of consumption patterns $(c(t), x(t))$ which maximizes the social utility functional (66).

Instead of solving the problem as presented here, which poses serious mathematical difficulties, we shall first reformulate the problem of optimum fiscal policy in a somewhat different manner which can be analyzed by standard techniques of optimum economic growth. Then we shall show that the solution to the latter problem may be used to find an optimum fiscal policy in the sense of the previous definition.

6 Optimum economic growth

To reformulate the problem of optimum fiscal policy, suppose that the public sector can determine not only the fiscal policy but also the allocations of capital and labor between sectors and the division of private goods between consumption and investment. The public sector then seeks for the feasible time-paths of factor and output allocations at which the utility functional (66) is maximized. Such time-paths will be called *optimum paths of economic growth.* The problem is more precisely defined as follows:

Find a time-path of $(K_C(t), K_V(t), L_C(t), L_V(t), C(t), Z(t), X(t))$ *for which the utility functional*

$$\int_0^\infty u\left[\frac{C(t)}{L(t)}, \frac{X(t)}{L(t)}\right]e^{-\delta t}\,dt \tag{67}$$

is maximized subject to the constraints:

$$C(t) + Z(t) \leqq F_C(K_C(t), L_C(t)), \tag{68}$$

$$X(t) \leqq F_V(K_V(t), L_V(t)), \tag{69}$$

$$K_C(t) + K_V(t) \leqq K(t), \tag{70}$$

$$L_C(t) + L_V(t) \leqq L(t), \tag{71}$$

$$K(t) = Z(t) - \mu K(t) \tag{72}$$

$$L(t) = vL(t), \tag{73}$$

with given initial capital $K(0)$ and labor $L(0)$ where all variables are nonnegative.

If we use small letters to indicate the quantities per capita and omit the time suffix, the problem of optimum economic growth is reduced to the following:

Maximize

$$\int_0^\infty u(c, x)\, e^{-\delta t} dt \tag{74}$$

subject to the constraints:

$$c + z = f_C(k_C) l_C, \tag{75}$$

$$x = f_V(k_V) l_V, \tag{76}$$

$$k_C l_C + k_V l_V = k, \tag{77}$$

$$l_C + l_V = 1, \tag{78}$$

$$\dot{k} = z - (v + \mu)k, \tag{79}$$

with given initial capital-labor ratio $k(0)$, where all variables are nonnegative.

The utility function $u(c, x)$ is assumed to satisfy the following conditions:

$$u(c, x) \tag{80}$$

is continuously twice-differentiable and has positive marginal utilities u_c and u_x for all positive c and x; $u(c, x)$ is strictly concave in the sense that the Hessian matrix

$$\begin{pmatrix} u_{cc} & u_{cx} \\ u_{cx} & u_{xx} \end{pmatrix} \tag{81}$$

is negative definite for all values of c and x.

Private and public goods are substitutes, in the sense that an increase in one of the two goods does not increase the marginal utility of the other, namely,

$$u_{cx} \leqq 0. \tag{82}$$

Private goods are not inferior; the income-consumption curve has a positive slope.

These conditions are summarized as:

$$u_c > 0, u_x > 0 \tag{83}$$

$$u_{cc} < 0, u_{xx} < 0, u_{cx} \leqq 0 \tag{84}$$

$$\Delta = u_{cc}u_{xx} - u_{cx}^2 > 0 \tag{85}$$

$$\frac{u_{xx}}{u_x} - \frac{u_{cx}}{u_c} < 0, \quad \frac{u_{cc}}{u_c} - \frac{u_{xc}}{u_z} < 0. \tag{86}$$

It may be noted that the optimum solution, if it exists, is always uniquely determined, because of the strict concavity of the utility function, $u(c, x)$, and the production functions, $f_C(k_C)$ and $f_V(k_V)$.

The problem now is solved by using a procedure similar to one developed in [19]. Let us introduce the auxiliary variables, $q_C(t)$, $q_V(t)$, $r(t)$, $w(t)$, and $q(t)$, corresponding to constraints (75), (76), (77), (78), (79), respectively, and form the Lagrangian:

$$\int_0^\infty \{u(c, x) + q(z - (v + \mu)k) + q_C(f_C(k_C)l_C - z - c) \\ + q_V(f_V(k_V)l_V - x) + r(k - k_Cl_C - k_Vl_V) + w(1 - l_C - l_V)\} e^{-\delta t} dt. \tag{87}$$

The variables $q_C(t)$ and $q_V(t)$ may be interpreted as the imputed prices of private and public goods at time t, while $q(t)$ is the imputed price of investment. The variables $r(t)$ and $w(t)$ are the rental of capital and the wage rate at time t (all measured in terms of private goods).

The problem of optimum growth will be completely solved once we find the time-paths of these imputed prices. We can show the following:

Lemma. Let $c(t)$, $x(t)$, $z(t)$, $k(t)$, $k_C(t)$, $k_V(t)$, $l_C(t)$ $l_V(t)$ give a feasible solution and let $q(t)$, $q_C(t)$, $q_V(t)$, $r(t)$, $w(t)$ be time-paths of imputed prices for which the following conditions are satisfied:

$q(t), q_C(t), q_V(t)$ are continuous positive and bounded (88)

functions of time t;

$r(t)$ and $w(t)$ are piece-wise continuous functions of time t; (89)

At each moment of time t, $(c(t), x(t), z(t), k_C(t), k_V(t), l_C(t), l_V(t))$ maximizes

$$u(c, x) + q(t)z + q_C(t)(f_C(k_C)l_C - z - c) + q_V(t)(f_V(k_V)l_V - x) + r(t)(k(t) - k_Cl_C - k_Vl_V) + w(t)(1 - l_C - l_V) \tag{90}$$

without any constraints (except for nonnegativity),

$$\dot{q}(t) = (v + \mu + \delta)q(t) - r(t). \tag{91}$$

Then the feasible path $c(t), x(t), z(t), k(t)$ is an optimum.

Since the Lagrangian is concave with respect to $c, x, z, k_Cl_C, k_Vl_V, l_C, l_V$, condition (90) is reduced to the following set of first order conditions:

$$\begin{cases} u_c(c(t), x(t)) = q_C(t) \\ u_x(c(t), x(t)) = q_V(t); \end{cases} \tag{92}$$

$$z(t) = 0, \qquad \text{if } q(t) < q_C(t), \tag{93}$$

$$\frac{w(t)}{r(t)}(\equiv \omega(t)) = \frac{f_j(k_j(t))}{f_j'(k_j(t))} - k_j(t), \qquad j = C, V, \tag{94}$$

$$r(t) = q_C(t)f_C'(k_C(t)) = q_V(t)f_V'(k_V(t)). \tag{95}$$

Let us now introduce

$$p = \frac{q_V}{q_C}, \tag{96}$$

$$p(\omega) = \frac{f_C'(k_C(\omega))}{f_V'(k_V(\omega))}. \tag{97}$$

Then conditions (92–95) together with the feasibility conditions (75–79) yield (omitting time-suffix t):

$$\begin{cases} \dot{k} = z - (n + \mu)k \\ \dot{q} = (v + \mu + \delta)q - r, \end{cases} \tag{98}$$

where

$$\begin{cases} u_c(c, x) = q_C \\ u_x(c, x) = pq_C, \end{cases} \tag{99}$$

$$q \leqq q_C, \tag{100}$$

with equality if $z > 0$,

$$p = p(\omega), \tag{101}$$

$$c + z = y_C(\omega, k) \equiv f_C(k_C(\omega)) \frac{k - k_V(\omega)}{k_C(\omega) - k_V(\omega)}, \tag{102}$$

$$x = y_V(\omega, k) \equiv f_V(k_V(\omega)) \frac{k_C(\omega) - k}{k_V(\omega) - k_V(\omega)}, \tag{103}$$

and

$$r = q_C f'_C(k_C(\omega)). \tag{104}$$

Since a one-to-one correspondence exists between p and ω through $p = p(\omega)$, $y_C(\omega, k)$, and $y_V(\omega, k)$ are often written as $y_C(p, k)$ and $y_V(p, k)$.

The pair of equations (99) uniquely determines (c, x) for given (p, q_C). We may use the notation:

$$c = c(p, q_C), \qquad x = x(p, q_C). \tag{105}$$

Differentiating (94), we get

$$\begin{pmatrix} u_{cc} & u_{cx} \\ u_{xc} & u_{xx} \end{pmatrix} \begin{pmatrix} dc \\ dx \end{pmatrix} = \begin{pmatrix} dq_C \\ pdq_C + q_C dp \end{pmatrix}. \tag{106}$$

Hence,

$$\begin{pmatrix} dc \\ dx \end{pmatrix} = \frac{1}{\Delta} \begin{pmatrix} u_{xx} & -u_{cx} \\ -u_{xc} & u_{cc} \end{pmatrix} \begin{pmatrix} dq_C \\ pdq_C + q_C dp \end{pmatrix}, \tag{107}$$

where

$$\Delta = det \begin{pmatrix} u_{cc} & u_{cx} \\ u_{xc} & u_{xx} \end{pmatrix} = u_{cc}u_{xx} - u_{xx}^2 > 0. \tag{108}$$

We have from (107) that

$$\frac{\partial c}{\partial q_C} = \frac{u_{xx} - pu_{cx}}{\Delta} < 0, \qquad \frac{\partial c}{\partial p} = \frac{-q_C u_{cx}}{\Delta} = 0, \tag{109}$$

$$\frac{\partial x}{\partial q_C} = \frac{-u_{xc} + pu_{cx}}{\Delta} < 0, \qquad \frac{\partial x}{\partial p} = \frac{q_C u_{cx}}{\Delta} > 0. \tag{110}$$

On the other hand, we have

$$\frac{\partial y_C}{\partial p} < 0, \qquad \frac{\partial y_C}{\partial k} > 0, \tag{111}$$

$$\frac{\partial y_V}{\partial p} > 0, \qquad \frac{\partial Y_V}{\partial k} < 0. \tag{112}$$

Now let us consider the equation

$$x(p, q_C) = y_V(p, k). \tag{113}$$

Since $x(p, q_C)$ is a decreasing function of p and $y_C(p, k)$ is a nondecreasing

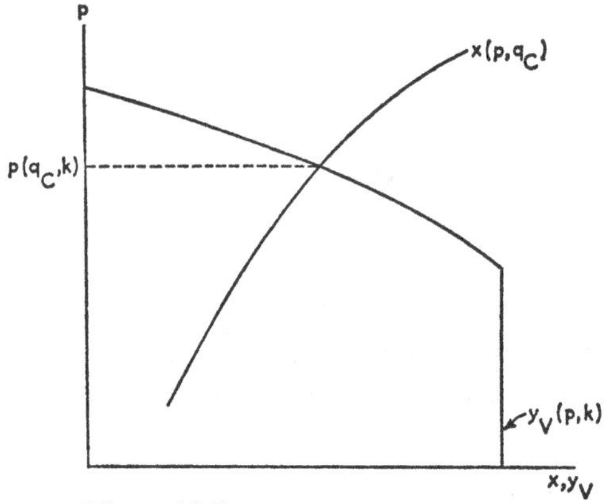

Figure 18.7

function of p, equation (113) has a unique solution, p, for any given pair of q_C and k, as described in Figure 18.7. We may simply write

$$p = p(q_C, k).$$

Let us first examine the phase in which the rate of investment $z(t)$ is always positive. Then the inequality (100) is satisfied by an equality, and we have

$$\begin{cases} \dot{k} = y_C(p, k) - c(p, q) - (v + \mu)k \\ \dfrac{\dot{q}}{q} = (v + \mu + \delta) - f_C'(k_C), \end{cases} \tag{114}$$

where $p = p(q, k)$.

The rate of change in the imputed price q of investment is zero if and only if

$$p(q, k) = p^* \tag{115}$$

where p^* is the relative price for which

$$f_C'(k_C(p^*)) = v + \mu + \delta. \tag{116}$$

We then have

$$\left(\frac{dq}{dk}\right)_{\dot{q}=0} = \left(\frac{dq}{dk}\right)_{p=p^*} = \frac{\partial y_V/\partial k}{\partial x/\partial q} > 0. \tag{117}$$

The $\dot{q} = 0$ curve thus has a positive slope everywhere, and it can be seen from (112) and (115) that the rate of change in the imputed price, q, is positive (negative) if (q, k) lies (below) above the $\dot{q} = 0$ curve.

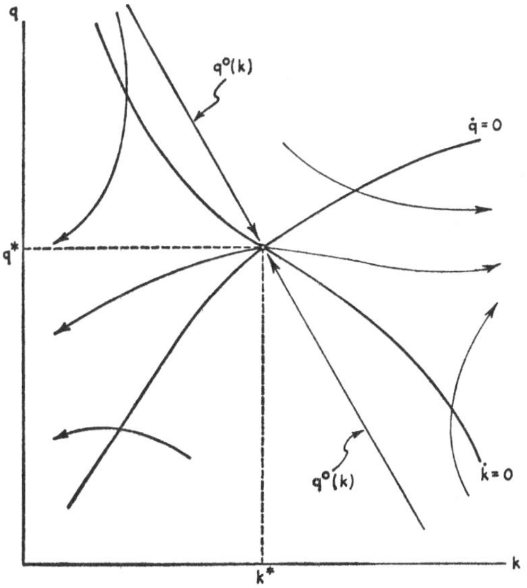

Figure 18.8

On the other hand, the slope of the $\dot{k}=0$ curve is given by

$$\left(\frac{dq}{dk}\right)_{\dot{k}=0} = \frac{\dfrac{\partial c}{\partial q} - \left(\dfrac{\partial y_C}{\partial p} - \dfrac{\partial c}{\partial p}\right)\dfrac{\partial p}{\partial q}}{\dfrac{\partial y_C}{\partial p} - \dfrac{\partial c}{\partial p}\dfrac{\partial p}{\partial k} + \dfrac{\partial y_C}{\partial k} - \nu - \mu}. \tag{118}$$

The sign of $\left(\dfrac{\partial q}{\partial k}\right)_{\dot{k}=0}$ is in general indeterminate, but it is negative at $p = p^*$, as is seen from (109), (111), and the following inequality:

$$\frac{\partial y_C}{\partial k} = \frac{f_C(k_C)}{k_C - k_V} = f'_C(k_C)\frac{k_C + \omega}{k_C - k_V} > \nu + \mu \qquad \text{if } f'_C(k_C) = \nu + \mu + \delta. \tag{119}$$

The typical structure of solution paths to the pair of differential equations (114) is illustrated in Figure 18.8, where the stationary point (q^*, k^*) is characterized by

$$\begin{cases} p(q^*, k^*) = p^* \\ y_C(p^*, k^*) = c(p^*, k^*) + (\nu + \mu)k^*. \end{cases} \tag{120}$$

Since the stationary point (q^*, k^*) becomes a saddle-point, there are two branches of solution paths which converge to the point (q^*, k^*). Hence, for

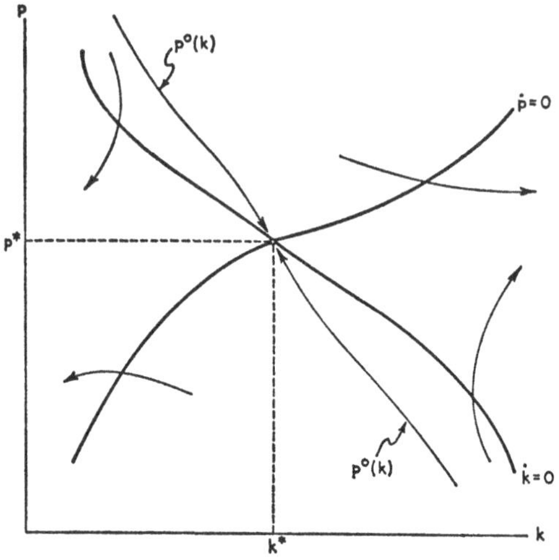

Figure 18.9

any capital-labor ratio, k^0, there exists an imputed price, $q^0 = q^0(k^0)$, such that the solution path going through (q^0, k^0) converges (q^*, k^*). The function $q^0 = q^0(k)$ is a decreasing function of k.

Since $p = p(q, k)$ is continuously differentiable, we can transform the system of differential equation (114) into one involving p and k. The structure of the solution path of the corresponding system is typically described in Figure 18.9.

It can again be shown that, for every capital-labor ratio, k^0, there exists a unique price ratio, $p^0 = p^0(k^0)$, such that the path going through (p^0, k^0) converges to (p^0, k^0). Such a curve, $p = p^0(k)$, has a negative slope.

In the discussion above, we have ignored the constraint that z must be nonnegative. The boundary of the domain on the (q, k) plane in which the resulting z is nonnegative is characterized by

$$\begin{cases} c(p, q) = y_C(p, k) \\ x(p, q) = y_V(p, k). \end{cases} \tag{121}$$

Hence, we have

$$\left(\frac{dq}{dk}\right)_{s=0} = \frac{\dfrac{\partial y_C}{\partial k}\left(\dfrac{\partial x}{\partial p} - \dfrac{\partial y_V}{\partial p}\right) - \dfrac{\partial y_V}{\partial k}\left(\dfrac{\partial c}{\partial p} - \dfrac{\partial y_C}{\partial p}\right)}{\dfrac{\partial c}{\partial q}\left(\dfrac{\partial x}{\partial p} - \dfrac{\partial y_V}{\partial p}\right) - \dfrac{\partial x}{\partial q}\left(\dfrac{\partial c}{\partial p} - \dfrac{\partial y_C}{\partial p}\right)} > 0. \tag{122}$$

Such a boundary is denoted by $q = q(k)$ and the corresponding boundary in

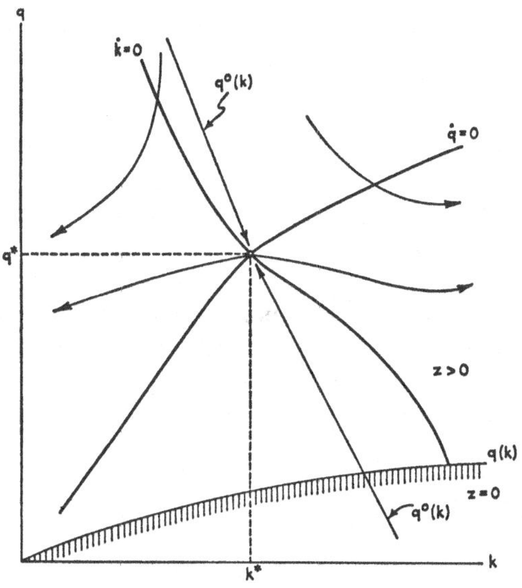

Figure 18.10

the (p, k) plane by $p = p(k)$. The stationary state (q, k) lies above the boundary.

If (q, k) lies below the curve $q = q(k)$, the optimum level of investment is zero. In this case (100) is satisfied with a strict inequality and we have

$$\begin{cases} \dot{k} = -(\nu + \mu)k \\ \dfrac{\dot{q}}{q} = \nu + \mu + \delta - f'_C(k_C), \end{cases} \tag{123}$$

where $k_C = k_C(p)$, $p = p(k, q)$.

There is a uniquely determined solution path to (123) such that it coincides with the $q^0(k)$ curve at the $q(k)$ curve (Figure 18.10). The $q^0(k)$ curve, as introduced above, then is modified so that below the $q(k)$ curve it satisfies the system (123). The $p^0(k)$ curve will be correspondingly adjusted.

It is easily shown that, for any initial capital-labor ratio, k_0, the optimum path is obtained by choosing the initial imputed price at the level $q_0 = q^0(k_0)$ and by allocating labor, capital, and private goods between consumption and investment so that (92–95) are satisfied at each moment of time, t.

The imputed relative price of public goods with respect to private goods is accordingly determined by $p_0 = p(q, k_0)$, and the allocations of labor and capital are also uniquely determined, together with the division of output between consumption and investment. The optimum relative share $1 - s^0(k)$ of the private output in the gross national product and the proportion of total private output to be invested $\beta^0(k)$ are uniquely determined as well:

$$1 - s^0(k) = y_C(p^0(k), k)/y(p^0(k), k), \tag{124}$$

$$\beta^0(k) = 1 - c(p^0(k), q^0(k))/y_C(p^0(k), k). \tag{125}$$

On the other hand, the path of optimum growth is uniquely determined by equating s and β with $s^0(k)$ and $\beta^0(k)$.

It is now possible, under some conditions, to achieve optimum growth by choosing an appropriate dynamic fiscal policy $(\tau(t), \theta(t))$. In particular, if the average propensity to save out of disposable income γ and the velocity of money λ are both constant, then the optimum rates, τ^0 and θ^0, of income tax and of increase in the money supply are determined by the following relations:

$$1 - s^0(k) = (1 - \tau^0(\lambda))(1 - \lambda\theta^0(\lambda)),$$

$$\beta^0(k) = 1 - \frac{\gamma}{1 - \lambda\theta^0(k)}.$$

Hence,

$$\theta^0(k) = \frac{1 - \dfrac{\gamma}{1 - \beta^0(k)}}{\lambda}$$

$$\tau^0(k) = 1 - \frac{1 - s^0(k)}{1 - \lambda\theta^0(k)} = 1 - \frac{1}{\gamma}(1 - s^0(k)(1 - \beta^0(k)).$$

References

[1] Brown, E. C. "Fiscal Policy in a Growing Economy: A Further Word," *Journal of Political Economy*, LXIV (1956), 170–72.

[2] Cass, D. "Optimum Economic Growth in an Aggregative Model of Capital Accumulation," *Review of Economic Studies*, XXXII (1965), 233–40.

[3] Gurley, J. G. "Fiscal Policy in a Growing Economy," *Jour. Pol. Econ.*, LXI (1953), 523–35.

[4] Hicks, J. R. "Mr. Keynes and the 'Classical'; A Suggested Interpretation," *Econometrica*, V (1937), 147–59.

[5] Inagaki, M. "A General Proof of Existence in Optimum Savings." Unpublished manuscript, 1964.

[6] Koopmans, T. C. "On the Concept of Optimal Economic Growth," *Semaine d'Etude sur le Role de l'Analyse Econometrique dans la Formulation de Plans de Development* (1965), 225–287.

[7] Kurz, M. "Optimal Paths of Capital Accumulation under the Minimum Time Objective," *Econometrica*, XXXIII (1965), 42–66.

[8] Metzler, L. A. "Wealth, Saving, and the Rate of Interest," *Jour. Pol. Econ.*, LIX (1951), 93–115.

[9] Mirrlees, J. A. "Optimal Planning for a Dynamic Economy." Unpublished manuscript.
[10] Musgrave, R. A. *The Theory of Public Finance: A Study of Public Economy*. New York: McGraw-Hill, 1959, especially pp. 472–500.
[11] Ramsey, F. P. "A Mathematical Theory of Savings," *Economic Journal*, XXXVIII (1928), 543–59.
[12] Smith, W. L. "Professor Gurley on Fiscal Policy in a Growing Economy," *Jour. Pol. Econ.*, LXII (1954), 440–41.
[13] Solow, R. M. "A Contribution to the Theory of Economic Growth," *Quarterly Journal of Economics*, XXXII (1956), 65–95.
[14] Srinivasan, T. N. "Optimal Saving in a Two-Sector Growth Model," *Econometrica*, XXXII (1964), 358–73.
[15] Stoleru, G. "An Optimal Policy for Economic Growth," *Econometrica*, XXXIII (1965), 321–48.
[16] Swan, T. W. "Economic Growth and Capital Accumulation," *Economic Record*, LXVI (1956), 358–73.
[17] Tobin, J. "An Aggregative Dynamic Model," *Jour. Pol. Econ.*, LXIII (1955), 103–15.
[18] Uzawa, H. "On a Two-Sector Model of Economic Growth, II," *Rev. Econ. Stud.*, XXX (1963), 105–18.
[19] ——— "Optimal Growth in a Two-Sector Model of Capital Accumulation," *Rev. Econ. Stud.*, XXXI (1964), 1–24.
[20] ——— "Optimum Investment in Social Capital." Paper presented at a NSF-Purdue Conference on Quantitative Methods in Economics, 1963.
[21] Von Weizaecker, C. C. "Existence of Optimal Programs of Accumulation for an Infinite Time Horizon," *Rev. Econ. Stud.*, XXXII (1965), 85–104.

CHAPTER 19

On the economics of social overhead capital

1 Introduction

Market mechanism and the private ownership of means of production are the two major instruments by which the working of a capitalistic society may be efficiently organized. On the one hand, markets stimulate information concerning demand and supply conditions that is relevant for an efficient allocation of scarce resources. The private ownership of means of production, on the other hand, creates a social environment in which individual members are motivated to seek their own profit or pleasure in accordance with the rules set by society.

Such an argument implicitly presupposes that all the scarce resources limitational to the economic activities engaged in by the members of the society may be privately appropriated, without involving significant costs either in the administration of such private ownership or in the resulting efficiency as for the productive organization of economic activities. However, in most contemporary capitalistic societies, a significant portion of scarce means of production is not necessarily privately appropriated, as typically illustrated by the existence of a large class of means of production usually termed social overhead capital.

Social overhead capital comprises all those scarce resources which are put in use for the members of the society, either free of charge or at a negligible price. They are either produced collectively by the society, as in the case of social capital such as highways or bridges, or simply endowed within the society, as in the case of natural capital such as air, water, and so forth.

Thus all the means of production may be classified into two categories: private means of production and social overhead capital. The classification is not absolute, but depends upon the historical, political, and social aspects

Translated from "Sur la théorie économique du capital collectif social," *Cahiers du Séminaire d'Économétrie*, 1974, pp. 103–22, with permission.

of the society in question. The same type of capital goods may be privately appropriated in one society, but not in another, while it is entirely possible that in a given society a capital good may be classified as private at one time and as social at another time, depending upon the economic and social climate. The present paper will not discuss the criteria by which means of production are classified into two categories, but will postulate that such a classification has already been made and will not change throughout the course of the present investigation.

2 The description of a national economy

As explained in the previous section, all the means of production existing in a society at a given moment of time are now classified into two categories: private means of production and social overhead capital.

Private means of production are appropriated to individual members of the society who are responsible for the management of those private means of production which they own. Individual members are concerned with attaining the maximum amount of profit or pleasure in accordance with the rules prevailing in the society.

On the other hand, social overhead capital in principle is put to use for any member of the society either free of charge or at a negligible cost. For the sake of simplicity, it will be assumed that social overhead capital is provided free of charge to every member of the society.

The services provided by social overhead capital belong to the category of public goods or services for which the formal analysis was presented by Samuelson in a number of articles (2, 3). The Samuelsonian analysis, however, is concerned with what may be termed pure public goods, which excludes most of the familiar examples of services provided by social overhead capital. I am particularly concerned with two aspects of social overhead capital which are not handled by the Samuelsonian approach.

The first is the range of freedom with which each member of the society may use the services of social overhead capital. Most of social overhead capital, such as highways, sewages, and so forth requires the input of certain amounts of private means of production, and each member of the society uses the services of such social overhead capital to the individually most desirable extent.

The second is related to the phenomenon of congestion. As illustrated by the example of roads, the benefit each individual gets from the use of a certain amount of social overhead capital depends upon the extent to which other members of the society are using the same social overhead capital. The Samuelsonian concept of pure public goods necessarily excludes the the phenomenon of congestion.

In the present paper, I should like to present a formulation of social overhead capital in which these two aspects are considered. I shall make a number of simplifying assumptions in order to bring forth essential aspects of the present approach. Most of these simplifying assumptions may be relaxed without substantially altering the nature of the analysis, but I shall not indicate precisely the extent to which they may be relaxed. It will be assumed that private means of production and social overhead capital are composed of homogeneous and measurable quantities. Social overhead capital may be used either in the processes of production or directly in the processes of consumption. However, it will be assumed that the economy is composed of a large number of economic units, each of which does not exercise any significant influence on the aggregate level of economic activities. Finally, it will be assumed that each consumption unit possesses a measurable utility which depends upon the amount of the services of social overhead capital as well as upon the amount of private goods being consumed.

3 Social overhead capital as a factor of production

To explain the essential nature of the present approach, I should like first to concentrate upon the case where social overhead capital is used as a factor of production only. Social overhead capital is assumed to be composed of a homogeneous and measurable quantity. Hence, it is possible to measure the amount of social overhead capital existing within the society at each moment of time. Let V be the stock of social overhead capital thus measured.

Production processes of each production unit in the society are affected by the amount of the services derived from social overhead capital as well as those provided by private means of production. That is, the output Q_β produced by a production unit β depends upon the amount of private means of production K_β and the services X_β derived from social overhead capital. Thus, the production function may be denoted by

$$Q_\beta = F^\beta(K_\beta, X_\beta). \tag{1}$$

However, as in the example of highways, the role of the services of social overhead capital is influenced by the amount of public services being used by other production units as well as by the amount V of social overhead capital existing in the society. Hence, the production function (1) may be rewritten as

$$Q_\beta = F^\beta(K_\beta, X_\beta, X, V), \tag{2}$$

where X stands for the aggregate amount of the services of social overhead capital used by all other production units existing in the society.

If it is assumed that there is a continuum of production units existing in the society, the label β may be assumed to range from 0 to 1. Thus, the aggregate level X of the services of social overhead capital used by all production units may be denoted

$$X = \int X_\beta d\beta, \tag{3}$$

where the integral is always taken from 0 to 1.

It may be assumed that private means of production and social overhead capital are complementary in the sense that the marginal product of private means of production is increased (or, at least not decreased) as the services rendered by social overhead capital are increased. Namely,

$$F^\beta_{K_\beta X_\beta} \geqq 0. \tag{4}$$

It is also assumed that social overhead capital becomes congested as more usage is made of it by other production units. The phenomenon of congestion may be explicitly stated by the following properties. First, the amount of output is decreased as the aggregate level X of social overhead capital being used is increased. Namely,

$$F^\beta_X < 0. \tag{5}$$

Second, the marginal product of either private means of production or social overhead capital is decreased as X is increased. In symbols,

$$F^\beta{}_{K_\beta X} < 0, \qquad F^\beta_{X_\beta X} < 0. \tag{6}$$

On the other hand, an increase in the endowment V of social overhead capital results in a shift upward of the production function. Hence, it may be assumed that

$$F^\beta_V > 0. \tag{7}$$

In addition to the properties specified above, it will be assumed that production function (2) satisfies the standard neoclassical conditions; that is, marginal rates of substitution are always diminishing and the law of constant rates of returns prevails when all the variables are taken into account. In particular,

$$F^\beta_{K_\beta K_\beta} < 0, \quad F^\beta_{X_\beta X_\beta} < 0, \quad F^\beta_{XX} < 0, \quad F^\beta_{VV} < 0, \tag{8}$$

and

$$\begin{vmatrix} F^\beta_{K_\beta K_\beta}, & F^\beta_{K_\beta X_\beta} \\ F^\beta_{X_\beta K_\beta}, & F^\beta_{X_\beta X_\beta} \end{vmatrix} > 0, \quad \cdots \tag{9}$$

I shall first examine how private resources and public services are allocated between individual production units under the competitive market mechanism.

4 Market allocation

Suppose production units all produce identical goods and markets for output and private means of production are both perfectly competitive. Each production unit then chooses the combination of private means of production and public services that will maximize the net profit. Let r be the price, quoted in terms of output, of the services rendered by private means of production prevailing in the factor market. The net profit of the production unit β is given by

$$\pi_\beta = Q_\beta - rK_\beta, \tag{10}$$

and the production unit β chooses the combination of K and X_β that maximizes the profit (10) for given levels of the endowment of social overhead capital V and the aggregate level X of the services of social overhead capital currently being used. Since social overhead capital is offered free of charge, the maximum profit is obtained when the following marginal conditions are satisfied:

$$F^\beta_{K_\beta} = r, \quad F^\beta_{X_\beta} = 0. \tag{11}$$

Demand for private capital K_β and social capital X_β by the production unit β is now uniquely determined by the rentals rate r. An increase in r results in a decrease in the demand for private capital K_β. In view of the complementarity assumption (4), the demand for social overhead capital X_β is shown to be decreased when the rentals rate r for private capital goes up.

The aggregate demand schedule for private capital is then given by summing up individual demand schedules:

$$K^D = \int K_\beta d_\beta. \tag{12}$$

Note, however, that the aggregate level X of social overhead capital being used is no longer an exogenous variable. An increase in the rentals rate r necessarily results in a decrease in the demand for the services of social overhead capital by *all* production units, thus resulting in a decrease in the aggregate level X of social overhead capital being used.

Thus, in order for market equilibrium to be reached, the following two conditions must be satisfied:

1 The rentals rate r for private means of production is so determined as to equate the aggregate demand with the supply of private means of production.
2 The aggregate demand for the services of social overhead capital is equal to the level at which the individual demand both for private means of production and social overhead capital is derived.

If the supply of private means of production is inelastically given at K, then the equilibrium conditions may be explicitly stated as follows:

$$F^{\beta}_{K_{\beta}} = r, \quad F^{\beta}_{X_{\beta}} = 0, \tag{13}$$

$$K = \int K_{\beta} d_{\beta}, \tag{14}$$

$$X = \int X_{\beta} d_{\beta}, \tag{15}$$

and

$$Q_{\beta} = F^{\beta}(K_{\beta}, X_{\beta}, X, V). \tag{16}$$

The aggregate real output (real net national product) Q then is given by

$$Q = \int Q_{\beta} d_{\beta}. \tag{17}$$

As mentioned above, the aggregate level of the services of social overhead capital being used X_{β} is related to the rentals rate r. To derive the aggregate demand schedule for private capital, it is necessary to take into account the adjustment in the aggregate use of social overhead capital. Mathematically, the system of equilibrium conditions (13) to (15) must be solved with respect to K, X_{β}, and X, for given levels of the rentals rate r and the endowment of social overhead capital V. It is easily shown that an increase in the rentals rate r is accompanied by a decrease in K_{β}, X_{β}, and X. Hence, the demand schedule for the aggregate level of private capital has a downward slope as a function of the rentals rate r.

The equilibrium rentals rate r, therefore, is uniquely determined by the equilibrium condition (14) for the given endowment of private capital K. The aggregate real output Q may accordingly be determined for the given amounts of private capital K and social overhead capital V.

The equilibrium rentals rate r is decreased as either the endowment of private capital K or that of social overhead capital being used tends to increase, because of the assumption that private capital and social capital are complementary.

One can easily infer from the existence of external economies with respect to social overhead capital that market allocation is not optimum. The problem then arises: Is it possible to devise a rule by which the optimum allocation of private and social means of production may be obtained? To examine this problem, we next consider the allocation scheme where social overhead capital may be priced for its usage.

5 Pricing of social overhead capital

Scarce resources are classified as social overhead capital because it is not desirable either from the economic or social points of view for private individuals to appropriate them. From the economic point of view, scarce resources are classified as social overhead capital because of the cost of excluding those who do not pay for using such resources. Hence, a pricing scheme for the usage of social overhead capital might at first glance not conform with the very definition of social overhead capital. Social overhead capital tends to be relatively more scarce than private means of production; the costs associated with the administration of the pricing scheme may become negligible compared with the social benefit, either in terms of efficiency or equity, derived from the resulting reallocation of scarce resources. In what follows, it will be assumed that such is in fact the case and that social costs associated with the pricing scheme are negligible.

Consider now the situation where private individuals are charged for the use of social overhead capital according to the amount of services being used. Private means of production are allocated in a prefectly competitive market.

Let θ be the price charged per unit of services derived from social overhead capital. The net profit of the production unit β now becomes

$$\pi_\beta = Q_\beta - rK_\beta - \theta X_\beta \tag{18}$$

instead of (10) as given in the previous situation. The net profit thus defined is maximized if the following marginality conditions are satisfied:

$$F^\beta_{K_\beta} = r, \quad F^\beta_{X_\beta} = \theta. \tag{19}$$

Other equilibrium conditions are identical with those obtained for the previous situation; namely,

$$K = \int K_\beta d_\beta, \tag{20}$$

$$X = \int X_\beta d_\beta, \tag{21}$$

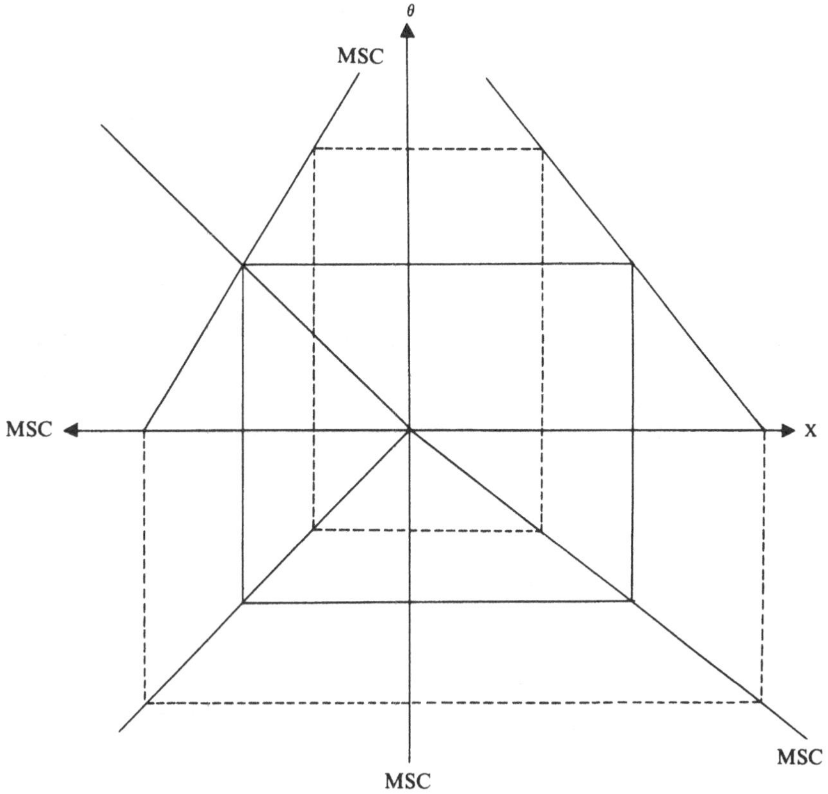

Figure 19.1

and

$$Q_\beta = F^\beta(K_\beta, X_\beta, X, V). \tag{22}$$

It is assumed, as in the previous situation, that private capital is inelastically supplied at the level K and the endowment of social overhead capital is given at V. For a given price θ for the use of social overhead capital, the equilibrium conditions (19 to 22) are solved to determine the equilibrium allocations of private capital and social overhead capital, K_β and X_β, together with the aggregate level of the services of social overhead capital X being used. It is easily shown that the equilibrium rentals rate r for private capital is also uniquely determined for a given price θ.

The relationship between the imputed price θ of social overhead capital and the aggregate level X of social overhead capital being used may be illustrated by the curve in the first quadrant in Figure 19.1. The complementarity assumption introduced above implies that the curve has a negative slope: as the imputed price θ is increased, the aggregate amount of the services of social overhead capital X is decreased.

Let $K_\beta(\theta)$, $X_\beta(\theta)$, and $X(\theta)$ be respectively the equilibrium allocations of private capital and of social capital, and the aggregate level of social capital being used, all corresponding to the imputed price θ. The resulting aggregate real output $Q(\theta)$ may be denoted by

$$Q(\theta) = \int Q_\beta(\theta) d_\beta, \tag{23}$$

where $Q_\beta(\theta)$ stands for the equilibrium output of production unit β.

Is the aggregate real output $Q(\theta)$ increased or not when the imputed price θ is increased? Indeed, the rate of change in the aggregate real output $Q(\theta)$ is easily calculated in view of equilibrium conditions (9 to 22). Differentiating (23) with respect to the imputed price θ, one obtains the following relationships:

$$\frac{dQ(\theta)}{d\theta} = \int \left[F^\beta_{K_\beta} \frac{dK_\beta(\theta)}{d\theta} + F^\beta_{X_\beta} \frac{dX_\beta(\theta)}{d\theta} + F^\beta_X \frac{dX}{d\theta} \right] d\beta. \tag{24}$$

In view of the equilibrium conditions (19 to 21), the relationships (24) may be reduced to the following:

$$\frac{dQ(\theta)}{d\theta} = \left[\theta + \int F^\beta_X d\beta \right] \frac{dX}{d\theta}, \tag{25}$$

which may be rewritten as

$$\frac{dQ(\theta)}{d\theta} = (MSC - \theta)\left(-\frac{dX}{d\theta} \right), \tag{26}$$

where

$$MSC = -\int F^\beta_X d\beta. \tag{27}$$

The expression (27) corresponds to the concept of the marginal social costs associated with the use of social overhead capital. It represents the loss in the aggregate real output due to the marginal increase in the use of social overhead capital.

Since an increase in the imputed price θ reduces the aggregate usage X of social overhead capital,

$$\frac{dX}{d\theta} < 0. \tag{28}$$

Hence, whether or not an increase in the imputed price increases the aggregate real output $Q(\theta)$ depends on the difference between the marginal social costs, MSC, and the imputed price θ. If the imputed price θ is less than the marginal social costs MSC, then the aggregate real output $Q(\theta)$ is increased if θ is increased. The maximum aggregate real output $Q(\theta)$ can be obtained when the imputed price θ is just equal to the marginal social costs MSC.

The complementarity condition again implies that an increase in the imputed price θ results in a decrease in the marginal social costs MSC, as illustrated by the curve in the fourth quadrant in Figure 19.1. By transforming the schedule of the marginal social costs from the fourth quadrant to the second quadrant, one may depict the relationships between the marginal social costs MSC and the imputed price θ by the two curves in the second quadrant.

Starting with the market solution which corresponds to the case where $\theta = 0$, the aggregate real output $Q(\theta)$ is increased until the imputed price θ is equated to the marginal social costs MSC. Hence, it is possible to devise an iterative procedure by which the maximum aggregate real output may be obtained provided the marginal social costs may be calculated from the known allocation of private and social capital among individual production units.

6 Optimum allocation

The procedure discussed above relies upon the price mechanism for the allocation of both private and social capital. Suppose it is possible, without incurring any costs, to make a centrally controlled plan for the allocation of scarce means of production. It is supposed for the moment that a central planning board possesses a complete knowledge about the production processes of each production unit. What would then be the allocation among individual production units of private and social capital that maximizes the aggregate real output? This problem may be mathematically stated as follows:

Let K and V be the given endowments of private capital and social overhead capital. Find the allocation of private capital among production units K and the levels of individual and aggregate uses of social overhead capital, X_β and X, so as to maximize the aggregate real output

$$Q = \int Q_\beta d\beta \tag{29}$$

subject to the constraints:

$$K = \int K_\beta d\beta, \tag{30}$$

$$X = \int X_\beta d\beta, \tag{31}$$

and

$$Q_\beta = F^\beta(K_\beta, X_\beta, X, V). \tag{32}$$

Such a maximization problem is easily solved in terms of Lagrange multipliers. Let r and θ be the Lagrange multipliers associated with the constraints (30) and (31) respectively, and introduce the Lagrangian form:

$$\int Q_\beta d\beta + \pi\left[K - \int K_\beta d\beta\right] + \theta\left[X - \int X_\beta d\beta\right]. \tag{33}$$

The optimum allocation may now be obtained by finding the allocation for which the Lagrangian may be maximized without any constraints.

Therefore, the optimum allocation may be obtained by solving the following equations:

$$F^\beta_{K_\beta} = r \tag{34}$$

$$F^\beta_{X_\beta} = \theta \tag{35}$$

$$\theta = -\int F^\beta_X d\beta, \tag{36}$$

together with the constraints (30 to 32).

These conditions are identical with those which have been obtained for the case where the imputed price for social overhead capital θ is equated to the marginal social costs MSC.

Hence, the allocative process discussed in the previous section results in an optimum allocation of scarce resources.

7 The presence of consumers

In the analysis presented in the previous sections, it has been assumed that the economy is composed of producers only, with consumers playing no role in the process of resource allocation. Consider now the general case where consumers are involved with the allocative process of both private capital and social overhead capital.

Let the consumers be denoted by the generic symbol α, ranging in continuous numbers from 0 to 1, as were the producers. It is assumed that the economy is composed of a large number of consumers each of whom plays a role negligible from the aggregative point of view. The process of aggregation again will be denoted by the integral.

The level of utility each consumer may enjoy is related to the amount of services realized from social overhead capital as well as private consumption. Again, we assume that there is only one kind of private consumption goods and that the services from social overhead capital are measurable. By adopting the Benthamite utility concept, it may be assumed that consumer α's utility U_α is a function of the level of private consumption C_α and the amount X_α of the services derived from social overhead capital. Considering the congestion phenomenon, the effectiveness of the services of social overhead capital to consumer α depends upon the aggregate level X of the services of social capital being used as well as upon the stock of social overhead capital V. It may be written as

$$U_\alpha = U^\alpha(C_\alpha, X_\alpha, X, V), \tag{37}$$

where the aggregative level X must be defined by

$$X = \int X_\alpha d\alpha + \int X_\beta d\beta, \tag{38}$$

where the integrals on the right-hand side of equation (38) cover all consumers and producers.

It is assumed that the utility function (37) is concave with respect to the variables C_α, X_α, X, and V, and that the marginal utility of private consumption is positive, while that of the services of social overhead capital is merely decreasing. Hence,

$$U^\alpha_{C_\alpha} > 0, \quad U^\alpha_{X_\alpha} \gtreqless 0 \tag{39}$$

$$U^\alpha_{C_\alpha C_\alpha} < 0, \quad U^\alpha_{X_\alpha X_\alpha} < 0, \quad U^\alpha_{XX} < 0, \quad U^\alpha_{VV} < 0. \tag{40}$$

If the services of social overhead capital are rendered to consumers free of charge, each consumer will use them up to the level where the marginal rate of substitution between social overhead capital and private consumption equals zero, that is,

$$\frac{\partial U'^\alpha / \partial X_\alpha}{\partial U^\alpha / \partial C_\alpha} = 0, \tag{41}$$

and all the consumer's income Y_α will be spent on private consumption C_α:

$$C_\alpha = Y_\alpha. \tag{42}$$

Market equilibrium will be attained when these conditions concerning consumers' equilibrium are satisfied with the producers' equilibrium conditions. It is obvious that the resulting pattern of resource allocation is neither efficient nor optimum.

Where consumers are present, one may have to be careful in defining the concept of optimum resource allocations. However, if the Benthamite concept of measurable and comparable utility is presupposed, then the social utility U is simply defined by the aggregate of individual utility levels U_α,

$$U = \int U_\alpha d\alpha, \tag{43}$$

where the integral ranges over all the consumers in the society.

A pattern of resource allocation and the accompanying income distribution may be defined as optimum if the social utility (43) is maximized among the feasible set of resource allocations. To be more precise:

At each moment of time, let the amounts of private and social capital be given by K and V, respectively. A pattern of resource allocation (C_α, X_α, K_β, X_β) is defined as optimum if the social utility U, given by (43), is maximized among the set of all feasible resource allocations:

$$\int C_\alpha d\alpha = \int Q_\beta d_\beta, \tag{44}$$

$$Q_\beta = F_\beta(K_\beta, X_\beta, X, V), \tag{45}$$

$$X = \int X_\alpha d\alpha + \int X_\beta d\beta, \tag{46}$$

$$K = \int K_\beta d\beta. \tag{47}$$

Let p, $p\theta$, pr, be the Lagrange multipliers associated with the constraints (44), (46), and (47) respectively. Then a simple calculation will show that an optimum allocation must satisfy the following conditions:

$$U^\alpha_{C_\alpha} = p, \quad \text{or} \quad U^{\alpha'}_{X_{\alpha'}}/U^{\alpha''}_{C_{\alpha''}} = 1, \qquad \text{for all pairs } \alpha' \text{ and } \alpha'' \tag{48}$$

$$U^\alpha_{X_\alpha}/U^\alpha_{C_\alpha} = \theta \tag{49}$$

$$\theta = \int - U^\alpha_X/U^\alpha_{C_{\alpha'}} d\alpha + \int - F^\beta_X d\beta \tag{50}$$

$$F^\beta_{K_\beta} = r, \quad F^\beta_{X_\beta} = 0. \tag{51}$$

The quantity on the right-hand side of equation (50) is nothing but the marginal social costs associated with the use of social overhead capital in the present context:

$$MSC = \int - U^\alpha_X/U^\alpha_{C_\alpha} d\alpha + \int - F^\beta_X d\beta. \tag{52}$$

An inspection of the optimum conditions (48–51) suggests that, to obtain an optimum resource allocation, it is necessary to introduce a transfer mechanism in such a manner that the marginal rate of distribution between any two consumers becomes unity

$$MRD_{\alpha'\alpha''}\left(\equiv \frac{U^{\alpha'}_{C_{\alpha'}}}{U^{\alpha''}_{C_{\alpha''}}}\right) = 1, \tag{53}$$

in addition to the pricing scheme for the use of social overhead capital according to the marginal social cost principle.

8 Optimum conditions from a dynamic point of view

The analysis in the previous sections has been concerned with the allocation of scarce resources where the stock of private and social capital has been assumed to be given. We now extend the analysis to the process of capital accumulation for both private and social capital, and examine the pattern of resource allocation over time which is optimum from a dynamic point of view. It will be shown that the principle of the marginal social costs may be extended to this dynamic case and the criteria for optimum allocation of investment between private and social capital will be obtained within the framework of the Ramsey theory of optimum growth.

To simplify the exposition, it will be assumed that the rate at which consumers discount their future levels of utility is constant and identical for all consumers in the society. Let δ be the rate of discount. The level of social utility U may now be expressed by

$$U = \int_0^\infty U(t)e^{-\delta t}dt, \tag{54}$$

where the utility level $U(t)$ at a point of time t may be given by

$$U(t) = \int U_\alpha(t)d\alpha, \tag{55}$$

with

$$U_\alpha(t) = U^\alpha[C_\alpha(t), X_\alpha(t), X(t), V(t)]. \tag{56}$$

Let V^o be the stock of social overhead capital existing at the initial point of time 0. The problem is to find a path of private consumption for each consumer, to allocate private and social capital between various economic units, and to adjust the accumulation of both private and social capital over time such that the resulting level of social utility (54) is maximized over all feasible paths. To address this optimum problem, we consider the difference between private and social capital with regard to the extent to which investment is used to increase the stock of capital (to be measured in the efficiency unit). In general, social overhead capital is difficult to reproduce since a rather significant amount of scarce resources must be used to increase the stock of capital. For private capital, investment may, without much difficulty, be converted into the accumulation of capital. It may be possible to formulate the relationship between the amount of investment and the resulting increase in the stock of capital in terms of a certain functional relationship. I have elsewhere discussed this problem for the case of private capital and a similar conceptual framework may be applied to social overhead capital (Penrose [1] and Uzawa [4, 5]).

Let I_V be the amount of real investment devoted to the accumulation of social overhead capital. If social overhead capital V is measured in a certain efficiency unit, the amount of real investment I_V may not necessarily result in an increase in the stock of capital by the same amount; instead there exists a certain relationship between the amount of real investment I_V and, on the one hand, the corresponding increase $\dot{V}$ in the stock of social overhead capital and the current stock of social overhead capital V on the other:

$$I_V = \phi_V(\dot{V}, V). \tag{57}$$

The relationships (57) may be interpreted as follows: to increase the stock of social overhead capital V by the amount $\dot{V}$, real investment I_V given by (57) must be spent on the accumulative activities of social overhead capital. In what follows it will be assumed that the function ϕ exhibits a feature of constant returns to scale with respect to $\dot{V}$ and V; thus one may write (57) as

$$I_V/V = \phi_V(\dot{V}/V). \tag{58}$$

Since it may be assumed that the marginal costs of investment increase as the level of investment increases, the function ϕ_V satisfies the following conditions:

$$\phi_V'(\cdot) > 0, \quad \phi_V''(\cdot) > 0. \tag{59}$$

Similar relationships may be postulated for the accumulation of private capital for each producing unit; for each producer β, the amount of real investment I_β required to increase the stock of capital K_β by the amount $\dot{K}_\beta$ may be determined by the following Penrose function:

$$I_\beta/K_\beta = \phi_\beta(\dot{K}_\beta/K_\beta), \tag{60}$$

where the Penrose function ϕ_β again satisfies the conditions:

$$\phi_\beta'(\cdot) > 0, \quad \phi_\beta''(\cdot) > 0. \tag{61}$$

Furthermore, it is assumed that the rate of depreciation of social overhead capital depends upon the extent to which it is used. Hence, the rate of depreciation μ may be written as

$$\mu = \mu(X/V), \tag{62}$$

$$\mu'(\cdot) > 0, \quad \mu''(\cdot) > 0. \tag{63}$$

The optimum problem may now be more precisely stated:

A path of resource allocation over time, $[C_\alpha(t), I_\beta(t), I_V(t), X_\alpha(t), X_\beta(t), K_\beta(t), V(t)]$, is defined as feasible if it satisfies the following consistency conditions:

$$Q(t) = \int C_\alpha(t) d\alpha + \int I_\beta(t) d\beta + I_V(t), \tag{64}$$

$$Q(t) = \int F^\beta[K_\beta(t), X_\beta(t), X(t), V(t)] d\beta, \tag{65}$$

$$X(t) = \int X_\alpha(t) d\alpha + \int X_\beta(t) d\beta, \tag{66}$$

$$\frac{I_\beta(t)}{K_\beta(t)} = \phi_\beta[z_\beta(t)], \qquad \frac{\dot{K}_\beta(t)}{K_\beta(t)} = z_\beta(t), \tag{67}$$

$$\frac{I_V(t)}{V(t)} = \phi_V[z_V(t)], \qquad \frac{\dot{V}(t)}{V(t)} = z_V(t) - \mu\left[\frac{X(t)}{V(t)}\right], \tag{68}$$

$$K_\beta(0) = K_\beta^o, \qquad V(0) = V^0 \qquad \text{given.} \tag{69}$$

Now find a feasible path of resource allocation over time which maximizes the social utility (54).

This optimum problem is in general extremely difficult to solve; instead let us find a path of resource allocation which approximates the optimum path to a reasonable extent. The one with the simplest structure will be obtained by examining the conditions which the imputed prices of private and social capital must satisfy.

Let $p_\beta(t)$ and $p_V(t)$ be the imputed prices at time t of private capital K_β and social overhead capital V respectively, and let $p(t)$ and $\theta(t)$ be the imputed prices of output Q and the use of social overhead capital X. These imputed prices correspond to the Lagrange multipliers associated with the constraints for the optimum problem. The Euler-Lagrange conditions which the optimum path must satisfy may be rearranged to yield the following conditions:

$$U^\alpha_{C_\alpha} = p, \qquad U^\alpha_{X_\alpha}/U^\alpha_{C_\alpha} = \theta, \tag{70}$$

$$F^\beta_{X_\beta} = \theta, \tag{71}$$

$$\theta = \int \frac{(-U^\alpha_X)}{U^\alpha_{C_\alpha}} d\alpha + \int (-F^\beta_X) d\beta + \frac{P_V}{p} \mu'(X/V), \tag{72}$$

$$\frac{\dot{p}_\beta}{p_\beta} = \delta - z_\beta - \frac{r_\beta - \phi_\beta(z_\beta)}{\phi'_\beta(z_\beta)}, \tag{73}$$

where

$$\phi'_\beta(z_\beta) = \frac{p_\beta}{p}, \qquad r_\beta = F^\beta_{K_\beta}, \tag{74}$$

$$\frac{\dot{p}_V}{p_V} = \delta - z_V - \frac{r_V - \phi_V(z_V)}{\phi'_V(z_V)}, \tag{75}$$

where

$$\phi'_V(z_V) = \frac{p_V}{p}, \qquad r_V = \int \frac{U^\alpha_V}{U^\alpha_{C_\alpha}} d\alpha + \int F^\beta_V d\beta. \tag{76}$$

Omission of the time suffix t will not cause any ambiguity.

The quantity on the right-hand side of equation (72) corresponds to the concept of the marginal social costs associated with the use of social overhead capital in the context of the dynamic optimization. It may be noted that the marginal costs associated with the depreciation of social overhead capital are evaluated in terms of its imputed price p_V/p measured in real terms. The quantity r_β defined in (74) is nothing but the marginal product of private capital, while the r_V defined in (76) is the marginal social product of social overhead capital measured in real terms. The r_V represents the marginal gain to society measured in real terms due to the marginal increase in the stock of social overhead capital V.

The conditions (72–74) suggest that, to attain an optimum allocation of scarce resources in the short run, one must impose the charges equal to the marginal social costs for the use of social overhead capital, the marginal social costs defined in the modified sense (74). On the other hand, the pattern of accumulation of private and social capital may be described by the conditions (73–76) delineating the rules by which the imputed prices change over time. To approximate the structure of the optimum path of capital accumulation, consider the case where the imputed prices are assumed as not changing at each moment of time. The rates of accumulation of private and social capital are obtained by assuming that equations (73) and (75) are equated to zero. It can be shown that the path of capital accumulation obtained by such a procedure reasonably approximates the optimum path, although the sense in which reasonable approximation is used needs a more complicated formulation.

If the imputed prices were assumed not to change over time, then the rates of capital accumulation z_β and z_V may be obtained by solving the

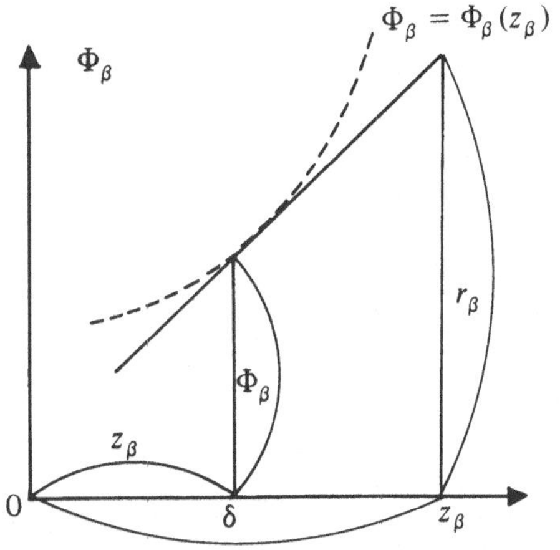

Figure 19.2

following conditions:

$$\frac{r_\beta - \phi_\beta(z_\beta)}{\delta - z_\beta} = \phi'_\beta(z_\beta), \tag{77}$$

$$\frac{r_V - \phi_V(z_V)}{\delta - z_V} = \phi'_V(z_V). \tag{78}$$

See Figures 19.2 and 19.3 for the determination of the rates of accumulation z_β and z_V.

Figures 19.2 and 19.3 clearly show that the rates of accumulation of private and social capital are uniquely determined, that the higher the marginal product of private capital, the higher the corresponding rate of accumulation for private capital, and that the higher the marginal social product of social overhead capital, the higher the rate of accumulation. On the other hand, an increase in the social rate of discount δ will lower the rate of accumulation for both private and social capital.

Thus, the (approximately) optimum rates of accumulation for private and social capital will be determined once the marginal private or social products of this capital are known. However, the marginal products of both private and social capital depend upon the extent to which social overhead capital is used by the members of society. The amount of the services of social overhead capital used is in turn related to the imputed price p_V/p of social overhead capital, as seen from the definition of the marginal social costs. To understand the general nature of the (approximately) optimum path of capital accumulation, consider the simplest case of only one

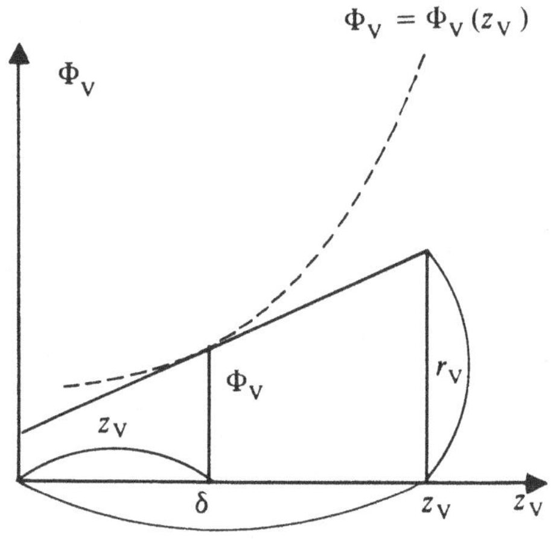

Figure 19.3

consumer and one producer in the society; the general case can be inferred from the conclusion of this simple case.

9. Optimum investment in private and social capital – the simplest case

The society is now composed of one consumer and one producer. Assume also that the services derived from social overhead capital exhibit the features of the Samuelsonian public goods. This assumption is introduced to facilitate the exposition; it is clear that the main conclusions are extended to the general case discussed in the previous sections.

Thus the level U of utility for the (representative) consumer is a function of private consumption C and the stock of social overhead capital V:

$$U = U(C, V). \tag{79}$$

On the other hand, the level Q of output produced by the (representative) producer is a function of private capital K and the stock of social overhead capital V:

$$Q = F(K, V). \tag{80}$$

Assume that the utility function $U(C, V)$ and the production function $F(K, V)$ are both linear homogeneous so that one may write as follows:

$$U = u(c)V, \; c = C/V \tag{81}$$

$$Q = f(k)V, \; k = K/V. \tag{82}$$

Let I_K and I_V be the amounts of investment (measured in real terms) in private and social capital respectively. Then the corresponding rates of increase in the stock of private and social capital may be described by the Penrose functions:

$$I_K/K = \phi_K(z_K), \qquad \dot{K}/K = z_K \tag{83}$$

$$I_V/V = \phi_V(z_V), \qquad \dot{V}/V = z_V. \tag{84}$$

The output Q will be allocated between consumption C, private investment I_K, and public investment I_V:

$$Q = C + I_K + I_V. \tag{85}$$

The social utility is now given by

$$\int_0^\infty U(C, V)\, e^{-\delta t}\, dt, \tag{86}$$

where δ is the social rate of discount.

A path of consumption C and capital accumulation K and V over time is then called optimum if it satisfies the constraints (80) and (83–85) and if it starts with the given initial condition K^o and V^o at time 0.

It is possible to solve this simple case in terms of the ratio of private capital over social capital, $k = K/V$. The approximately optimum path (k, c) may be obtained by solving the following equations.

First, the marginal product r_K of private capital K is given by

$$r_K = f'(k), \tag{87}$$

while the marginal social product r_V of social capital V is given by

$$r_V = \left[\frac{u(c)}{u'(c)} - c\right] + [f(k) - kf'(k)]. \tag{88}$$

The rates of capital accumulation z_K and z_V are determined by the following conditions:

$$\frac{r_K - \phi_K(z_K)}{\delta - z_k} = \phi'_K(z_K), \tag{89}$$

$$\frac{r_V - \phi_V(z_V)}{\delta - V} = \phi'_V(z_V). \tag{90}$$

The imputed prices p_K and p_V of private and social capital and the imputed price of output p are related by the following conditions:

$$p = u'(c), \tag{91}$$

$$p_K = p\phi'_K(z_K), \qquad p_V = p\phi'_V(z_V). \tag{92}$$

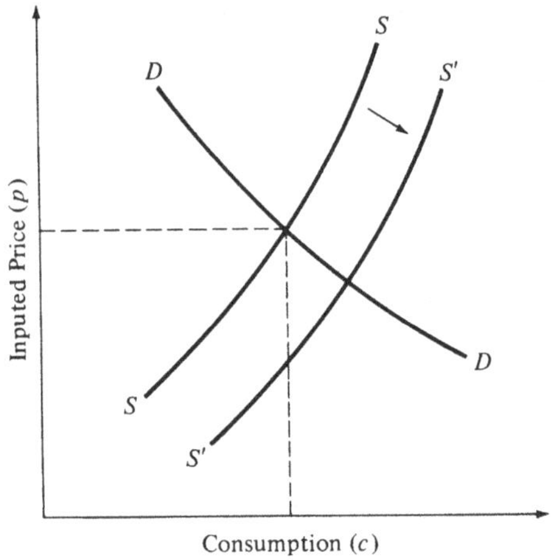

Figure 19.4

Finally, the equilibrium conditions for the goods and services market may be stated as

$$c + \phi_K(z_K)k + \phi_V(z_V) = f(k). \tag{93}$$

For the given level of capital ratio k, it is possible to solve uniquely the values of c, z_K, z_V, p, p_K, and p_V which satisfy the equations (87–93).

Let the imputed price p be temporarily given. The equation (91) determines the level of consumption c at which the consumer is in a sense in equilibrium. Hence, the demand schedule for consumption may be described by the curve DD in Figure 19.4, which has a downward slope due to the assumption of diminishing marginal utility $u''(c) < 0$.

On the other hand, the supply condition may be obtained by equation (93), where the rate of capital accumulation r_K and r_V must be obtained from (89) and (90), with (87) and (88).

Clearly, an increase in the imputed price p induces a decrease in c [from (91)], resulting in a decrease in the marginal social product r_V of social capital. Hence, an increase in the imputed price p is accompanied by a decrease in the rate of accumulation r_V of social capital, and a resulting increase in the supply of consumption [from (93)]. Therefore, the supply schedule, a positive slope, is depicted by the curve SS in Figure 19.4. The equilibrium level of consumption c and the imputed price p are uniquely determined by the two curves DD and SS.

The approximately optimum rates z_K and z_V of private and social capital and the corresponding level of consumption c are therefore all uniquely determined for a given capital ratio k.

When the capital ratio k becomes higher, then the SS curve will shift to the right, while the DD curve remains fixed. Hence, an increase in the capital ratio k is always accompanied by an increase in the level of consumption and a decrease in the imputed price of output p. Therefore, the approximately optimum rate z_K of accumulation for private capital is decreased, while that of social capital z_V is increased.

10 Concluding remarks

This paper has presented an introductory analysis of social overhead capital, with emphasis on the implications of the presence of such an overhead capital on the process of resource allocation and the ensuing pattern of real income distribution. Two aspects of social overhead capital not readily covered by the standard Samuelsonian concept of pure public goods have been emphasized. Each individual member of society is free to use the services of social overhead capital to the extent to which he or she desires. However, the effectiveness of the services used crucially depends on the way other individuals are using the same services, thus incorporating the phenomenon of congestion.

We have considered principally the pattern of resource allocation which results in an optimum allocation of social as well as private resources, from both static and dynamic points of view. From the static point of view, the given stock of social overhead capital may be efficiently used if each individual member is charged a price equal to the marginal social costs for the use of social overhead capital, provided the administrative costs associated with such a pricing scheme are negligible. For optimum allocation from the dynamic point of view, first modify the concept of the marginal social costs for the use of social overhead capital, taking into account the value of the marginal depreciation of social overhead capital due to the marginal increase in the use of social overhead capital. The evaluation of the marginal depreciation of social overhead capital has been based upon the imputed price of social overhead capital. The imputed price of social overhead capital, being the discounted present value of the marginal social product or benefits from a marginal increase in the stock of social overhead capital, is also a crucial factor in the determination of the optimum rate of accumulation and corresponding investment in social overhead capital. The optimum rate of accumulation of social overhead capital (although only an approximately optimum pattern has been discussed in this paper) is closely related to the ease or difficulty with which such social overhead capital may be reproduced. Obviously, the more difficult and more costly is reproduction of social overhead capital, the smaller is the amount devoted to its accumulation.

These propositions have been discussed in terms of the Penrose relationships which equate the amount of real investment with the rate by which social overhead capital is accumulated.

The analysis has been presented for the case where there is only one kind of social overhead capital. Most of the propositions obtained may be extended, however, with slight modifications, to the general case of a variety in social overhead capital – merely replace V by a vector of the stock of social overhead capital having a number of components, as many as there are kinds. In particular, it is possible to extend the analysis to the case where there are two distinct social overhead capitals – one increasing the marginal products of private factors of production and the other directly increasing the economic welfare of the members of society.

Finally, we have assumed only one kind of private factor of production, private capital, however, the analysis can be applied without modification to situations where there are a number of variables as well as fixed factors of production which are privately approximated.

References

[1] E. T. Penrose, *The Theory of the Growth of the Firm*, Oxford, Blackwell's, 1959.
[2] P. A. Samuelson, "The Pure Theory of Public Expenditures," *Review of* Expenditures," *Review of Economics and Statistics*, Vol. XXXVI (1954), pp. 387–9.
[3] P. A. Samuelson, "Diagramatic Exposition of a Pure Theory of Public Expenditures", *Review of Economics and Statistics*, Vol. XXXVII (1955), pp. 350–6.
[4] H. Uzawa, "The Penrose Effect and Optimum Growth," *Economic Studies Quarterly*, Vol. 19 (1968), pp. 1–14.
[5] H. Uzawa, "Time Preference and the Penrose Effect in a Two-Class Model of Economic Growth," *Journal of Political Economy*, Vol. 77 (1969), pp. 628–52.

Index